Vienna Metropolitan Area

Mapping the Zero Carbon City Region

Roland Krebs
Stefan Mayr
Cédric Ramière
Claudia Staubmann
(eds.)

jovis

METROLAB
RESEARCH | DEVELOPMENT | SERVICE

THE ZERO CARBON CITY REGION

EMERGING PHENOMENA ATLAS

INTERNATIONAL PERSPECTIVE

MAPPING FUTURE SCENARIOS

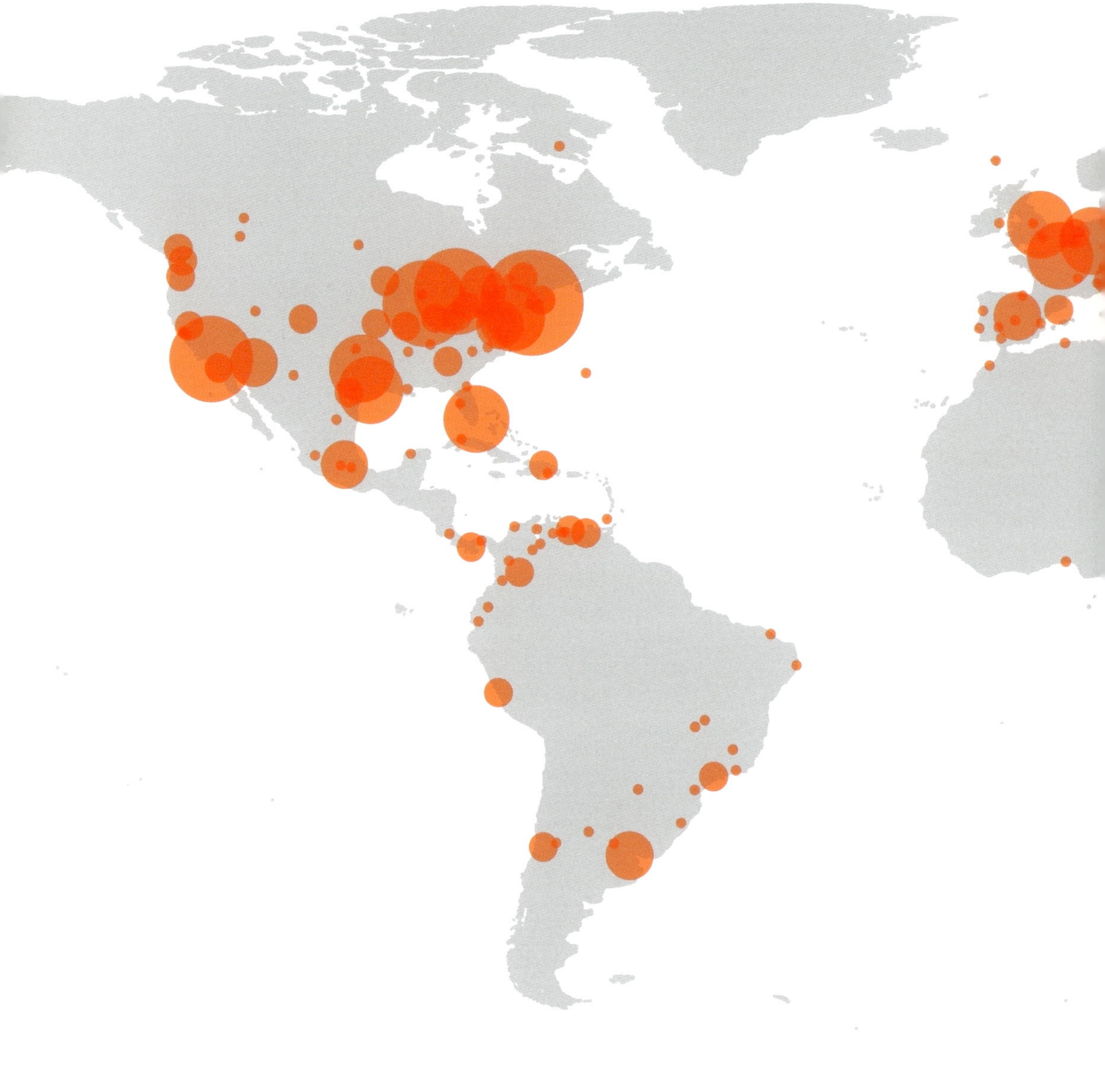

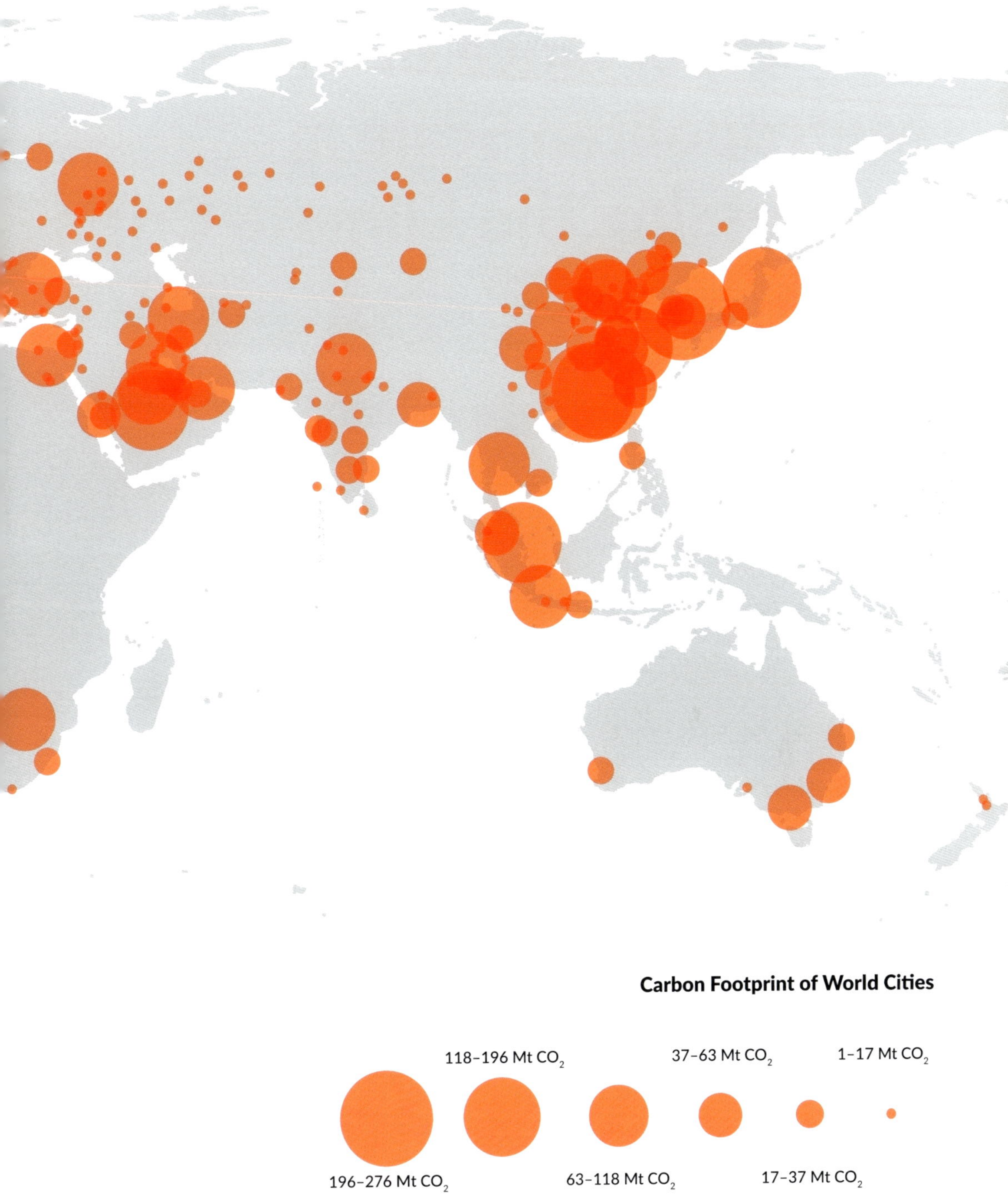

Moran, D., Kanemoto, K., Jiborn, M., Wood, R., Többen, J., and Seto, K.C. (2018) Carbon footprints of 13,000 cities. Environmental Research Letters DOI: 10.1088/1748-9326/aac72a.

The Importance of the Metropolitan Scale in Addressing the Climate Crisis

Climate change severely affects cities and their surrounding areas, highlighting the priority of climate neutrality and the need for innovative solutions in various facets of our lives. Metropolitan areas around the world contribute significantly to the climate crisis as they are responsible for the majority of greenhouse gas emissions due to high concentrations of industry, transportation, and residential activities. Reducing emissions in these areas is critical to mitigating climate change.

The metropolitan scale is therefore essential to addressing climate challenges. Our urban centers and their suburban regions are highly interconnected and have strong functional and spatial relationships that are often inadequately considered, as they share critical infrastructure systems such as transportation, water supply, and energy networks. Climate issues such as air pollution, water and waste management often transcend city boundaries, making the metropolitan scale the most effective level at which to address these challenges holistically. Focusing at this scale allows for more efficient allocation of resources and strengthens regional synergies through collaborative projects, such as regional public transportation systems or joint renewable energy projects.

Mitigating and adapting to climate change requires coordinated action across sectors and levels of government. At the metropolitan level, it is possible to coordinate common policies and regulations to ensure that climate policies are consistent across the region, avoid the pitfalls of fragmented regulations, and strengthen cooperation among different municipalities, regional authorities, and stakeholders to promote a unified approach to climate action.

Metropolitan areas encompass both urban and rural regions, each facing unique climate challenges. Addressing climate change at the metropolitan scale allows for balanced strategies that benefit both urban and rural areas, ensuring that climate solutions are inclusive and equitable by supporting sustainable land use, reducing urban sprawl, preserving natural habitats, and promoting sustainable agricultural practices.

Addressing climate change at the metropolitan scale enables coordinated action over a larger geographic area, integrates infrastructure and resource management, and facilitates multisectoral governance. By focusing on the metropolitan scale, we can develop and implement solutions that are not only more effective, but also more sustainable and equitable.

GOVERNANCE FRAME FOR CLIMATE NEUTRALITY

To achieve climate neutrality in Europe's metropolitan regions, the EU has established a governance framework that focuses on key legislative and policy measures. The European level is essential for setting a common goal of climate neutrality. This scale is crucial for tackling climate change because it can provide a unified policy framework, increase impact through consistency across borders, and coordinate climate action. It is also in a position to influence substantial reductions in greenhouse gas emissions, provide global leadership and strategically allocate resources. This EU level approach ensures that climate policies are effective, equitable and consistent with broader international and regional objectives.

The **European Climate Law & Green Deal** is legally binding since 2021 – EU institutions and member states are bound to take the necessary measures at EU and national levels to meet determined targets. As part of the European Green Deal, the goal is to reach climate-neutrality until 2050. Until 2030, greenhouse gas emissions need to be reduced by at least 55% compared to the levels of 1990. After 2050, the climate law includes a commitment for negative emissions (European Commision, n.d.-b).

The **Green Deal** is a package of policy initiatives that aim to set the EU on the path to a green transition, with the ultimate goal of reaching climate neutrality in 2050. It comprises the "Fit for 55" package, that sets out proposals to revise climate-, energy- and transport-related legislation and align EU laws with the EU's climate goals (European Council 2022).

The **European Emissions Trading System (EU-ETS)** is in place in all member states of the EU, Norway, Iceland as well as Liechtenstein and aims to reduce industry, energy, and transport emissions. It is a legally binding European directive, ratified into national laws, in Austria in form of the "Emission Allowance Act". It was implemented in 2005 to comply with the Kyoto Agreement and is currently in its fourth trading period (2021–2030).
Around 9,000 plants in the energy and industry sector throughout Europe are covered by the system, these plants account for around 40% of all greenhouse gas emissions in Europe. Since 2012, intra-european air traffic is also covered by the ETS.

The system functions according to the "Cap & Trade" principle: The "Cap" determines how many greenhouse gas emissions, measured in CO_2-equivalents, may be emitted by the concerned plants in a certain period. The member states then issue emission allowance for the permission of emitting one ton of CO_2-equivalents. These allowances are partly issued for free, partly auctioned. They can then be traded freely on the market. This system has been criticized because in the past, too many certificates were given away, leading to very low prices: At its lowest, an emission allowance for one ton of CO_2 equivalents was traded at a prize of three Euros. Meanwhile, the "Cap" has been continuously reduced in the frame of the "Fit for 55" program, leading to higher prices of over a hundred Euros. Until 2030, the cap will be yearly reduced (Environmental Agency Germany 2021).

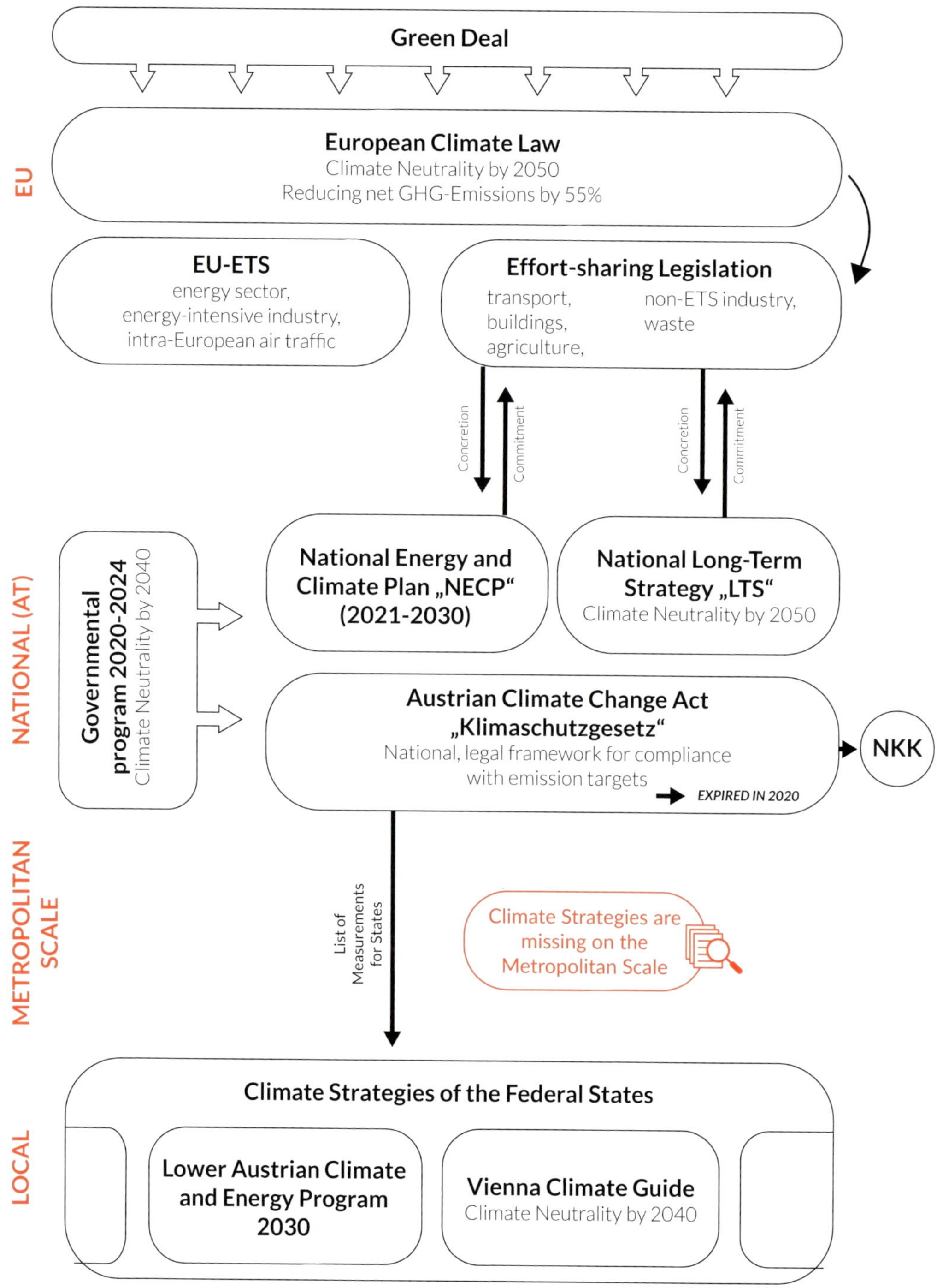

Green Deal
EU
European Climate Law
Climate Neutrality by 2050
Reducing net GHG-Emissions by 55%
EU-ETS
energy sector,
energy-intensive industry,
intra-European air traffic
Effort-sharing Legislation
transport,
buildings,
agriculture,
non-ETS industry,
waste
Concretion
Commitment
Concretion
Commitment
NATIONAL (AT)
Governmental program 2020-2024
Climate Neutrality by 2040
National Energy and Climate Plan „NECP" (2021-2030)
National Long-Term Strategy „LTS"
Climate Neutrality by 2050
Austrian Climate Change Act „Klimaschutzgesetz"
National, legal framework for compliance with emission targets
EXPIRED IN 2020
NKK
METROPOLITAN SCALE
List of Measurements for States
Climate Strategies are missing on the Metropolitan Scale
LOCAL
Climate Strategies of the Federal States
Lower Austrian Climate and Energy Program 2030
Vienna Climate Guide
Climate Neutrality by 2040

The **Effort-Sharing-Legislation** means that EU member states have binding annual Greenhouse gas emission targets for 2021–2030 for the economy sectors that are outside of the EU-ETS scope. These sectors account for almost 60% of domestic EU emissions. The Effort sharing regulation says that the economy non covered by the ETS must reduce their emissions by 30% until 2030 compared to the levels of 2005. The regulation translates this commitment into binding annual greenhouse gas emission targets for each member states for the period 2021–2030 (European Commission, n.d.-a).

The **Austrian Climate Change Act** ("Klimaschutzgesetz") defines the process of preparation and implementation of measures, with defined emission ceilings for six sectors (Energy and Industry outside the ETS, transport, buildings, agriculture, waste management, fluorinated gases) with annual progress reports: but since 2020, there are no defined emission ceilings. In 2024, the situation is still the same (BMK 2022).

The National Energy and Climate Plan (NECP) (2021–2030) is a climate and energy policy framework that sets out the goals until 2030 to reduce greenhouse gas emissions outside of the ETS by 36% compared to 2005, it yet needs to be adapted to comply with the goal of climate neutrality until 2050.

The **Vienna Climate Roadmap** is not legally binding but it was adapted by the Vienna City Government in 2020. The program sets out goals and actions for sectors to reduce their emissions and become climate neutral by 2040. This however does not include industries and energy plants that are part of the EU-ETS system.

MISSING THE METROPOLITAN SCALE

As shown above, European climate governance frameworks focus primarily on overarching regional and national policies. While these frameworks are critical for setting broad goals and coordinating large-scale efforts, they often overlook the metropolitan scale, which is the level at which many climate-related problems are most acutely felt and addressed.

Incorporating the metropolitan scale into climate governance is crucial for several reasons. Metropolitan areas are where many climate impacts are directly experienced, including air pollution, traffic congestion, and heat islands. Tailored policies at this scale can address these issues more effectively than broad, regional or national policies. Furthermore, metropolitan regions have unique characteristics and challenges. Addressing these specific needs requires policies and strategies that are customized to the local context.

Additionally, coordinated urban planning can lead to more efficient use of resources, such as implementing green infrastructure and promoting sustainable building practices, which can be more effectively managed at the metropolitan level. Regarding the local governance, metropolitan governments and local authorities have a better understanding of local conditions and can implement policies more effectively. They are better positioned to engage with communities and tailor solutions to their specific needs.

Finally, local governance structures are closer to the community, which facilitates greater public participation and buy-in for climate initiatives. This can lead to more successful and sustainable outcomes.

MetroLab Approach in Mapping the Viennese Zero Carbon City Region

Holistic transformation requires the integration of climate considerations into all facets of urban planning and development. Building on its previous work in metropolitan planning and design, MetroLab developed an innovative and visionary metropolitan mapping approach to address the climate crisis at the metropolitan scale with the project "Mapping the Zero Carbon City Region". The creative mapping tool shows relevant spatial pathways towards climate neutrality and aims to promote a more integrated and visionary approach to achieve a climate neutral Vienna metropolitan region. This creative, cross-sectoral, interdisciplinary approach can be applied to other city regions, making the necessary measures tangible and stimulating the discussion on integrated metropolitan urban planning in the context of climate neutrality at the metropolitan scale.

This book presents the work of MetroLab on the project "Mapping the Zero-Carbon City Region". The publication is divided into three main parts.

The first part introduces the MetroLab approach and describes how the publication is organized into five different areas of life that are most responsible for greenhouse gas emissions in the metropolitan area of Vienna: Living, Moving, Producing, Consuming and Wasting.

The second part presents the results of an extensive data mining process. This phase involved a comprehensive data collection and analysis of the distribution and origin of greenhouse gas emissions in relation to the different areas of life as well as the demographic, spatial, social and economic context in the Vienna metropolitan area. The result of this process is the Emerging Phenomena Atlas, a visual synthesis of the complex spatial and social connections and interdependencies that makes complicated relationships accessible and easy to understand. The Emerging Phenomena Atlas is organized according to the five areas of life that are the largest emitters of greenhouse gases in the Vienna metropolitan region. It visually communicates key trends and concrete emerging phenomena in greenhouse gas emissions that form the basis for development transformation strategies.

The third part synthesizes the emerging phenomena into integrated strategies towards a zero-carbon city region and spatializes the strategies into concrete tools for more integrated transformations at the metropolitan scale. The tools are applied to the spatial context of the Vienna metropolitan region and finally result in scenarios that visualize new pathways towards climate neutrality, visually communicating how climate goals can be achieved through integrated cross-border development.

LEARNING FROM OTHERS

Since the beginning, MetroLab has emphasized the importance of learning from others. By fostering dialogue with other experts and different disciplines, cities and regions, a wider range of knowledge can be gained, shared and made accessible.

The MetroLab Podcast: To learn from experts in different disciplines and contexts, the MetroLab podcast was created, with each episode focusing on a different greenhouse gas emitting sector. Renowned international experts from science and research, business and politics were invited to discuss key challenges on the path to climate neutrality, the status quo and best-practice solutions that have already been implemented in various subject areas. The format thus enabled Metrolab to expand its knowledge and perspective, enter into public discourse and address a broad, interested audience. The contributions of the experts from the podcast are also included in this publication.

International Webinar: An international webinar on "Integrated Planning for livable, compact and sustainable metropolises" was held in cooperation with the Àrea Metropolitana de Barcelona (AMB). The event combined focal points of MetroLab's work of Mapping the Zero Carbon City Region with focal points of the Barcelona, Porto and Thessaloniki metropolitan regions and discussed these in a European context. Topics included the governance of metropolitan regions in the climate crisis, sustainable mobility strategies and the relevance of urban-regionally planned green spaces. The webinar was organized as an official side event of the European Week of Regions and Cities of the EU.

Cooperation and Design Studios with Technical University of Vienna: MetroLab also cooperated with the Institute for Urban Planning, Landscape Architecture and Design at the Technical University of Vienna to design a joint course entitled "MetroLab—Zero Carbon City Region". Based on the emerging phenomena identified by MetroLab, the students developed innovative spatial models and scenarios on a metropolitan scale, embedded in a future climate-neutral urban region.

Zero Carbon City Region Forum: In May 2024, MetroLab organized an international forum in Vienna to discuss different perspectives on the role of metropolitan regions in the climate crisis with several international experts and local stakeholders. The aim was to facilitate and exchange ideas on the transformation towards a zero-carbon metropolitan region, to engage in a collaborative exchange and sharpen solutions and insights through constructive dialogue and collaboration. A number of international experts from different metropolitan regions were invited to give keynote speeches and valuable insights on their approaches and paths towards climate neutrality. The subsequent panel discussion with relevant local stakeholders from planning and design applied the international approaches to the Viennese context and discussed possible solutions to the major challenges. In addition, a site visit and tour of biofabrique Vienna—a project that focuses on the joint development of a bioregional design approach to transform unused local resources into materials for architecture and design—rounded out the program and contributed to the exchange of knowledge.

Five Areas of Life in the Vienna Metropolitan Area

THE SPATIAL CONTEXT

In order to analyze spatial phenomena, develop strategies and test tools, the visioning and mapping approach of this book focuses mainly on the Viennese metropolitan context. Our research revealed significant challenges in collecting data on the Vienna metropolitan region, as it lacks defined boundaries, a unified data set and a consistent strategy for data collection. Without an official designation, the Vienna metropolitan region does not exist as a distinct entity, making coordinated data collection difficult. The "Stadtregion+" defined by the PGO (Planungsgemeinschaft Ost) covers three federal provinces: Vienna, Lower Austria and Burgenland. Therefore, in our definition of the Vienna metropolitan region, we have combined the three entire federal states of Vienna, Lower Austria and Burgenland and worked with these three datasets to create a common entity by merging the data into one metropolitan region dataset. This posed new challenges, however, as all three provinces have different programs, for example in terms of climate strategies and climate-related measures. This highlights the importance of creating a common metropolitan dataset as an important step in promoting integrated projects and planning processes at the metropolitan scale.

MAIN EMITTING SECTORS: FIVE AREAS OF LIFE

During our research on the main emitters of greenhouse gases in the Vienna metropolitan region, it became clear that two sectors in particular are responsible for the majority of emissions in Vienna, Lower Austria and Burgenland: Industry & Energy and Transport account for three quarters, almost 72%, of the region's greenhouse gas emissions. The building sector is the third largest emitter with more than 12% of the emissions, followed by Agriculture with about 8,5% of the emissions and Waste and fluorinated gases (F-gases) with 7%. While the industry and energy sectors also have large technical components that need to be addressed to reduce emissions and have planned reduction paths defined on the European level within the EU Emissions Trading System (see also European Emissions Trading System), the remaining sectors such as transport, buildings, agriculture and waste have a stronger spatial dimension. Their flows and systems are strongly intertwined between Vienna and the surrounding suburban regions, which means that reducing their emissions could be most efficiently addressed at the metropolitan level. To solve the complex and diverse challenges of the climate crisis, it is necessary to look more closely at these five areas and address them with integrated solutions to become a zero carbon city region.

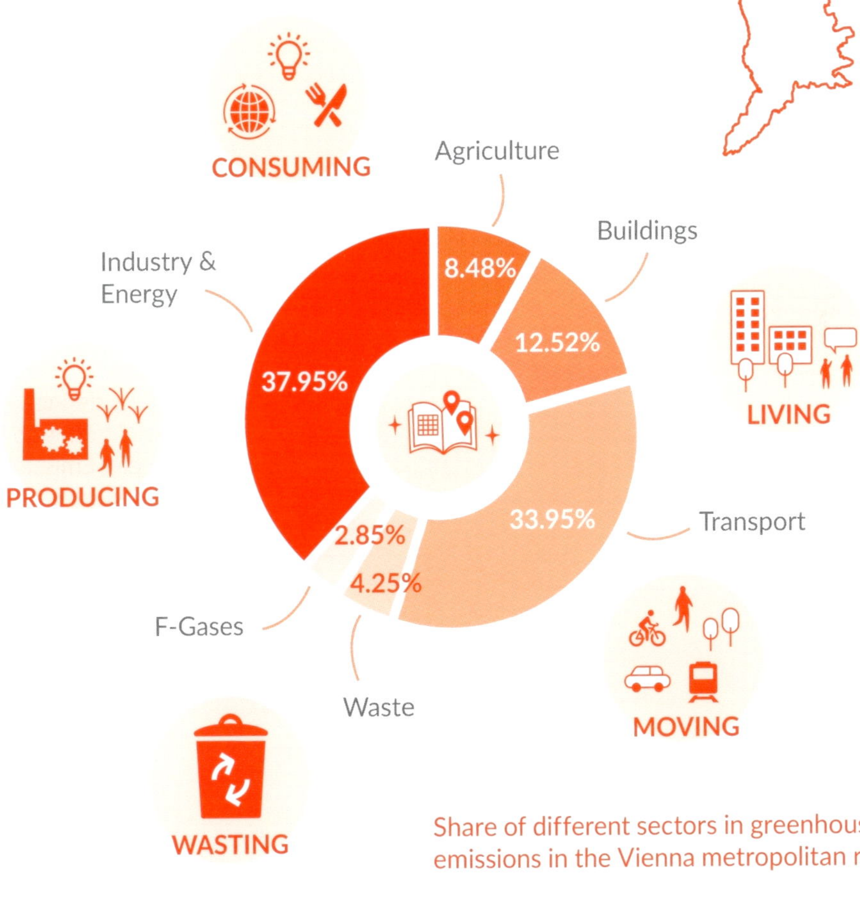

Share of different sectors in greenhouse gas emissions in the Vienna metropolitan region

Environment Agency Austria (2022 b): Federal states air pollutant inventory 1990–2020

Emerging Phenomena Atlas

Mapping Emerging Phenomena

Climate relevant topics can be complex and difficult to grasp: emissions are somewhat abstract, often invisible, but always tied to our human behavior in space. The Emerging Phenomena Atlas simplifies complex information by distilling diverse data into a visual representation. It helps to quickly grasp relationships, trends, and spatial patterns that may be difficult to see in purely textual or statistical formats. The atlas reveals the spatial dimension of the climate neutral challenges of the metropolitan area of Vienna by looking at five different areas of daily life: Moving, Living, Producing, Consuming, and Wasting. These areas of life are related to the major emitting sectors within the region.

With these five themes and five chapters, the Atlas presents the status quo of climate-neutral development in the metropolitan region. It is structured around key trends—"Emerging Phenomena"—that are explained through easy-to-read maps and graphics. MetroLab defines Emerging Phenomena as spatial trends and challenges related to greenhouse gas emissions, which result from a detailed analysis of the emissions in the Vienna metropolitan region. All phenomena have a spatial dimension and provoke spatial interrelationships, which the atlas aims to visualize.

Furthermore, the Emerging Phenomena Atlas creates a new image of the region as a common territory (Vienna, Burgenland and Lower Austria) with common challenges to be solved, and serves as a basis for the further development of visionary scenarios.

MOVING

M1 Greenhouse Gas Emissions
M2 Commuting
M3 Networks & Policy
M4 Air & Rail Travel
M5 Freight Transport
» Interview with Jacqueline Grassl & Nicolas Fontaine

LIVING

L1 Density & Emissions
L2 Vacancy Rate
L3 Construction & Land Use
L4 Typology & Energy
» Interview with Andrea Jany & Yoann Gorostiaga

PRODUCING

P1 Biggest Emitters
P2 Land Footprint Food Production
P3 Food Diversity
P4 ETS – EU Emissions Trading System
» Interview with Helene Pattermann & Alexander Prinsen

CONSUMING

C1 Food Emissions
C2 Lifestyle Emissions
C3 Resource Consumption
» Interview with Carolyn Steel, Yvonne Lötscher & Martin Strele

WASTING

W1 Waste Management
W2 Recycling Goals
W3 Waste in Landfills
W4 Construction Waste
» Interview with Dominik Wiedenhofer, Carolin Bellstedt & Felix Heisel

“It is not only a question of convincing people, but also of changing structures”

Interview with Helga Kromp-Kolb & Lautaro Iriarte

Helga Kromp-Kolb is a meteorologist and climate scientist who has been researching climate change since the early 1990s. Formerly head of the Austrian Climate Change Centre and professor emerita at the University of Natural Resources and Applied Life Sciences, Vienna (BOKU), she is one of the most important contributors to the public debate on the climate crisis in Austria.

Lautaro Iriarte is the communication coordinator of the Austrian Klimavolksbegehren, an initiative advocating for more ambitious climate politics in Austria. Since 2019 he has been active at the Fridays for Future movement.

MetroLab: Language affects our perceptions. For example, we feel a different kind of urgency when we talk about the climate crisis as opposed to climate change. When we talk about the climate crisis, we are confronted with different terms and expressions, such as “climate friendly”, “climate neutral”, “carbon neutral”, “net zero emissions”, just to name a few.
How could you describe these different goals, do these terms really mean the same thing?

Helga Kromp-Kolb: Perhaps the first is the question of climate change or climate crisis. There’s no real rule about which term to use. Personally, I use the term climate change when I’m talking about nature and processes in the atmosphere, and I use the term climate crisis, or at least I try to, when I’m talking about impacts on humans or interactions with humans. Because nature itself has experienced quite a lot of climate change and can certainly adapt in some way, maybe in a different way than we like, and maybe it harms us a lot through these adaptations, but nature as such is not threatened. It’s human beings that are threatened, so it’s a crisis for human beings, but not for nature. If I were very cynical, I could say that it would be beneficial for nature if humans disappeared. It could be a kind of healthy reaction of nature to get rid of us. So that’s where I see the difference between climate change and climate crisis. But this is my personal approach.

Now about climate neutrality and the other terms you mentioned: Neutrality always means that the input is somehow equal to the output, that they are balanced. You can either balance carbon dioxide or you can balance greenhouse gas emissions as a whole, depending on what you are doing, you should be talking about carbon dioxide, CO_2 budget, CO_2 net zero or CO_2 neutrality or greenhouse gas neutrality. It's often not so clear what you mean, but even if you're very precise about what you're talking about, there are still a lot of additional assumptions you have to make in order to really talk about neutrality.

It is not a very clear or well defined term unless you add a lot of footnotes to what you mean. But it's a term that's sort of easy to understand, easy to communicate, even if it's not very precise. It's more than just being neutral. I mean, it's not enough to be neutral in a given year. We have to do more than that.

MetroLab: Do you think that the fact that there are so many terms, or that the definitions are often vague and not very precise, might be holding us back from getting certain messages across?

H.K.-K.: It can happen that people think that neutrality is enough. And it is not, we also need to talk about the budget, because at the time we reach neutrality, greenhouse gas concentrations in the atmosphere will remain at the same level. As long as we put more greenhouse gases into the atmosphere than we take out, greenhouse gas concentrations will rise.

From the point of neutrality, it will remain constant, and if we go beyond neutrality, the concentration can be reduced, nature will help us to reduce the carbon concentration or the greenhouse gas concentration in the atmosphere. If we talk about carbon neutrality on a global scale by 2050, it means that the concentration of carbon dioxide in the atmosphere will be maybe 430 parts per million (PPM). That is definitely too much, we should be closer to 350 PPM. We really need to go beyond neutrality to allow nature to take carbon dioxide out of the atmosphere and reduce the concentration. This is something that I'm pretty sure most people do not realise. They think that once we reach carbon neutrality, the job is done and everything is fine. On the other hand, achieving carbon neutrality is already such a challenge that if we go beyond that, we run the risk of losing everyone because people think it is already hopeless and give up.

MetroLab: If neutrality is not enough, is there another terminology to define the goal we are trying to achieve?

H.K.-K.: There is a 350 PPM movement, but people normally have absolutely no sense of carbon dioxide levels in the atmosphere. Even the 2 degree target is difficult to communicate, although temperature is something we know. But we are talking about the concentration of a gas that cannot be smelled or seen. Maybe we should ask a psychologist or a communication scientist about this.

Lautaro Iriarte: One idea might be to call it a larger goal, such as the goal of an ecological or sustainable society. That would be a very broad terminology, but it might be more appealing to people.

H.K.-K.: But that is a bit of a problem: "sustainable", the word, has been so misused. Almost everything is sustainable these days, at least according to the marketing teams. Sustainable gas, sustainable cars, all sorts of things that are definitely not sustainable. There is a problem with that term, but also with other terms like "footprint", which is very visual and good for communication. Whatever term we come up with in our current economic system will be misused to promote some kind of product or service that really has nothing to do with it.

The Climate Change Centre Austria (CCCA) has published a paper on the notions of neutrality and net zero emissions for Austria, so at least now there is a scientific basis to refer to when calling something "CO_2 neutral". We have tried to take some of the ambiguity out of these terms by publishing something where we really come up with numbers, including the assumptions behind those numbers. Hopefully this will make some things easier, or at least stop everyone using the term regardless of what ▸

they really mean. It's really quite frightening because there's so little greenhouse gas or carbon dioxide left that we're allowed to put into the atmosphere if we're going to do our part to meet the Paris target of 1.5 degrees Celsius, we're going to have to move extremely fast.

I agree that one of the key things to do this is to look at the issue not just from a climate perspective but from a broader perspective. To see the climate issue as part of a broader issue, because there are a lot of co-benefits that come with change that are more important to people than the climate benefits. We have a lot of synergies with a lot of other issues that need to be changed apart from climate. I think it's perhaps not communicated enough that climate policy is not a "do nothing" agenda, but a quality of life agenda. And that could be a way of framing things that would encourage people to do more to gain that quality of life.

MetroLab: The Klimavolksbegehren points out that there are no binding climate targets anymore in Austria since December 31st 2020. What would you say are the most pressing consequences of this situation?

L.I.: To give an example, this is like studying for a big exam without a plan of when and what to study. You cannot check if you are preparing well, or if you are behind, what you are missing. The government says it is acting in a climate-friendly way, but we cannot prove if it is true, only in retrospective. There is no legally binding way.

The government argues that certain laws are more beneficial to the climate than the law that lays out the path to net zero. While I understand their argument, I think it is wrong: We need to plan, we need to have a context where we need to go, otherwise we are navigating blind. What we really want is an institutional pathway and a control body that has the authority to tell the government if it is falling short of its targets.

MetroLab: Why do you think that, despite the efforts of so many people and organisations, we are still unable to persuade many people, especially decision-makers, of the urgency of the situation?

L.I.: In the conservative part of our government, there is still a fear of losing votes in elections, or losing the support of businesses or key players in society if they move too quickly. And that will continue unless we find a way to promote climate action, to see it as something positive and visionary.

The European Union is moving forward on climate change. Commission President von der Leyen is presenting the European Green Deal as Europe's "man on the moon" moment, and I think that is what we need, not to debate what we would lose because of climate policy. Not to wait until China and the US act, but to act now for a good life here in Europe, with health care, good public transport and so on. Then maybe people will see that as something achievable and something they want to have.

H.K.-K.: It is not only a question of convincing people, but also of changing structures. The way Austrian society is structured, especially the economy, with a lot of institutions representing industry, companies and workers, is rather inflexible. I think we need this bottom-up movement, which is why initiatives like the Klimavolksbegehren are so important. If we do not change these structures, we will have difficulties in achieving our goals, because structures also determine the actions of individuals.

MetroLab: There are different policy structures at different spatial levels, for example, European, national or local. At which of these levels would change be most effective?

H.K.-K.: I think the biggest impact at the moment would be at the national level, Europe still needs unity on many issues. But I think the easiest way to make change is at the local level. We have to work upwards, bring individuals together into a broad movement of individuals, to change local government, local structures, and work upwards from there. And at the same time try to work at the top, but I think that will be more difficult and will take more time. We have to attack this problem from all sides. There are a lot of small cities that are already doing quite well in terms of mitigation and adaptation. The more of them there are, the harder it will be for regional or national policymakers to ignore them.

L.I.: We need to work at all levels, from the EU to the local level. The Klimavolksbegehren initiative is working very strong on the national level. I see great opportunities there, because the Climate Change Act and the framework of our climate policy is made at the national level, so it is a kind of starting point for other laws and changes in different institutions.
But when I see projects happening at the local level, I am very hopeful because I see what is possible when you gather people around you. We have regions that are very advanced and moving forward, and then they serve as a model for other regions. It is very important to have pioneers who show in reality that it works. We could be a pioneer at the national level, making a strong climate law that could show other countries and the EU an example of how to make a strong law that moves the institutions.

H.K.-K.: Theoretically, it is clear that a national climate law is essential, but I do not see it happening in the near future, in this legislature. But we cannot just wait for the next government and hope that they will do more for the climate.

Right now, with this economic war with Russia, people are really afraid that they will not have a warm home tomorrow or the day after tomorrow. In this crisis mode there is no time for deep reflection, it is a time for panic action. A lot of people have understood that now would be the time to really switch to renewables, and although some of these actions are going in the right direction, our government is still talking about where we are going to get gas and oil, and they are even talking about fracking and nuclear energy. To some extent this is ambiguous at government level, moving forward but some are still looking backwards, trying to revive something that is not completely dead.

MetroLab: How do you think regional cooperation can advance climate action across administrative boundaries?

H.K.-K.: For Vienna in particular, I really do see a hopeful aspect. There are still problems in the mobility sector, but on the other hand it is really moving forward. A city like Vienna trying to get rid of coal, oil and gas for heating is a really ambitious task, but they are working on it. They have decided to run a carbon dioxide budget parallel to the euro budget, they are working on it and trying to integrate it into the administrative process. Once you get that right, you get a lot of climate-friendly decisions because you look at the carbon cost of decisions and whether you can afford it or whether you need to find a different solution.

Vienna has a history of combining social issues with other issues: It would be a great achievement if Vienna manages to combine the social issue with the climate issue, to show that climate protection does not deprive the socially weak, on the contrary. Vienna is doing more than our national government and represents almost a quarter of the Austrian population, so if it works here, it will have an important impact on many other cities in Austria. ▪

MetroLab Podcast
Episode Climate Neutral City Regions

Listen to our podcast on all platforms!

MOVING
in the Metropolitan Region

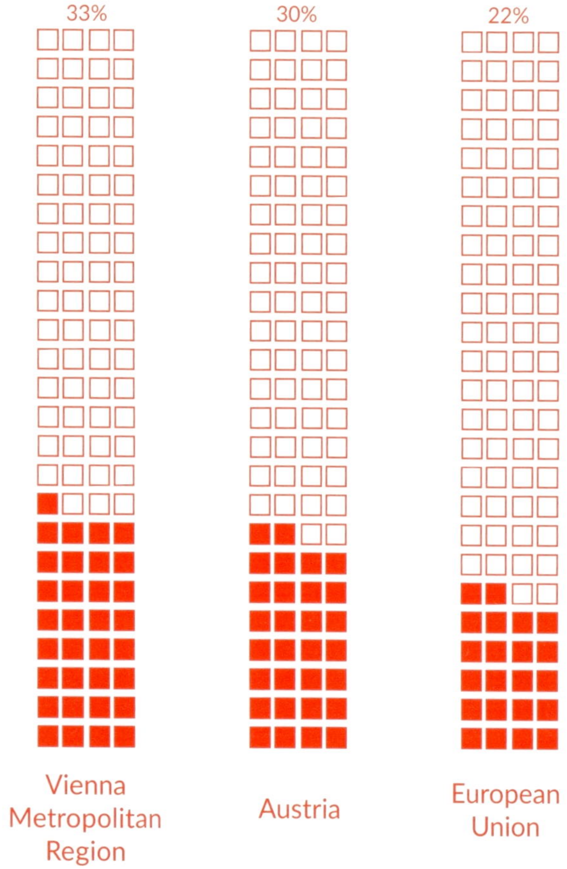

Share of the mobility sector in total greenhouse gas emissions

Environment Agency Austria (2022 b): Federal states air pollutant inventory 1990–2020

The way we move has a significant impact on our carbon emissions. In this chapter of the Emerging Phenomena Atlas, we explore the profound impact of transportation and mobility on carbon emissions in the Vienna metropolitan area. The movement of people and goods—whether by road, rail or air—is a major driver of greenhouse gas emissions, and the transportation sector is one of the world's largest consumers of fossil fuels. From daily commuting to international trade, our reliance on carbon-intensive modes of transportation contributes to air pollution, resource depletion, and the acceleration of climate change. Transportation is the only sector where Austria and the Vienna metropolitan area have failed to reduce emissions since 1990. Understanding the complex interactions between transportation infrastructure, energy use, and urban planning is critical to developing innovative solutions that reduce emissions, promote sustainable mobility, and support the transition to a low-carbon economy.

Greenhouse gas emissions are increasing further, we are still failing to change the modal split towards climate-friendly mobility

The mobility sector is responsible for 33,9% of the metropolitan region's greenhouse gas emissions. Since 1990, greenhouse gas emissions from the transport sector have increased by 66%, along with the number of private cars. Across Austria, more than half of all journeys, on an average working day are made by car. The share of trips made by public transport within Vienna is comparatively high at 38%, while in Lower Austria it is only at 14%.

Environment Agency Austria (2022 b): Federal states air pollutant inventory 1990–2020
European Environment Agency (2024): Greenhouse gases viewer

Shopping Center south of Vienna. Source: basemap.at

Metropolitan Structures Changing over Time

Stadtlau
Vienna

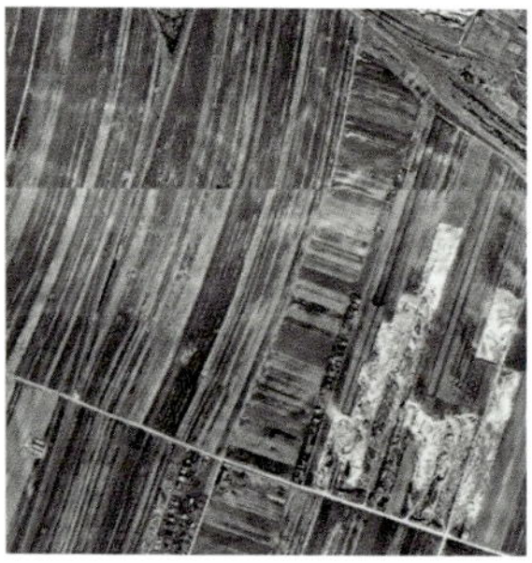

YEAR 1956

YEAR 1976

YEAR 2021

Wienerberg
Vienna

YEAR 1956

YEAR 1976

YEAR 2021

Vienna
main train station

YEAR 1956

YEAR 1976

YEAR 2023

City of Vienna (2024): Geodata viewer of the Vienna City Survey

Greenhouse gas emissions in the mobility sector increased dramatically between 1990 and 2020. The number of private cars per inhabitant increased along with greenhouse gas emissions.

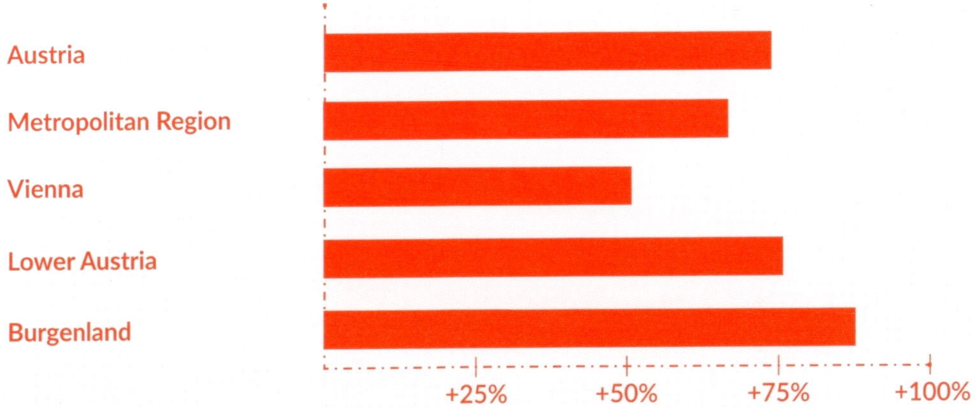

Change in Greenhouse Gas Emissions in the Mobility Sector between 1990 and 2020

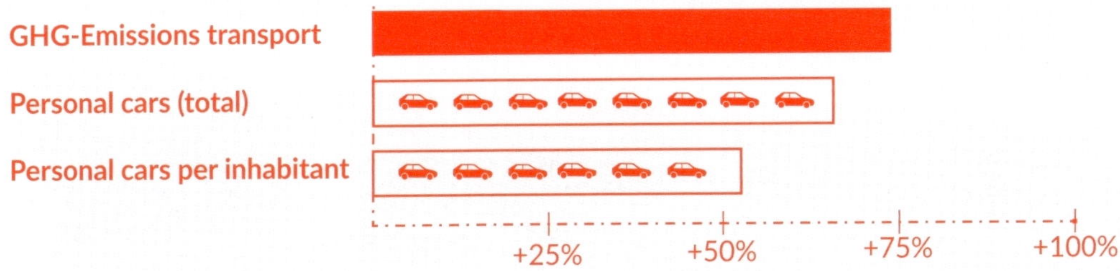

Increase in personal cars and Greenhouse Gas Emissions in Austria

Environment Agency Austria (2022 b): Federal states air pollutant inventory 1990–2020
Federal Ministry for Transport, Innovation and Technology (2016): Austria on the move 2013–2014
Statistics Austria (2023): Population
Statistics Austria (2023): Stock of motor vehicles

Greenhouse gas emissions from daily mobility vary widely between urban, suburban and rural areas: In Lower Austria, emissions per inhabitant are twice as high as in Vienna.

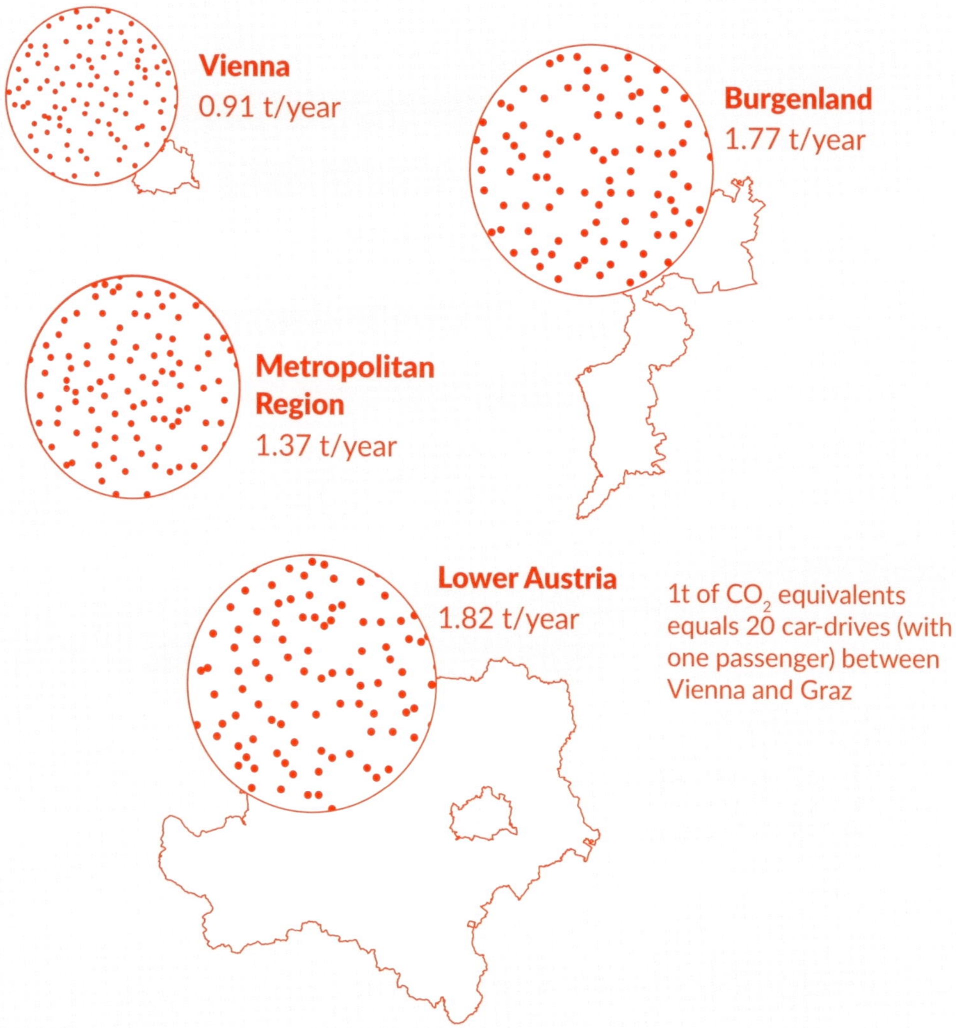

Greenhouse Gas Emissions of Everyday Mobility per Capita

Abart-Heriszt (2022): Energiemosaik Austria
Statistics Austria (2023): Population

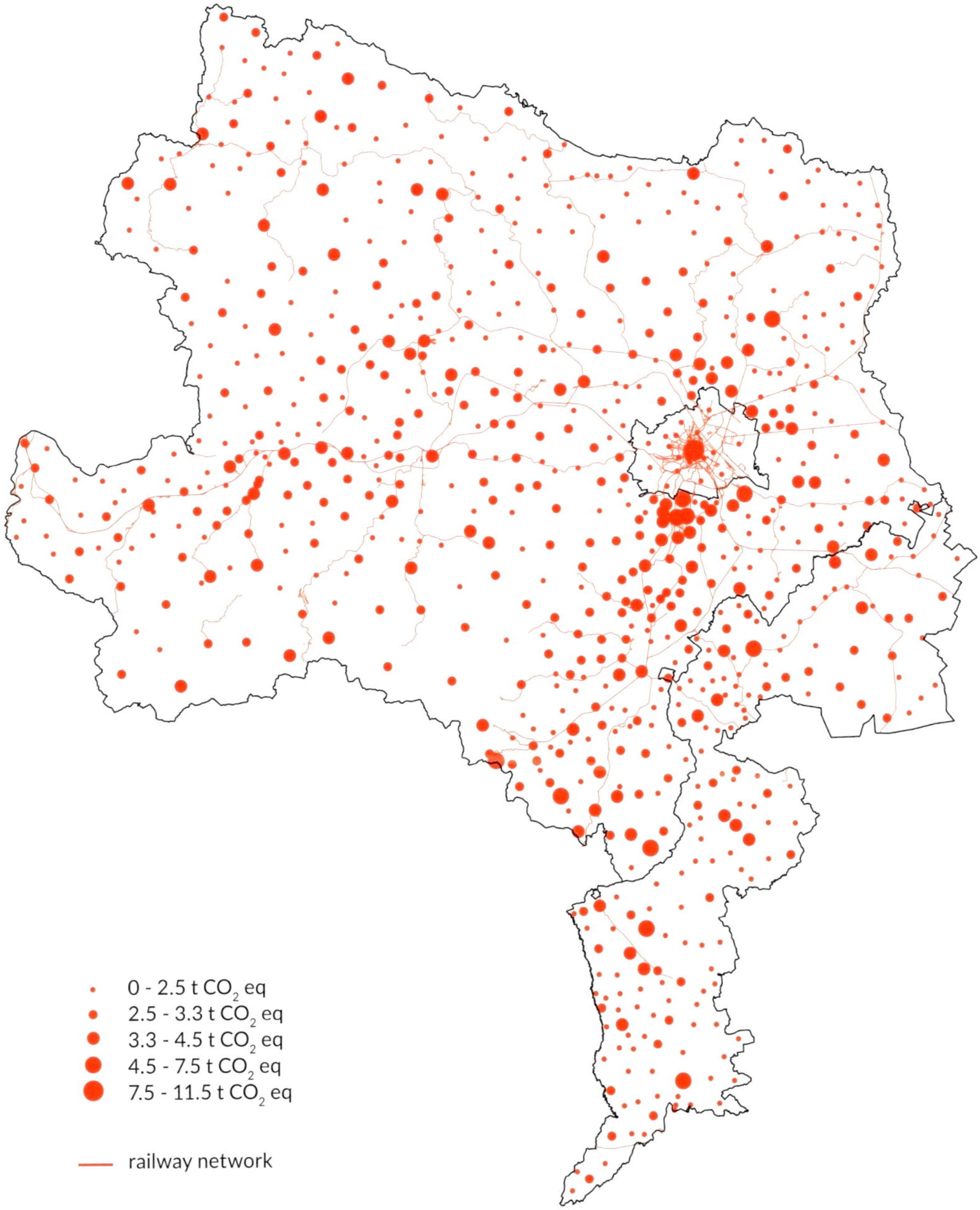

Greenhouse Gas Emissions of Everyday Mobility per Year and Inhabitant

Abart-Heriszt (2022): Energiemosaik Austria

On an average working day, a person in Austria makes 2.8 journeys. Differences in greenhouse gas emissions from daily mobility between urban, suburban and rural areas are related to differences in modal split: In Lower Austria and Burgenland, most journeys are still made by car, in contrast to Vienna, where public transport is the preferred mode.

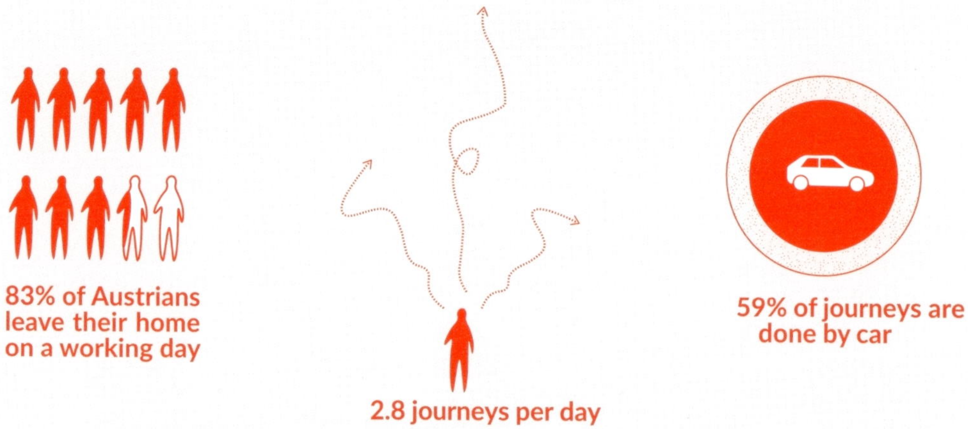

Modal Split 2013/2014 Austria

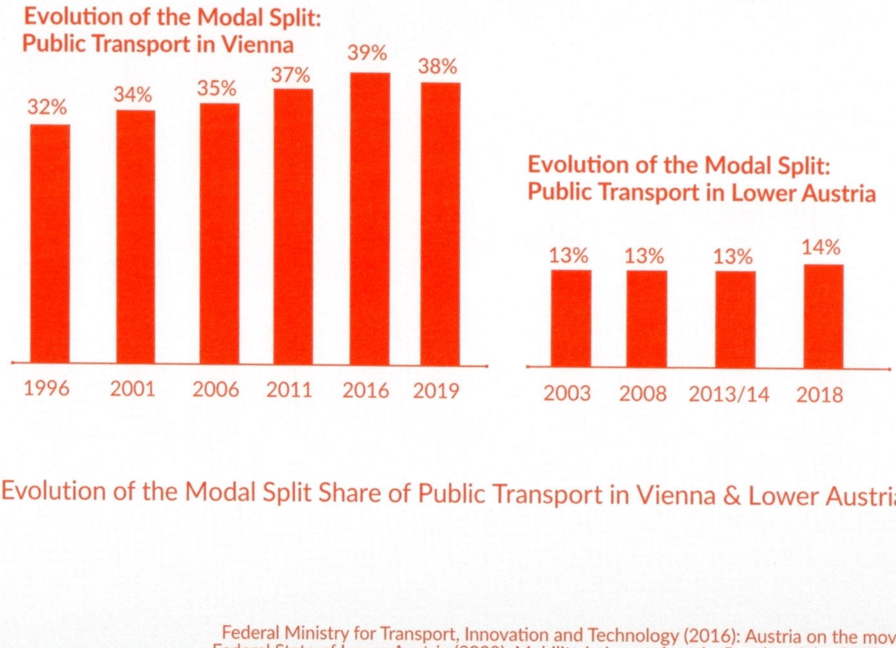

Evolution of the Modal Split Share of Public Transport in Vienna & Lower Austria

Federal Ministry for Transport, Innovation and Technology (2016): Austria on the move 2013–2014
Federal State of Lower Austria (2020): Mobility in Lower Austria. Results of the 2018 mobility survey

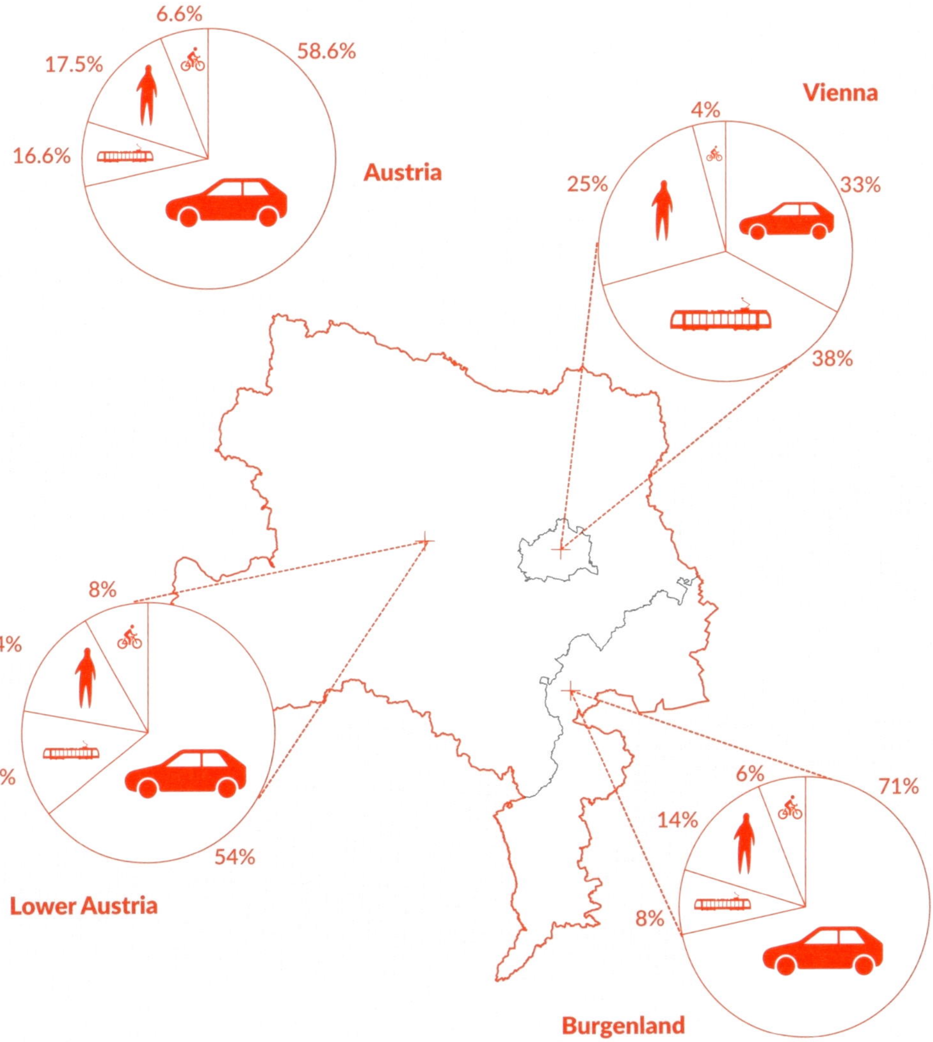

Modal Split 2013/2014 Average Working Day

Federal Ministry for Transport, Innovation and Technology (2016): Austria on the move 2013–2014

Private cars require about 31 km² of parking space in the metropolitan region. A collective parking garage for all private cars would have to be larger than Favoriten, the most densely populated district of Vienna.

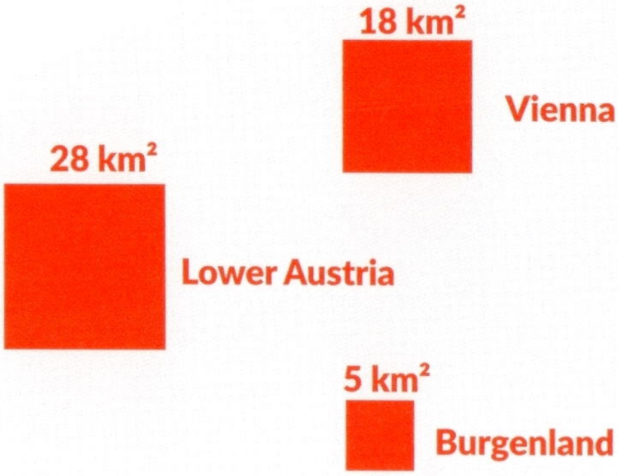

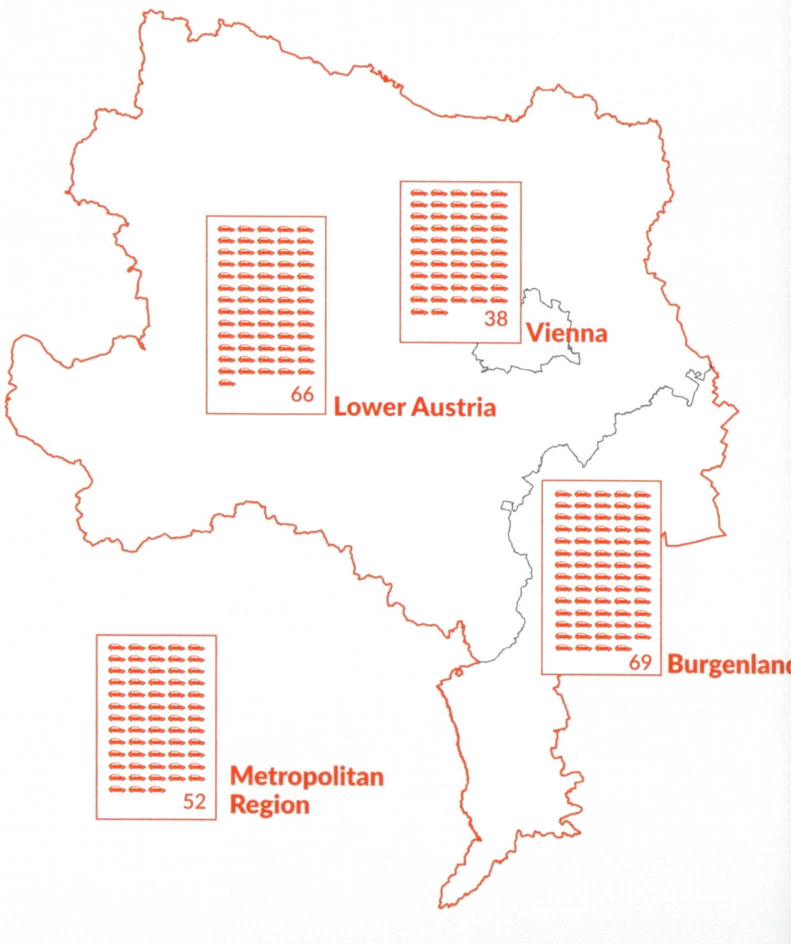

Statistics Austria (2022): Stock of motor vehicles
Wüstenrot Stiftung (Ed.) (2012): Raumpilot Basics

M2 Commuting

Most trips between Vienna and the region are made by car, and the number of commuters and the distances traveled in the region are increasing

Commuter flows between Vienna and Lower Austria show the highest numbers and with 77%, most of these trips are made by private car. While the number of commuters with short distances to work has not increased noticeably in recent years, the number of commuters travelling medium to long distances has increased significantly.

Technical University Graz, ISV (2023): Kordonerhebung Vienna 2022
Statistics Austria (2023): Commuters (place of work)

Highway Intersection at St.Marx in Vienna, Source: basemap.at

Nearly half of the working population does not live and work in the same municipality, indicating strong functional ties between the three states in the metropolitan region. This trend has increased over the past decade.

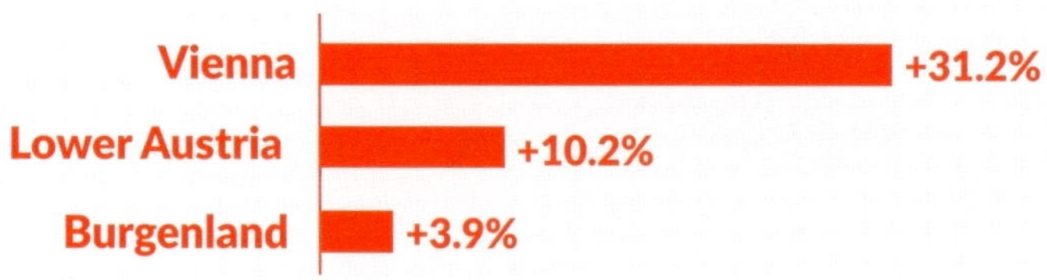

Development of commuters to another municipality 2010–2020

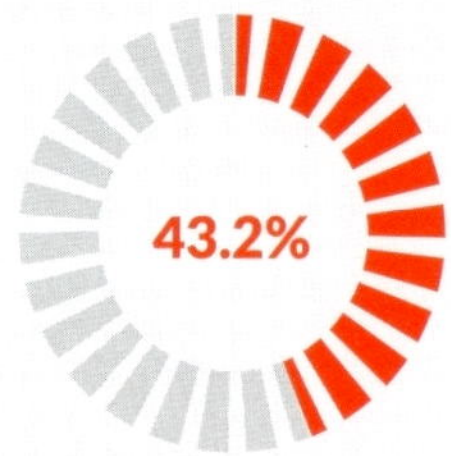

Percentage of working population living and working in a different municipality

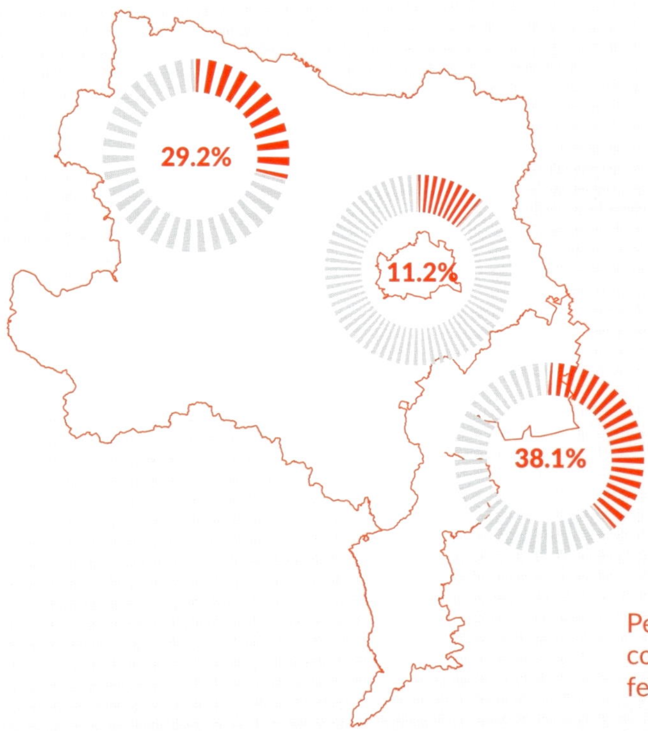

Percentage of workers commuting to a different federal state

Statistics Austria (2023): Commuters (place of work)

The majority of commuters commute short distances, between 0 and 30 kilometers. There are differences within the region: In Vienna, commuting distances are shorter than in Lower Austria and Burgenland.

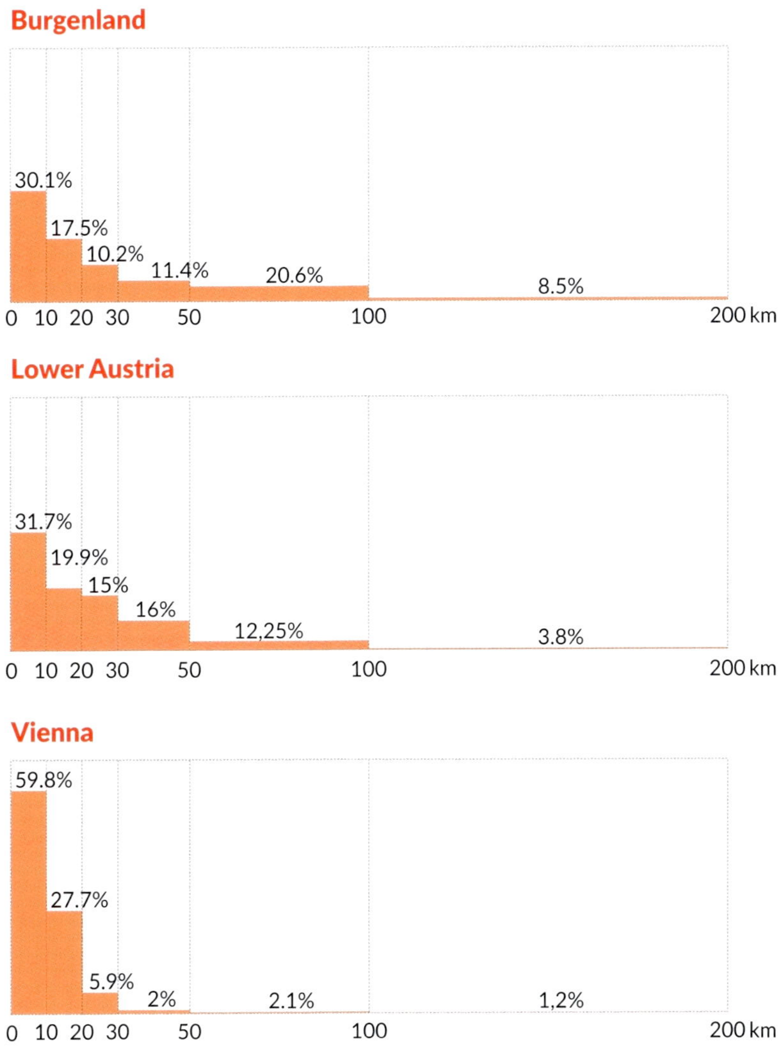

Commuter Distances

Statistics Austria (2023): Commuters (place of work)

In the region, 45.1% of commuters commute within 0–10 kilometers and 68.1% commute within 0–20 kilometers.

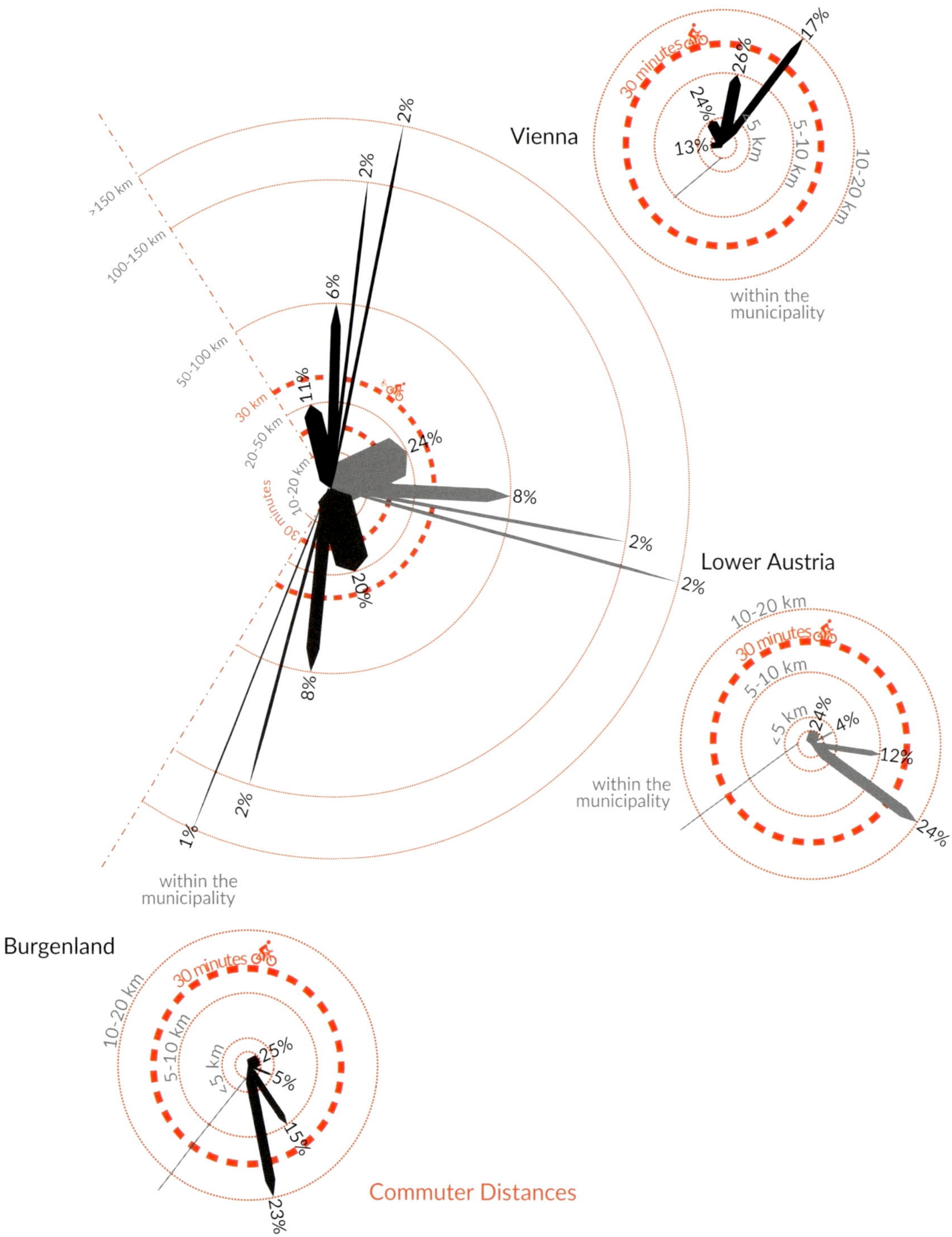

Statistics Austria (2023): Commuters (place of work)

By car, 34.1% of commuters can reach their workplace within 15 minutes and 71.7% within 30 minutes. In some cases, switching to public transport or active mobility is already an attractive option. Switching commutes to public transport represents a significant CO_2 savings potential.

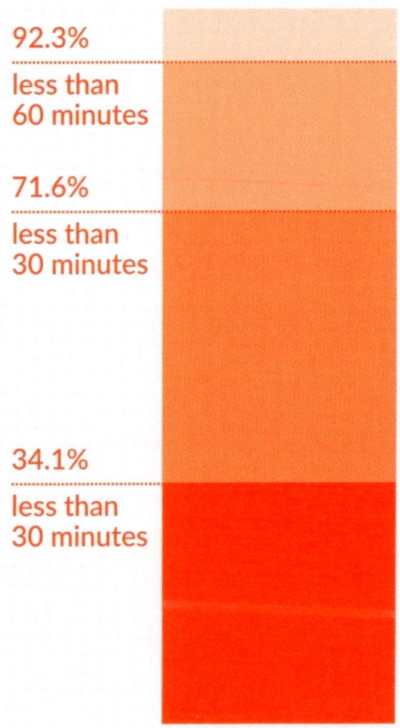

Commuter Times

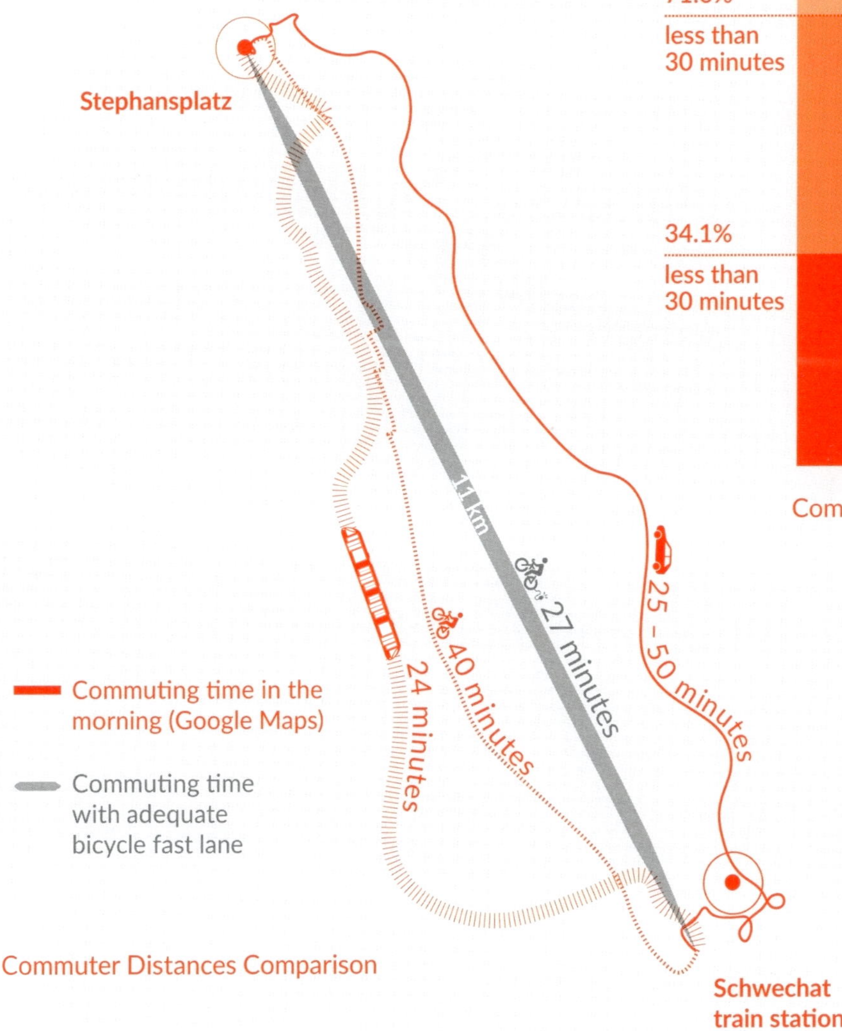

Commuter Distances Comparison

Statistics Austria (2023): Commuters (place of work)
Google Maps (2023)

The Vienna metropolitan region experiences strong daily commuter flows. There is a particularly strong connection between Vienna and Lower Austria, with many people commuting to Vienna.

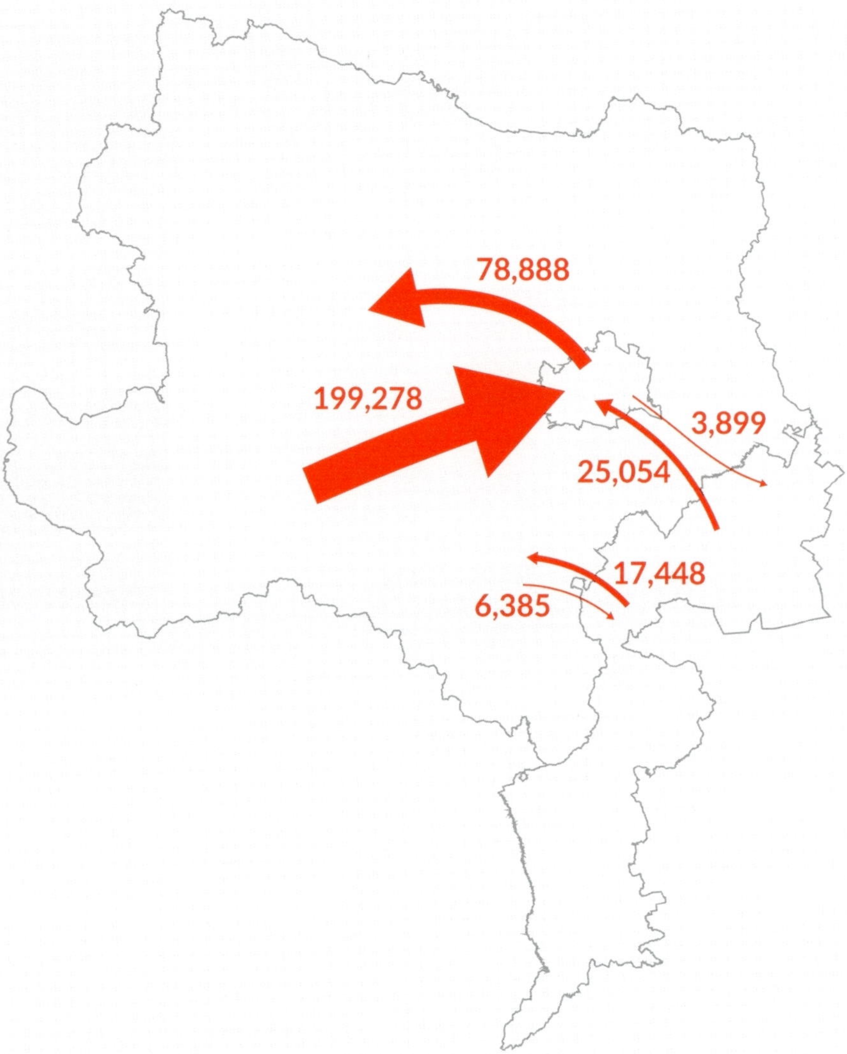

Commuter Flows between Burgenland, Lower Austria & Vienna in Passangers per Day

Statistics Austria (2023): Commuters (place of work)

Most commuting is done by car: This trend has not changed in recent years. While car use has been reduced within Vienna, it has not been reduced for trips to Vienna: Car use is a metropolitan problem.

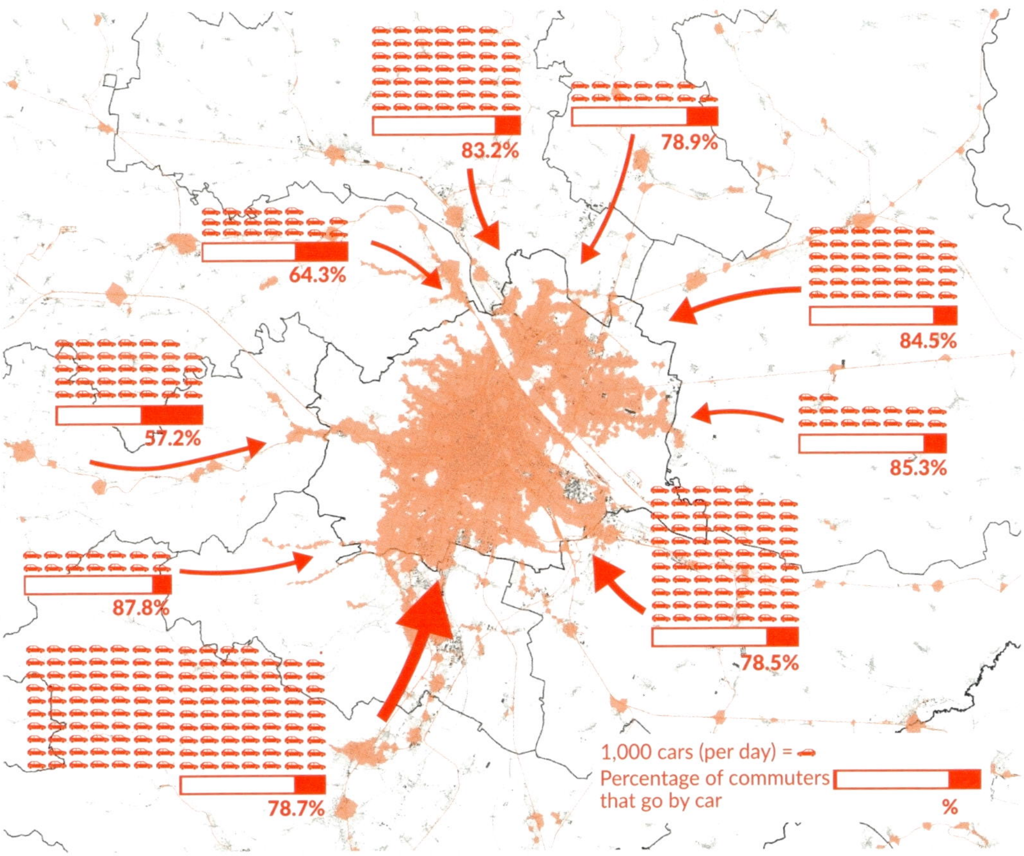

Everyday Commuter Flows to Vienna

Technical University Graz, ISV (2023): Kordonerhebung Vienna 2022

Adequate bicycle connections increase average speed and reduce trip duration by about 17% for bicycles and 25% for e-bikes.

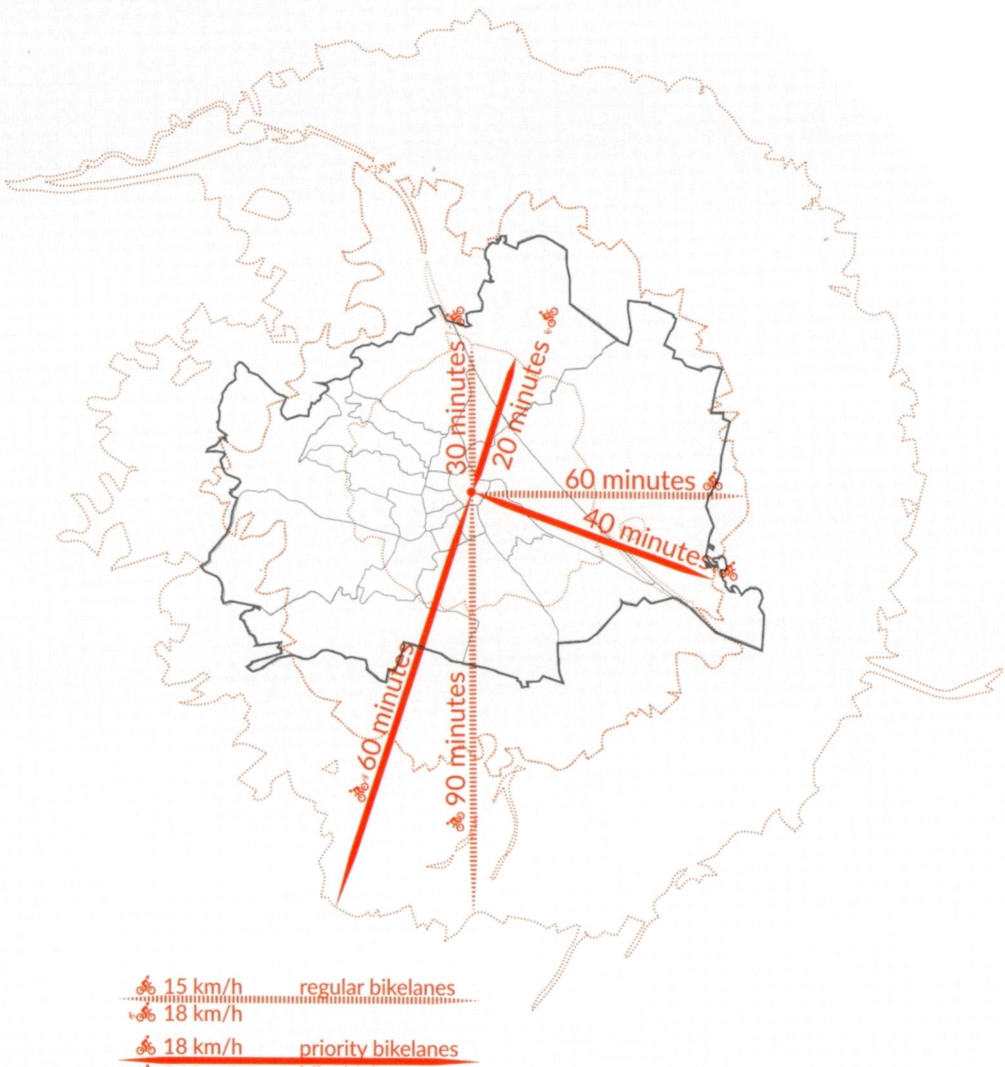

Bike Distances

calculated with Iso4App (2023)

Our networks are not ready for a mobility transition and our policies continue to fund carbon-intensive mobility

The annual land use for road infrastructure is increasing, while parts of our rail network are dismantled. The public transport is partly fragmented and there is a lack of fast and adequate bike connections.

Legislation and funding are incentivising an unsustainable way of mobility. 75% of the government's climate-damaging subsidies in the mobility sector go to road transport. The amount spent is between 1.87 and 3 billion euros.

Environment Agency Austria (2021): Land take in Austria 2020
WIFO (2022): Analysis of climate-counterproductive subsidies in Austria

Construction of the "Stadtstraße" Vienna. Source: basemap.at

Every year in Austria, several square kilometers of land are used to build new roads, while the rail network stagnates or is even reduced.

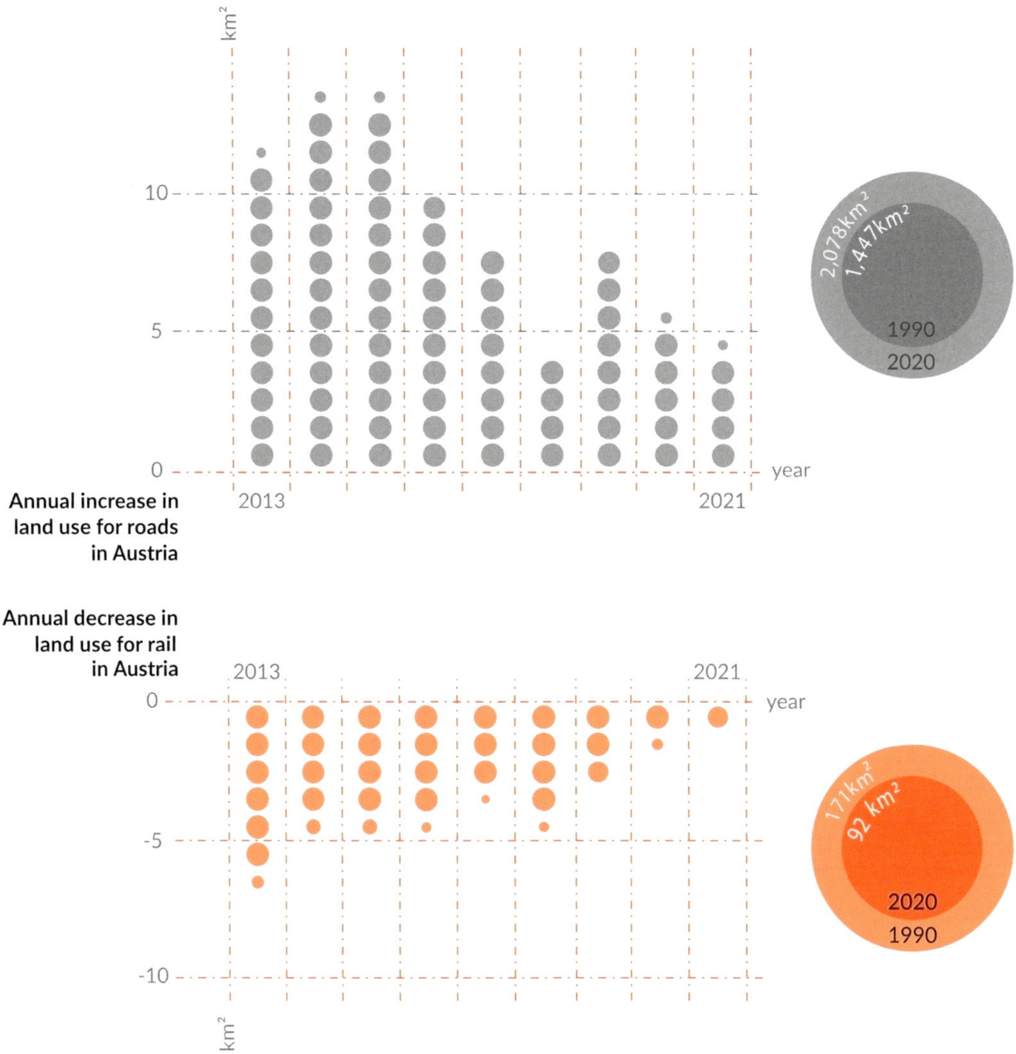

Development of Land used for Traffic Infrastructures

Environment Agency Austria (2021): Land take in Austria 2020

Between 2010 and 2020, 16.4 km² of new land was used for transportation in the metropolitan region.

Land taken between 2010 and 2020
for New Traffic Areas

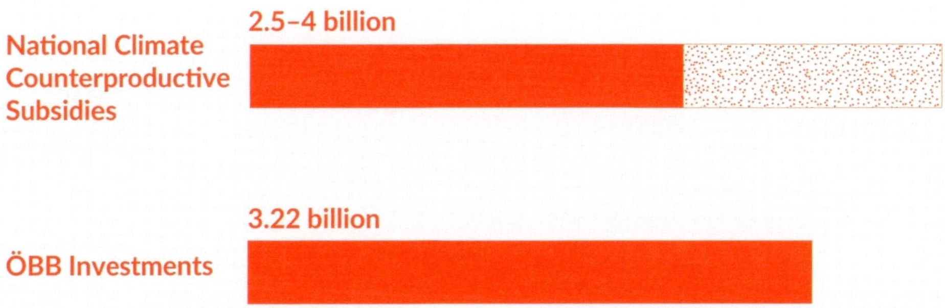

National Climate Contra Productive Subsidies
vs. ÖBB Investments

Technical University Graz, ISV (2023): Kordonerhebung Vienna 2022
Austrian Parliament (2022): Parliamentary Correspondence No. 1267

Public policies such as the commuter allowance encourage car commuting and long commutes: There is no incentive to live near your workplace.

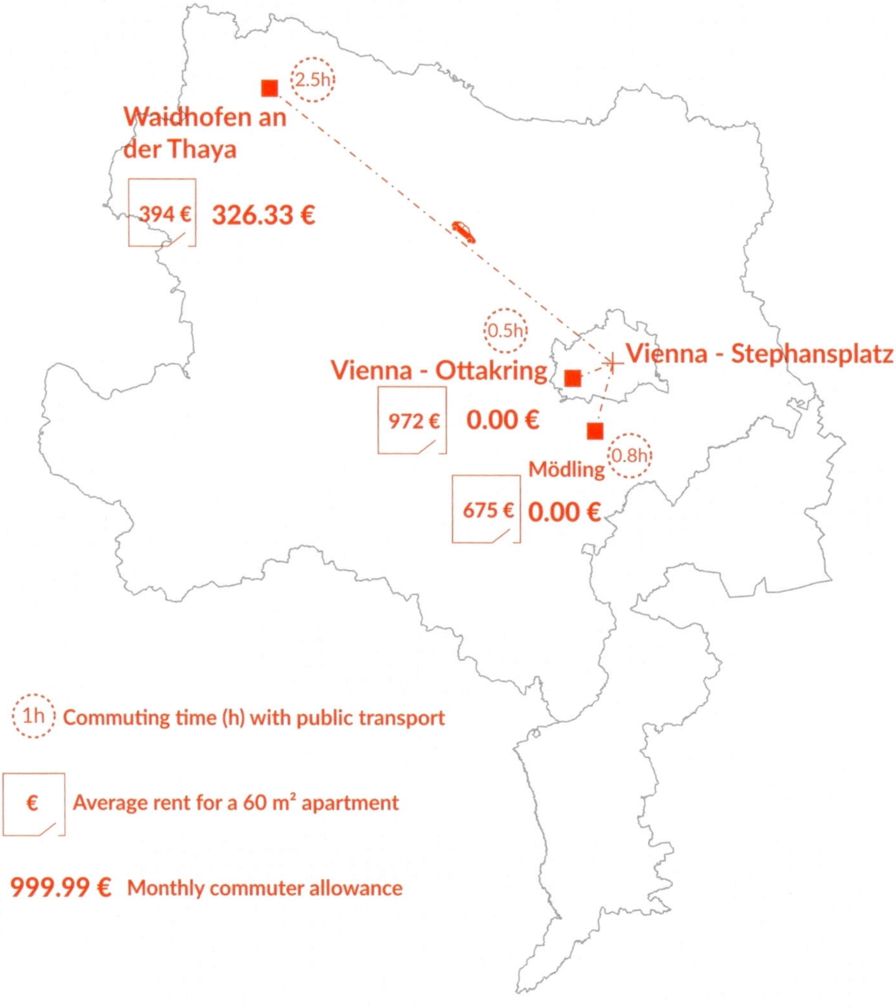

Financial Commuter Allowance

BMF (2023): Commuting Calculator
Wohnungsbörse (2023): Rental prices Vienna 2024
Wohnungsbörse (2023): Rental prices Weidhofen an der Thaya (Lower Austria) 2024

The total amount of commuter allowance spent in Lower Austria and Burgenland is very high compared to Vienna. The amount for Vienna is only 15% as high.

75% of the climate counterproductive government subsidies in the mobility sector are spent on road traffic. The amount spent is between 1.87 and 3 billion Euros.

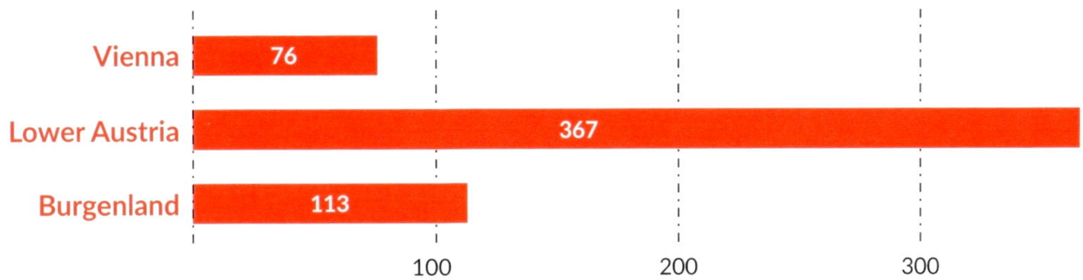

Commuter Allowance in Million Euros

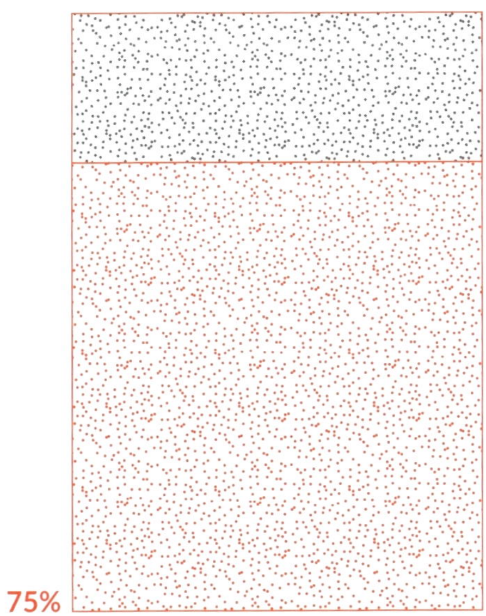

Share of Climate Contra Productive Subventions in the Mobility Sector for Road Infrastructure

Agenda Austria (2018): Commuters
WIFO (2022): Analysis of climate-counterproductive subsidies in Austria.

The international rail network still cannot compete with air connections from Vienna International Airport

There are several destinations around Vienna that can be reached by train within 8 hours without having to change trains, but these represent only a mere fraction of the destinations that can be reached by a direct flight from Vienna International Airport.

The year 2019 (before the pandemic) was a record year for Vienna International Airport with more than 31 million passengers: More than 8-times the population of the region.

Statistics Austria (2023): Aviation
Flightconnections B.V. (2023): Flights from Vienna (VIE)

Vienna International Airport in Schwechat, Source: basemap.at

Passenger traffic at Vienna International Airport has increased by more than 150% in ten years, impacting aviation emissions. In 2019, it counted 31 million passengers, more than 8 times the population of the metropolitan region.

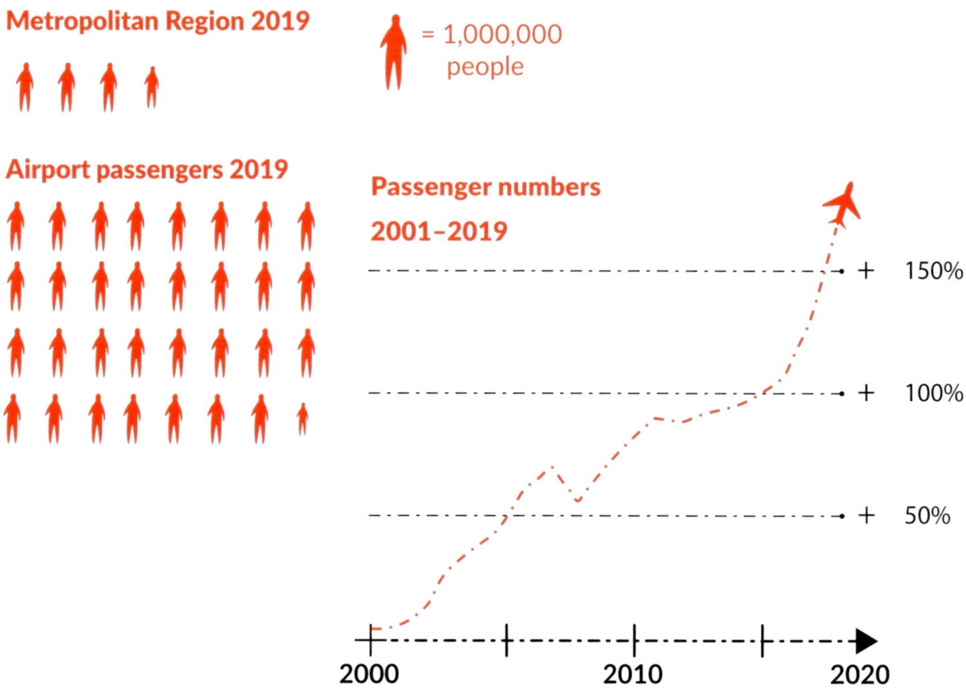

Inhabitants in the Metropolitan Region & Passengers from Vienna International Airport in 2019

Vienna Airport (2023): Traffic figures

Popular destinations include Germany and Italy, some of which can be reached within a few hours by train.

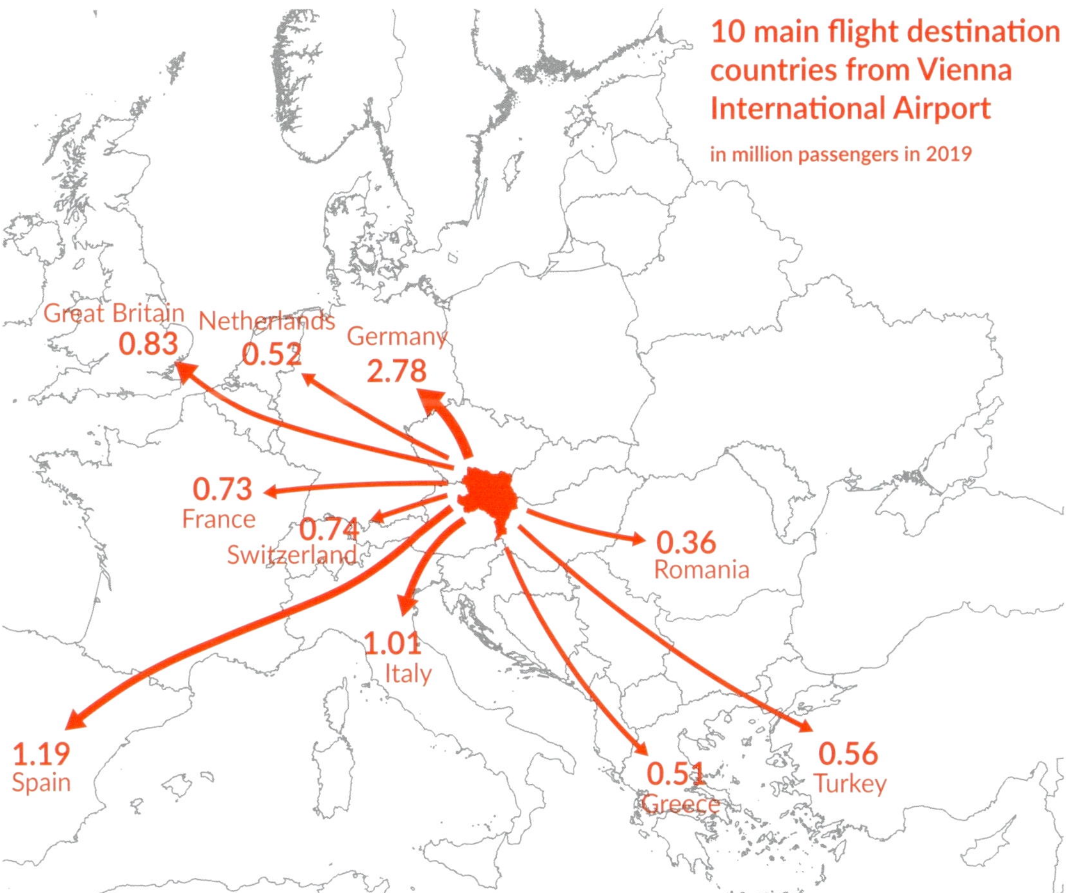

Flight Destinations

More than 50 cities in Europe can be reached by plane within a few hours from Vienna International Airport. In comparison, the number of cities that can be reached by train within 8 hours or by night train is much smaller.

Direct Connections by Plane

Flightconnections B.V. (2023): Flights from Vienna (VIE)

Direct Train Connections within 8 Hours or by Night Train

Interrail (2023): Timetable

If we shift our perspective from a time budget to a carbon budget, the network of connections changes significantly. For example, flying from Vienna to Frankfurt emits almost 14 times as much CO_2 as taking the train.

Destinations Reachable with ≤50 kg of CO_2 by Plane

Environment Agency Austria (2022a) : Emissions figures data basis 2022
SNCF Connect (2022): Calculation of CO2 emissions on your train journey

Connections by Train with a max. of one Change and ≤50 kg CO_2

Environment Agency Austria (2022a) : Emissions figures data basis 2022
SNCF Connect (2022): Calculation of CO2 emissions on your train journey

M5 Freight Transport

In Austria, 78% of goods are transported by road

On average, trucks produce about 39 times more emissions than rail transport. Nevertheless, road transport is the most important mode of freight transport in Europe, and Austria is no exception at 78%. Switching to rail transport would be much more efficient, as one freight train can replace about 40 trucks carrying 80 standard containers. One ton of goods can be transported almost 30 times further by rail than by road, with the same amount of greenhouse gas emissions.

Eurostat (2021): Freight Statistics – Modal Split
WKO (2022): Rail freight transport

Logistic Hub in Vienna, Source: basemap.at

The metropolitan region sits at the intersection of three Trans-European Network corridors.

Trans-European Network Corridors

European Commission (2021): Ten-T Core Network Corridors

The transportation of goods is mainly done by road, and Austria is no exception.

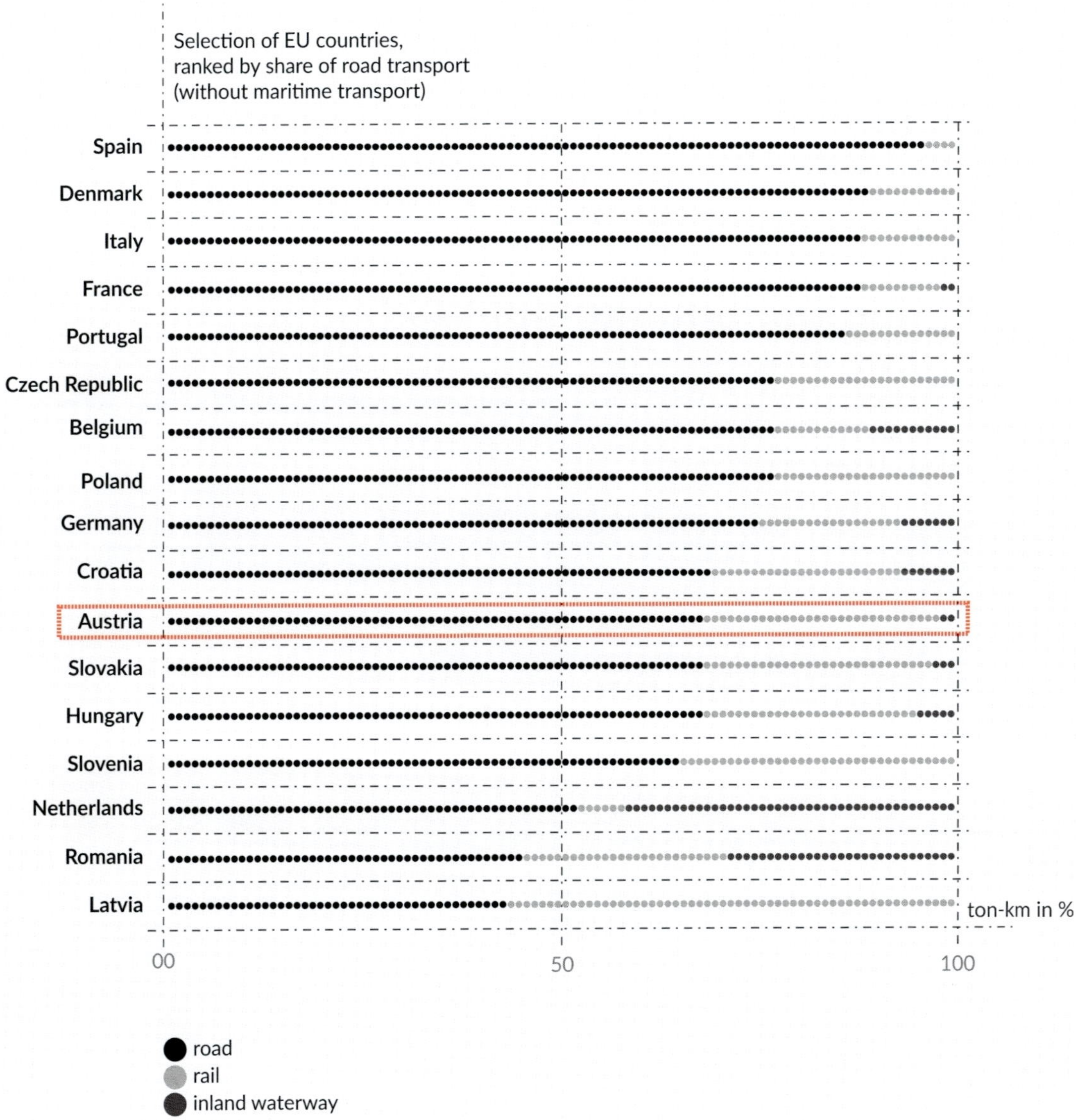

Distance with the Same Energy Consumption: Rail Freight Transport vs. Trucks

Eurostat (2021): Freight Statistics – Modal Split

Shifting to rail transport is more efficient: One freight train can replace 40 trucks carrying 80 standard containers. A ton of goods can be transported nearly 30 times farther by rail than by truck with the same amount of greenhouse gas emissions.

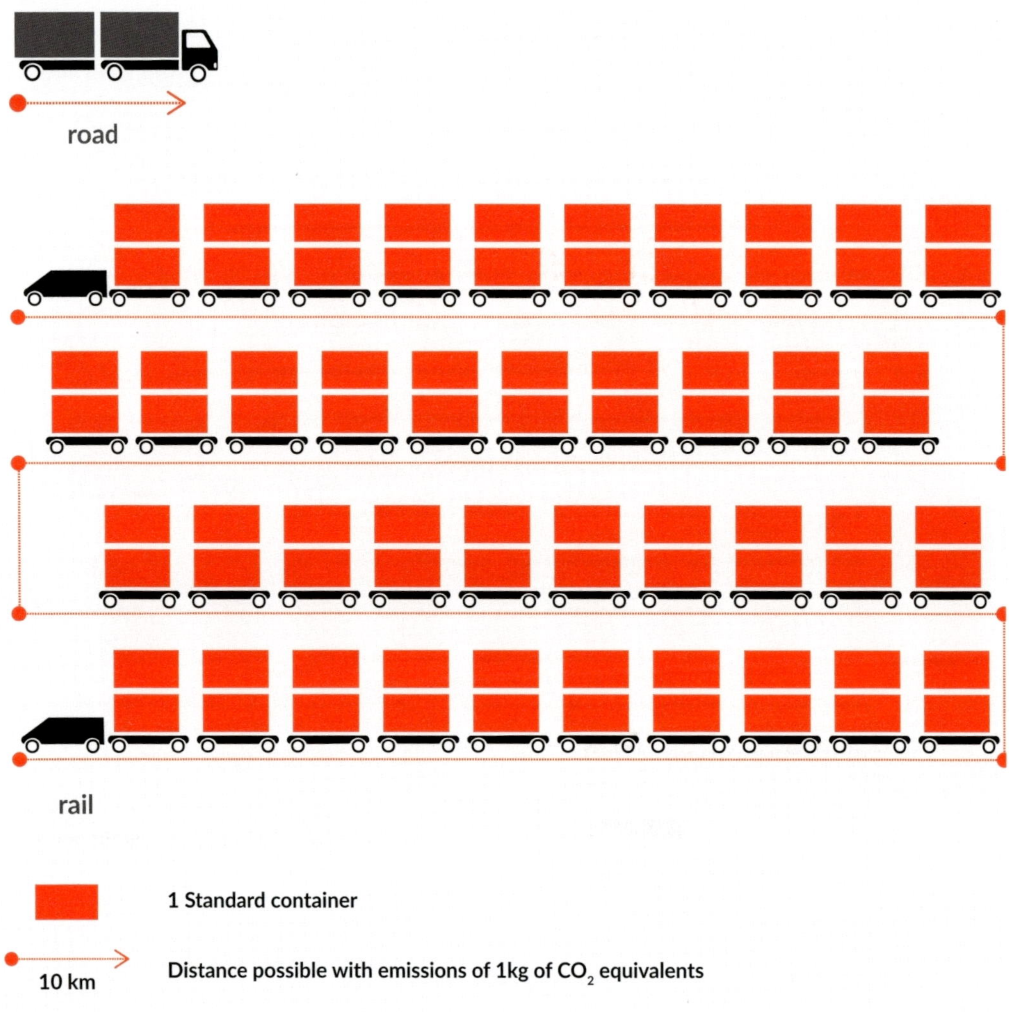

Freight Train Capacity

EcoTransit (2021): Methodology Report EcoTransIT World
Environment Agency Austria (2022a) : Emissions figures data basis 2022
WKO (2022): Rail freight transport

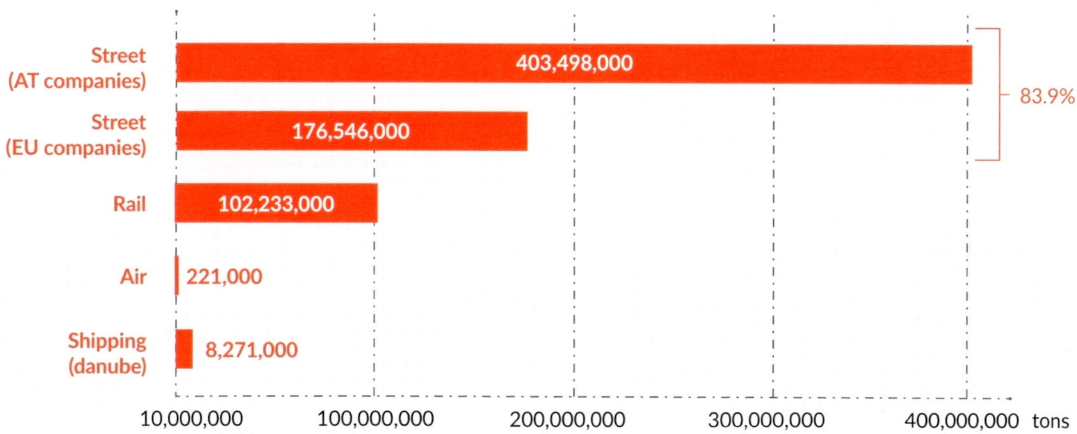

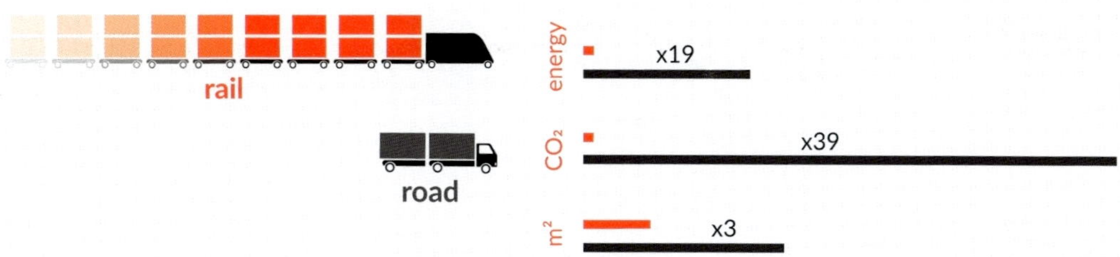

Statistics Austria (2022): Transport statistics
WKO (2022): Rail freight transport

Goods coming in by road

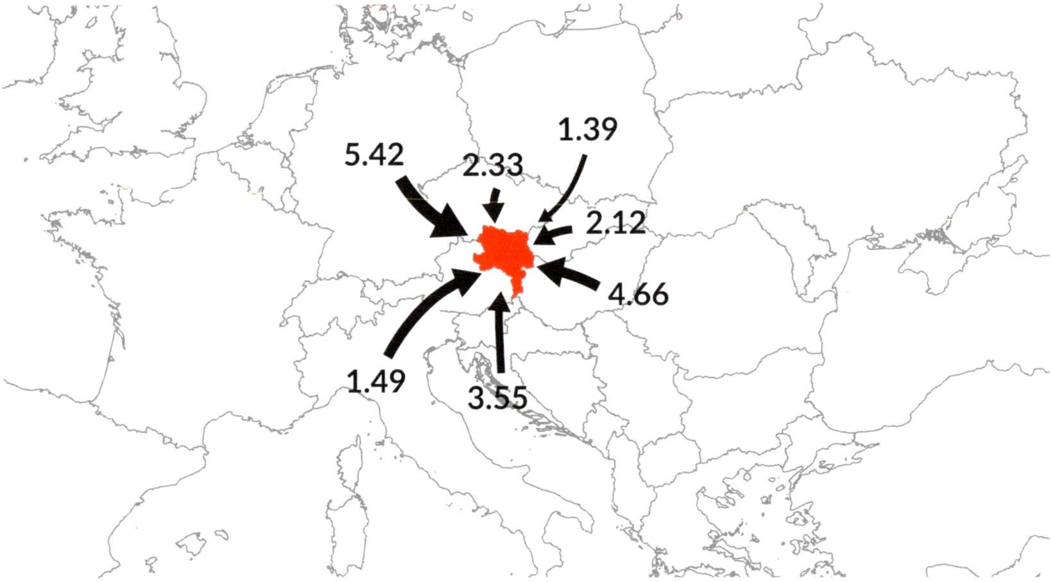

Main freight destinations to the metropolitan region by road

in million tons transported in 2021

Goods going out by road

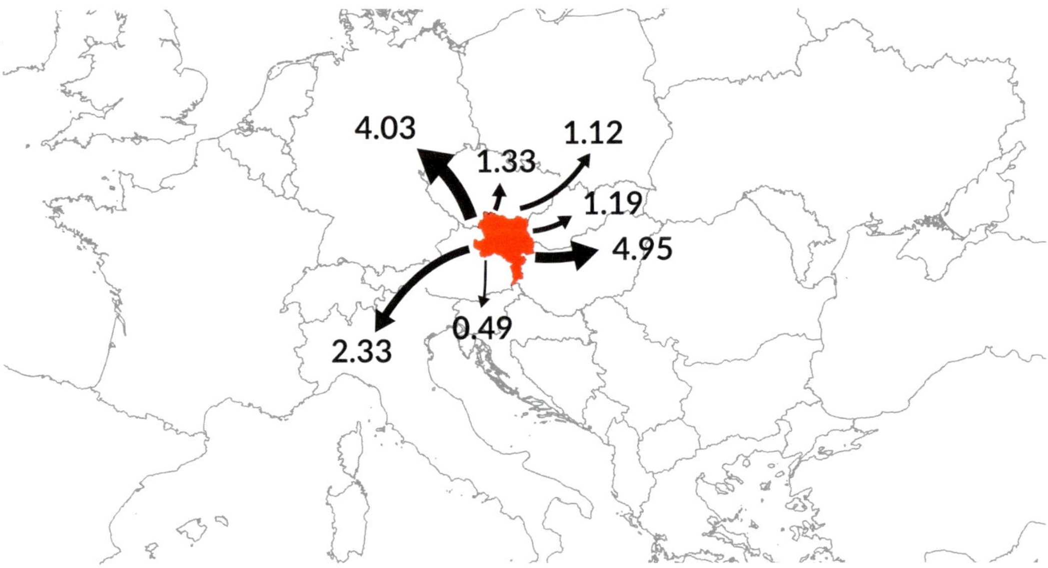

Main freight destinations from the metropolitan region by road

in million tons transported in 2021

Goods coming in by rail

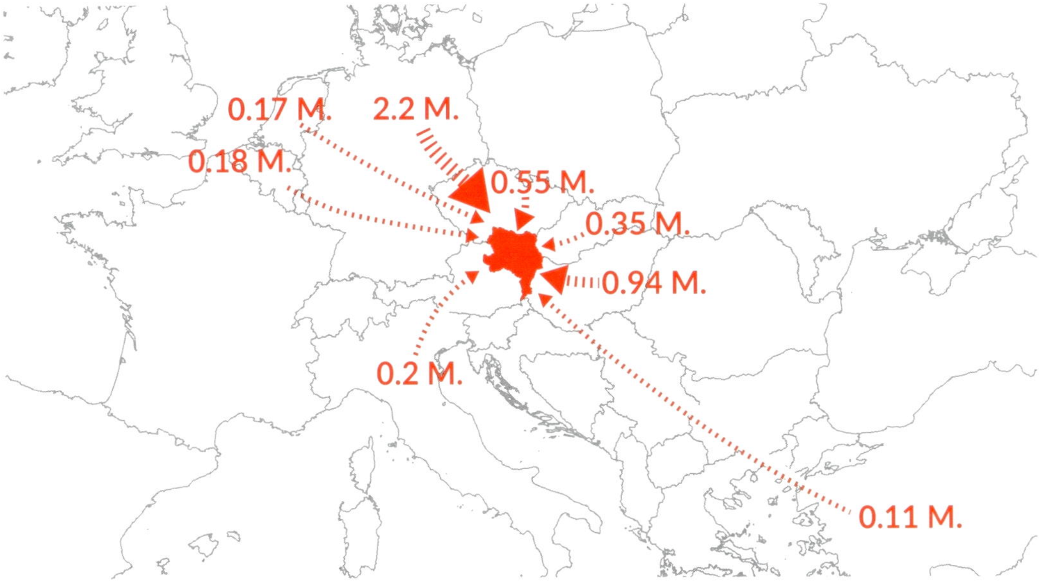

Main freight destinations to the metropolitan region by rail

in million tons transported in 2021

Goods going out by rail

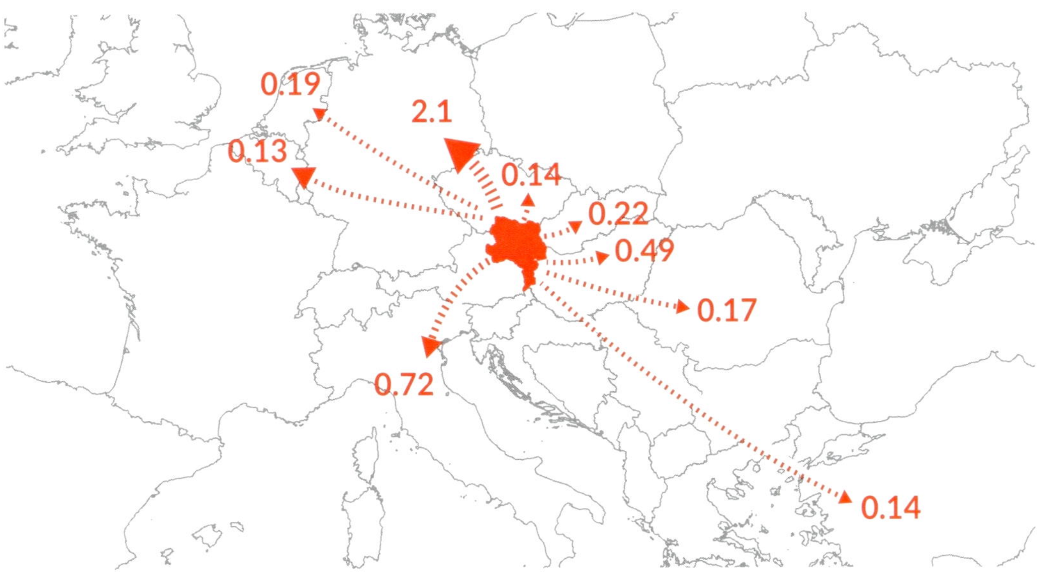

Main freight destinations from the metropolitan region by rail

in million tons transported in 2021

Statistics Austria (2022): Transport statistics

“We need to work with other sectors to create a holistic approach to mobility”

Interview with Jacqueline Grassl & Nicolas Fontaine

Jaqueline Grassl works at the Austrian Federal Ministry for Climate Action as head of the Mobility and Transport Technologies Department.

Nicolas Fontaine was the general manager of the Grenoble Mobility Authority, France and has been working in the field of mobility since 20 years throughout France. He is now the head of the territorial planning for the Val d’Oise department in France.

MetroLab: In Austria, the mobility sector is responsible for about one third of total greenhouse gas emissions, and emissions are even higher than in 1990 and are still growing. Mobility plays an important role in our daily lives, as most of us have to travel for work, education, leisure and shopping, among other things. Austria aims to be carbon neutral by 2040, but as the Austrian Federal Ministry of Environment points out, this goal will not be achieved with current measures alone. Could you tell us about Austria’s goals and strategies for achieving climate neutrality in the mobility sector?

Jaqueline Grassl: Becoming climate neutral is probably the most or the biggest challenge that man and womenkind were ever facing.

Austria has set itself quite ambitious goals, our ministry has introduced the Mobility Action Plan 2030. It is really a combination of different measures to avoid traffic on the one hand and to shift and improve traffic on the other.

We have several main objectives: Reversing the trend of steady growth in passenger and freight transport. A clear shift towards public transport and rail. And to promote new technologies with maximum efficiency. The first priority is certainly to create an attractive public transport system. We are working to have a demand-driven public transport system, to improve our rail network, to have a public transport system that is easy to use.

We have invented the climate ticket, an annual ticket for a maximum of three euros a day for almost all public transport in Austria. This is just one incentive, but a very powerful one to change people’s behaviour. Other priorities are certainly forms of active mobility such as walking or cycling. We have launched an e-mobility offensive. We are investing a lot of money in rail freight.

Another important economic instrument is the CO_2 pricing system that we introduced last year, where we are focusing on creating cost transparency for CO_2 emissions.

MetroLab: A new urban mobility plan has been introduced in Grenoble for 2019: Can you tell us about the pillars of this mobility plan and your experiences and lessons learned during its implementation?

Nicolas Fontaine: In 2019, the Grenoble Mobility Authority adopted a very ambitious mobility plan, which was awarded a prize by the European Commission. However, the authority was soon working on a brand new plan. Because the territory of the Mobility Authority was expanding, the plan was too ambitious for the financial situation, and the Covid-19 pandemic happened in between.

So what are the challenges we face today? We have a problem with the way public mobility policies were conceived in the 1970s and 1980s. Cities decided to focus their mobility policies on a single instrument, the tramway. In France, there were no trams in the 1970s. Now, every city, even small ones with around 50,000 inhabitants, has at least one line. The problem with this system is that it is very expensive to build. And after 40 years, a lot of maintenance has to be done, it is time to change the rolling stock, which is a huge investment. We are not talking about creating new services, just maintaining what we have. And we have found that the tram works very well for short trips, short distances, between one and four kilometres. For these distances, car use in Grenoble has really declined and the share of public transport has become very high.

But beyond five kilometres, if you are not travelling in the centre of the city, we realise that we are not offering people any solutions. We now really want to focus on those trips and develop new solutions for those trips. And that's the main challenge we're going to face in our new mobility plan.

MetroLab: It is interesting to discuss the challenges of implementing public transport. Mobility measures can be difficult because they require several factors to be in place before they can be effective. An important part is the acceptance of the population to change or adapt. Mobility habits are closely linked to individual behaviour and are therefore an emotive issue. How can we raise public awareness of new measures that affect our daily lives?

J.G.: There are many factors involved in changing personal behaviour and mobility habits, but I'll focus on two of the most important ones. The first important factor is accountability or responsibility. People often find it difficult to relate to national greenhouse gas emissions or their reduction because these concepts are too vague and distant from their personal lives. People don't really feel the need to change their behaviour in response.

In our research projects, we've found that a mobility budget, for example, can be an effective way to create a transparent picture of an individual's or company's CO_2 emissions. This approach makes people more aware of their impact and encourages them to think about whether their mobility choices are conscious or harmful to the environment. It is about making the issue personal, rather than focusing on the broader, less tangible concept of national greenhouse gases.

The second key factor is incentives or co-benefits. People need to see that changing their behaviour is not only good for the environment, but also good for them. If we can link mobility habits to personal health or well-being, it becomes easier to convince people to change. For example, if we count commuting time spent on active mobility, such as cycling, as part of the working day, it provides a tangible benefit. This kind of incentive can motivate people to change their behaviour. Companies can also be motivated by the fact that employees who cycle to work are often more productive, healthier and ▸

take fewer sick days. These are just two examples, but they show how incentives and co-benefits can play an important role in encouraging behaviour change.

N.F.: In Grenoble, we have never really struggled with public acceptance. We are lucky to have a fairly progressive population. People here are really keen to cycle and change their behaviour. As I mentioned, they were the first in the country to reintroduce the tram system. There's always been a strong relationship between the local authorities and the public.

One example is the Climate Citizens' Assembly that took place in Grenoble last year. We modelled it on the National Assembly that took place in 2021. We invited several citizens to work with technicians and politicians from the Grenoble Urban Community to propose measures and an action plan to achieve the goals of the Paris Agreement and contribute to the fight against climate change. These citizens spent several weekends working with us, learning about policies, and in the end they produced a very insightful list of action plans. We were pleased to see that more than 85% of the mobility-related measures they proposed were in line with what we're already working on and trying to improve.

This is a good example of how people often come up with the best solutions when you take the time to explain changes to them, allow them to interact with experts and give them space to reflect and discuss. These solutions are then much easier to implement because they are widely understood and supported by both local authorities and the public.

MetroLab: On the subject of freight transport, Austria occupies a central position, particularly within the European Union, so that it has to deal not only with domestic traffic but also with significant transit traffic. We would like to talk about the role of innovative and sustainable mobility solutions in freight transport. You have mentioned the National Freight Transport Plan, but what are the specific plans and strategies for freight transport at metropolitan or city level in Austria?

J.G.: We need to address not only greenhouse gas emissions, but also air pollution and noise associated with freight transport. Our Ministry has launched an RTI Mobility Strategy, which focuses on technical improvements for vehicles, improving digital infrastructure, increasing data availability and implementing governance measures. In addition, the National Freight Transport Plan will be published soon. To ensure sustainable freight transport, it is essential to increase the use of rail, especially for long-distance transport of heavy goods.

We also need to consider the integration of electric and hybrid vehicles on the road. For city centres, cargo bikes are an effective option for first and last mile deliveries. Digitalisation also has a key role to play. For example, optimising processes along logistics chains and developing multimodal hubs can reduce the number of empty trips, which is a significant problem. Improving interoperability between different systems and enhancing collaboration between companies is also crucial. In summary, freight transport needs to explore new ways to improve existing mobility solutions and consider new technologies and digital advances. Finding sustainable and efficient ways to handle deliveries is crucial, given the growing volume of online orders, especially with the COVID-19 pandemic.

MetroLab: In terms of the spatial impact of transport, the car still dominates and occupies a significant amount of space compared to other modes of transport.
Could you explain the spatial impact of the urban mobility plan in Greater Grenoble and why the metropolitan scale is crucial for the implementation of this new plan?

NF: Created in 2020, the Mobility Authority is the result of the merger of three previous authorities. The Grenoble agglomeration is relatively small, about 20 kilometres wide, which limited our ability to address the challenges of daily medium-distance travel.

Previously, we effectively encouraged short trips by getting people out of their cars and onto the tram. However, we struggled to provide solutions for those who travelled 5 to 20 kilometres a day due to the limitations of our smaller authority. In 2020, the three areas decided to merge and shift their focus. We now prioritise improving services and developing new transport modes for journeys between 5 and 25 kilometres. This is a major metropolitan challenge, as our previous structure was too limited in scope. In the future, we plan to focus on improving express bus services and developing an "S-Bahn" system in Grenoble. We see this as a key tool for transforming mobility on a metropolitan scale.

MetroLab: Where do you see the importance of promoting cooperation between cities, metropolitan areas and their immediate surroundings?

N.F.: In France, the situation is quite complex, with different public authorities responsible for different aspects of transport. For example, while we are responsible for urban transport, the regional authority in Lyon manages the regional rail networks. It's clear that we need to work closely together because our efforts are interdependent. The region and the metropolitan area have been working together for about 20 years. We've developed an integrated ticketing system, a single information system and a single fare system.

Our next challenge is to work out how to fund and manage these regional networks, which is proving difficult due to shared financial constraints. On a smaller scale, it's also crucial to work with individual cities as they control parking, a key lever for influencing mobility behaviour. The balance between the regional authority and the cities is not always easy, but it is essential. Our Mobility Authority serves as an ideal platform to manage this cooperation effectively.

MetroLab: In Austria, looking specifically at Vienna and the surrounding municipalities in Lower Austria and Burgenland, is there strong cooperation in the mobility sector between the city and the surrounding regions?

J.G.: I'd say there's still potential, but we're seeing a lot of cooperation at the moment, and we're supporting that kind of cooperation. We have what we call real-world laboratories, which provide a good environment for experimentation and fostering cooperation in both urban and regional contexts. We support research by providing funding to both rural areas and cities to encourage them to work together on new mobility services, and at the city level we're working on different concepts such as superblocks and the 15-minute city.

The 15-minute city concept, for example, means that everything you need for your daily life is just around the corner. It's a concept we find very attractive and actively support. This includes active mobility, public transport and shared mobility at city level. Real-world labs are valuable because they bring together decision-makers, users and the general public. They help to break down barriers and address people's concerns about new mobility services. This approach facilitates effective collaboration and participation.

MetroLab: How do you see the future of the mobility sector as a driving force towards climate neutrality?

N.F.: I must admit that I may seem old-fashioned, but I still strongly believe in the importance of infrastructure development. I do not think that digital services will change everything and be the solution to everything, I think they need a solid infrastructure foundation to be truly effective. In Grenoble, we want to change our mobility paradigm. In France, in the 1970s and 1980s, ▸

the focus was very much on trams. But we've seen that other countries, particularly in northern Europe—such as the Netherlands and Copenhagen—have prioritised active modes of transport such as walking and cycling. They have invested heavily in infrastructure for these modes, and we want to take a similar approach.

Our aim in Grenoble is to become the "Copenhagen of the Alps". This shift will be a key driver for changing mobility and achieving climate neutrality in the coming years. We also recognise the need to invest in infrastructure for longer journeys, particularly those between 5 and 25 kilometres. A key initiative here is the development of an "S-Bahn" system for the Grenoble area. By combining cycling for short trips with rail for medium distances, we believe we can transform mobility in Grenoble and move closer to carbon neutrality.

J.G.: I completely agree. The future of mobility must be multimodal and inclusive. It's important that people can easily access and use different modes of transport without being overly dependent on their own car.

In Austria, we often discuss the concept of a mobility guarantee, which is in line with this vision. People should be able to rely on mobility services regardless of their income, background or disability. We need to build a system that allows everyone to use different mobility options effortlessly.

But let's not forget that mobility is not an end in itself. As you mentioned, no one uses a train just for the sake of it; we use it to get where we want to go, whether it's to work, school or leisure activities. So we need to work with other sectors such as health, tourism and education to create a holistic approach to mobility. Ultimately, it's about improving quality of life and making mobility work seamlessly for everyone. ▪

MetroLab Podcast
Episode MOVING in Climate Neutral City Regions

Listen to our podcast on all platforms!

LIVING
in the Metropolitan Region

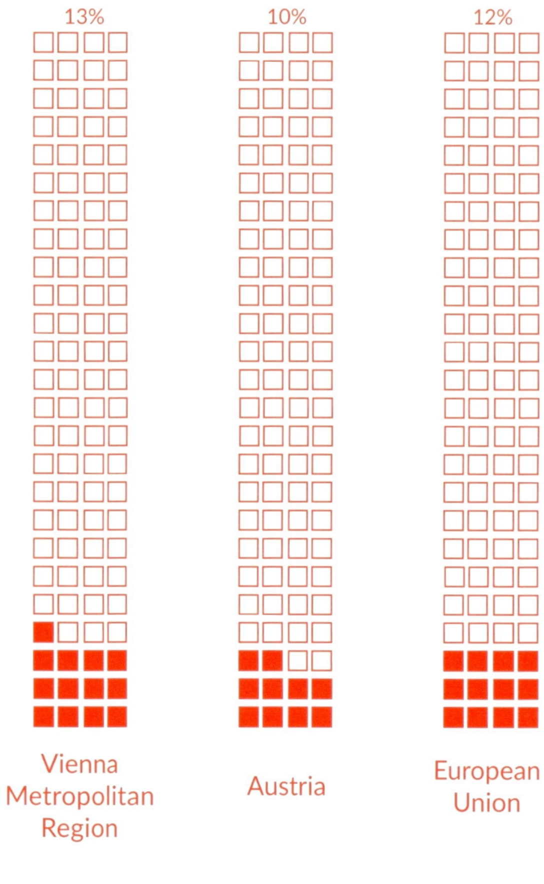

Share of the housing sector in total greenhouse gas emissions

Environment Agency Austria (2022 b): Federal states air pollutant inventory 1990–2020

The way we live and build has a significant impact on our carbon emissions. In this chapter of the Emerging Phenomena Atlas, we explore current trends in the building sector, which plays a critical role in greenhouse gas emissions. This sector is responsible for a significant proportion of energy consumption and carbon emissions. Despite efforts to improve energy-efficient typologies and adopt sustainable practices, the building sector remains a significant challenge in the quest to reduce emissions. Understanding the complex interactions between building practices, density, typologies, and urban planning is essential to reimagining a more sustainable future for our living spaces.

Metropolitan Structures Changing over Time

Oberes Hausfeld, Vienna

YEAR 1956

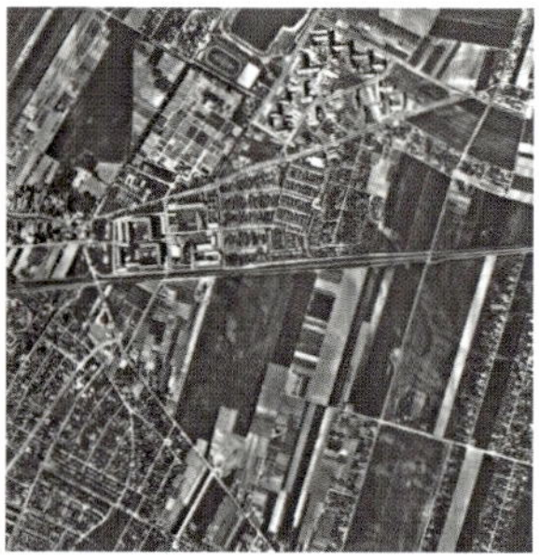

YEAR 1992

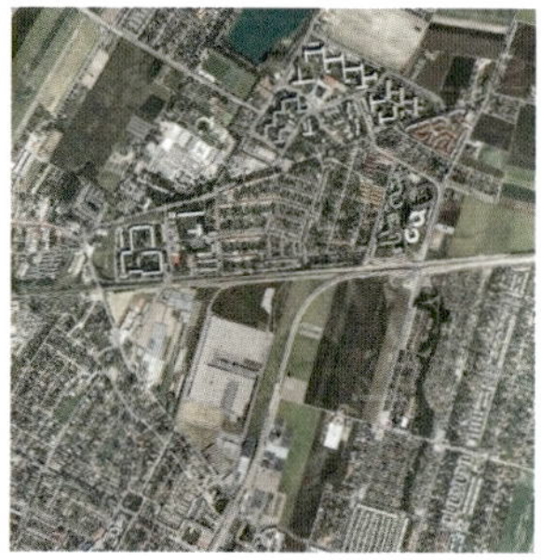

YEAR 2021

Altmannsdorf, Vienna

YEAR 1956

YEAR 1976

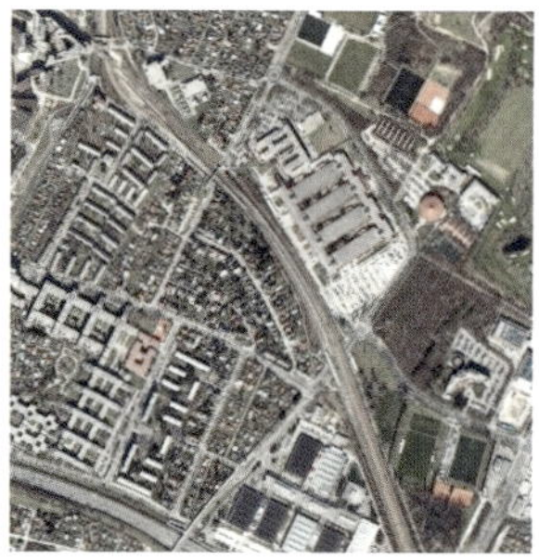

YEAR 2021

Siebenhirten, Vienna

YEAR 1956

YEAR 1976

YEAR 2021

City of Vienna (2024): Geodata viewer of the Vienna City Survey

Since the beginning of the new millennium, the metropolitan region has experienced a steady increase in its population, which is expected to reach 4.45 million in 2050. Thus, the metropolitan region will have to cope with an increase of 1 million inhabitants in 50 years.

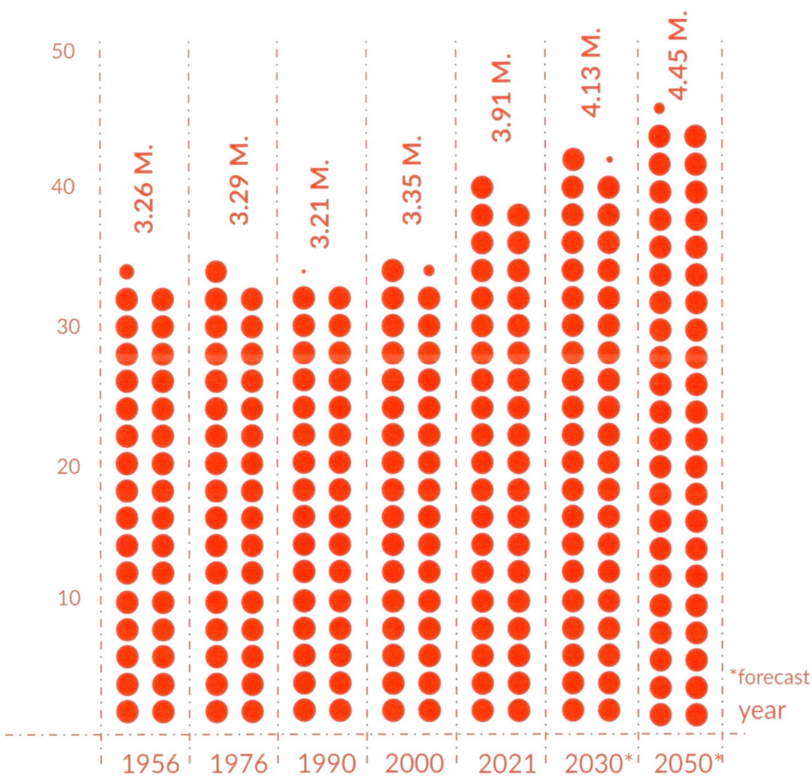

Population of the Metropolitan Region 1956–2050

Statistics Austria (2023): Population

Areas with a high population density have lower greenhouse gas emissions per person

More densely populated areas within the metropolitan area have lower housing-related emissions per inhabitant. Municipalities with a higher population density also emit fewer greenhouse gases per person: This is partly due to smaller living spaces (the average living space per person in Lower Austria and Burgenland is 43.5% higher than in Vienna), but also due to shorter distances and a reduction in greenhouse gas emissions from mobility.

Abart-Heriszt (2022): Energiemosaik Austria
Environment Agency Austria (2021): Land take in Austria 2020

2nd District Vienna, Source: basemap.at

The different population densities also reflect very different living conditions within the metropolitan region: In Lower Austria and Burgenland, people live on average in larger houses, most of which are owned. In Vienna, despite a particularly high proportion of single households, the majority live in rented apartments in a denser area.

Population Densities 2022

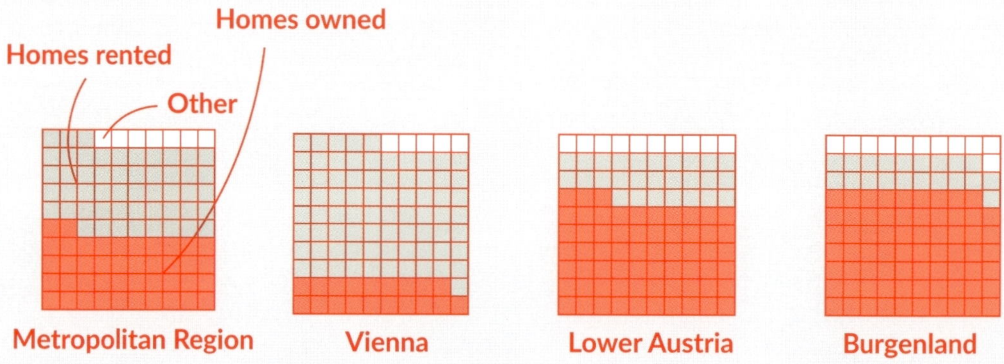

Home Ownership & Rent

Statistics Austria (2023): Private households
Statistics Austria (2023): Regional division
Statistics Austria (2023): Population

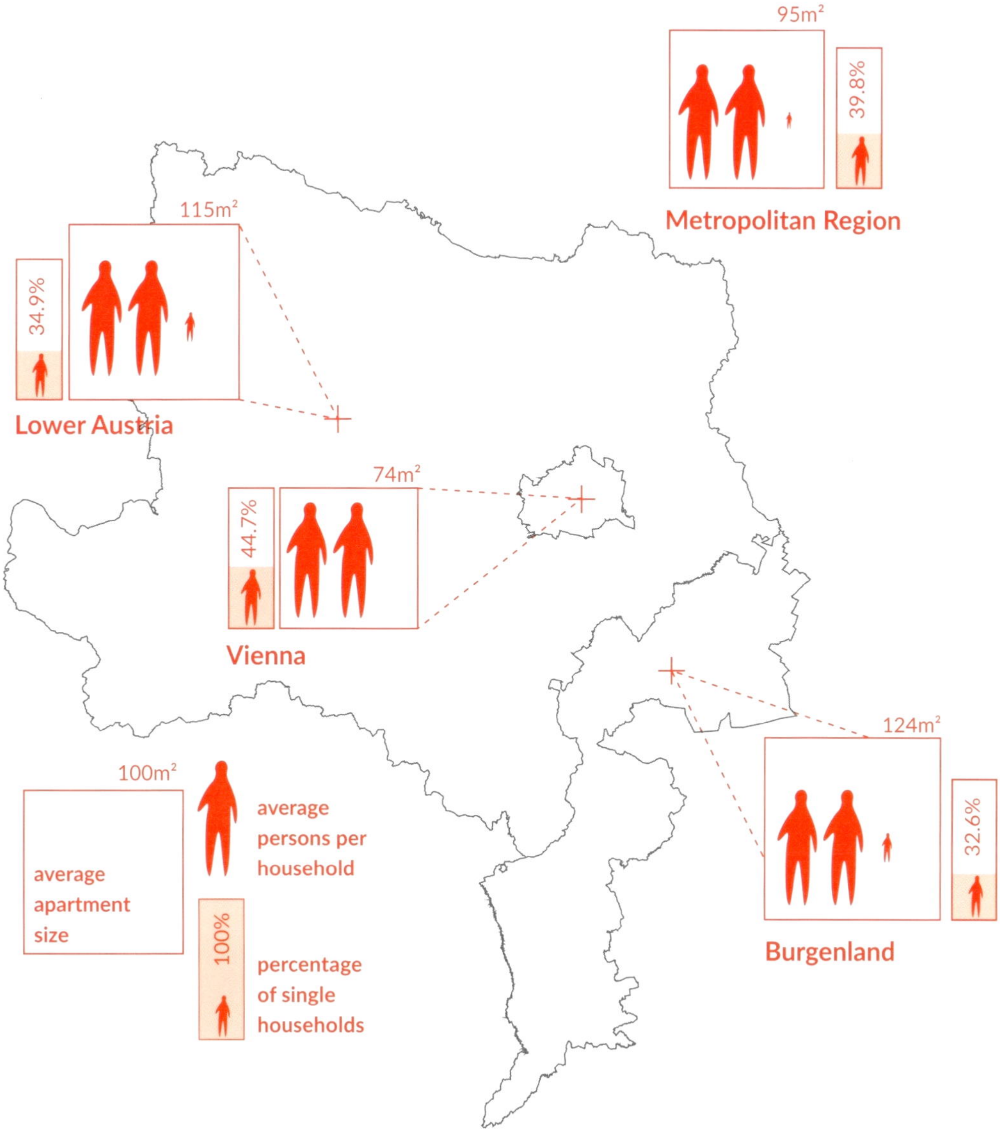

Housing Conditions 2022

Statistics Austria (2022): Housing Conditions
Statistics Austria (2023): Private households

Different population densities have a strong impact on energy consumption for housing and thus on greenhouse gas emissions. Vienna has by far the highest population density in the metropolitan region.

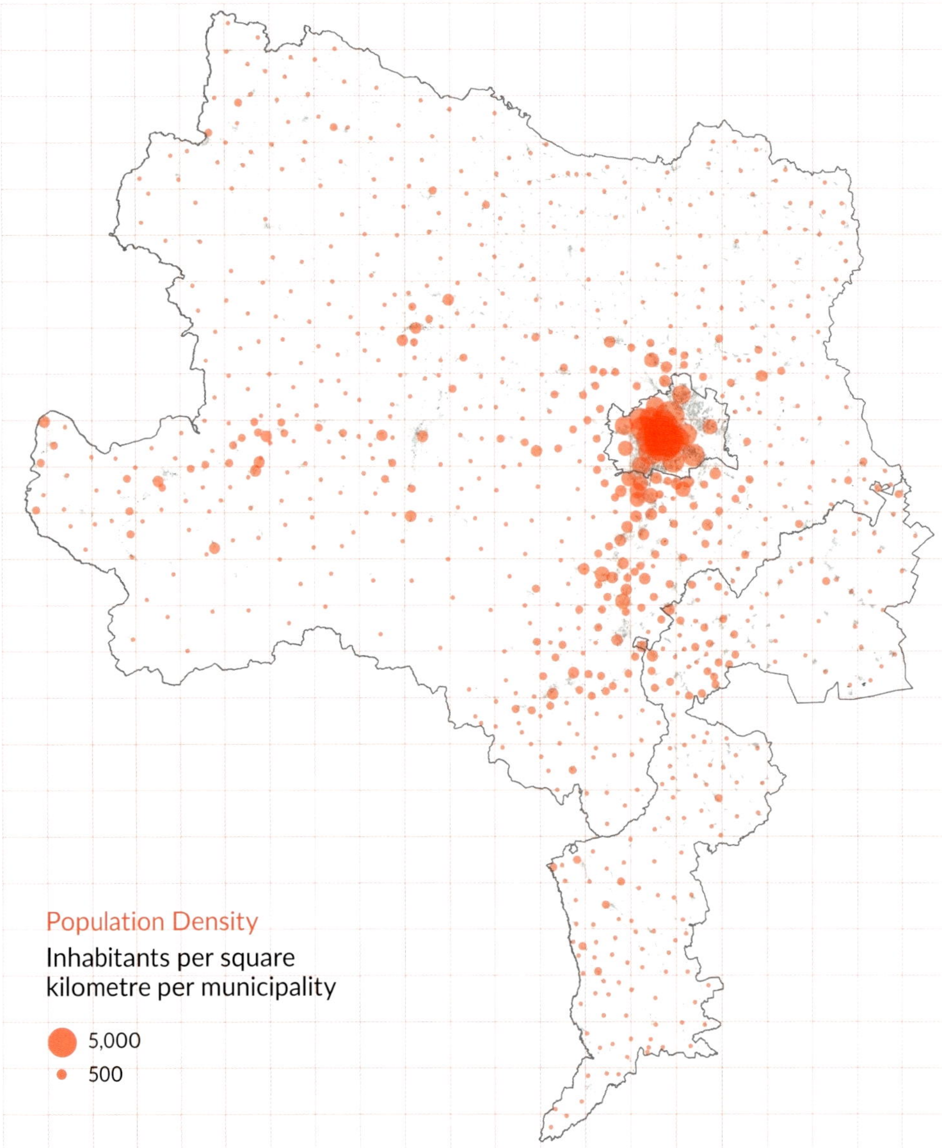

Population Density

At the same time, Vienna has the lowest greenhouse gas emissions from the housing sector. In contrast, the least densely populated, more rural areas have the highest greenhouse gas emissions from this sector.

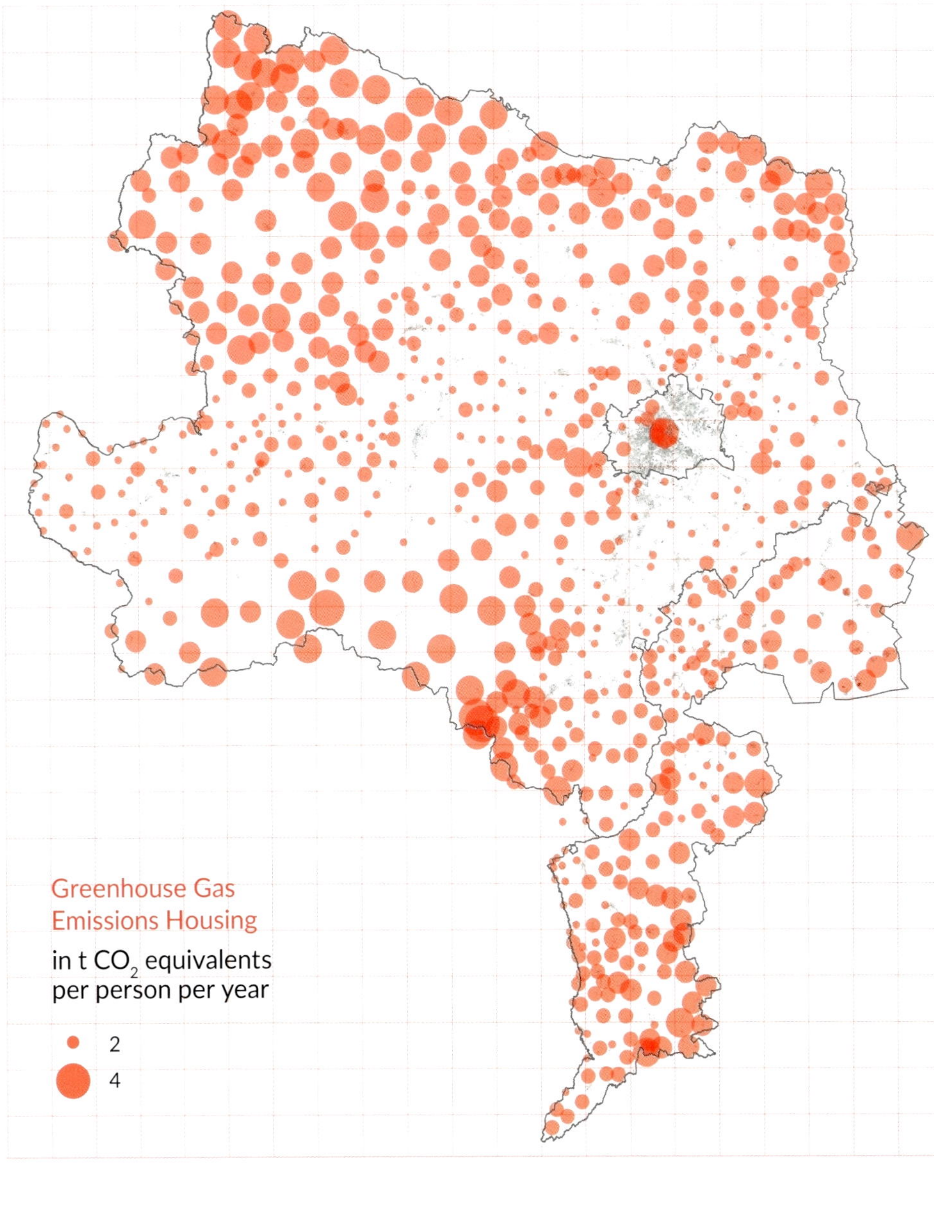

Greenhouse Gas Emissions in the Housing Sector

Density saves precious land: Although 35% of Vienna's permanent settlement area is sealed, the average sealed area per inhabitant in Lower Austria and Burgenland is more than 7 times higher.

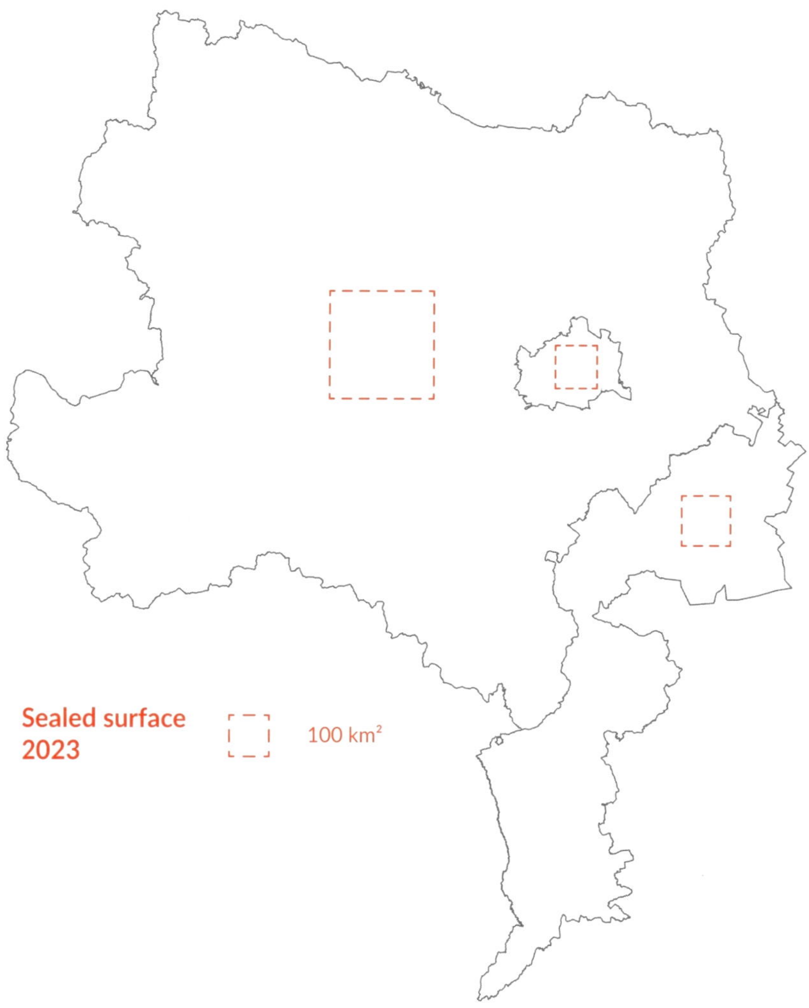

Sealed Surface in Vienna, Lower Austria and Burgenland

Environment Agency Austria (2021): Land take in Austria 2020

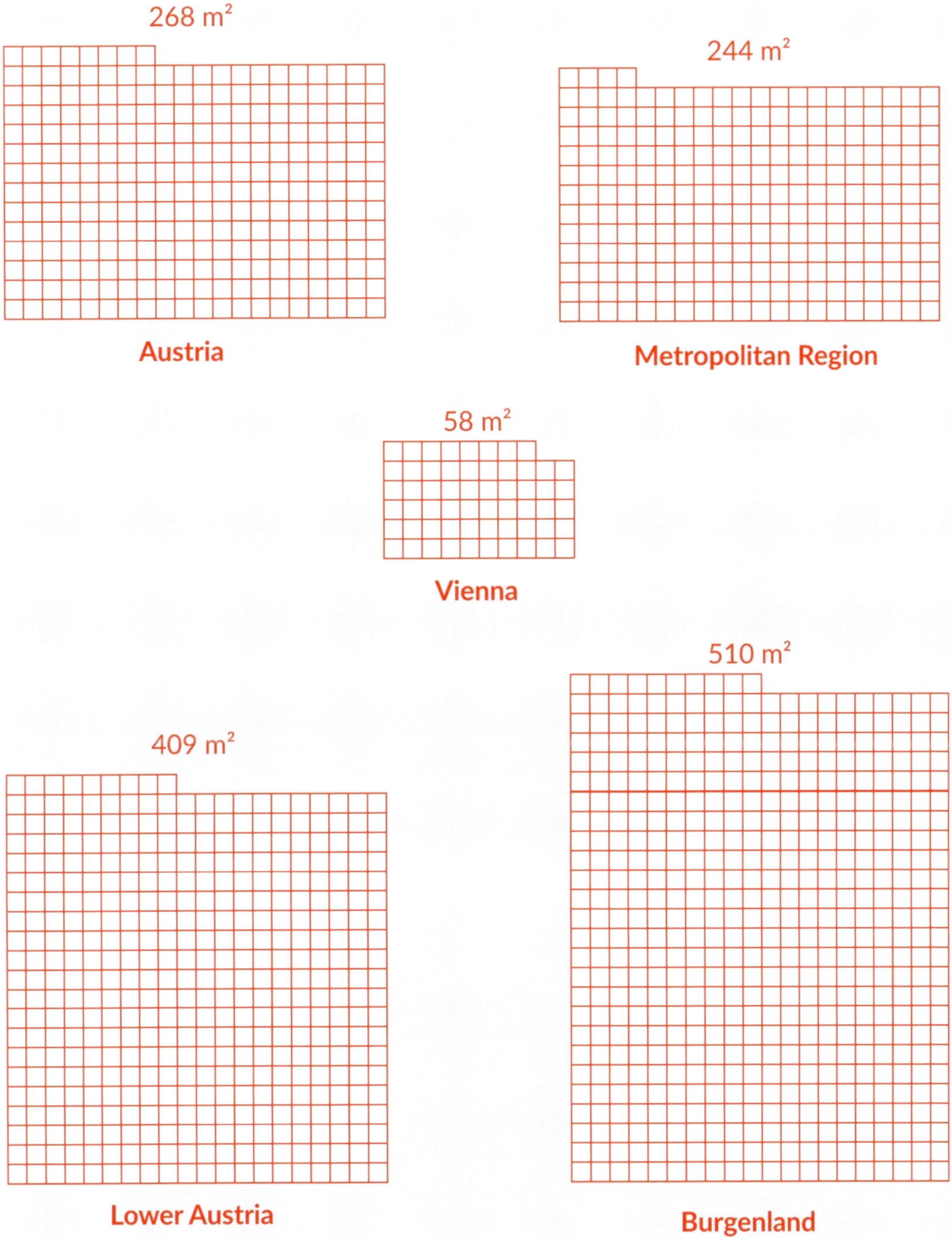

Sealed Surface per Person

L2 Vacancy Rate

The region is not able to keep track of its vacancy rate and, as a result, does not know its current statistics

Due to the lack of knowledge about vacancy rates throughout Austria, no adequate measures can be taken to address the problem, nor can a true reflection of housing demand be made for newly constructed buildings. It is only known that 12% of dwellings have no registered occupants.

Statistics Austria (2023): Microcensus; Main Residence Dwellings as of 2004

High Rise Devlopment St. Marx Vienna, Source: basemap.at

There is no official count of empty dwellings in Austria. This also means that there is no basis for deciding how much new construction is needed to meet population growth.

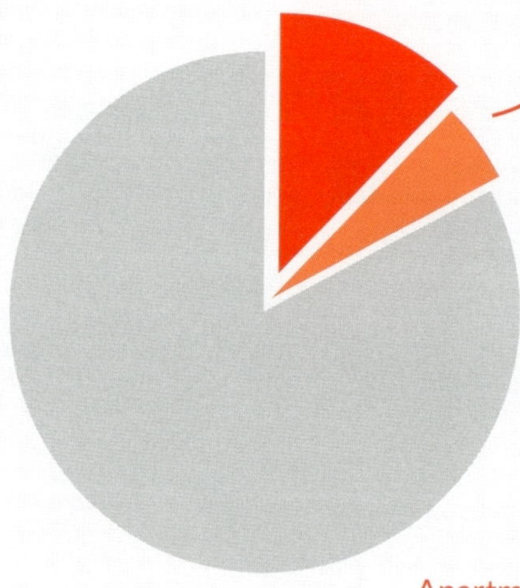

In Vienna, 20% of newly constructed apartments are empty.

Vacant Apartments

Chamber of Labour Vienna (2022): Housing boom in Vienna 2018–2021

Ongoing construction is increasingly taking up space on undeveloped land. The trend toward larger homes and more living space results in land use, energy consumption, and carbon emissions

Average living space per person has more than doubled since 1971. We continue to build single-family homes, each of which occupies an average of 162.8 square meters of land in the metropolitan area. If the region continues at this rate, by 2058 an area larger than the city of Vienna will have been consumed. This also impacts the effectiveness of our carbon sinks.

BMAW (2022): Housing policy and the housing industry in Austria.
Abart-Heriszt (2022): Energiemosaik Austria

The Municipalities Wiener Neustadt and Neudörfl growing together, Source: basemap.at

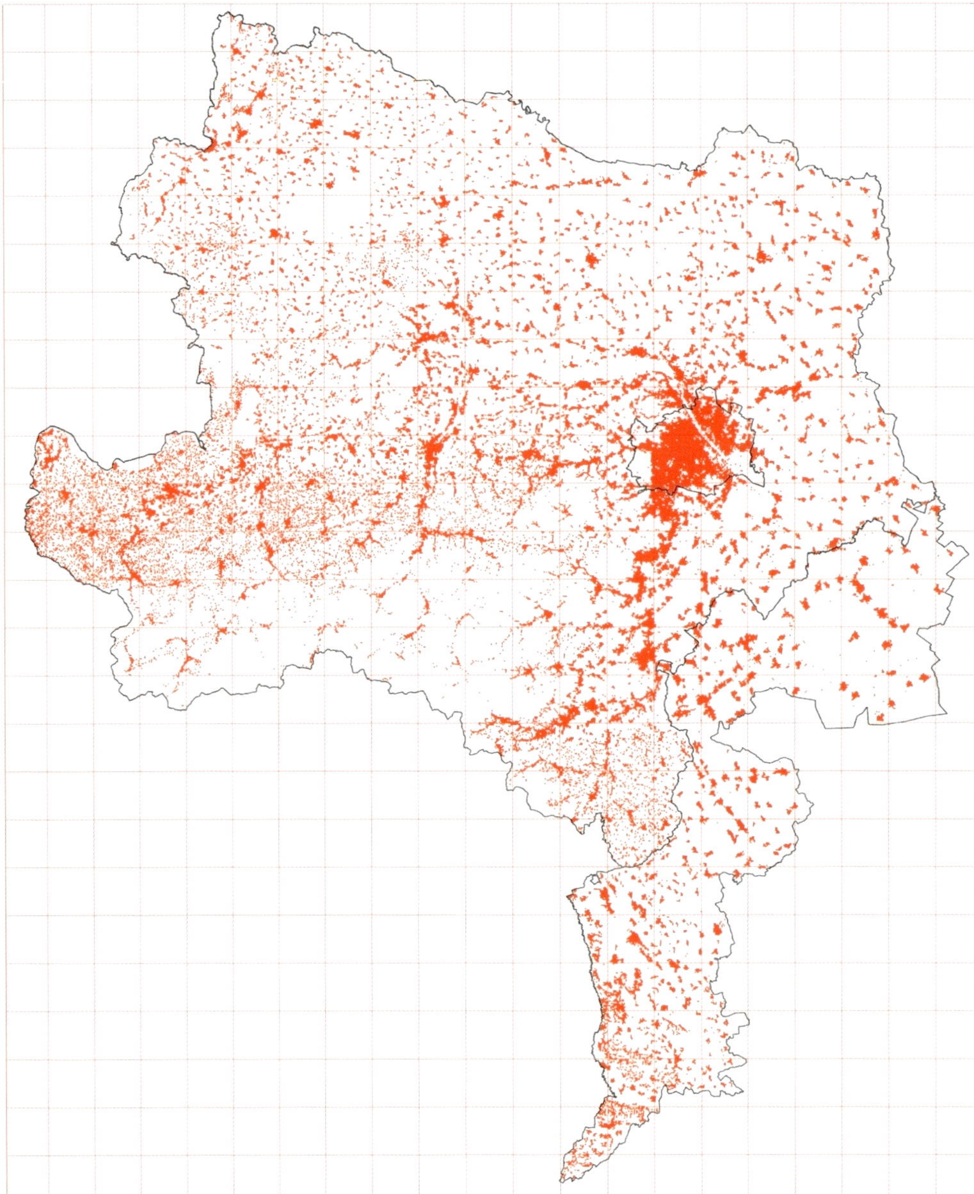

Settled Areas

OpenStreetMap (2022)

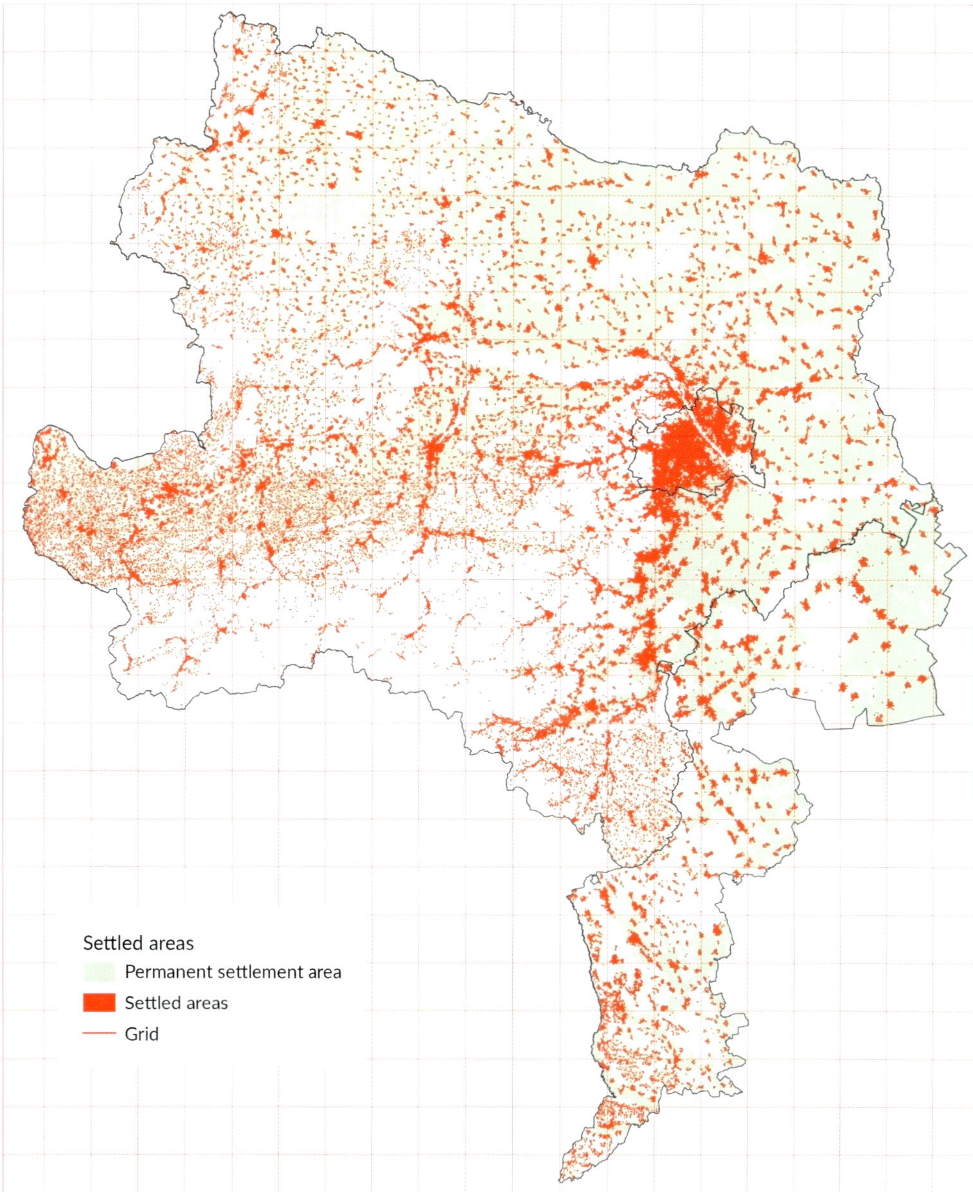

Permanent Settlement Areas

The average living space in Austria has more than doubled since 1971. The percentage of single households in Austria has risen from 26.5% to 38%. Single households require a lot of living space: the living space per person in single households is 67% higher than the general average.

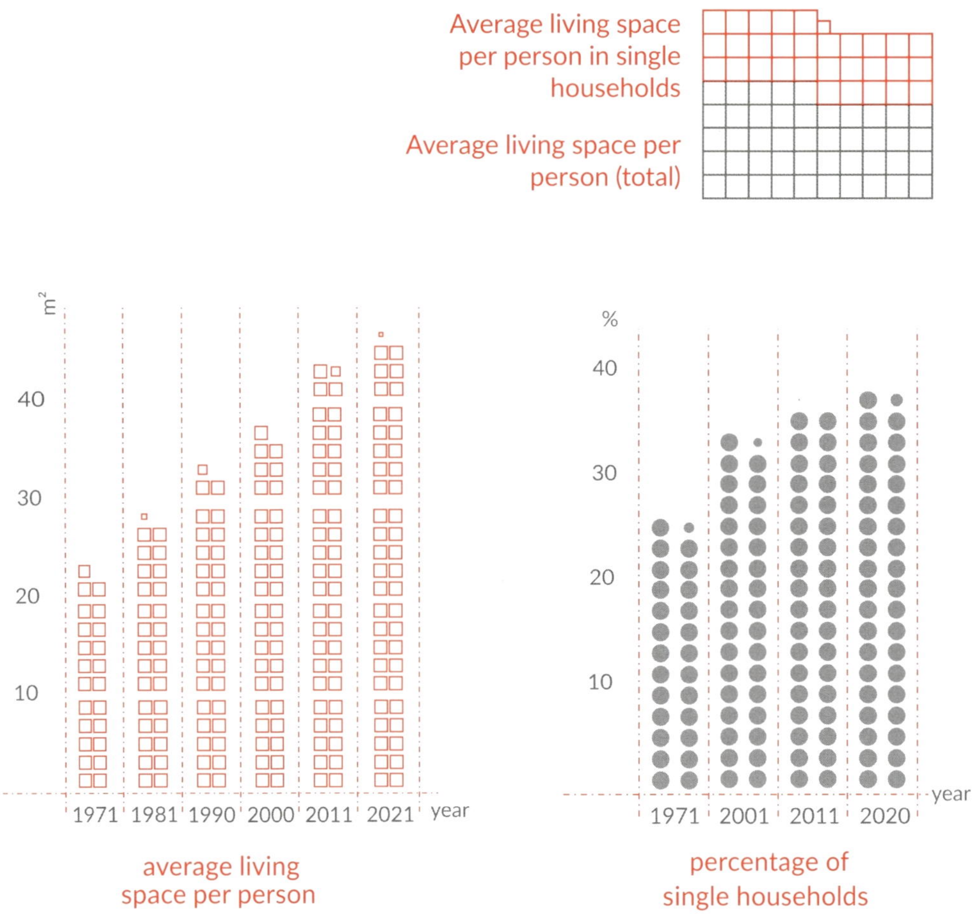

Average Living Space per Person in Austria

In recent years, the trend in the metropolitan region has been towards even more single households, smaller households, and larger apartments. According to statistical projections, the trend towards single households will continue in the coming decades. This means that there is still a demand for more housing, which contradicts ecological limits.

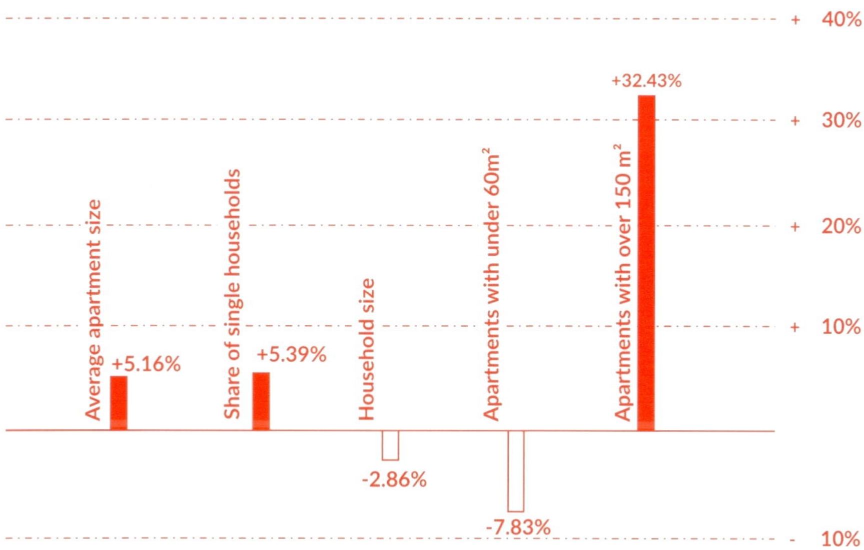

Tendencies in the Metropolitan Region 2005–2021

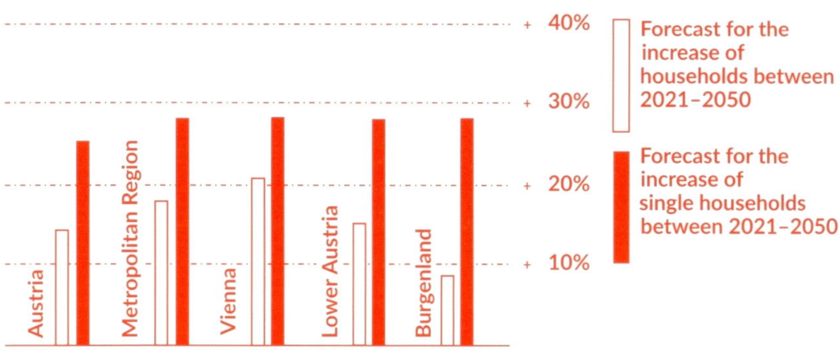

Increase in Households 2021–2050

Statistics Austria (2023): Private households

Between 2005 and 2021, an additional 162.8 square meters per single-family or two-family dwelling were permitted in the metropolitan area, contributing significantly to land consumption. Between 2016 and 2021, more than 26% of new housing units in the region were built in one- or two-family homes.

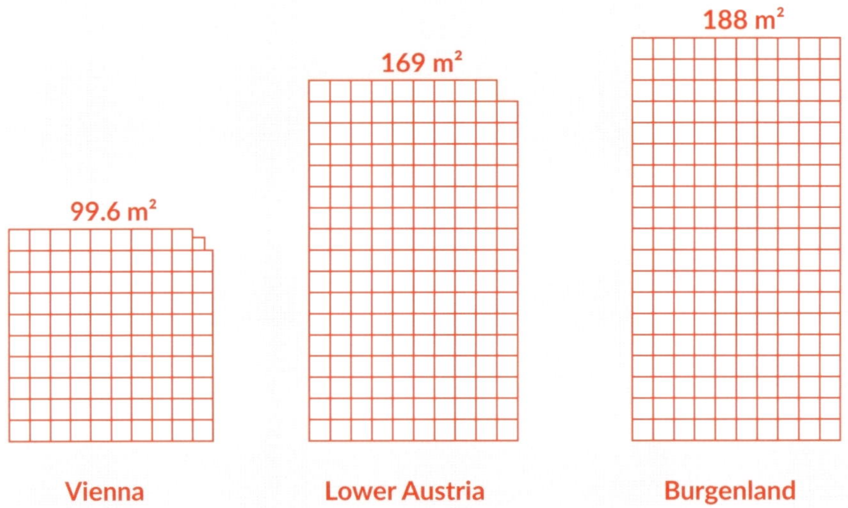

Average Surface Permitted to be Overbuilt per Single/Two-Family Home

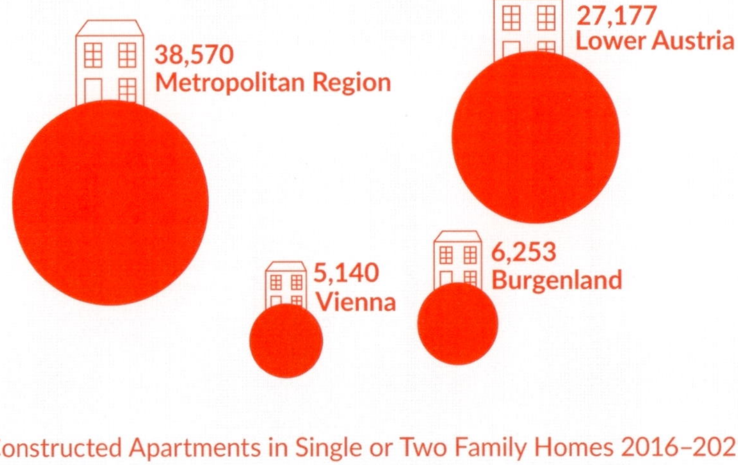

Newly Constructed Apartments in Single or Two Family Homes 2016–2021

Statistics Austria (2023): Building permits, dwellings as of 2010

If we continue to use the same amount of land as we have in recent years, by 2050 we will have used an additional area larger than the permanent settlement area of Vienna. That means fewer carbon sinks, less space for food production, less green space, less space for recreation.

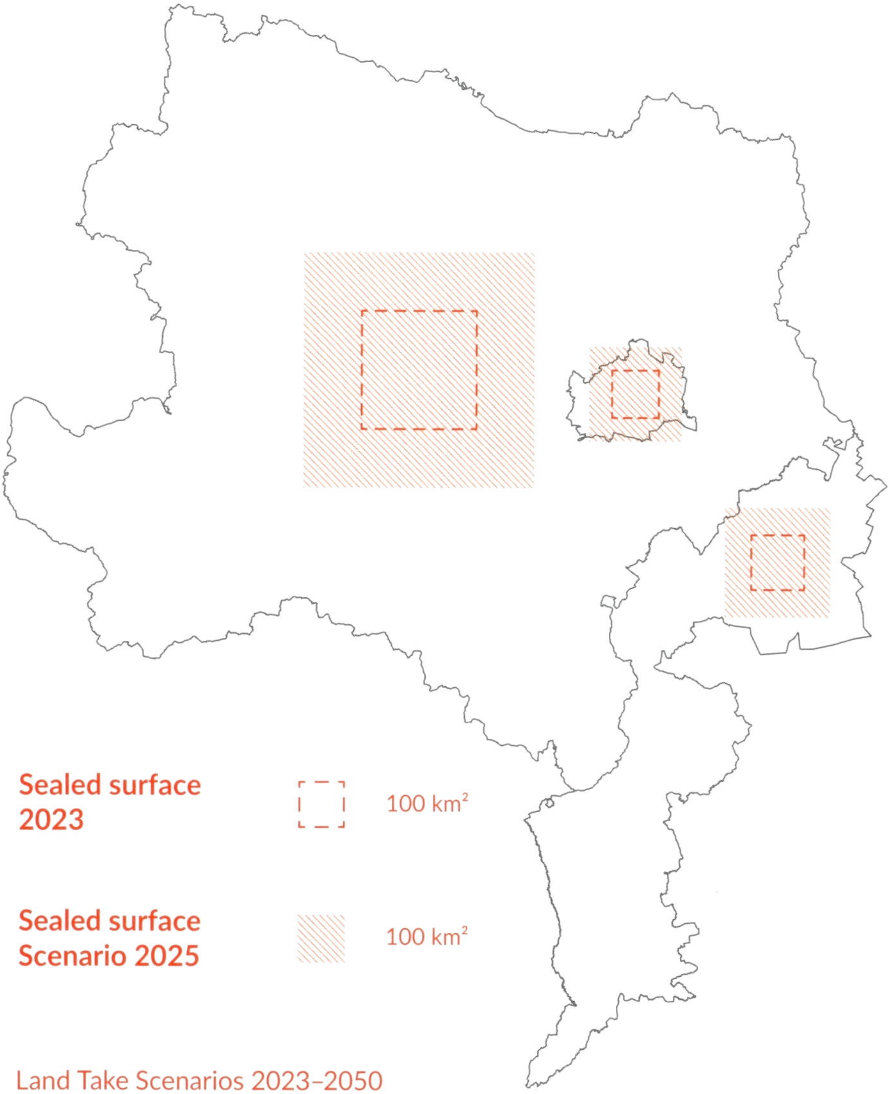

Land Take Scenarios 2023–2050

The typology and size of our dwellings significantly influence our energy consumption, and we are still highly dependent on fossil energy to heat our living spaces

Single-family homes consume almost twice as much energy per square meter as compact multi-story buildings, and space heating accounts for about 2/3 of the carbon emissions associated with the residential sector. This is particularly true in Vienna, where a significant number of households rely heavily on non-renewable sources such as gas and district heating. Despite a reduction in greenhouse gas emissions in the residential sector since 1990, energy demand is still increasing.

Eurostat (2023): Built-up areas
Climate Dash Board (2023): Facts and figures on the climate crisis in Austria

Housing Development near Velm in Lower Austria, Source: basemap.at

Nearly 30% of the housing in the metropolitan region is single-family homes, and in Burgenland and Lower Austria it is even the majority. In addition to being inefficient in terms of space, single-family homes are a significant emission factor, emitting more greenhouse gases than other dwellings.

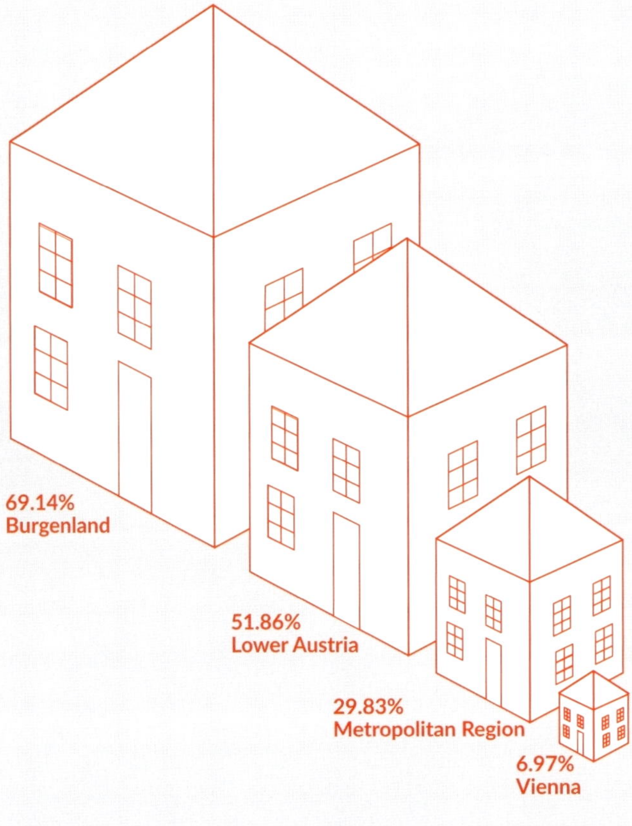

Share of Residencies in Single-Family Homes

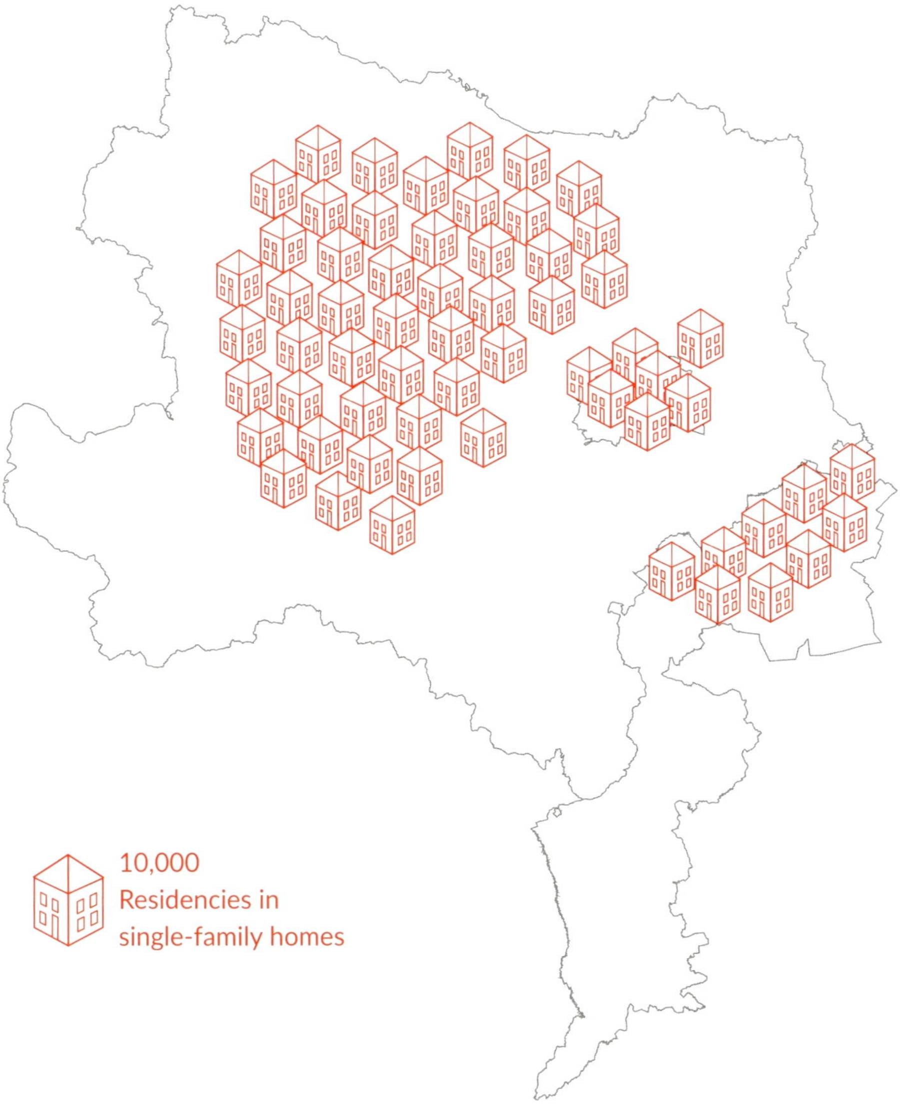

Residencies in Single-Family Homes

Statistics Austria (2022): Microcensus – main residence dwellings as of 2004

In suburban and rural areas, the majority of homes are single-family dwellings. They consume nearly twice as much energy per square foot as a compact multi-family dwelling.

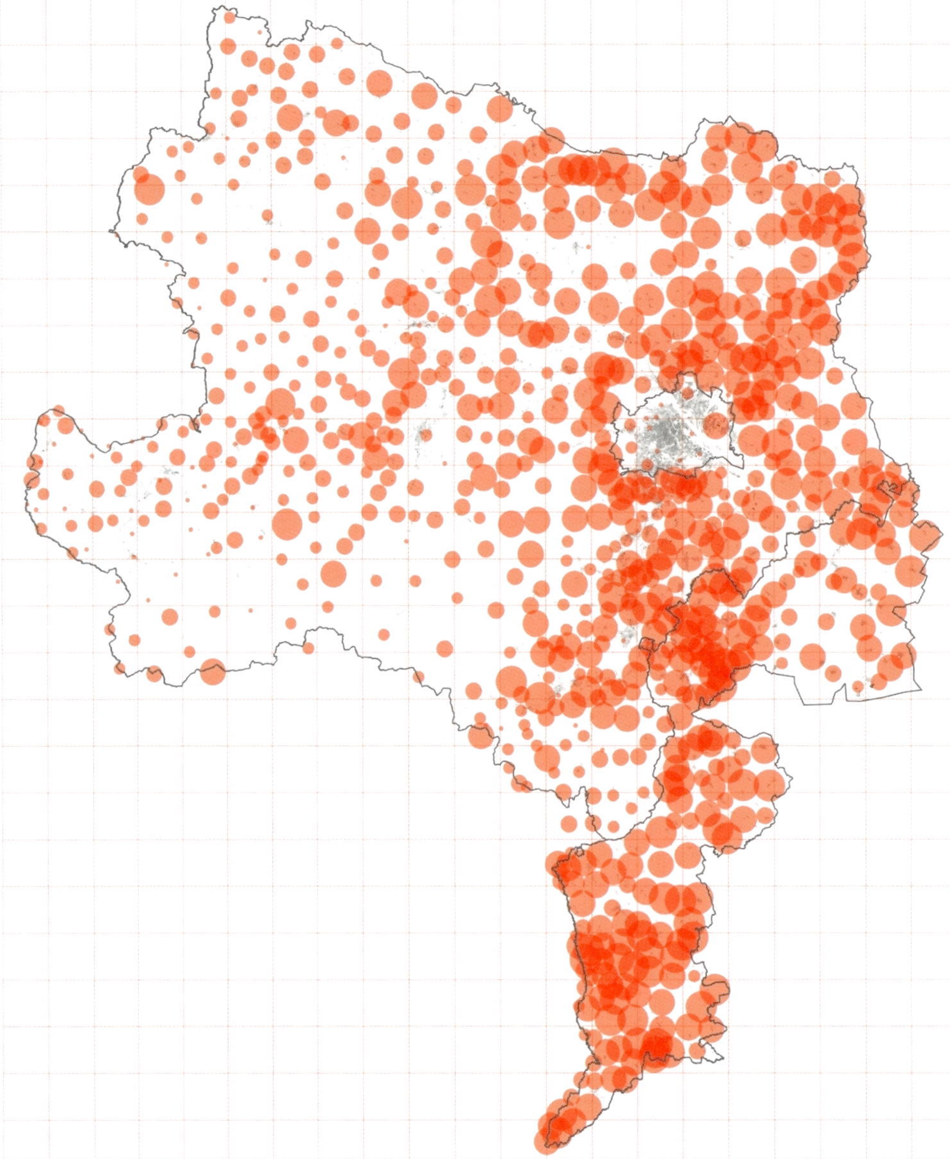

Share of Single-Family Homes

Statistics Austria (2022): Housing census

The construction period as well as the typology makes a big difference in the heating demand per square meter. Depending on the construction period, a single-family house requires almost twice as much energy per square meter for heating as a multi-family house. Space heating is responsible for the largest share of greenhouse gas emissions in the residential sector.

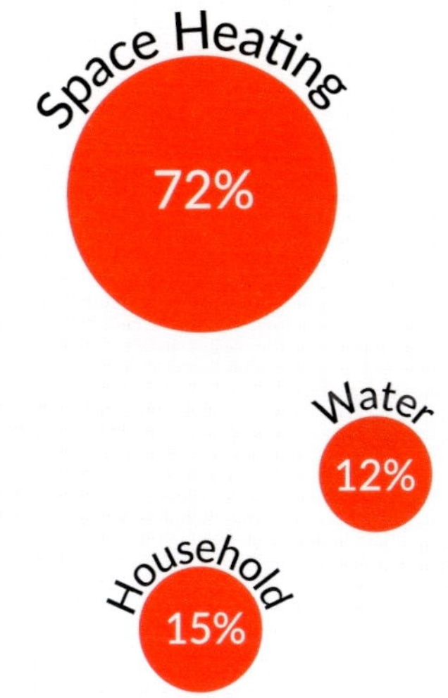

Greenhouse Gases Housing

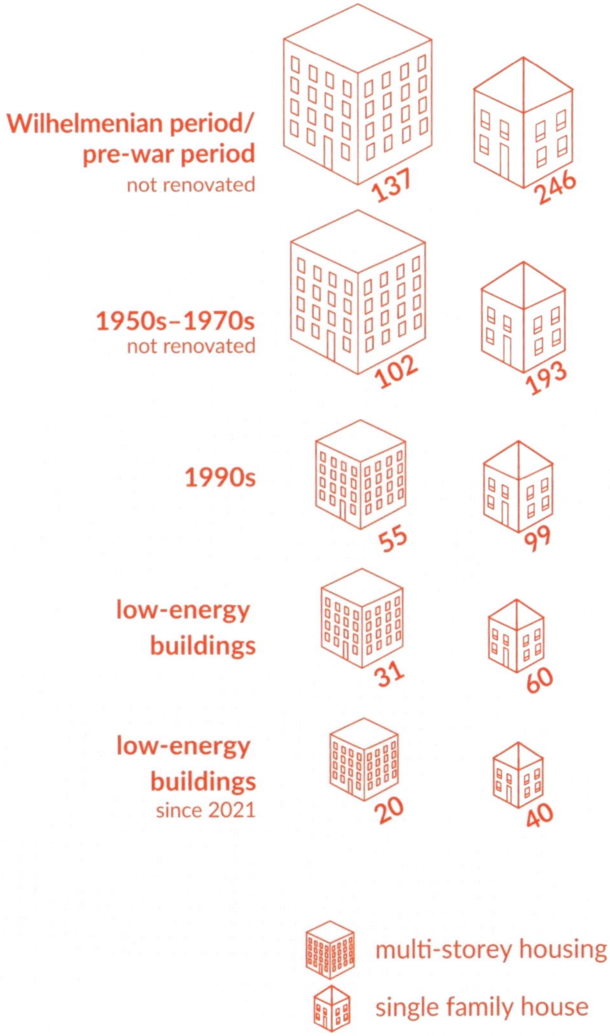

Heating Demand (in kW/h per m²)

Although most households use fossil fuels to heat their homes and residential energy use is increasing, greenhouse gas emissions have decreased since 1990.

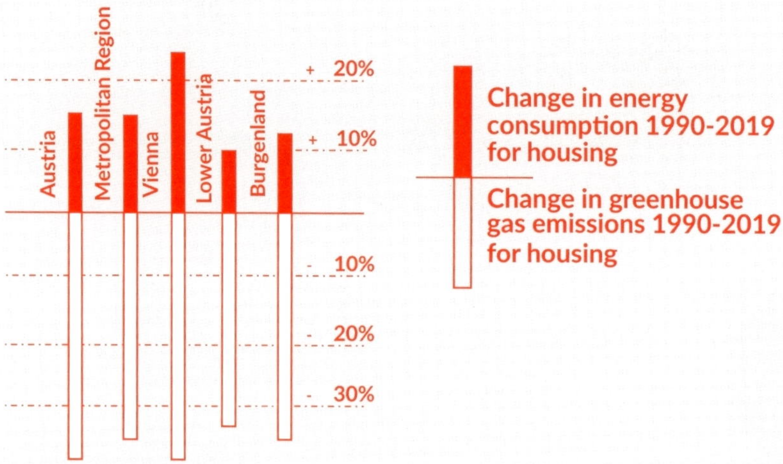

Change in Energy Consumption and Greenhouse Gas Emissions 1990–2019

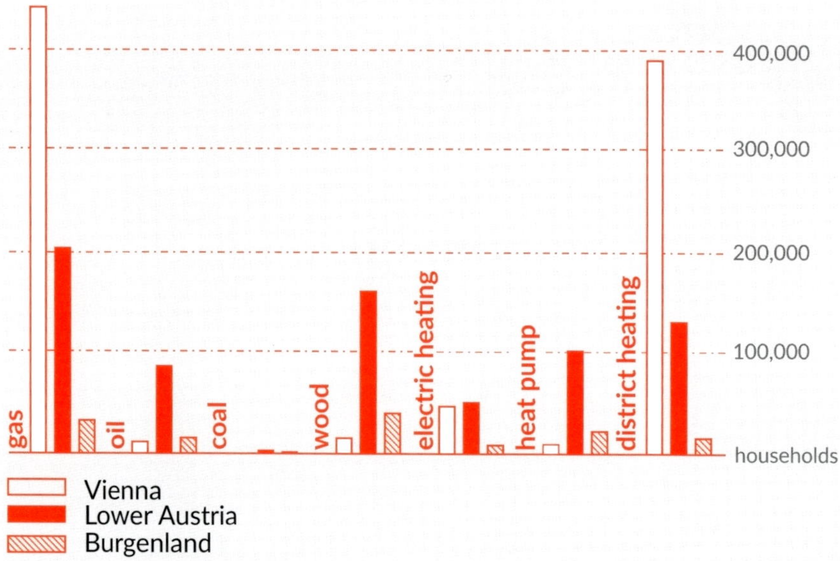

Primary Heating System Based on the Main Energy Sources

Environment Agency Austria (2022 b): Federal states air pollutant inventory 1990–2020
Climate Dash Board (2023): Facts and figures on the climate crisis in Austria

To accelerate the low-carbon transition, a high rate of renovation is needed. But only 26% of housing subsidies support renovation rates.

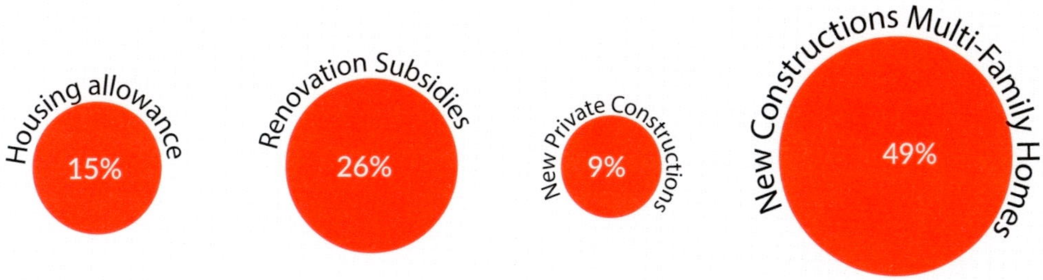

Housing Subsidies in Austria 2021

Renovation Rates in Austria

WKO (2023): Housing subsidies
Environment Agency Austria (2020): Renovation rate in Austria: proposal for new calculation

“We need to switch our focus from new constructions to retrofitting.”

Interview with Andrea Jany & Yoann Gorostiaga

Andrea Jany is currently researching and teaching at the Wegener Center for Climate and Global Change at the University of Graz. In her research, she focuses on current and future housing needs in urban and rural regions. In 2023, she coordinated the chapter on housing in the Austrian Panel on Climate Change report on structures for climate-friendly living.

Yoann Gorostiaga is a project manager working on sustainable and energy efficient buildings at NOBATEK INEF4 in France, a private applied research centre that seeks to develop solutions for the energy transition in the construction sector.

MetroLab: In Austria, our average living space has more than doubled in the last 50 years, from around 22 square metres to over 45 square metres per person today.
What has caused this development and what are the environmental consequences?

Andrea Jany: There is a desire for more, the idea of living better, bigger and nicer than we grew up with is deeply rooted in our society, which can be seen, among other things, in society’s constant desire for single-family homes. According to statistics, all the people currently living in Austria could live in all the existing one- and two-family houses with an average occupancy rate of 4.8 people: We have a lot of space in our existing buildings.

The construction industry needs to change to focus more on retrofitting and redesigning buildings and existing spaces.

MetroLab: The construction of houses also leads to an increase in the artificialisation of soil and greenhouse gas emissions due to construction. What do you see as the biggest challenge in the construction sector?
And could you explain the regulations in place in France to reduce the carbon impact of buildings?

Yoann Gorostiaga: As Andrea said, we need to change the ratio between new construction and retrofitting. In France, in 2021, we only retrofitted about 65,000 homes, whereas we need to do 370,000 per year to get to net zero by 2050, so we are only at about 20% of what we need to do. And at the same time, in 2021, planning permission has been granted for 470,000 new homes.

The main issue for me is that I think we really need to shift our focus from new construction to retrofitting. The second issue is energy costs: I think it is necessary for future projects to think more about how much I have to invest now and how much I will have to pay later. And then, of course, there is a third challenge, which is obviously choosing the right materials in the right place.

The new French regulation, which unfortunately only applies to new buildings at the moment, makes us look at both the energy impact of a project and the carbon footprint. So we have to look at how much greenhouse gas is emitted by our consumption and how much is emitted by the materials we use. We have different timeframes, 2022, 2025, 2028 and 2031, for the construction sector to adapt to these new changes. The first target in 2022 does not change much: Just using a little bit of low-carbon concrete is enough to meet the target. But then the target goes on to reduce emissions by 20%, and then again by 20%. So if today we emit about one tonne of CO_2 per square metre to build an office building, by 2031 it will be about 600 kg. This 40% reduction will favour bio-based solutions, building mainly with wood and timber, and finding solutions to replace materials like clinker that emit a lot of CO_2. But in my view, this is a slow process.

MetroLab: Since the construction of new buildings is the largest contributor to emissions, we could have a huge impact by extending the lifespan of existing buildings rather than building new ones. But how would buildings need to be adapted to meet our current housing needs and standards?

Y.G.: We have to use less energy: All the scientific reports show that we are going to exceed the limits of our planet. But I don't think that focusing only on technological solutions will solve the problem.

I think the most important thing is to focus on the essentials of building. Thermal, visual and acoustic comfort. If you design a building that is as passive and bioclimatic as possible, you're going to use less: Less air conditioning and therefore less greenhouse gas emissions and impact. Otherwise, you're using a lot of cooling, which releases heat outside, it gets warmer outside, then you have to cool the building even more. It is a cycle that never ends.

I think we need to focus on what the users really need: Do we really need 200 m² for a family of four, or can we share spaces? Could we have guest rooms or a shared kitchen, for example in an apartment block? I think we have to look at that too.

A.J.: I think that the social agenda needs to be addressed more. The quality of the social environment is important, for example the question of meeting places outside one's own home.

In my view, this cannot be done in a copy and paste way, but must be planned with the people who use the buildings. We need to rethink the design process from the perspective of the future occupants to understand their needs. It is important to include community-based factors and not create isolated housing in a standardised way. From my point of view, it is important to promote social interaction and a sense of belonging, so that people really feel a sense of belonging to a neighbourhood, also in terms of resilience: They can help each other in an emergency.

Keeping housing flexible allows it to adapt to changing needs: Flexible space can be used for different purposes throughout the life of the building. From a design perspective, it is too narrow to focus only on the floor plan, as we do today.

When people are involved in the design and development process of the neighbourhood, they take more care of the space and this extends the life of the whole existing community and the building itself. ▸

MetroLab: If you involve a lot of people and opinions in the building process, it takes a lot of time, does that necessarily make it more expensive to build that way? Do we need to think about putting a carbon price tag on every material we use to value a better way of building?

Y.G.: I think it makes it easier to convince customers to opt for sustainable solutions: Sometimes it is difficult to convince clients to invest in solutions that will save them money over a number of years. The big players in the construction industry need incentives to change the way they build, and unfortunately the industry is not moving fast enough.

If you use unconventional construction methods, they tend to cost more and take too long, even though they have a very low carbon impact.

MetroLab: If you could think of a law, a ban or an initiative that could be implemented immediately, what would be the biggest lever to change something?

Y.G.: At the moment, the laws in France are not strong enough, but they do include the idea of zero artificialisation of land. Today, you can compensate for the amount of land you artificialise. We have about three million vacant dwellings in France—we do not need to build any more.

A.J.: I would agree and say in a more drastic way that we should stop building now. We already have the existing buildings, the housing stock. We also need to raise awareness and encourage people to maintain and extend the life of their homes by retrofitting and using what we already have.

Y.G.: Of course we have to make an effort in all sectors: But I think everybody has to make an effort, people have to start to understand that maybe living in a smaller apartment where you share space with people is just as good and probably even better than living alone in a house with a pool: Awareness is important. But of course industry and governments have to make an effort.

MetroLab: In Austria, we are sealing more than 11 hectares of land every day—the federal target is to reduce this to 2.5 hectares by 2030. Meanwhile, the number of building permits for residential buildings continues to rise, as does the number of permits for detached and semi-detached houses. Our existing settlements and housing types are not suitable for climate-neutral development, how can we change them?

A.J.: Unfortunately, there is still a strong desire for single-family houses in Austria. And these typologies do not meet the requirements of climate-neutral development, because they are mostly new buildings, the sealing of the soil is progressing, new resources in terms of materials have to be used for new spaces that have to be supplied with energy. It seems like a spiral that has not yet been broken. But I think it is important for people to create communal areas where people can engage and interact outside their own homes. ▪

MetroLab Podcast
Episode LIVING in Climate
Neutral City Regions

Listen to our podcast on all platforms!

PRODUCING
in the Metropolitan Region

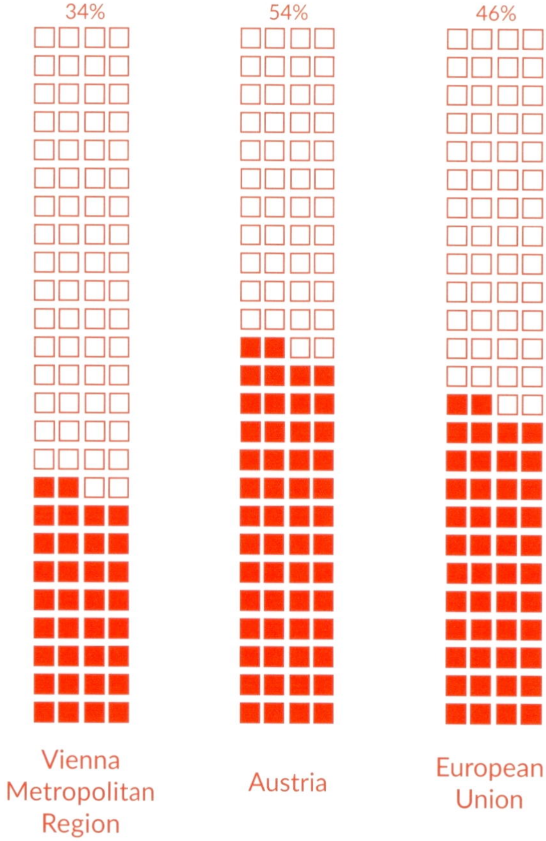

Share of the productive sector of the total greenhouse gas emissions

Environment Agency Austria (2022 b): Federal states air pollutant inventory 1990–2020

The way we produce has a significant impact on our carbon emissions. In this chapter of the Emerging Phenomena Atlas, we examine current trends in the production sector, which is a major contributor to greenhouse gas emissions. This sector, which includes manufacturing, agriculture, and resource extraction, accounts for a significant portion of global energy consumption and carbon emissions. Despite advances in technology and efficiency, many production processes remain heavily dependent on fossil fuels and are associated with high levels of waste and pollution. Understanding the complex relationships between production methods, supply chain dynamics, and resource management is critical to developing innovative strategies to minimize emissions and transition to a more sustainable and circular economy.

P1 Biggest Emitters

P2 Land Footprint Food Production

P3 Food Diversity

P4 ETS – EU Emissions Trading System

» Interview with Helene Pattermann & Alexander Prinsen

P1 Biggest Emitters

Nearly 20% of the regions emissions are due to two production sites and energy plants

Oil, energy and cement companies are the biggest emitters in the metropolitan region: Together, the four biggest emitters are responsible for 19.5% of the metropolitan regions greenhouse gas emissions.

WIFO (2020): A (De-)Carbonisation Map for Austrian Manufacturing

OMV Oil Refinery in Schwechat, Source: basemap.at

Industry emits more greenhouse gas emissions than electricity and district heating and is the largest emitter in Austria.

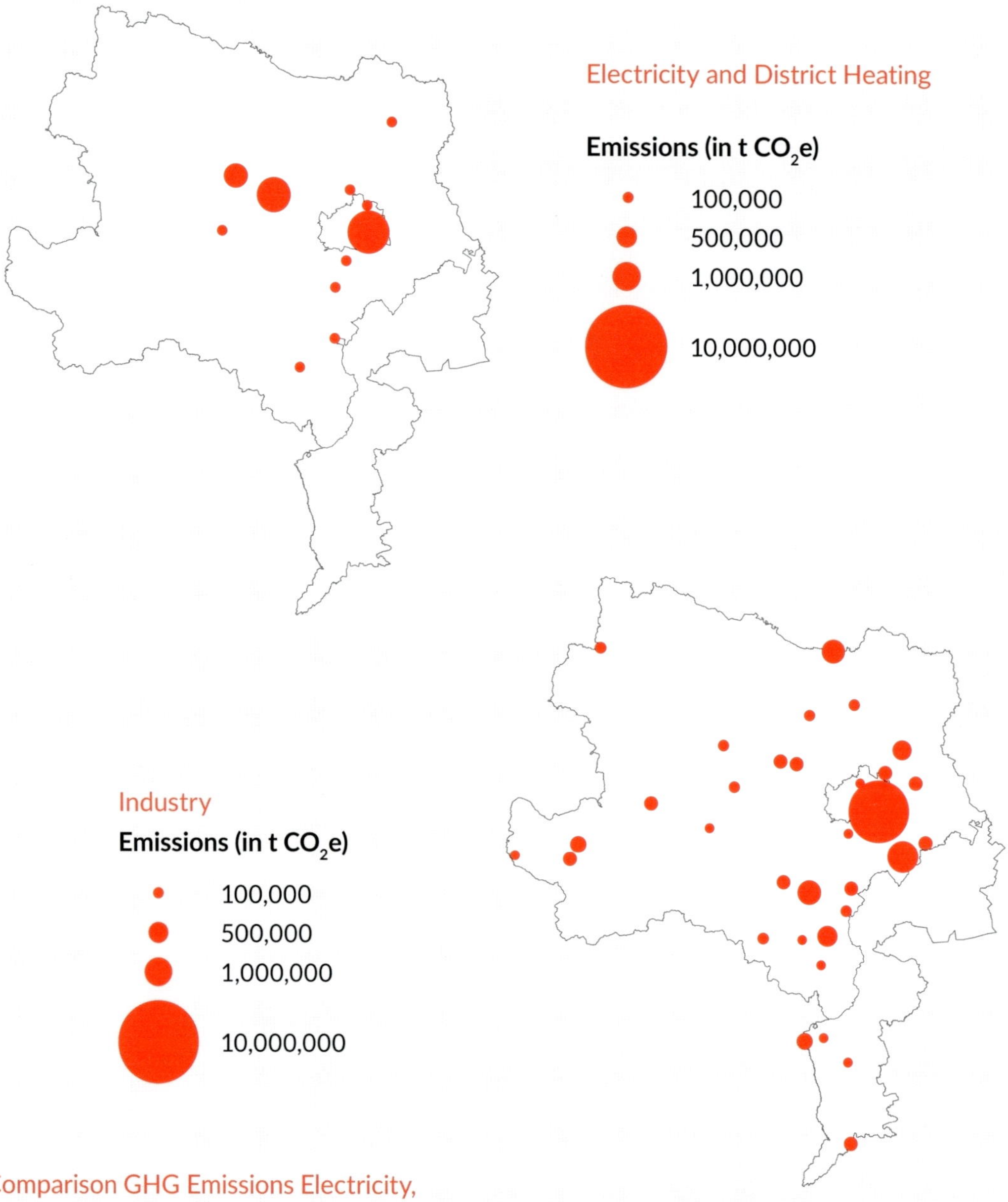

Comparison GHG Emissions Electricity, District Heating and Industry

In the metropolitan region, oil and energy companies are the largest emitters.

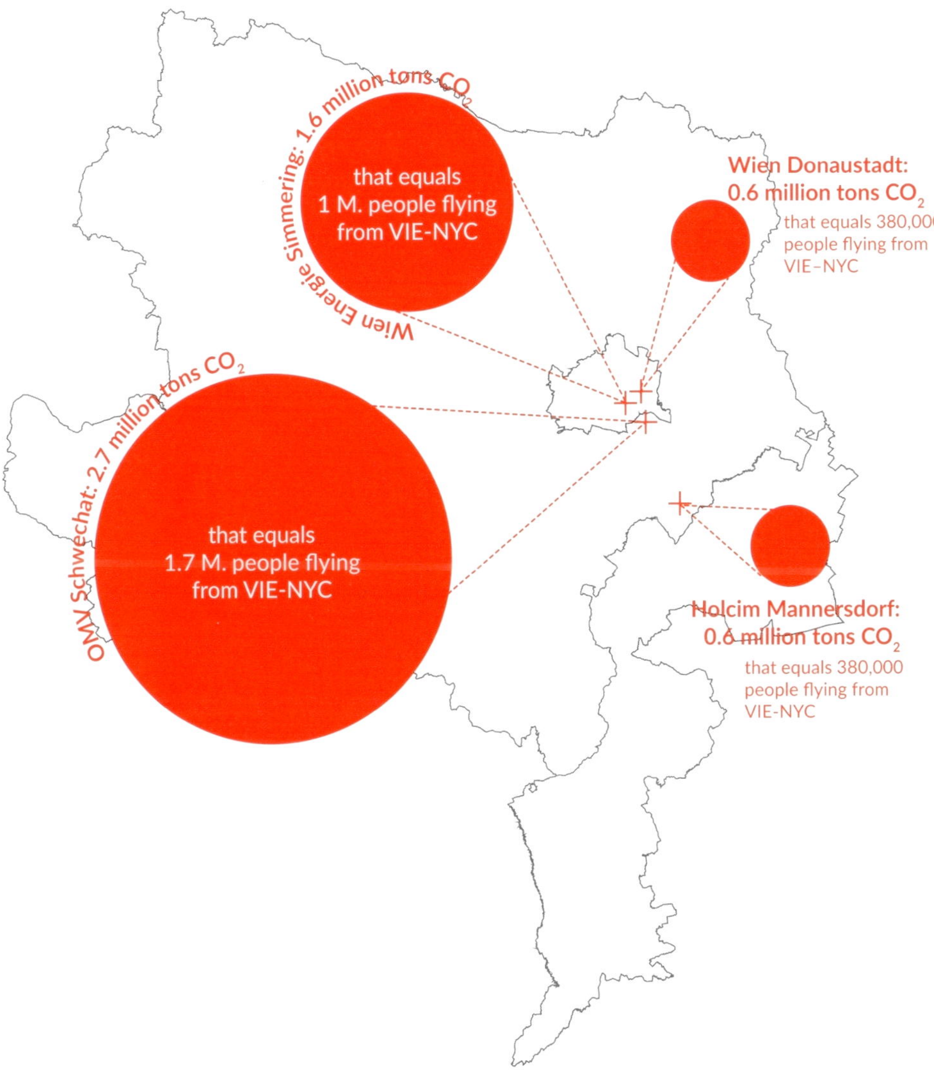

Main Emitters

Basic needs such as housing, energy, mobility and food account for almost 2/3 of the CO_2 emissions of an average Austrian.

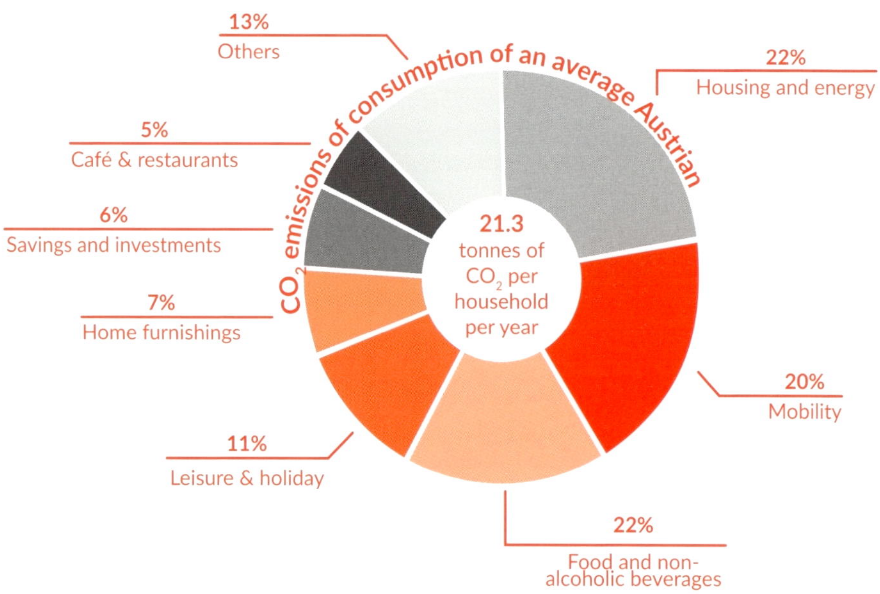

CO_2 Emissions per Household

Industrial emissions account for a good third of Austria's greenhouse gas emissions in 2021. Iron and steel is the largest emitter of greenhouse gas emissions, followed by energy and heat, and building materials.

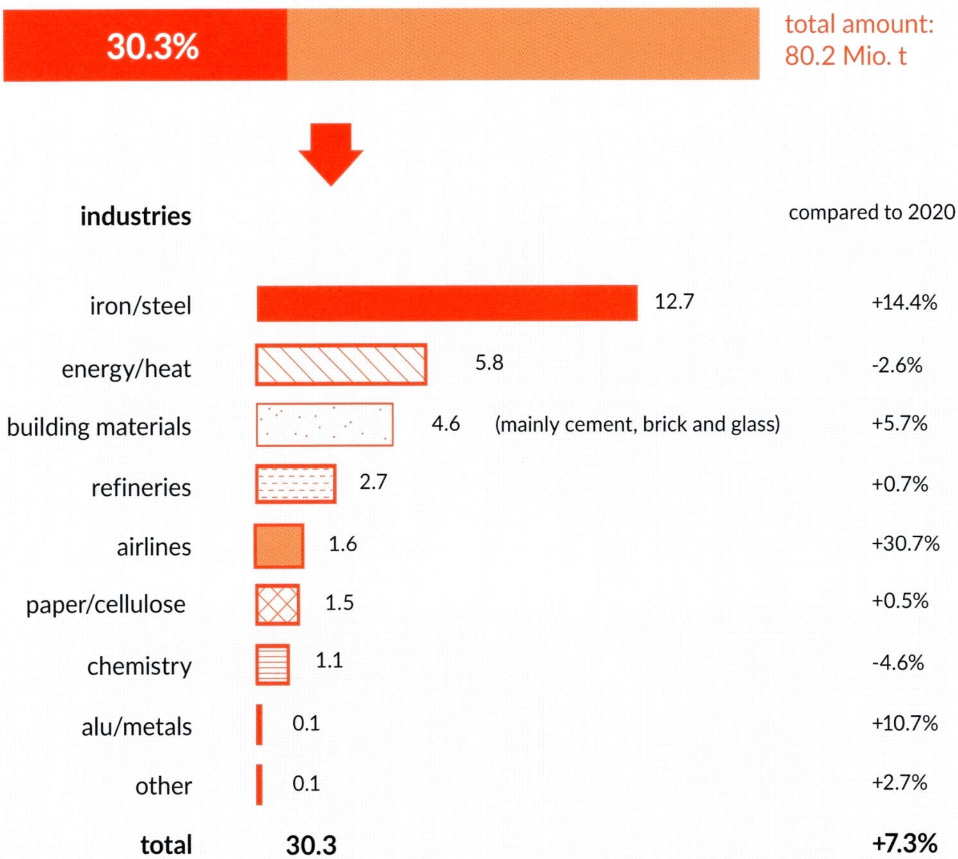

Austria's Total Greenhouse Gas Emissions by Industry (2021)

ERCST et al. (2021): 2021 State of the EU ETS Report

Austria's electricity is generated primarily from hydropower, with increasing imports, and from photovoltaic, wind, and geothermal sources. The Vienna metropolitan area produces mainly hydro and thermal energy.

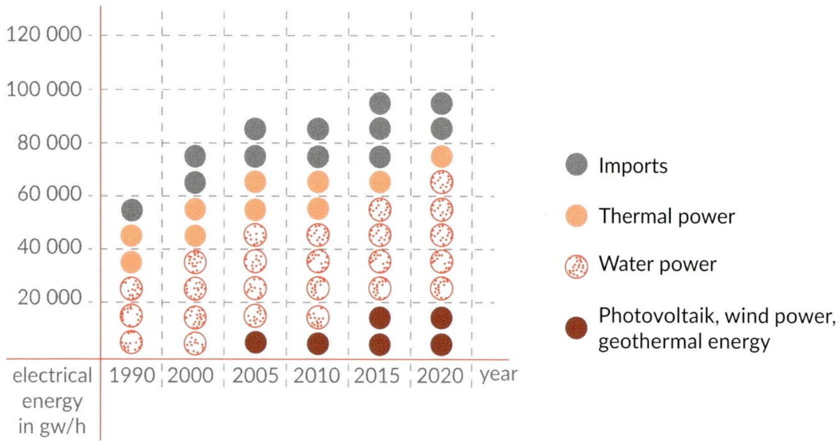

Generation of Electrical Energy in Gigawatt Hours (gw/h) in Austria between 1990 and 2020

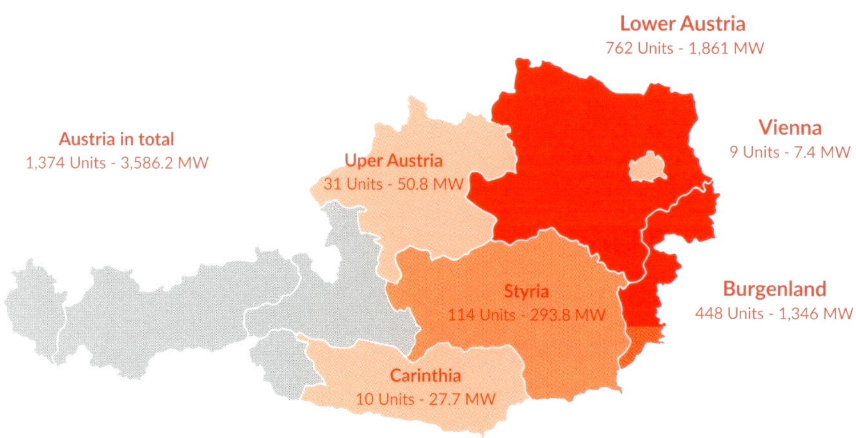

Regional Distribution of Wind Energy Production in Units and Megawatts

BMK (2022): Renewable energies 2020
IG Windkraft (2022): Wind power in Austria

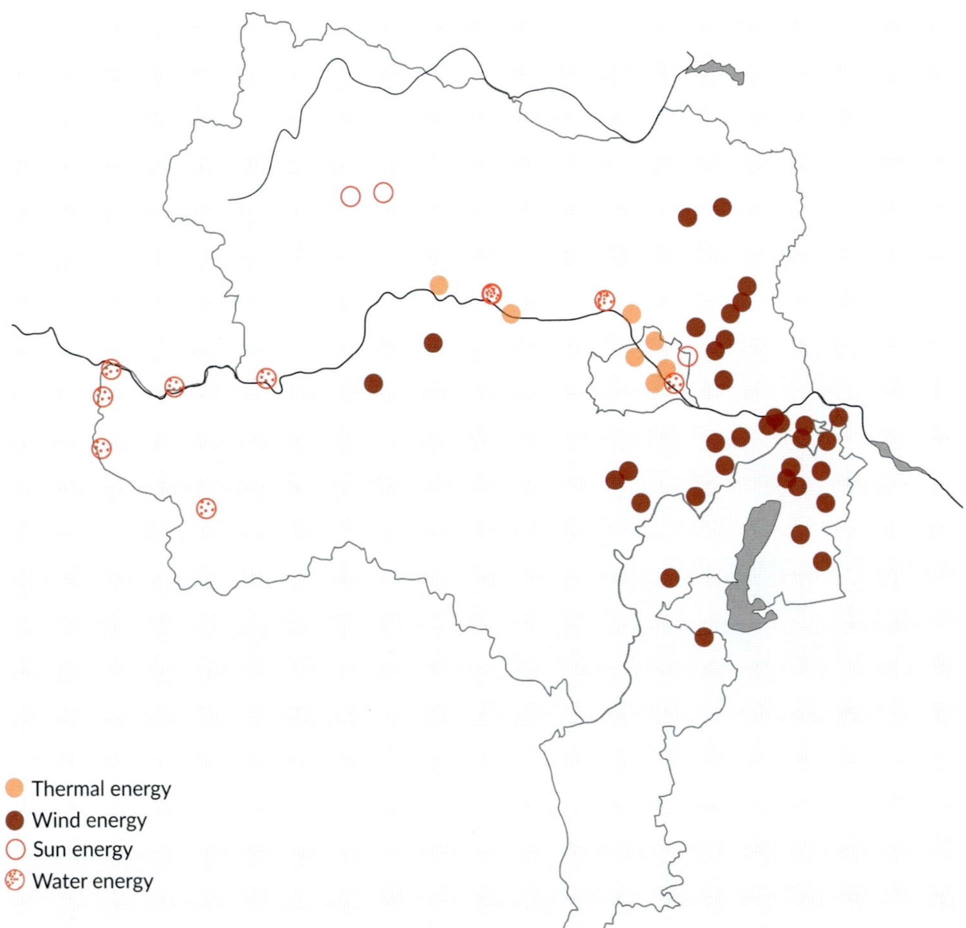

Renewable Electricity Generation in the Metropolitan Region

Food production requires a lot of land, but most of the land needed is not available in the region

The production of the food consumed in Vienna alone requires a total of 639,000 ha of agricultural land, which corresponds to about 60% of the agricultural land in the metropolitan region. However, only 8% of this required land is actually located within the region, 24% in the rest of Austria, 49% in the rest of Europe and 19% outside Europe.

Statistics Austria (2022): Supply balance sheet for vegetables 2020/21
Lauk et al. (2022): Demand side options to reduce greenhouse gas emissions and the land foot-print of urban food systems: A scenario analysis for the City of Vienna.

Agricultural Production Sites in Lower Austria, Source: basemap.at

Food production has a major impact on greenhouse gas emissions and land use. Animal products, in particular, require a large amount of land, and with current consumption patterns, this demand for land cannot be met within the metropolitan region. Even Vienna alone requires 15 times the amount of agricultural land to sustain its population.

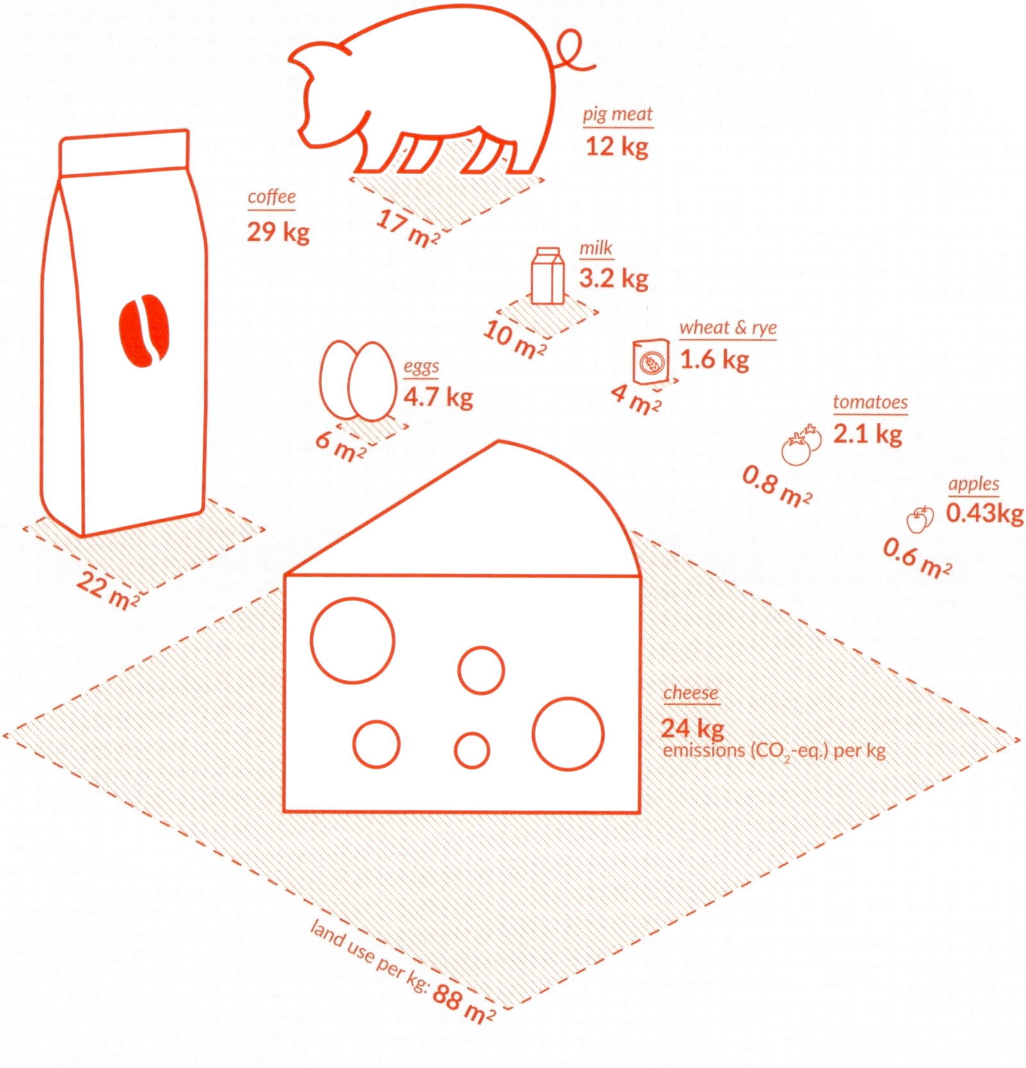

Greenhouse Gas Impact of Food Production

Ritchie, H. & Roser, M. (2022): Environmental Impacts of Food Production

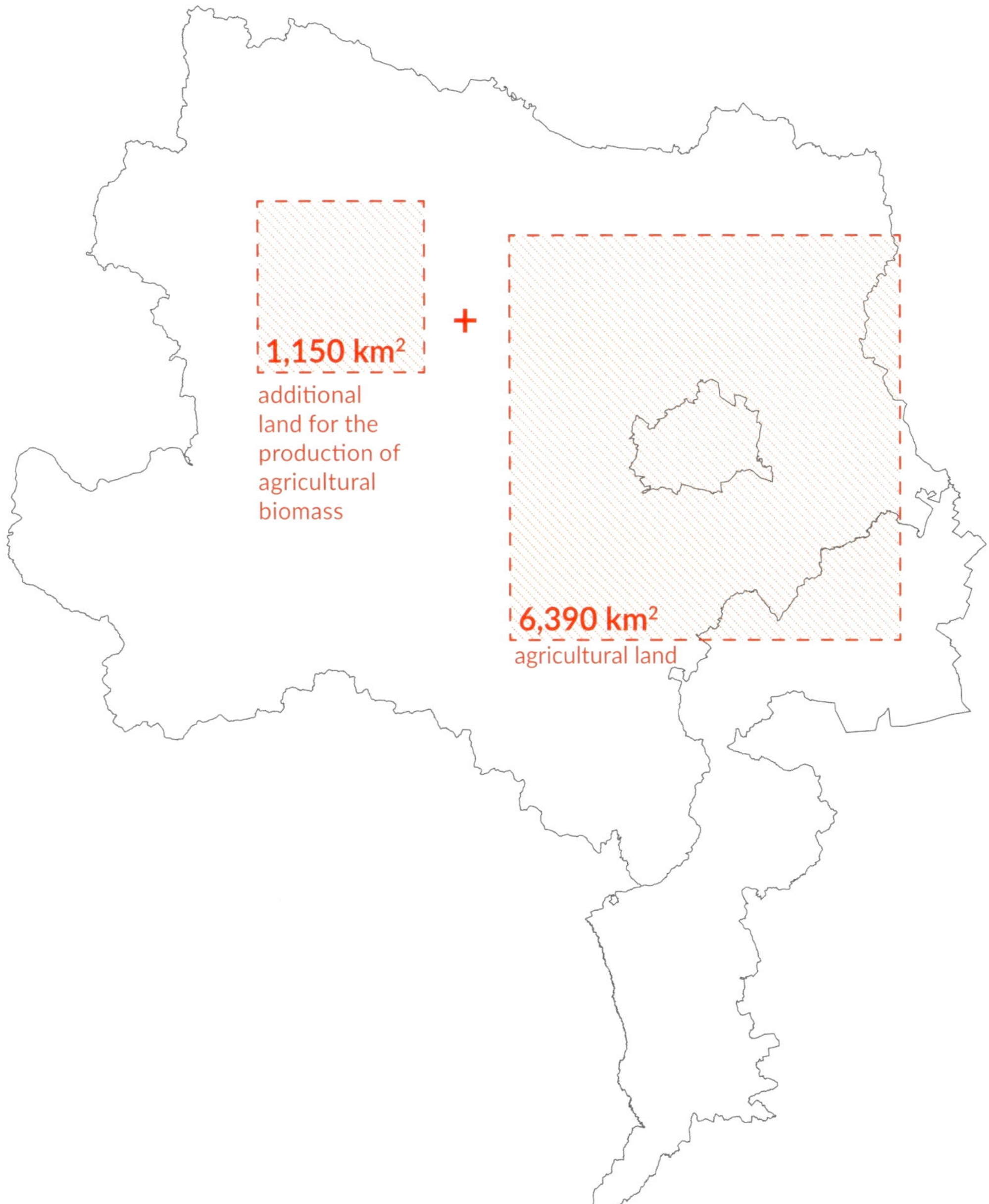

Amount of Agricultural Land Required to Sustain Vienna's Food System

Lauk et al. (2022): Demand side options to reduce greenhouse gas emissions and the land foot-print of urban food systems: A scenario analysis for the City of Vienna

Agricultural and forest land cover the majority of the metropolitan area, but since 1990, agricultural land has been urbanized.

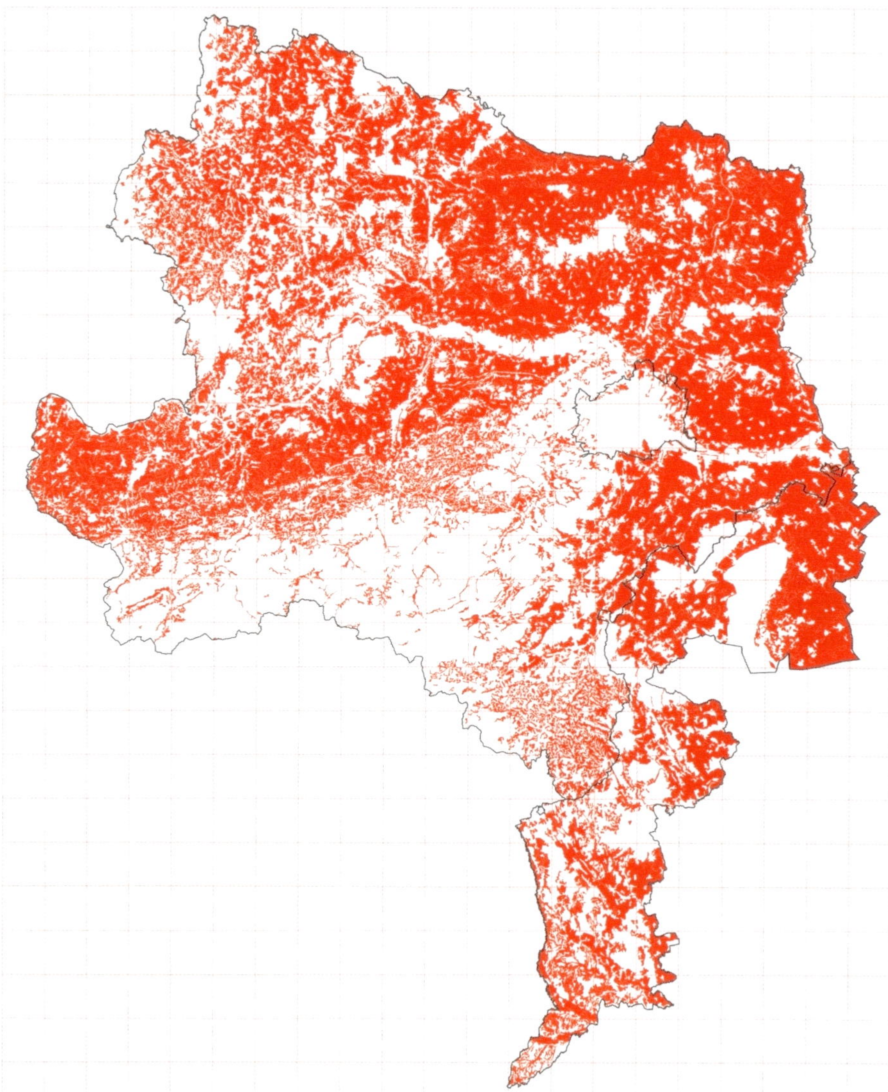

Agricultural & Forestry Land

European Environment Agency (2023): Copernicus Land Monitoring, CORINE Landcover

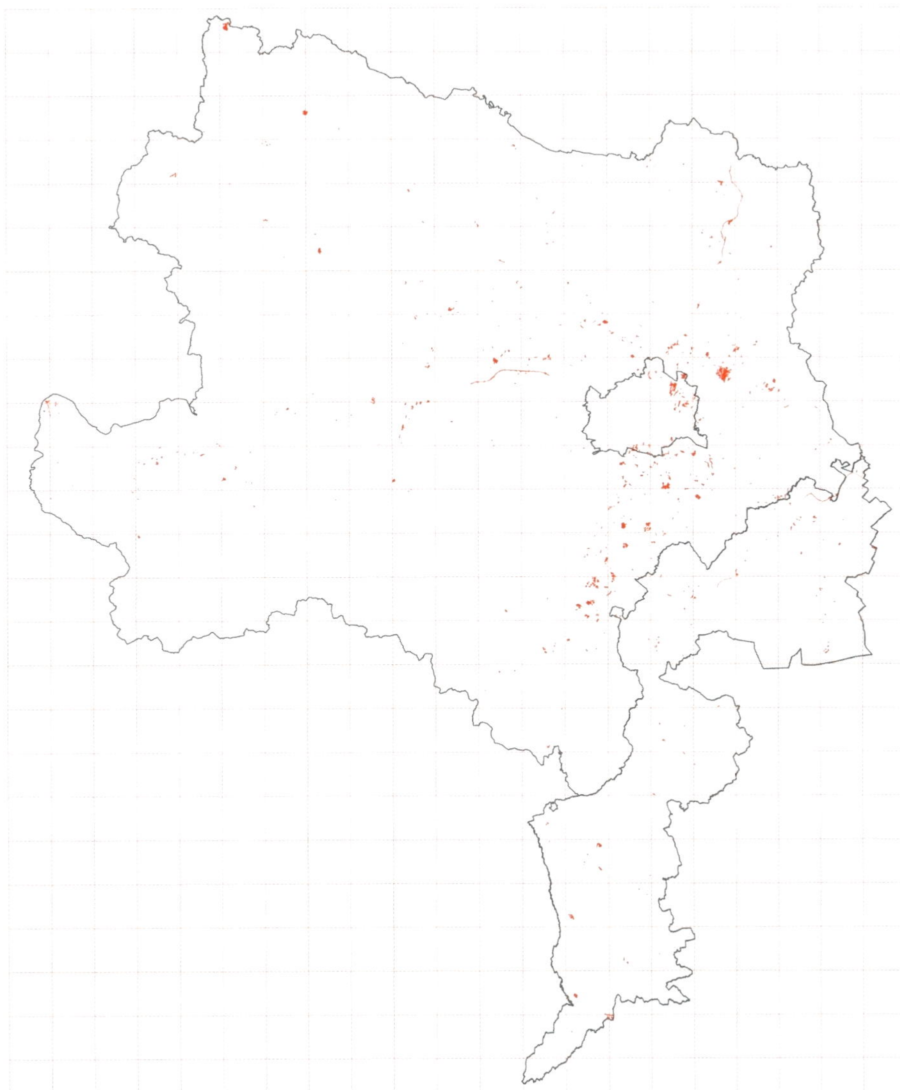

■ converted land since 1990

Urbanization of Agricultural Land

European Environment Agency (2023): Copernicus Land Monitoring, CORINE Landcover

The metropolitan region does not produce the diversity of food that it consumes, resulting in inefficient import-export flows

Domestic agriculture in Austria was able to cover 100% of the demand for wine, 87% for cereals, 86% for potatoes, 57% for vegetables, 50% for oilseeds, 41% for fruits and 33% for vegetable oils.

The value of agricultural imports exceeded the value of agricultural exports in 2021/22. The value of agricultural imports increased from € 13.0 billion to € 15.2 billion (+17%), while the value of exports increased from € 13.2 billion to € 15.0 billion (+13%).

Statistics Austria (2022): Supply balance sheet for vegetables 2020/21

Agricultural Production Sites in Vienna, Source: basemap.at

The economic value of plant-based production is twice that of animal-based production. The share of total agricultural production is also higher than the share of emissions produced.

Share of the Metropolitan Region in Austria's total GHG Emissions and Economic Value from Agricultural Food Production

Statistics Austria (2023): Economic Accounts for Agriculture

The value of plant-based agricultural products exceeds the value of animal-based agricultural products in all three federal states within the metropolitan region, with Vienna showing the largest difference.

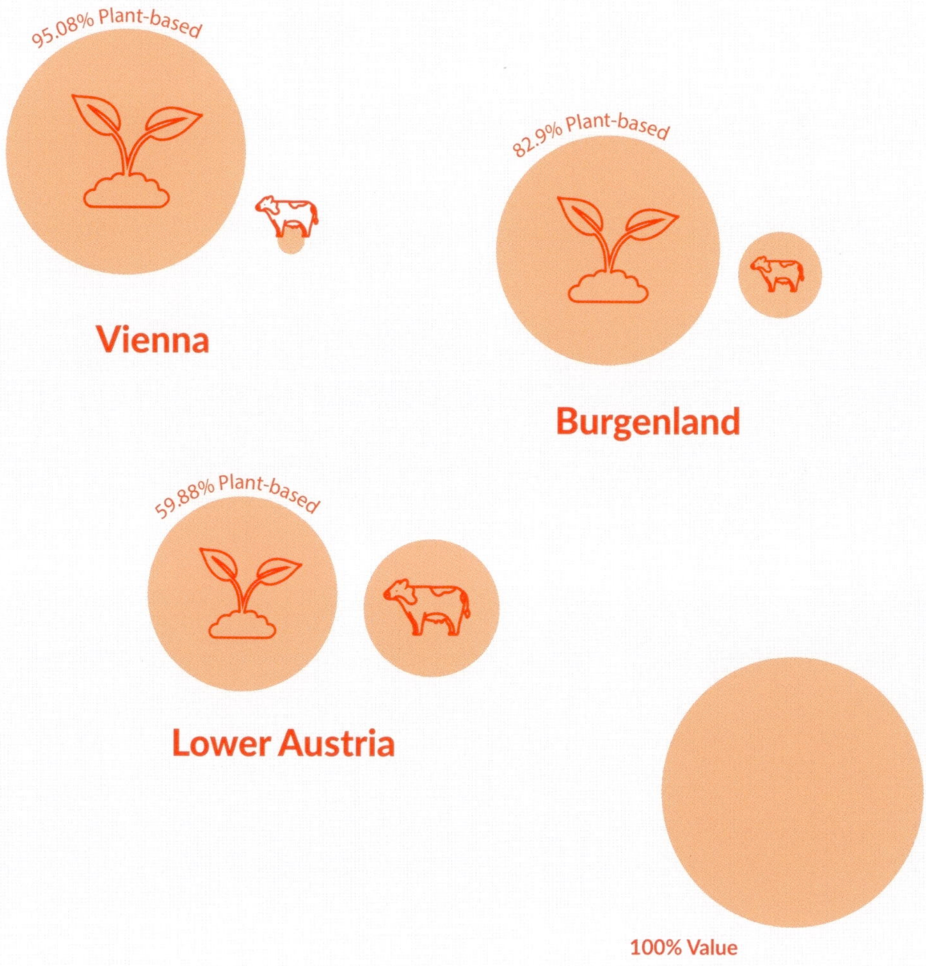

Share of the Value of Plant-Based and Animal-Based Products in Total Agricultural Goods

Statistics Austria (2023): Economic Accounts for Agriculture

The western part of the region, called Marchfeld, is by far the largest vegetable producer in the region, while the south and east are more focused on animal-based production.

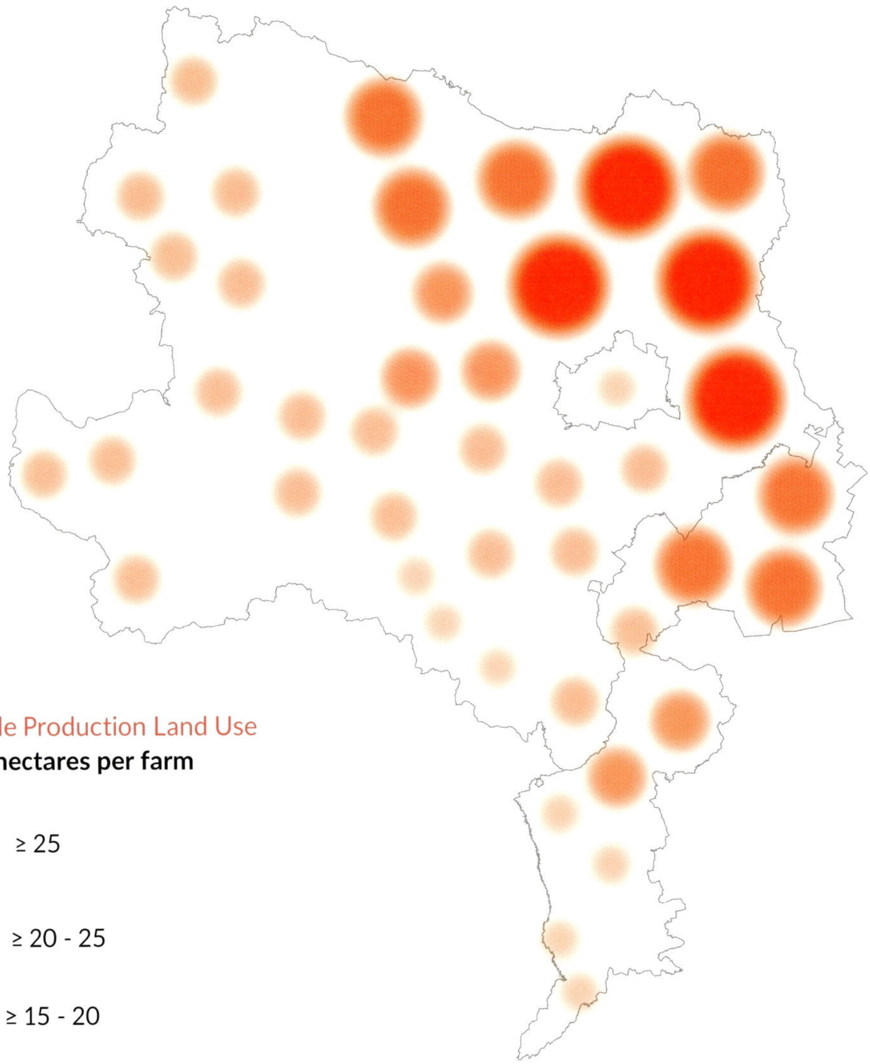

Vegetable Production Land Use

Land in hectares per farm

≥ 25

≥ 20 - 25

≥ 15 - 20

≥ 10 - 15

< 10

Distribution of Agricultural Land used for Vegetable Production

Statistics Austria (2022): Harvest survey

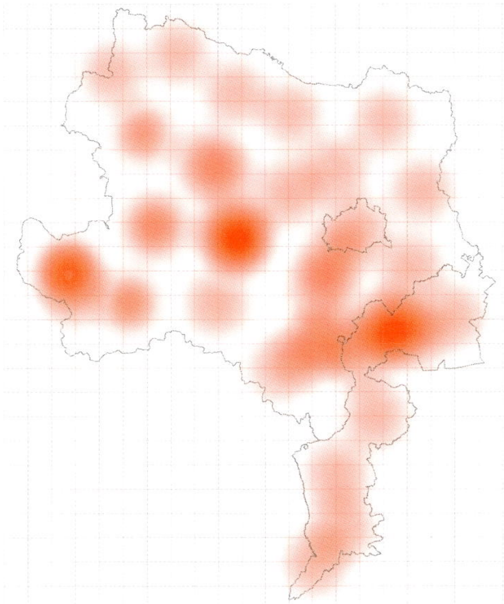

Land Use for Animal Production

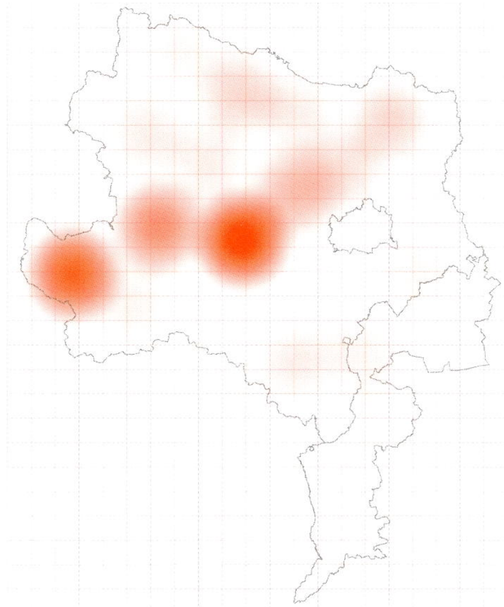

Land Use for Pig Breeding

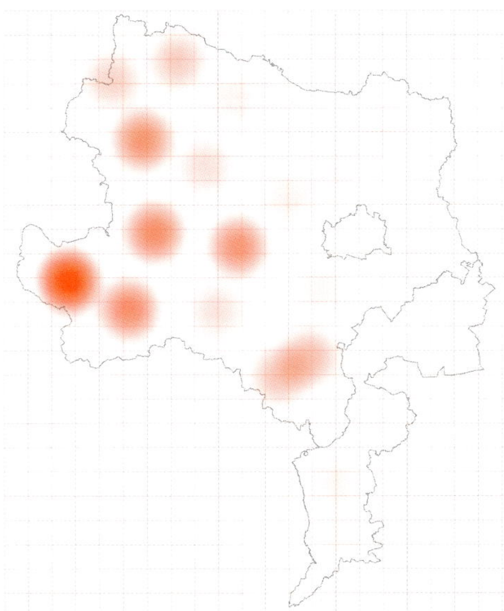

Land Use for Cattle Breeding

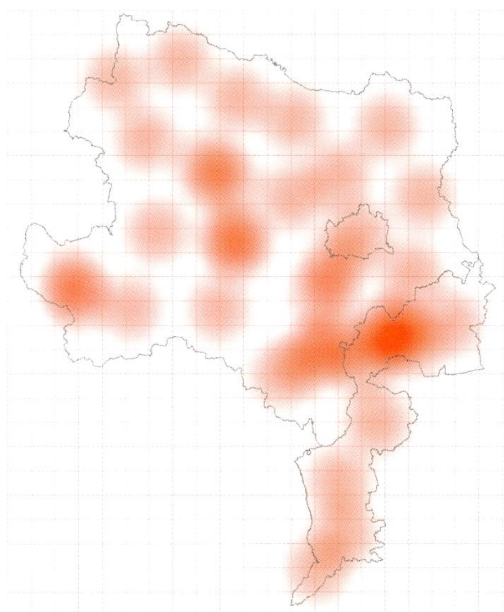

Land Use for Poultry Breeding

Distribution of Agricultural Land for Livestock Farming

Statistics Austria (2020): Farm Structure Survey 2020: Agricultural and forestry holdings increased in size

Free allocations within the EU Emissions Trading System to industry have hindered substantial reductions of emissions in the region

The EU Emissions Trading System (ETS) monitors emissions from approximately 10,000 energy and energy-intensive industrial installations in Europe. Together, these installations account for approximately 36% of Europe's greenhouse gas emissions.

Approximately 26.6 million tons of CO_2 equivalent are emitted in Austria under the ETS trading system and are therefore not included in most emissions calculations.

Environment Agency Germany (2021): European Emissions Trading
WWF (2023): EU emissions trading

Industrial Area in Vienna, Source: basemap.at

The Emissions Trading System monitors emissions from approximately 10,000 energy and energy-intensive industrial installations in Europe. Together, these installations account for approximately 36% of Europe's greenhouse gas emissions.

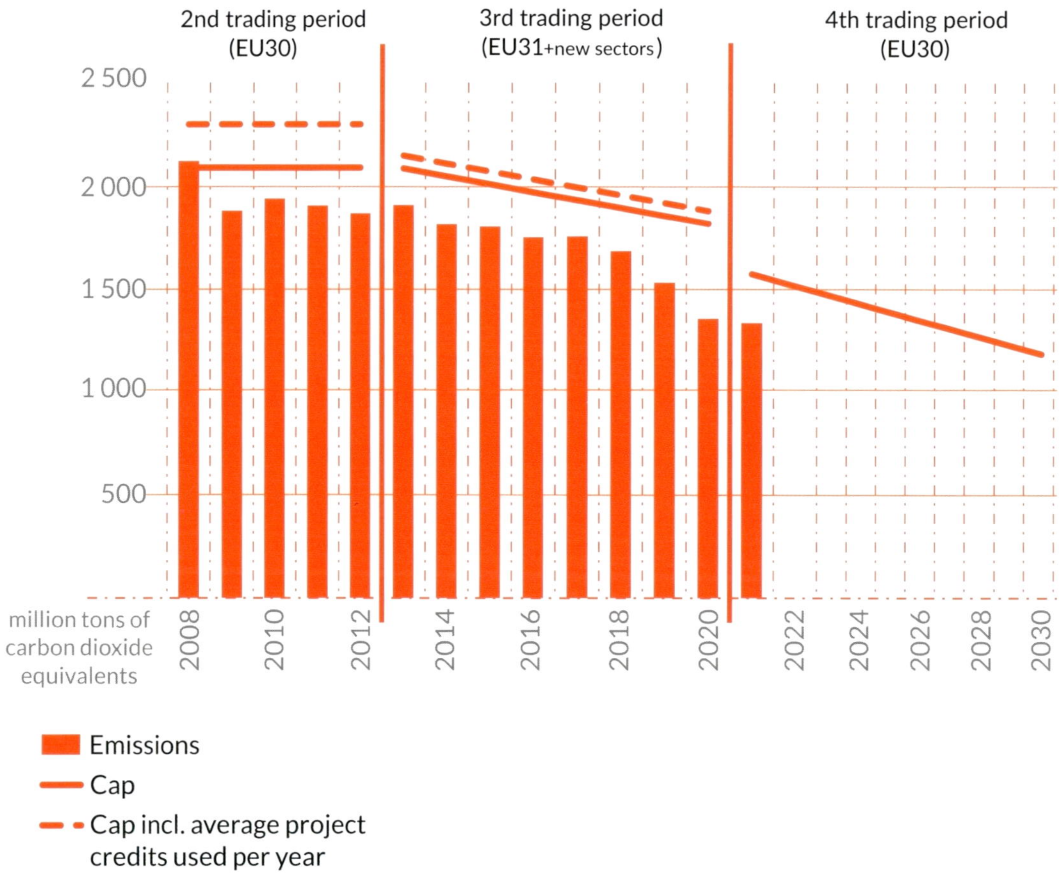

Total Cap and Emissions in European Emissions Trading

Environment Agency Germany (2021): European Emissions Trading
WWF (2023): EU emissions trading

The Trading Emissions System operates under the “Cap & Trade” principle, setting a limit on greenhouse gas emissions for participating installations. Member states allocate emission allowances accordingly, which can be freely traded. Each allowance permits the emission of 1 ton of CO_2 equivalent.

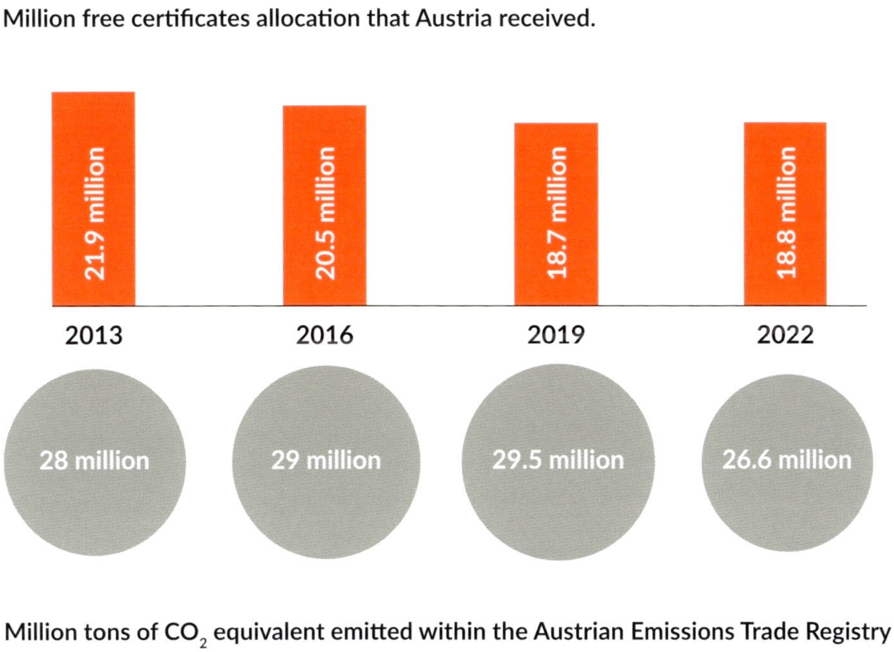

Free Certificates given and Emissions actually caused by these Units in Austria

Austrian Emissions Trading Registry (n.d.): Copliance status

"The issue lies in the outdated business model of producing, wasting, and selling as much material as possible"

Interview with Helene Pattermann & Alexander Prinsen

Helene Pattermann is Circularity Director at the Climate Lab Vienna, an innovation space that brings together a community of climate pioneers, public institutions and big industry players with an impact on climate neutrality in Austria.

Alexander Prinsen is founding and managing partner of Scope Matters, where he advises companies on strategies for regenerative and resilient business models together with other innovation and transition experts.

MetroLab: The climate crisis imposes profound challenges on companies to restructure their way of producing and their business models. Helene Pattermann, in the Climate Lab, you are connecting companies, start-ups and innovators to collaborate across industries and sectors. Where do you see the biggest benefits of these collaborations, and what are the opportunities for working with companies across different sectors?

Helene Pattermann: We have a clear focus on climate neutrality in our community, with a focus on mobility, construction and energy. We really wanted to focus on where we could have the biggest impact on CO_2 emissions.

We cannot solve the big challenges within one sector or one company, no matter how big. You need to share with more innovative ideas from small start-ups and other companies, learn from different sectors and apply things that make sense to you.

Alexander Prinsen: It is about the coalition of the willing—do you trust each other to do something new? Innovation is only possible in the context of a community where partners want to move forward together, then they will be able to overcome the problems.

It is not easy to innovate, and the challenges we face require a restructuring of regulations, legislation and the way we do business. That requires dialogue between everyone. We tend to be comfortable with discussion, which is always yes and no, but it is only in dialogue that you build on each other.

MetroLab: Economic growth is often referred to when talking about the state of an economy, or even as a driver for decision making. To what extent should economic growth influence decisions about business models, does it hinder or enable our aspirations for a future within our planetary boundaries?

A.P.: The word economy comes from the Greek and means the bookkeeping of the house. So if economics means the bookkeeping of our houses and our planet, then it is about the bookkeeping of our planet. Then the connection to planetary boundaries is quite easy to make. Interestingly, it also relates to how nature does its bookkeeping. If you look at growth, it is a kind of measure of how much we produce. We produce in a linear way and we produce a lot of waste. The more waste we produce, the more economic growth we create, which is strange in a way. If you look at it from a natural point of view, nature always grows in abundance, whereas economics, especially from a micro point of view, wants to create scarcity and move towards monopoly. Nature does not have that, it strives for biodiversity, for abundance, and growth is the result of a complex system with many interactions.

The economy is bound by its planetary boundaries, there is no endless growth, it will always level off. Growth as we know it is exponential. There are economies with zero GDP that are still thriving, but not by the economic standards that use economic growth. It is no longer the right measure because we know that our economies are flattening. We have forgotten to recycle our waste streams and that is cascading into climate change and other issues that we are facing today.

H.P.: We are destroying our planet with the way we have been doing business for the last hundred years, but people are not happy either: This materialistic way of thinking in the economy, where we tie our happiness to what we own. We see that what we have at the moment is clearly not working, but we need to shift for a major social transformation. Right now, our economy is tied to resources that we buy and things that we waste. We should be renting instead of buying, paying for a service we do not own. This alone could save resources that could be shared. We need to rethink how it can be and have positive images of how it could be.

A.P.: Most companies just focus on selling more and more. For example, the iPhone used to be easy to fix, but not anymore. There is a new model every year or two. The business model has run its course, the phones and the technology are there. Ideally their business should be that people use their phone as long as they can and they can make replaceable parts. I find it ridiculous to throw away my phone when the software is no longer updated.

Businesses are taught that the only way to have a sustainable business model is to sell as much as you can and find new upgrades. Convince people that a new phone is better than the old one. Marketing departments are a big problem with this. They tend to make you feel that certain things are better than other things. As Helene says, our wellbeing is not defined by what we have, it's about who we are. But business is defined by what we have, because then you can show that you are different. And yet we are all the same.

MetroLab: Do you have main pillars or characteristics of a regenerative and resilient business model that you advise your clients on?

A.P.: It is just to apply common sense: Physics, biology and chemistry tell us and define everything we need to know. The word "sustainable" means the ability to sustain. It all derives from how nature operates. We should not produce stuff that cannot degrade, nature makes everything able to degrade, even if takes a long time. We designed chemicals, polymers which cannot break down ▸

under natural circumstances, which is ridiculous. We now have plastics in our body, because we designed it to outlive ourselves. It is ridiculous because plastic needs around one or two weeks to go from the producer to the consumer, then it can be gone. So we should stop designing for eternity, but for the short cycle, according to its purpose. Let materials degrade by sunlight, salt or other chemical interaction, it is not more difficult than that.

MetroLab: But in your experience, what are the main concerns of companies that are embarking on this change? Is it mainly the idea of growth?

A.P.: No, they have more practical concerns, its innovation capacity, if the goods are available. For instance, IKEA announced that they finally have a bio-based binder for their plywood. This is an innovation from a Canadian company that has been working on it for 20 years, and suddenly it is ready for the market, and IKEA's plywood will be almost 100% bio-based and biodegradable. These innovations take time and require a value chain that dares to be different. Then the technology can be scaled up as costs come down and you can start to compete with existing polluting polymers.

It is a long road and there is a lot of reluctance from incumbents because taking a risk means you can lose. And if you look at the innovation graveyard, there are a lot of start-ups and ideas that have not made it because of a lack of funding, the wrong team, the wrong investors, the wrong time. There are a lot of reasons why something does not work.

MetroLab: And Helene, what is your experience with companies when they have concerns, or do most companies already come to you as if they already have this mindset that they want to change?

H.P.: Many of our partners are industry leaders with an innovation department. They know what regulations are coming and they know they need to act now to be ready for the future. But not many people are early adopters and want to be the first, because there is a lot of risk involved and a lot of uncertainty about how the market will react. Most people want to play it safe and see if others are making the first move. So I think it is important to showcase best practice and raise awareness. Most companies are not fully aware of what is changing, what is coming and what lies ahead, especially smaller companies. As Alexander said, they are more likely to respond if you convince them that it is important, not just for their children and grandchildren, but for the existence of their business. That they will have a big advantage if they already know how to deal with change and invest in innovation, because they will be the first to react if, for example, CO_2 prices change. There is still a large part of our society that is not fully aware that big changes are coming.

MetroLab: We just have to flip the switch pretty quickly, because if we want to change the whole system, it takes time. It doesn't work from one day to the next. It's very important that we start soon on a large scale.

A.P.: We should have started yesterday. Many companies will do everything in their power to drag this transition. Because it is not in their interest, because their business model will be destroyed. Companies need to recognise and be honest about the fact that their business model is not going to be successful in the future. If you want to move in a certain direction, you have to acknowledge where you have come from, and that requires reflection.

The change of transition that we are going through is also a leadership challenge. And requires some visionary leadership from these companies. The question is, do we really want to continue burning fossil fuels as we do now, with all the challenges of sourcing them? This is at the heart of the climate change issue, which we often refer to as emissions. If you think about it, wasting molecules is the most irrational thing we can do, even from a business perspective—you're paying for these resources and then just throwing them away. That's simply bad business. The smart approach is to turn all waste streams into new product streams, adding value in the process. So, if you have significant emissions, the idea is to convert those emissions into chemicals, which can then be transformed into reusable products, ideally into biodegradable polymers. This is a materials science challenge, but it's one we can meet. We don't need more fossil fuels because everything we need is already available. By converting emissions, wastewater, and solid waste back into products, we effectively close the material loop.

The issue lies in the outdated business model of producing, wasting, and selling as much material as possible, which drives unnecessary consumption, whether it's smartphones, bicycles, or other goods. The weakest point of combustion is that we've overlooked the fact that the emissions themselves are actually a wasted product, those who designed the car forgot to put an extra tank to collect the emissions. We create combustion because it produces the energy we need in the short term, but we forget that the output is also a product.

MetroLab: We focus mainly on the metropolitan scale. In order to get all these pieces moving, do you think that organisations like the Climate Lab can be scaled up? That maybe every metropolitan region should organise some kind of cooperation centre?

H.P.: I think so, because I think we've only been running Climate Lab for a couple of months and we're getting a lot of positive feedback and a lot of things are happening, it is very useful for a lot of different players. But I think apart from that, we have the plan to not only focus on projects or partners that are based in Vienna, but also to include all of Austria and always have the international perspective to bring them into online events and to learn and study other things.

If you provide innovation centres, you have a very big potential to create local jobs and keep the industry in a certain area, to help your businesses thrive. I think it's very important to provide space for innovation and to connect it with companies, but also with SMEs, because they are the majority of the economy.

A.P.: Sharing a common vision of the future is essential. Do we tolerate waste? Do we tolerate emissions? If the answer is no, that's an incentive to change, that's an incentive to close the loop. Nature is very clear about design principles, about how to design a functioning ecosystem, or a functioning bookkeeping system, if you go back to economics. It wrote a book on economics a long, long time ago, about three 3.8 billion years ago. Nature knows how economics works, natural bookkeeping works. If we adapt to it and follow it, it can be done.

Having hubs like Climate Lab is good because it helps people to talk to each other, to talk about a common future, to talk about perspectives. You can only do that if you have a community structure where there is trust and respect for each other. Local action is the only way forward. Most innovators are somewhere in a shed making beautiful things, and only their local community knows about it. But if you have a group of people who understand that this could be the solution or the things we need, then it can grow. ▪

MetroLab Podcast
Episode PRODUCING in Climate Neutral City Regions

Listen to our podcast on all platforms!

CONSUMING
in the Metropolitan Region

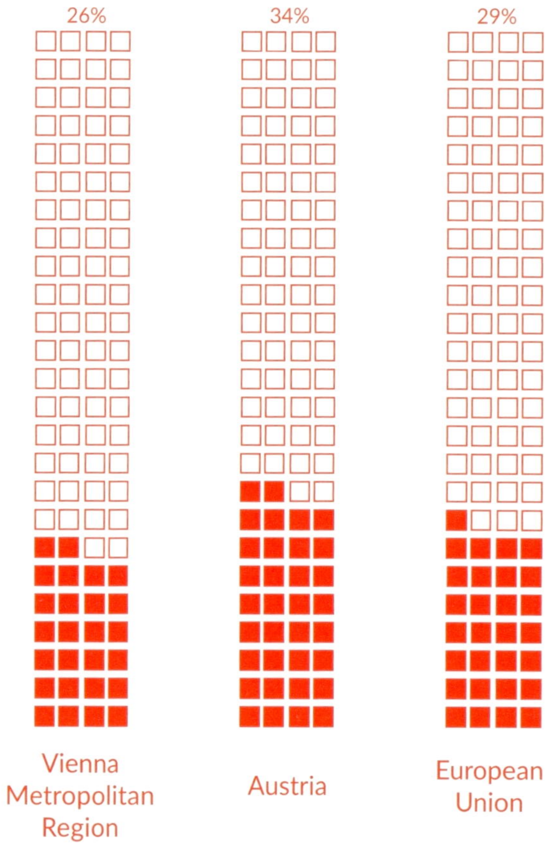

Share of the consumption sector of the total greenhouse gas emissions

Environment Agency Austria (2022 b): Federal states air pollutant inventory 1990–2020

The way we consume has a significant impact on our carbon emissions. In this chapter of the Emerging Phenomena Atlas, we explore the central role of consumption patterns in driving carbon emissions in the Vienna metropolitan area. This sector, which encompasses everything from the products we buy, to the energy we use, to the food we eat, is responsible for a significant share of greenhouse gas emissions. Demand for goods and services often leads to increased production, resource depletion and waste, perpetuating a cycle of environmental degradation. As global consumption increases, so does the pressure on natural resources and the carbon-intensive systems that support them. By understanding the links between consumption patterns, resource use and carbon footprints, we can develop more sustainable lifestyles and policies that reduce emissions and promote a greener, more equitable future.

C1 Food Emissions

C2 Lifestyle Emissions

C3 Resource Consumption

» Interview with Carolyn Steel, Yvonne Lötscher & Martin Strele

C1 Food Emissions

Only part of the emissions due to food consumption are in reality emitted in Austria, and 90% of these emissions are caused by animal-based products

Austrians eat 12.5 times as much red meat and twice as much poultry as recommended by the EAT-Lancet Planetary Health Diet. Our current average diet causes a total of 1,467 kg CO_2 equivalent/person/year and requires an average of 1,832 m2/person/year. The average diet in Austria can be classified as unhealthy, with excessive consumption of meat and insufficient consumption of fruits and vegetables. These dietary imbalances have negative environmental and health effects. Reducing meat consumption to the recommended amount would save 523.7 kg of CO_2 equivalents and 0.5 ha of land per person per year.

Wolbart, N. (2019): Greenhouse gas emissions of Austrian diets in comparison
Schlatzer et al. (2020): DIETCCLU

Farms in Lower Austria, Source: basemap.at

Austria imports agricultural products worth €14 billion annually. Germany is Austria's most important trading partner.

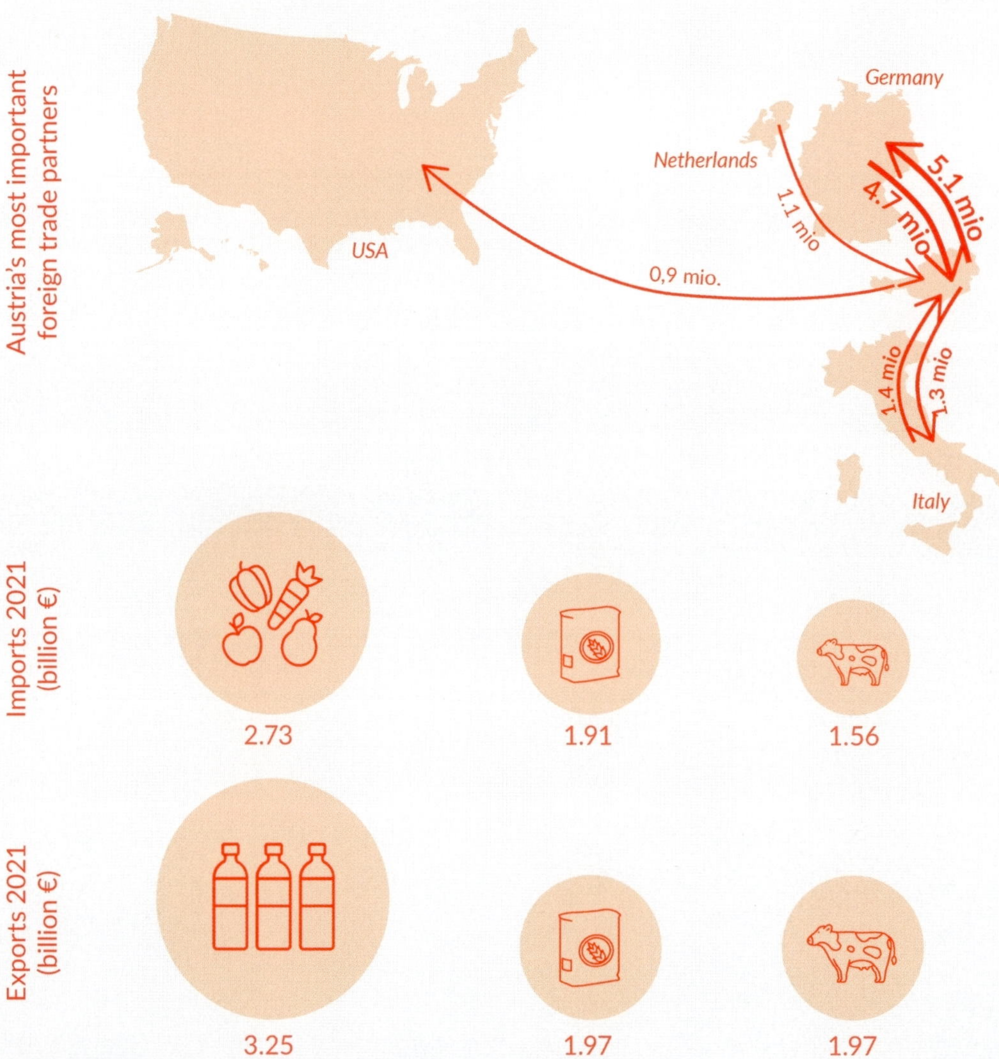

Import and Export Relations of Austria

 Frey et al. (2021): The global carbon footprint of Austria's consumption of agricultural (food- and non-food) products

In Austria, the main emissions associated with animal products are from enteric fermentation, while in other countries the main contributors are the cultivation of soybeans, maize and other feed crops for livestock. The current land footprint of Vienna's food consumption is about 15 times the size of the city and two orders of magnitude larger than the available agricultural land within the city limits.

Only 36% of Austria's emissions related to food products originate in Austria

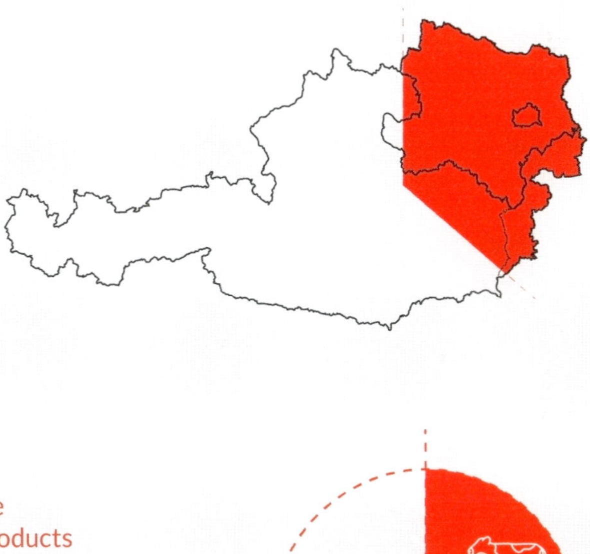

90% of these emissions are caused by animal-based products

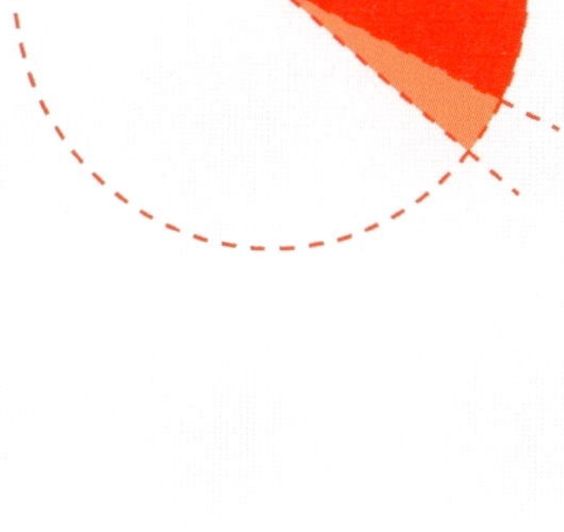

Emissions Due to Our Food Consumption

Frey et al. (2021): The global carbon footprint of Austria's consumption of agricultural (food- and non-food) products
Environmental Agency Austria (2017): SUM-Food

In recent decades, meat consumption in Austria, as in other countries, has increased dramatically. In order to reduce greenhouse gas emissions from food consumption, it is necessary to change the current diet to a non-meat diet.

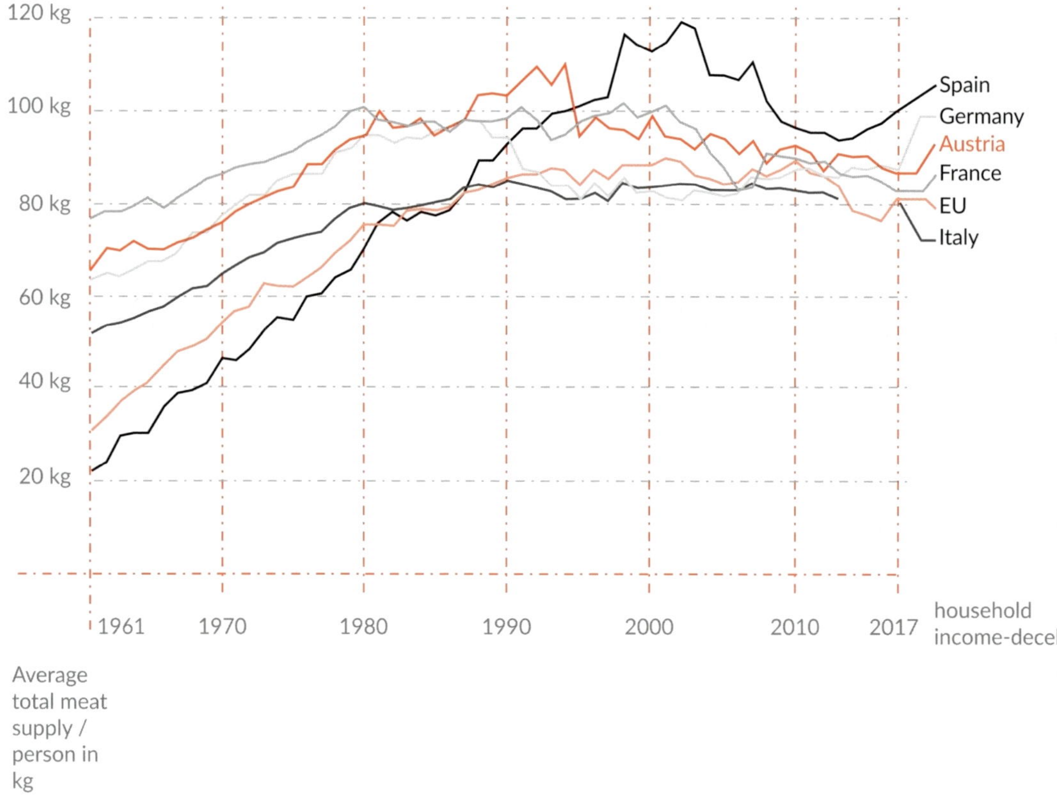

Meat Supply per Person

FAO (2023): Per capita consumption of meat

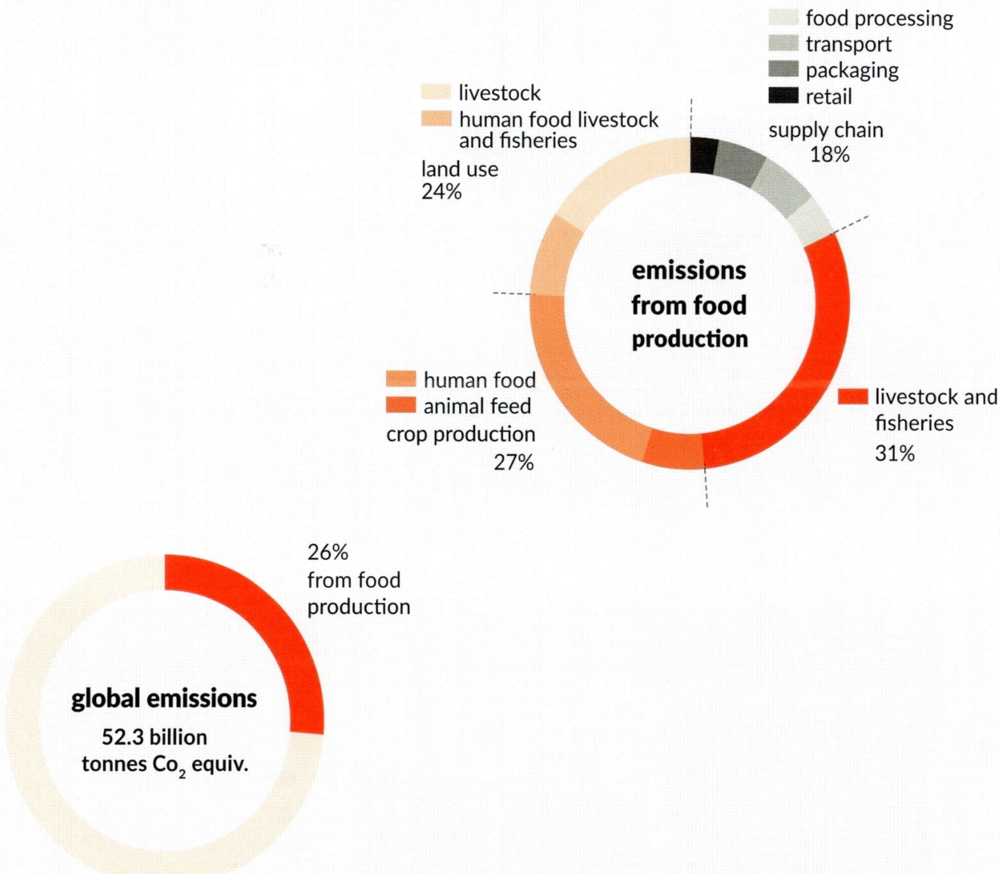

Global Emissions from Food Production

Ritchie, H. & Roser, M. (2022): Environmental Impacts of Food Production

Switching to a vegan diet could reduce Vienna's food-related greenhouse gas footprint by 57%. Vienna's land food footprint could be reduced by 54%. Although the land required for Vienna's food system accounts for less than a quarter of Austria's total agricultural land, only 32% of the land required for Vienna's food system is actually located in Austria.

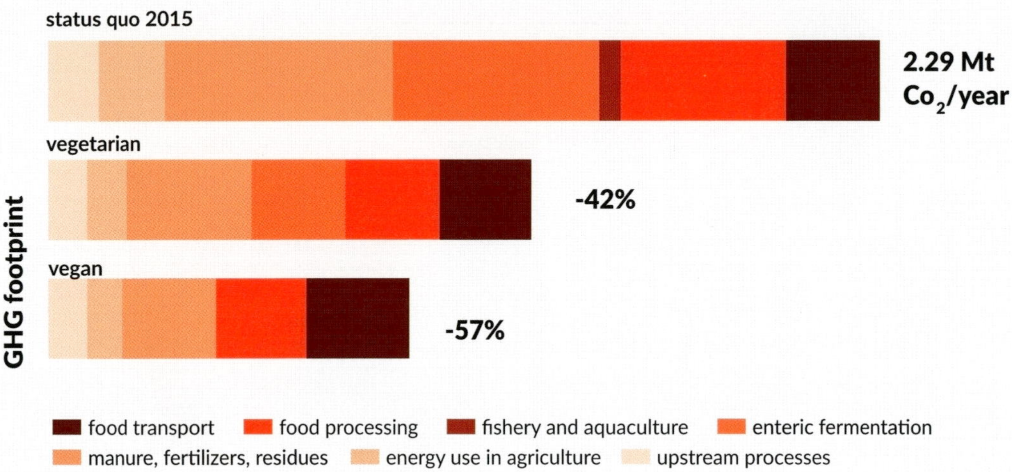

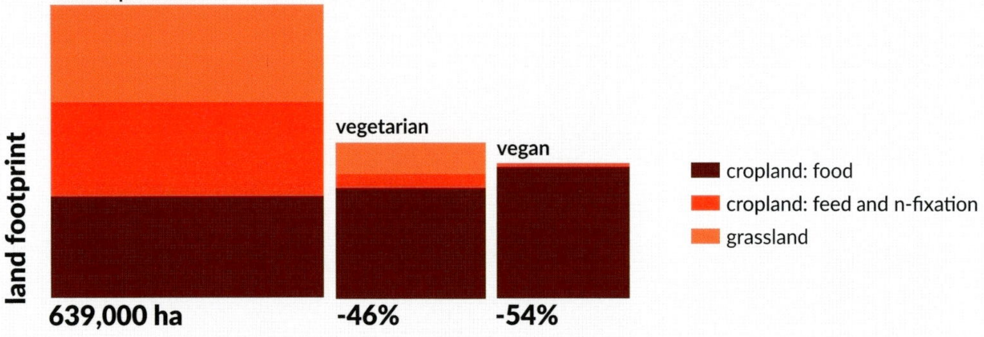

Footprint Reduction Potentials through Dietary Changes

Lauk et al. (2022): Demand side options to reduce greenhouse gas emissions and the land foot-print of urban food systems: A scenario analysis for the City of Vienna

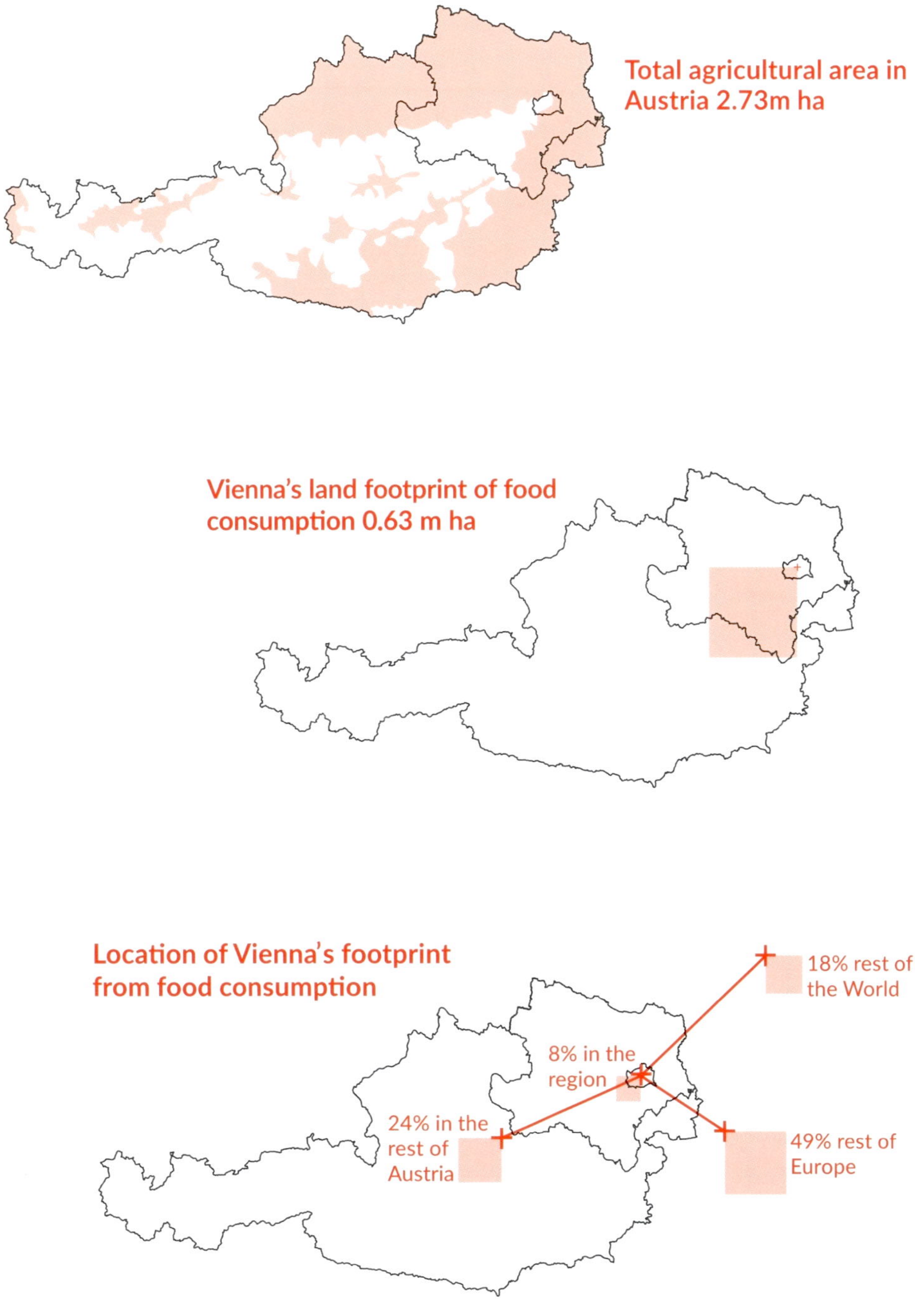

Location of the Land Footprint of Vienna's Food System

Lauk et al. (2022): Demand side options to reduce greenhouse gas emissions and the land foot-print of urban food systems: A scenario analysis for the City of Vienna

Consumption-based emissions are highly influenced by our lifestyle choices

The richest 10% of households in Austria have twice the emissions of the average household, with transport, leisure and holidays being the main contributors to this large difference. Holidays alone contribute 16% of our carbon footprint, as we tend to be less mindful during these times, and transportation plays a significant role in these holiday-related emissions.

Greenpeace (2020): Climate injustice in Austria

Housing Development "Fontana" in Oberwaltersdorf, Source: basemap.at

Eliminating all spending on vacations and eating out results in an average carbon intensity of 1.17 kg CO_2e per hour. This suggests that these expenses contribute about 16% of carbon emissions.

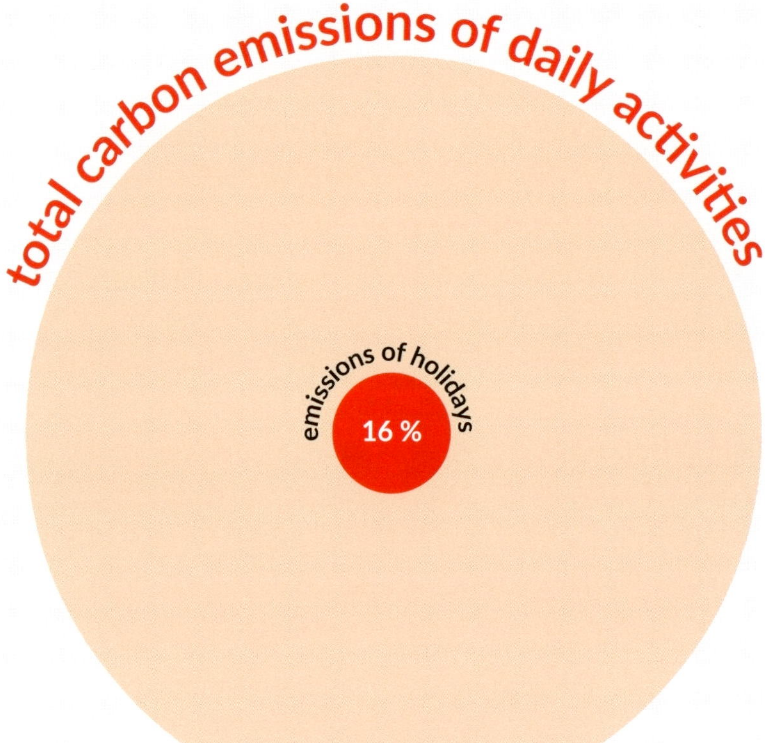

Total Carbon Emissions of Daily Activities

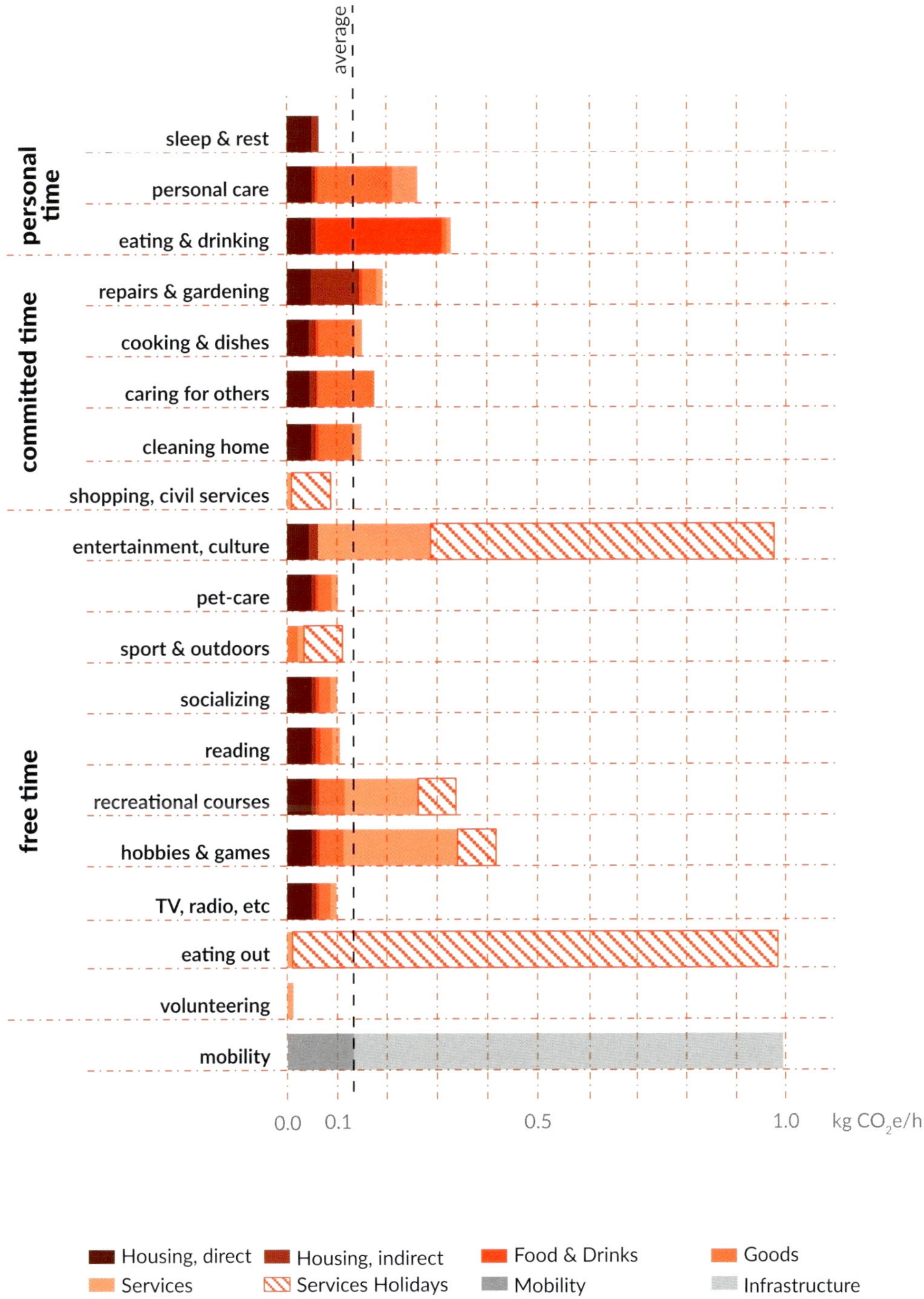

CO_2 Footprint of Everyday Activities in Comparison

The carbon footprint of different types of travel varies significantly. Traveling by car or train does not vary much, but traveling by air multiplies the carbon footprint exponentially.

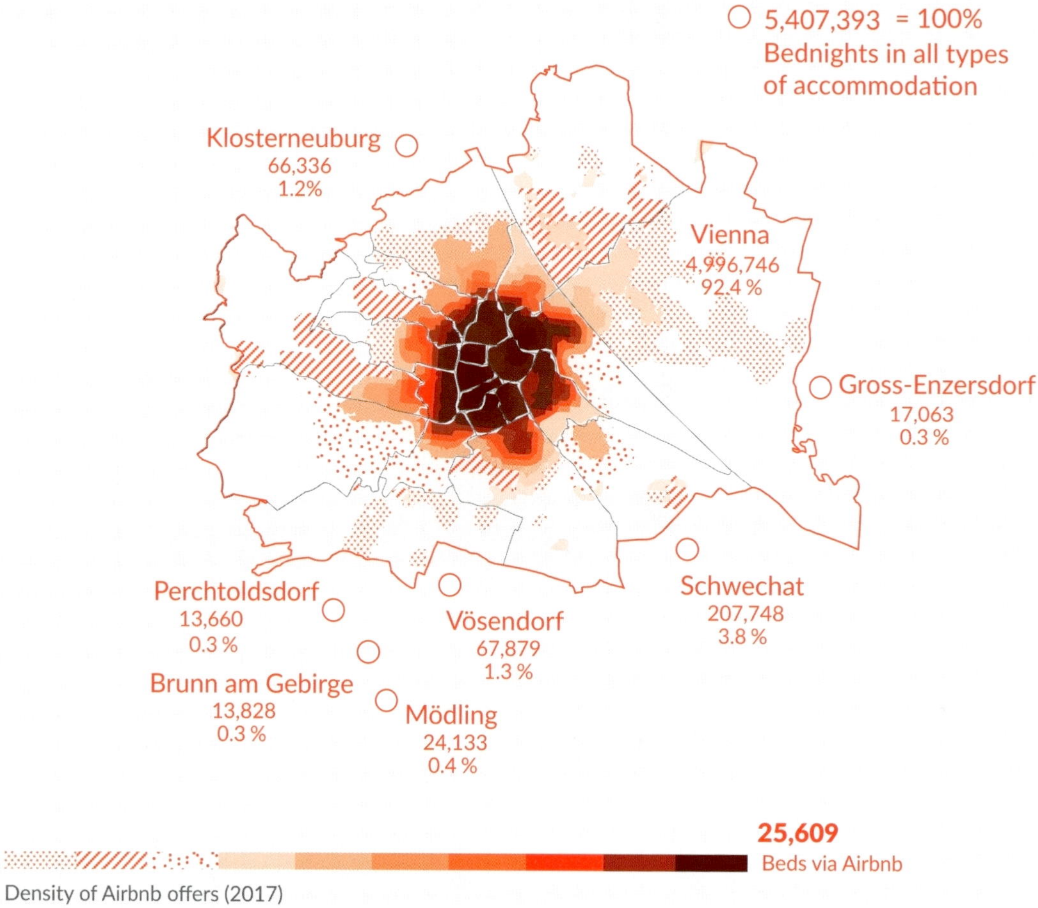

Overnight Visitors in Accommodation Facilities and Airbnb

Seidl et al. (2017): Airbnb in Vienna: An analysis. Interactive research report 2017

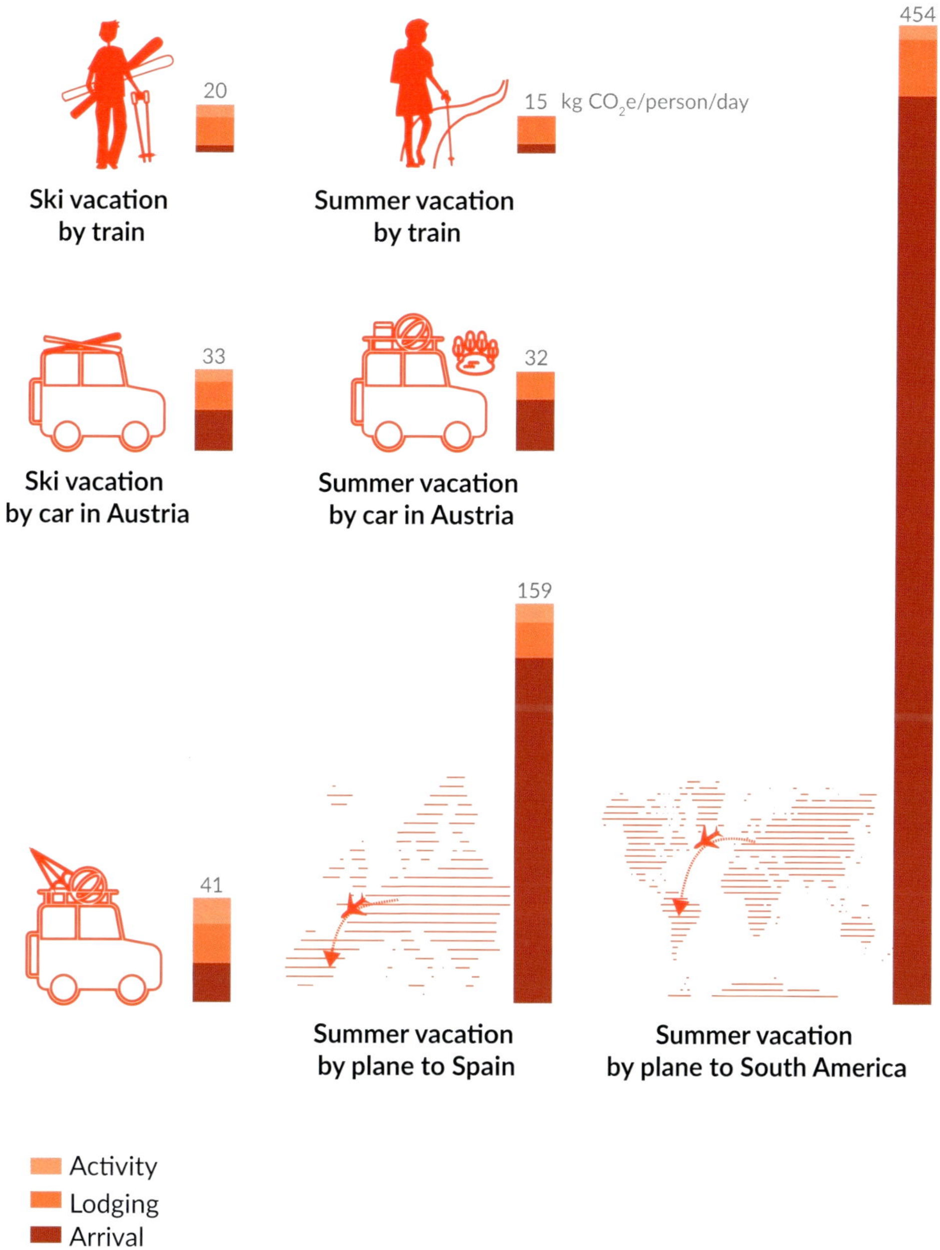

CO_2 Footprint of Vacation Types in Comparison

Environment Agency Austria (2018): Factsheet greenhouse gas balance: a comparison of vacation types

The consumption of resources in the metropolitan region is responsible for resource consumption in other parts of the world

Austrian consumption has a significant impact on global resource use, with 40% of the materials used in Austria being imported. In 2011, Austria's greenhouse gas emissions amounted to a significant 80.3 million tons, or 9.6 tons per person.

However, when Austria's total consumption is taken into account, emissions rise to 123.6 million tons, resulting in a per capita share of 14.7 (54% higher than conventional measurements).

Steininger et al. (2018): Austria's consumption-based greenhouse gas emissions: Identifying sectoral sources and destinations

United Nations in Vienna, Source: basemap.at

Material use has increased by 160% since the 1960s. The construction sector (14%), mining (13%) and food production (9%) are the sectors with the largest material footprints.

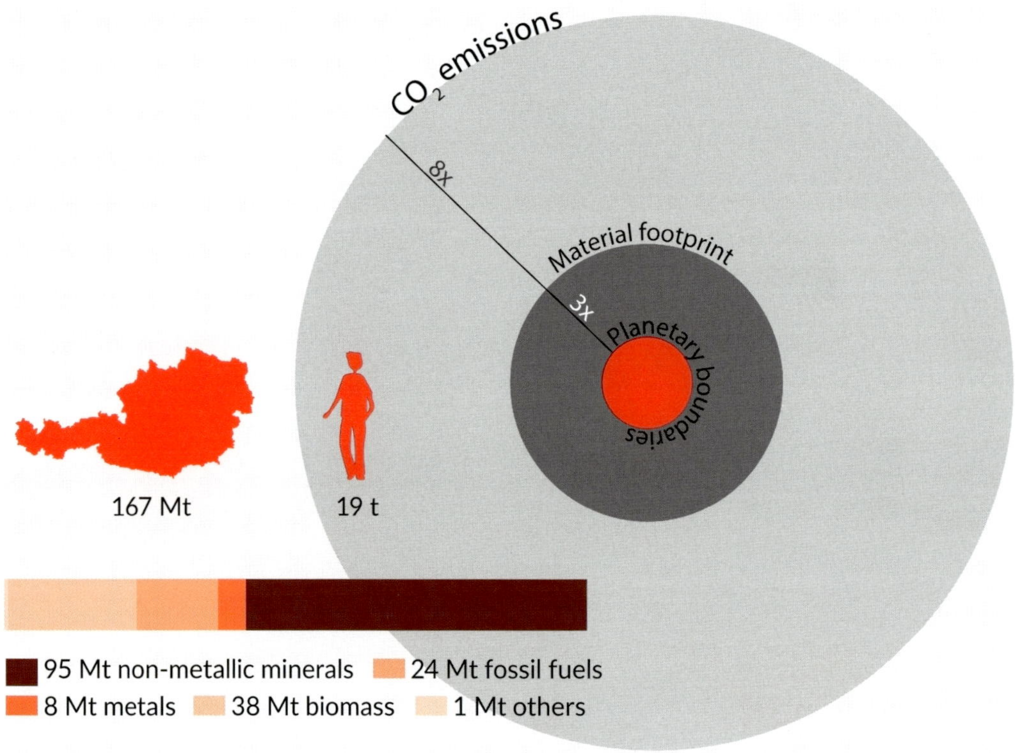

Material Resource Consumption in Austria

40% of Austria's material consumption in production and consumption comes from abroad. 98% of the biomass Vienna needs for food, energy and the economy comes from outside, mostly from the surrounding areas.

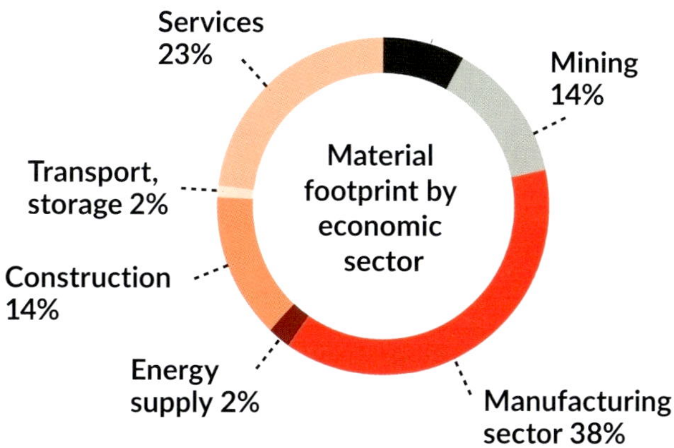

Material Footprint by Economic Sector

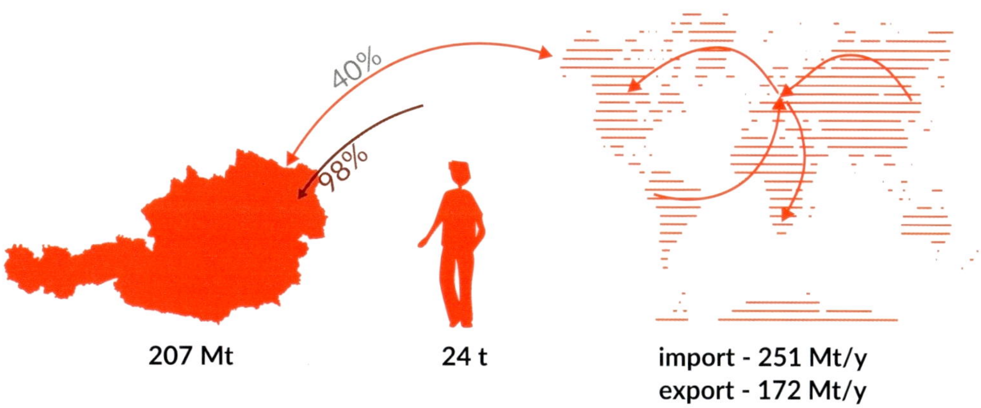

Material Footprint of Austria

The approximately 170 metric tons per year are consumed in Austria in production and consumption or tied up in buildings, infrastructure or durable goods.

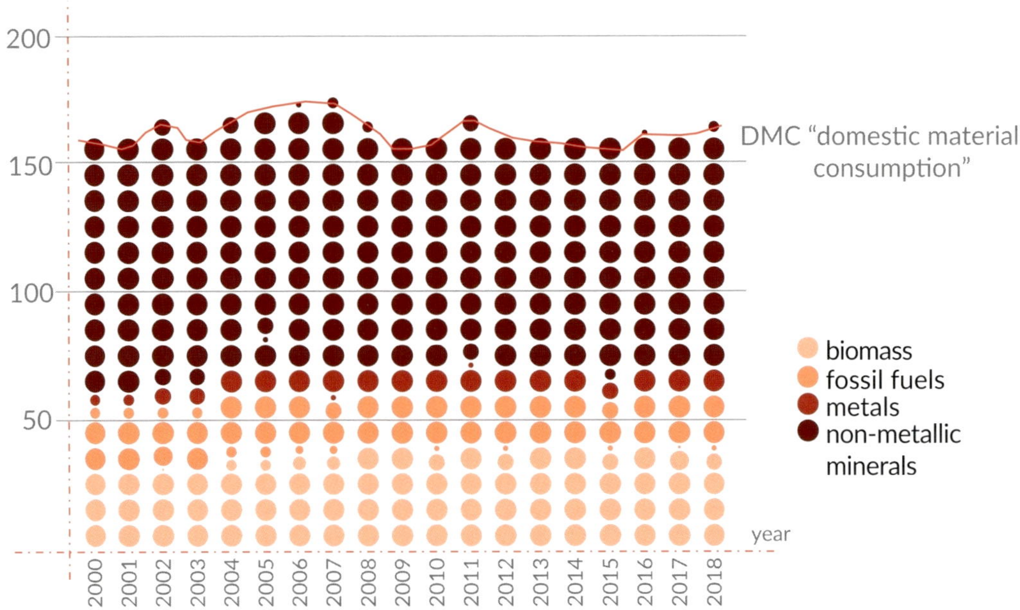

Domestic Material Consumption in Austria

Austrian consumption has a significant impact on global resource use, as 40% of the materials used in Austria are imported. This is due to the fact that Austria imports more than it exports, resulting in the outsourcing of production and the associated environmental impacts to other countries. The concept of the Material Footprint allows the allocation of resource use along the entire production and supply chain, identifying the countries where the end use takes place.

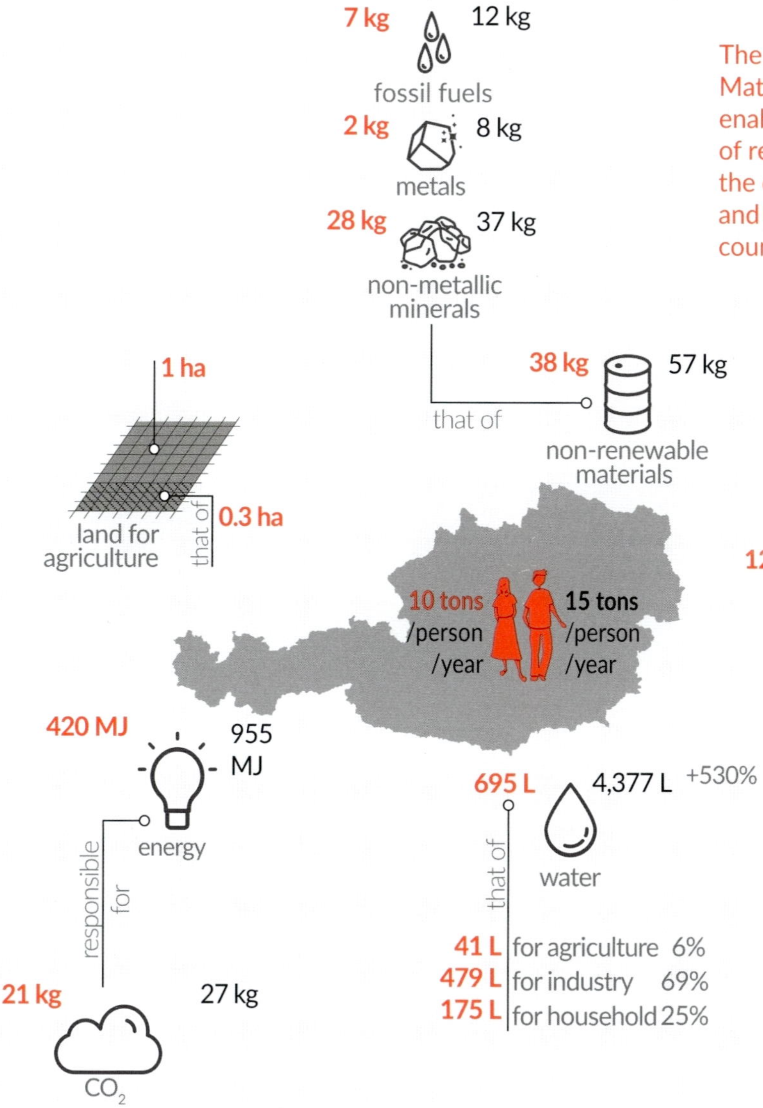

The concept of the Material Footprint enables the allocation of resource use across the entire production and supply chain to the countries of end use.

Worldwide Material Consumption / Person / Day

BMK (2020): Resource Use in Austria 2020
Steininger et al. (2018): Austria's consumption-based greenhouse gas emissions: Identifying sectoral sources and destinations

“There is no such thing as cheap food, we have just externalised all the costs of trade”

Interview with Carolyn Steel, Yvonne Lötscher & Martin Strele

Carolyn Steel is an architect and leading author of several books on food. She has spent past decades investigating how food shapes our lives and our environment.

Yvonne Lötscher led the development of the Sustainable Food Strategy for the City of Zurich, focusing on sustainable food production and consumption and raising public awareness on a city-wide scale.

Martin Strele is the managing director of Kairos, a private research centre in Bregenz, which focuses on impact research and development. He is also the founder of Bodenfreiheit, an initiative against land consumption.

MetroLab: In July comes the day when humanity has used up all the resources that the earth could regenerate in a year. In Austria, because of our lifestyle, that day will come in April. Especially in the global North, we are consuming far more than we can produce in a truly sustainable way. Are we consuming too much or the wrong things?

Yvonne Lötscher: I think part of it is that people are consuming too many goods that are only used once, we are not yet in a circular economy. We need to learn how to make products more sustainable, more circular, so that the single product does not use so many resources. We need to think about circularity, efficiency, but also sufficiency, I think.

Martin Strele: The main problem is that our consumption patterns do not make us happier. It does not lead to a more fulfilling life. And that was the basic idea of consumption in the past. People tried to produce things to consume in order to make their lives better, happier, healthier. And since the late 1960s or early 1970s, we have left that path of growth, the gap between better life and more consumption has been widening since then. The fundamental question for us is, do we promote less consumption or do we promote a good, a good life, well-being, a happy life, a fulfilling life? And it's a very important question because we still have a lot of areas in our world where people are eager to consume more in order to have a good life.

Carolyn Steel: It's a very well-established, long-lived cultural evolution that we've gone through. It comes out of the Enlightenment and after the Industrial Revolution, with a whole Western idea of what a good life looks like. And very famously it is at odds with many Eastern philosophies, for example Buddhism, a philosophy which absolutely says that a good life is a life lived in balance with nature, and in which finding out what is enough is the good life.

We need to ask a deeper question; find out why we have developed this idea of a good life that requires us to consume. If you want to reduce consumption and bring it more into balance with nature, you have to think about how we can replace the things in people's lives that we have taken away from them. What can make people happier with their lives so that they don't have to consume to feel that they have a good life. This is massively complicated and intertwined, it has deep historical roots. The answer will never be to make people feel bad about themselves or to put the vegetables at the front of the supermarket. That is just scratching the surface of a deeply rooted problem. But I think recognising the nature of the problem and asking the question again, what does a good life look like in the 21st century, is essential to finding answers to these kinds of questions.

M.S.: We have been asking ourselves for a long time: When was there a time in history, in our cultural areas, when we lived within planetary boundaries and our consumption patterns lasted all year round, rather than using up resources in April or May as we do today? But this was not a time of dark stone ages—the average Swiss lifestyle in 1968 was one that the whole population of today could live within planetary boundaries: So this is not a very long time ago in history, and makes us optimistic that the goals we need to achieve are not out of reach.

C.S.: You have to look at the whole question of power: Who is driving this development? On the one hand, you have an economic model that says GDP equals happiness and growth equals business. On the other hand, you have corporations whose entire modus vivendi is to get us to buy more stuff in order to make profits. There are engines that are driving this kind of crazy development that is not making us happier, but making our lives unsustainable. But until you identify what those engines are and start to dismantle or change them, we are never going to change anything.

MetroLab: Food is a central part of our consumption. If we ate according to the Planetary Health Diet recommended by the EAT-Lancet Commission, it would not only benefit public health, but also significantly reduce our greenhouse gas emissions.
Studies have shown that in Vienna, if the entire population followed these recommendations, food-related greenhouse gas emissions would fall by a third. What influences the consumption patterns of our society? And why is it so difficult to change them, even when we have the basic knowledge about sustainable and healthy food choices?

Y.L.: The influence on food choices is largely influenced by habits, by the foods that we know, that we grew up with, that we eat regularly. Changing habits is a really long process and it's not done by giving people information. The key to changing habits is to give people alternatives that they like. Providing alternatives in an easy way, so that in the end the sustainable choice is the logical choice that comes naturally.

And that is part of what we can do with the Zurich Sustainable Food Strategy at the restaurant level, or when we design our offerings, so that we can really give people an easy choice and the opportunity to try new dishes. This is an opportunity especially in ▸

private restaurants, where people go to enjoy something that they do not cook at home: Gastronomy can really be a pioneer and part of the change, we are already seeing that.

MetroLab: We still waste large amounts of food. Is the process of seeing how food is grown or produced and by whom, understanding the amount of labour behind certain products a possible factor in changing the way we consume?

C.S.: Value is what this all comes down to. In our industrialised world, we expect food to be cheap. Food is made up of living things that we kill so that we can live. So food is life. If you treat food as cheap, you treat life as cheap.

The second issue is visibility, and that's also very important. I often talk about the development that we have gone through since industrialisation, which has separated the city from the productive hinterland that used to feed it. And it's not surprising that people do not think very much about the impact of their consumption on those landscapes, because they are literally not in their world. They create the illusion of cheapness by externalising the true cost of food production.

Y.L.: In Switzerland, too, far too much food is still wasted in an institutional way. There is too much product available, but we also have to think about the consumers, they are the biggest part of the food waste, responsible for about 40% in Switzerland. And I think we can only address that if people appreciate it, I don't think it works in terms of money.

M.S.: We developed an exhibition a few years ago and came up with three suggestions to help people appreciate food: The first was to cook for yourself. When you cook your own food, you learn how much effort it takes to make good food. The second was to meet a farmer, someone who produces the raw materials for food. Because we don't know many farmers, we don't see them around us, they are pushed to the edge of our settlements. The last one was growing your own food. Even if it's just a small herb plant, just to be in contact with the living plants and to realise how much effort you have to put in.

Y.L.: That's why in Zurich we are also investing a lot of energy in urban farming, urban gardening, so that people can participate, we need to make our green spaces accessible to a wider range of people. There are interesting new forms such as community gardens and regenerative farming concepts that encourage participation.

C.S.: I absolutely believe in the idea of making food more visible, of designing a place where the processes or the spaces that support them are all present to people, either physically or transparently, as something they can encounter in their everyday lives.

Y.L.: I think it's important to reflect on your own behaviour because I think the vast majority of people don't realise how much food they waste. I think it helps a lot to see what you are wasting, so I encourage people to really measure their food waste for a week or two, it can really be an eye-opener to be able to add it up and see the value and the amount of food that you have actually wasted.

MetroLab: Consider the spatial relationships between cities and their surrounding areas or within metropolitan regions: Where would you see the most important points of connection between a city and its productive countryside?

M.S.: Spatial planning should be about freeing up the space needed to produce our food, our energy and much more. Nobody cares where this land is located: Mainly in Asia, Africa and other parts of the world. In my opinion, spatial planning should focus more on the complementary open spaces that need to go hand in hand with our living spaces. If we set aside a certain amount of land for housing, we need to set aside a hundred times that amount of land for food, fibre and energy production.

Open spaces are just waiting to be marked as building sites, and that's not enough.

C.S.: Cities have always had strong links with the countryside, and the place where they came together was the market. These were not only places to get fresh food, but also places of great sociability. At a market, food is real, physical, from a real place, made by real people, and meant to be shared with other people. Over the last 50 years, food has increasingly come into the city, but through supermarkets with their own invisible distribution system. Markets are increasingly necessary as a social counterpoint to the kind of increasing distance and resignation in our social lives. They allow small farmers to exist, we need to encourage regenerative and small-scale mixed farming. Cities need to allow markets, protect them, subsidise them, and in the end there are so many social and environmental benefits that come from them.

Y.L.: We teamed up with a vegetable vendor and started a Foodsave market in Zurich, where people can buy leftover vegetables at a really affordable price, making healthy vegetables accessible to everyone. You don't have to be a member of an association or a discussion group or have a lot of time. You can just go to the market and be part of saving food.

MetroLab: Since Climate Change is progressing very fast, we need to make changes quickly: Where do you see the greatest leverage to act now? Should we focus more on bottom-up approaches or on existing regulations and legislation?

M.S.: I'm afraid there is no fast solution – small initiatives as well as political decisions are needed. It's a matter of being active at all levels.

C.S.: We need bottom up as well as top down, to restructure our planning and tax system. Over the last 150 years we have created a society based on the existence of cheap food. But there is no such thing as cheap food, we have just externalised all the costs of trade. If you want to move to a society that is based on good food and everyone being able to eat, then obviously you have to internalise the true cost of food. That is the only way to get the market to do the work for you.

Basically, the true cost of locally grown organic food is already in it, whereas the true cost of industrial food is all over the world. We are paying the consequences in terms of climate change, habitat destruction, loss of biodiversity. We just don't pay for it in the supermarket bill. Planning has massive power: take the green belt around London, for example, a protected area of agricultural land. It simply does not feed London at the moment because of the economic landscape we have created.

MetroLab: Do you think your sustainable food strategy in Zurich can serve as a model for other cities to adopt the same approach? Where do you see the positive impacts?

Y.L.: In Zurich, we are far from being self-sufficient, but we really want to promote the participatory element in food production, that people can be part of it, to have experimental spaces like community gardens and solidarity concepts, and then help them to multiply. We also see the strategy as a climate strategy for urban agricultural spaces. When we give spaces to farmers, we demand that they farm organically. We also need to think about how much of the available space we want to use for animal production, and think about the potential for plant-based production. ▪

**MetroLab Podcast
Episode CONSUMING in Climate Neutral City Regions**

Listen to our podcast on all platforms!

WASTING
in the Metropolitan Region

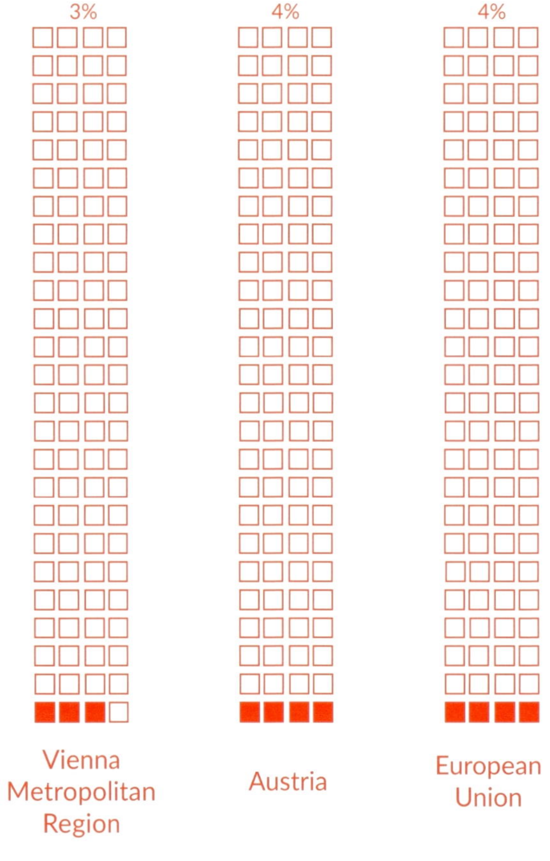

Share of the waste sector of the total greenhouse gas emissions

Environment Agency Austria (2022 b): Federal states air pollutant inventory 1990–2020

The way we waste has a significant impact on our carbon emissions. In this chapter of the Emerging Phenomena Atlas, we explore the critical issue of waste generation and its significant contribution to global carbon emissions. Waste in its various forms—whether food, plastics, excavation materials or industrial by-products—represents not only lost resources, but also a significant source of greenhouse gases. When products and materials are discarded, the energy and resources invested in their production are effectively wasted, resulting in additional emissions throughout their lifecycle, from production to disposal. Landfilling, incineration and inefficient waste management practices compound the problem by releasing methane and other potent greenhouse gases into the atmosphere. Understanding the intricate links between waste generation, resource inefficiency, and carbon emissions is essential for developing strategies to reduce waste, increase recycling, and transition to a circular economy where resources are reused and emissions are minimized.

W1 Waste Management

W2 Recycling Goals

W3 Waste in Landfills

W4 Construction Waste

» Interview with Dominik Wiedenhofer, Carolin Bellstedt & Felix Heisel

Austria produces 8 tons of waste per inhabitant per year, it’s municipal waste generation is above the EU-average

59% of the total waste generated in Austria is excavation material, while construction and demolition waste accounts for about 16%. Austria imports almost as much waste as it exports, more than half of it to neighboring countries.

BMK (2023): Bundes-Abfallwirtschaftsplan Statusreport 2023

Landfill in Vienna. Source: basemap.at

A large proportion of the waste generated in Austria is due to excavation materials, while the amount of municipal waste is also considerably high compared to other countries.

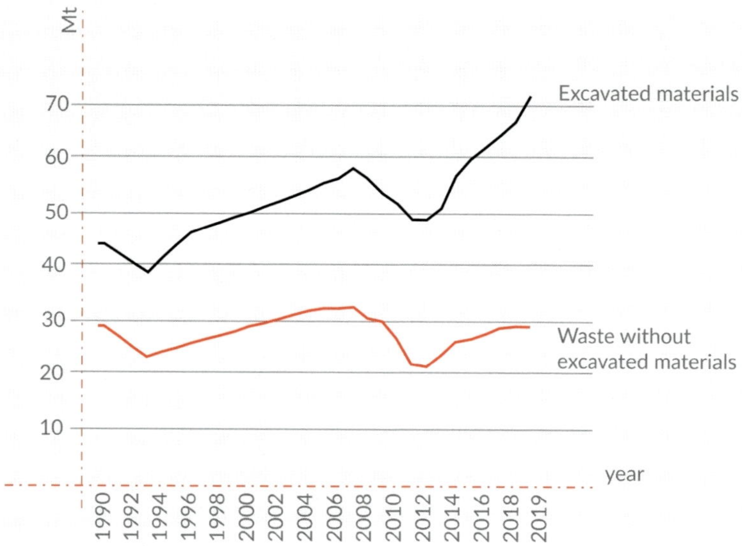

Waste Generation in Austria

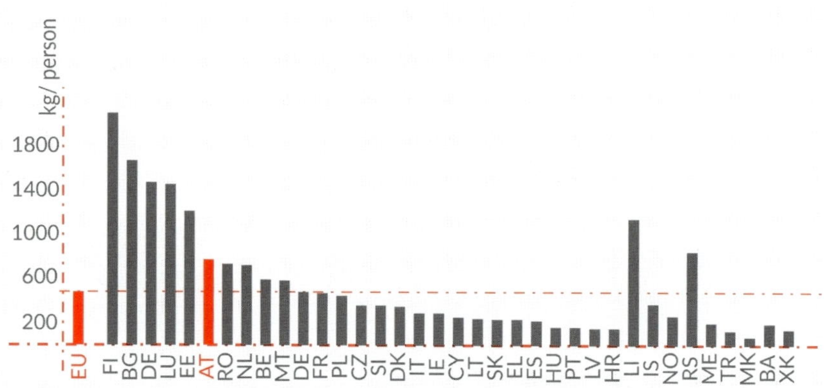

Municipal Waste in EU countries

BMK (2023): Bundes-Abfallwirtschaftsplan Statusreport 2023

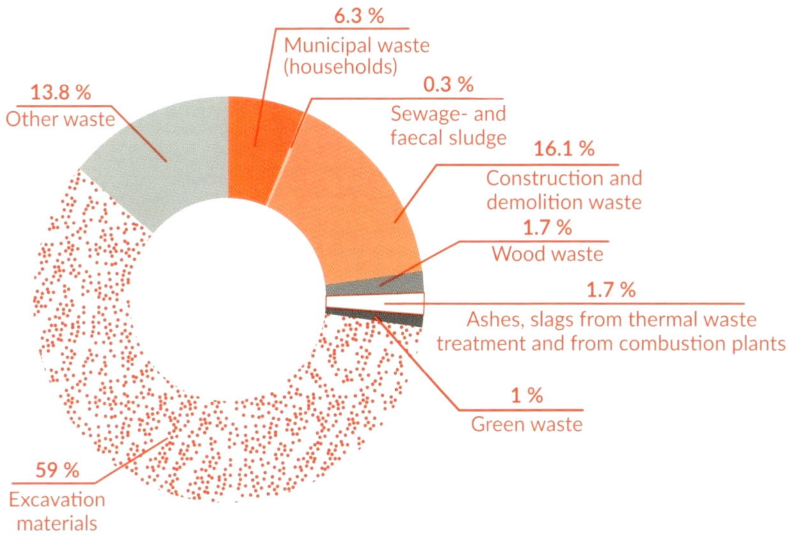

Total Waste Generation by 2019 in Waste Groups

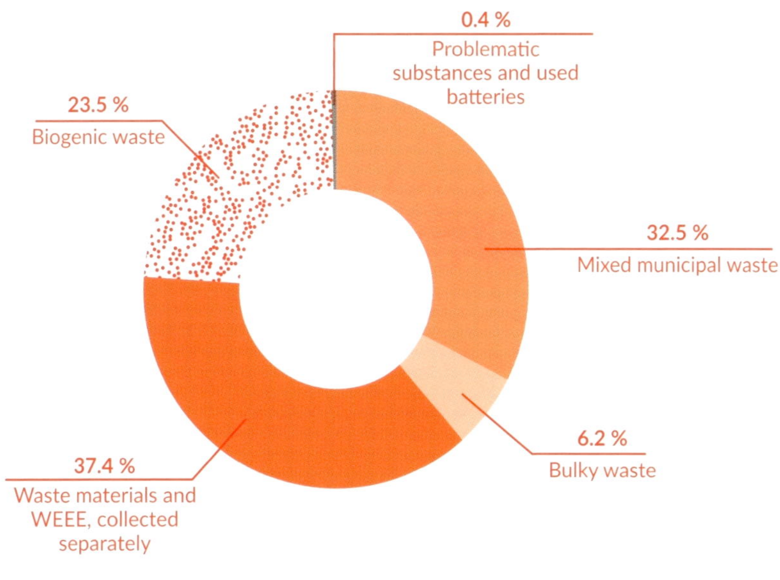

Municipal Waste from Households and similar Establishments (2019) in Austria

Eurostat (2022): What are the main destinations of EU export of waste?

Austria imports almost as much waste as it exports, more than half of it to neighboring countries. It is part of a global waste network.

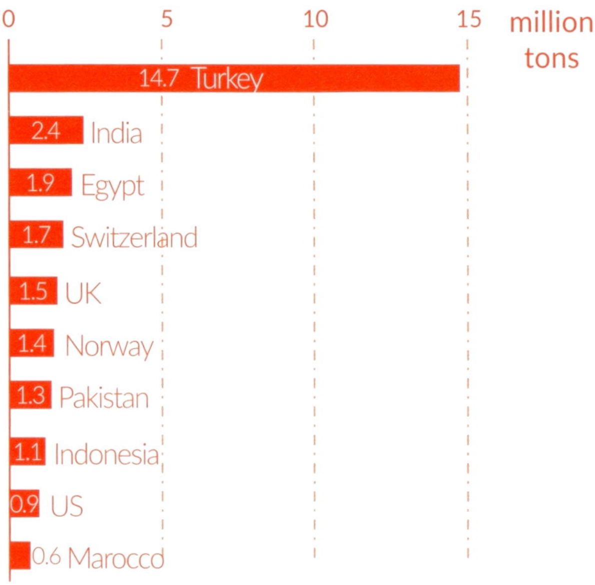

Main Destinations of Waste from the EU

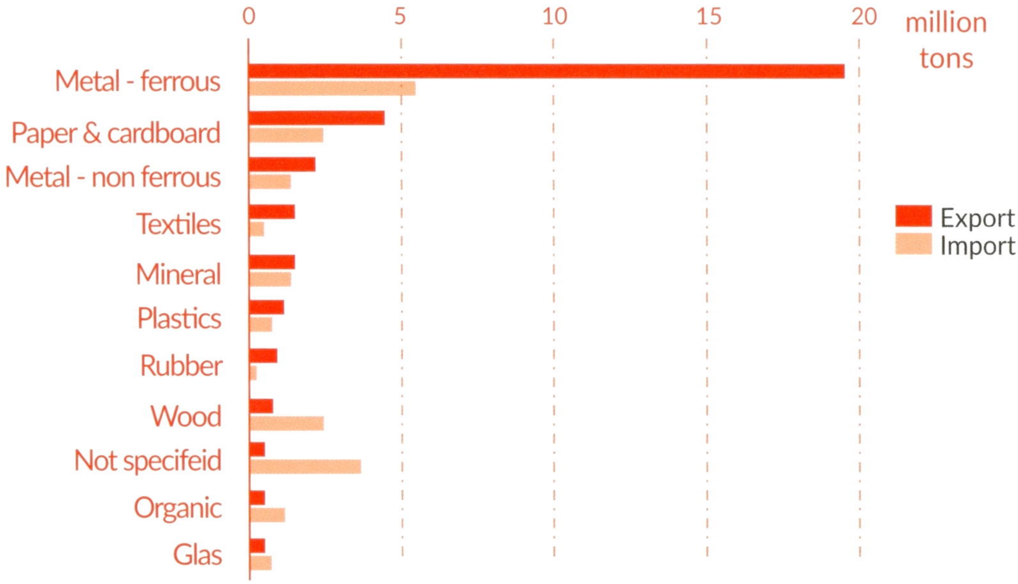

EU Exports and Imports by Type of Material

Eurostat (2022): What are the main destinations of EU export of waste?

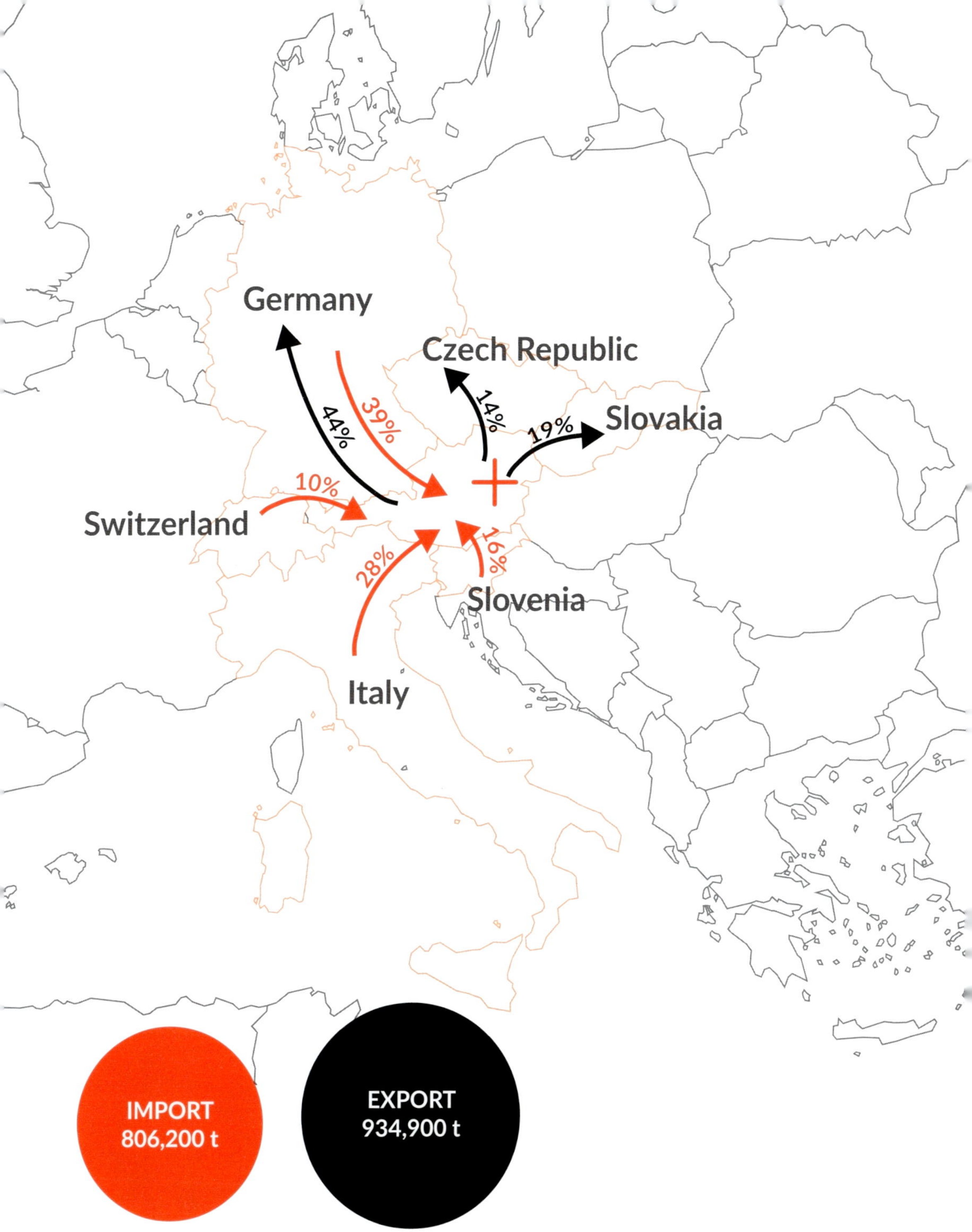

mainly:
Residues from mechanical
waste processing (181,100 t)
clean wood waste (170,000 t)

mainly:
Substitute fuels (180,000 t)
dusts, ashes & drosses from
melting processes (113,700 t)

Waste Streams

Austria has only achieved its 2025 recycling goals for certain materials, others are still well below EU average

Austria has the second highest recycling rate of household waste in the EU. Recycling rates for paper, glass and metal have reached Austria's 2025 targets, but only 30% of Austria's plastic packaging waste is recycled.

Current financial incentives and infrastructure are not sufficient to meet all recycling targets. The legal framework and capacities need to be improved and targets already achieved need to be re-evaluated.

BMK (2023): Bundes-Abfallwirtschaftsplan Statusreport 2023

Waste Collection Center in Vienna, Source: basemap.at

According to the EU, more than 50% of plastic waste should be recycled by 2030. The current financial situation and infrastructure are not sufficient to achieve this goal. Legal frameworks and capacities need to be improved.

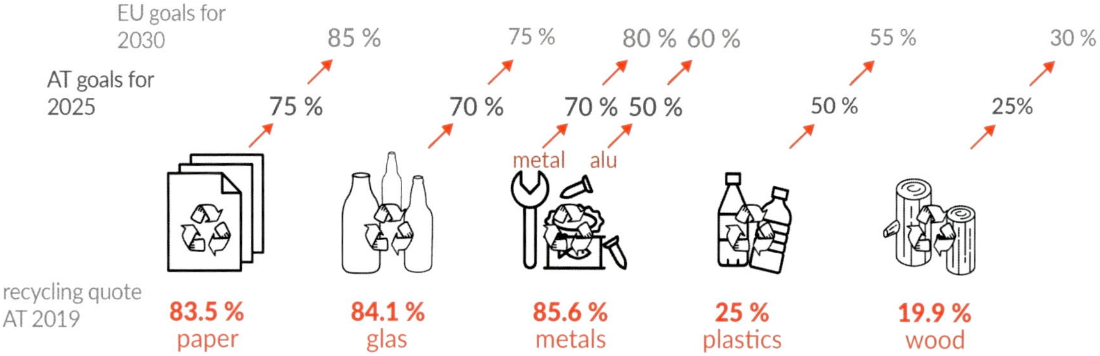

Recycling Rate & Recycling Targets

BMK (2023): Bundes-Abfallwirtschaftsplan Statusreport 2023
ÖWAV (2020): Recycling targets 2025/2030

Austria has the second highest recycling rate of household waste in the EU, yet only 30% of Austrian plastic packaging waste is recycled.

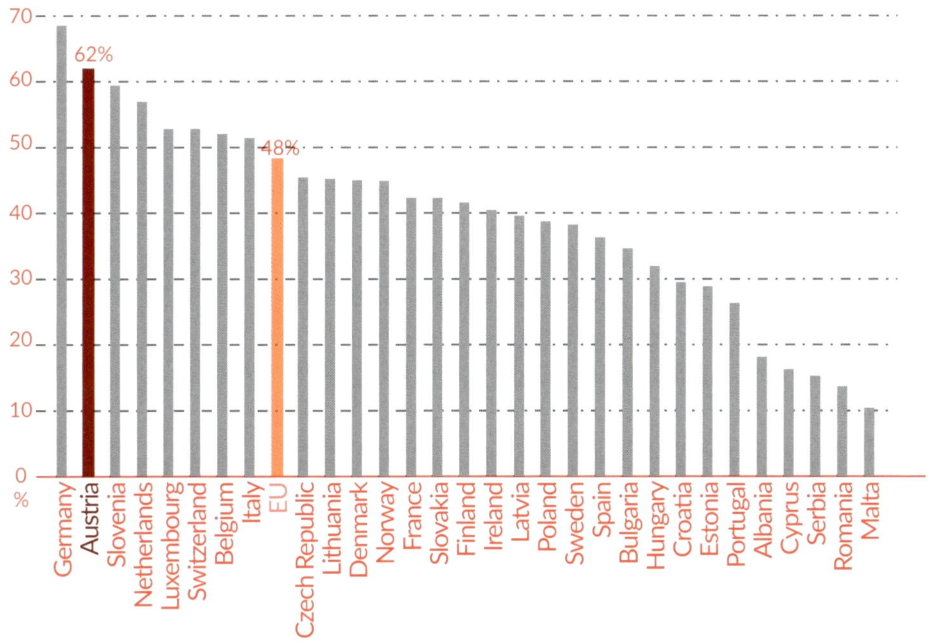

Residential Waste EU Comparison

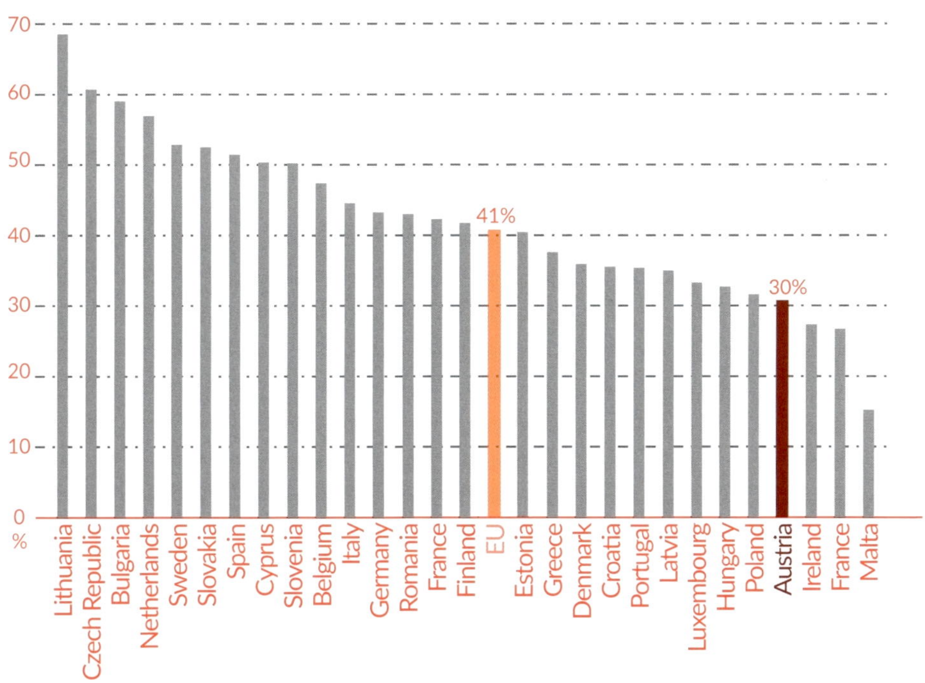

Plastic Packaging Waste EU Comparison

Eurostat (2022): What are the main destinations of EU export of waste?

W3 Waste in Landfills

46% of Austria's total waste volume goes to landfill, but the majority of household waste is incinerated

Although municipal waste is now incinerated rather than landfilled, nearly half of Austria's waste still ends up in landfills.

BMK (2023): Bundes-Abfallwirtschaftsplan Statusreport 2023

Waste Incineration Plant in Vienna. Source: basemap.at

Municipal waste from individual households accounts for only 6% of Austria's total waste. Only 34% of all waste is recycled. However, this figure rises to 64% if waste from excavations, the largest contributor to the waste volume, is excluded.

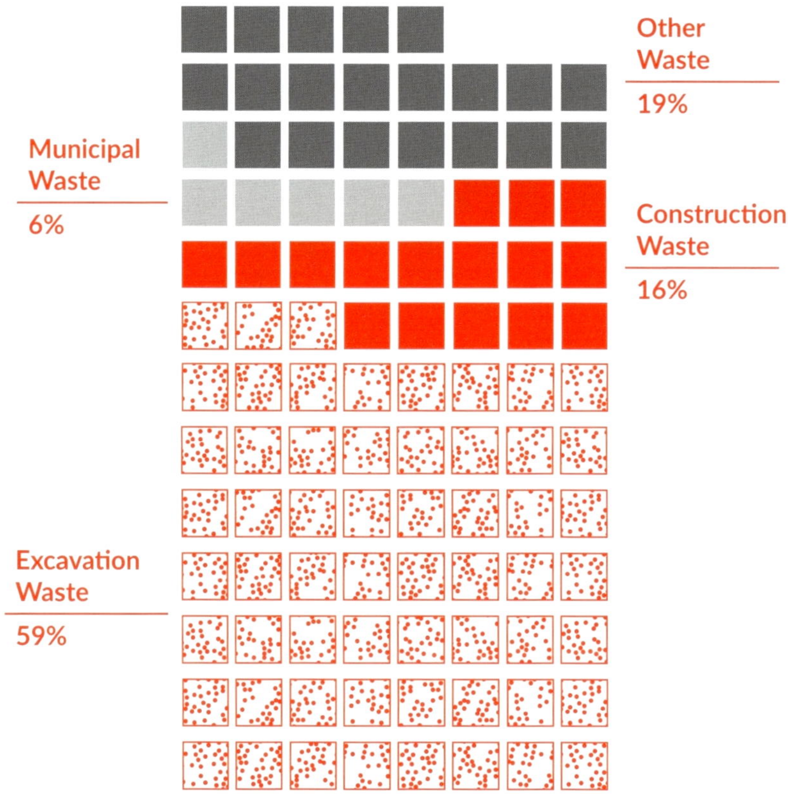

Waste Volume in Austria by Types of Origin

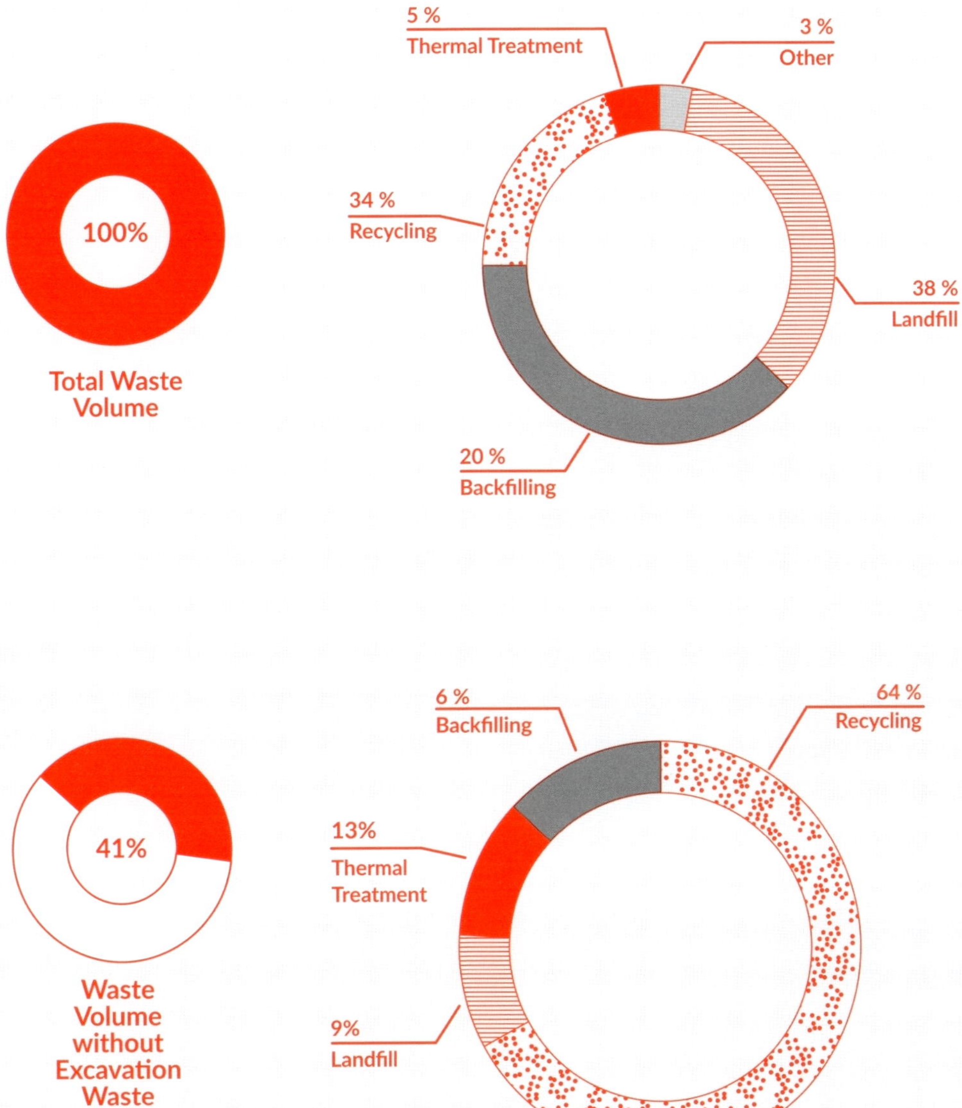

Waste Treatment in Austria

BMK (2023): Bundes-Abfallwirtschaftsplan Statusreport 2023

Austria processes more than 4.2 million tons of municipal waste per year, but with only a small percentage recycled, significant improvements in waste reduction and recycling are needed.

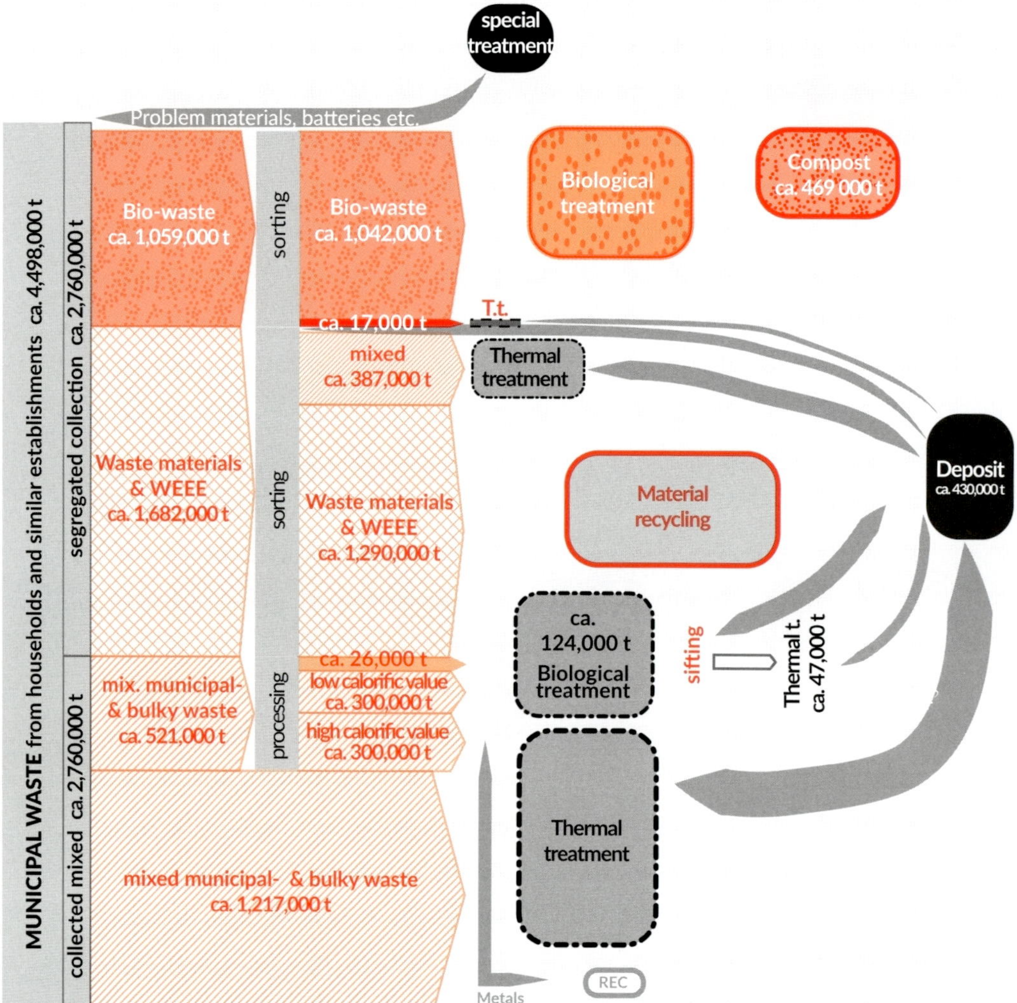

Treatment Procedure of Municipal Waste in Austria

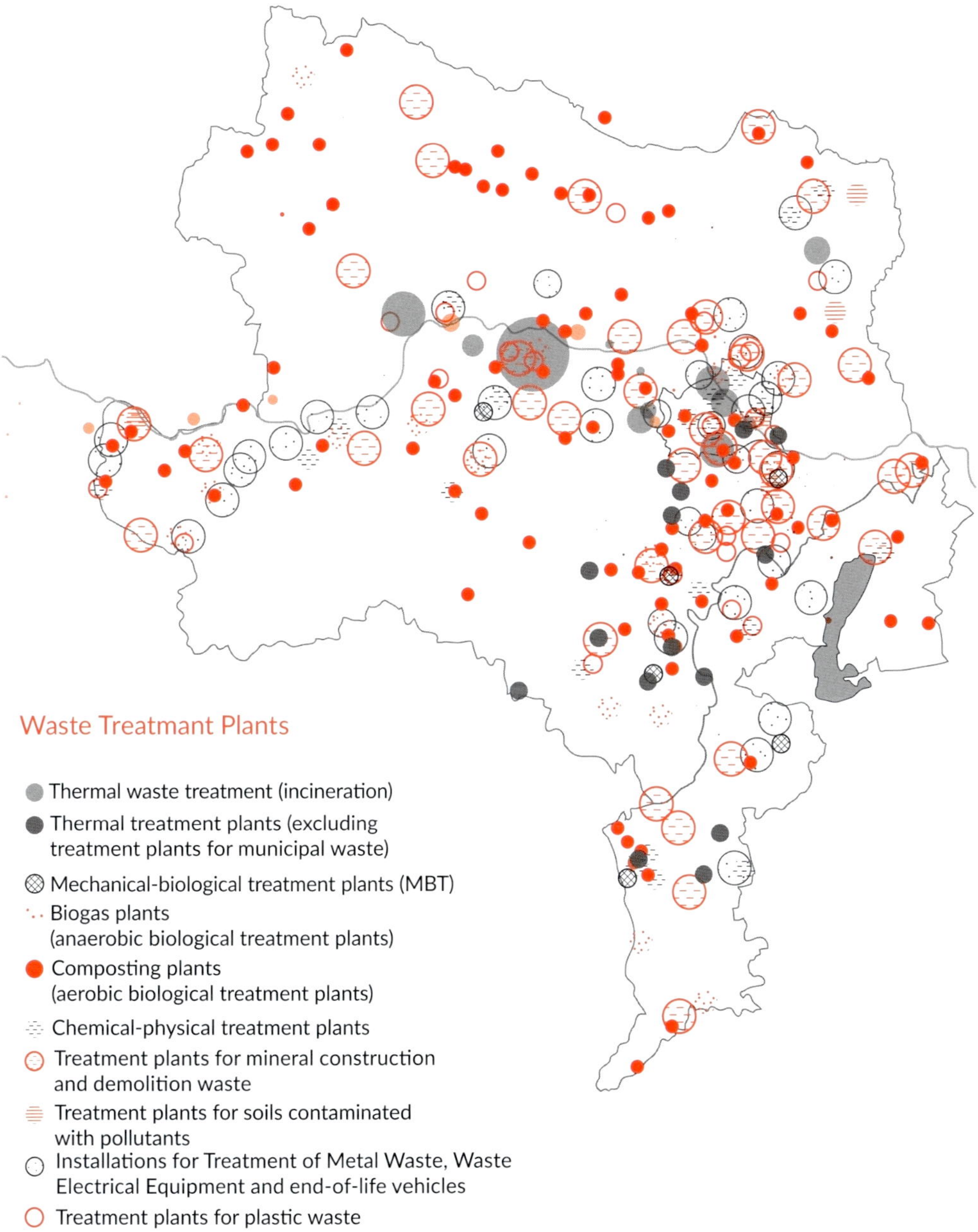
Waste Treatmant Plants
Thermal waste treatment (incineration)
Thermal treatment plants (excluding treatment plants for municipal waste)
Mechanical-biological treatment plants (MBT)
Biogas plants (anaerobic biological treatment plants)
Composting plants (aerobic biological treatment plants)
Chemical-physical treatment plants
Treatment plants for mineral construction and demolition waste
Treatment plants for soils contaminated with pollutants
Installations for Treatment of Metal Waste, Waste Electrical Equipment and end-of-life vehicles
Treatment plants for plastic waste

Construction waste, including waste from excavations accounts for three fourths of Austria's waste volume

The construction industry is the main source of waste in Austria. For several years, the amount of waste from the construction industry has been increasing.

BMK (2023): Bundes-Abfallwirtschaftsplan Statusreport 2023

Expansion of a Shopping Center in Parndorf, Source: basemap.at

Construction and demolition waste accounts for 16.1% of Austria's waste volume. If excavation waste is also included, the construction sector is responsible for 75.1% of the waste volume.

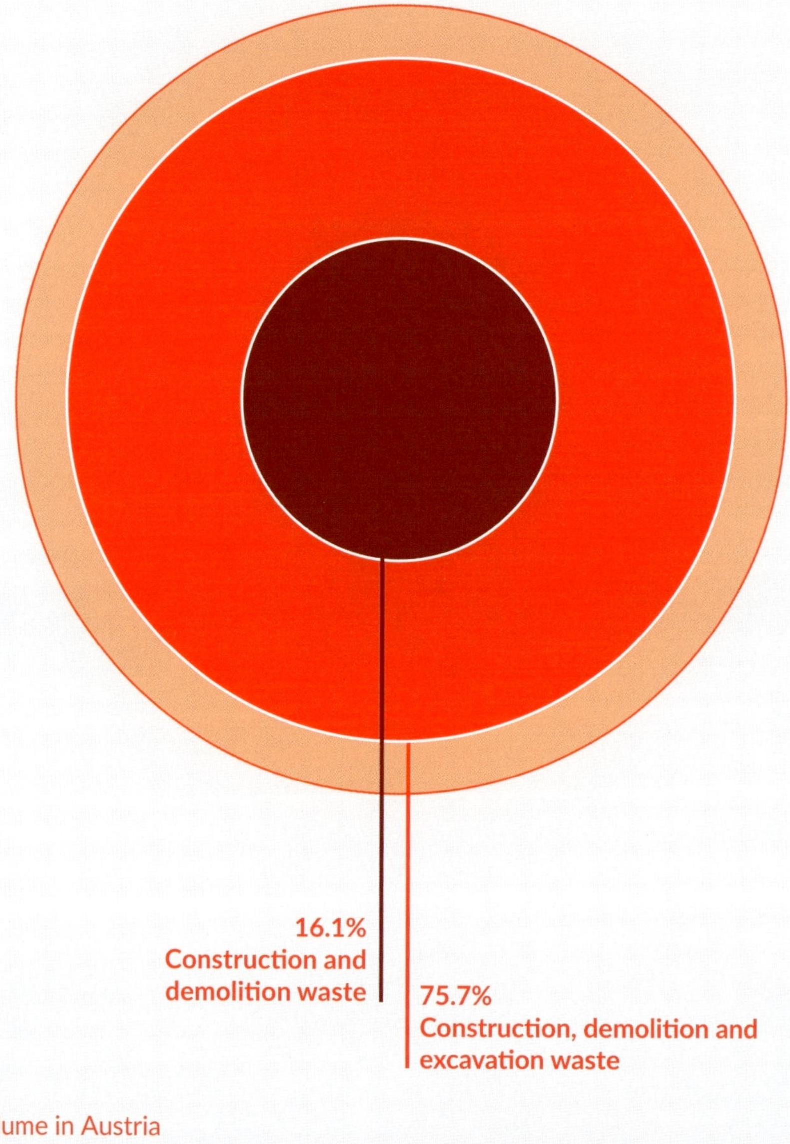

Waste Volume in Austria

BMK (2023): Bundes-Abfallwirtschaftsplan Statusreport 2023

The volume of waste in these sectors is growing rapidly: Since 2015, the volume of construction waste has increased by 25%, while excavation waste has increased by 40.6%.

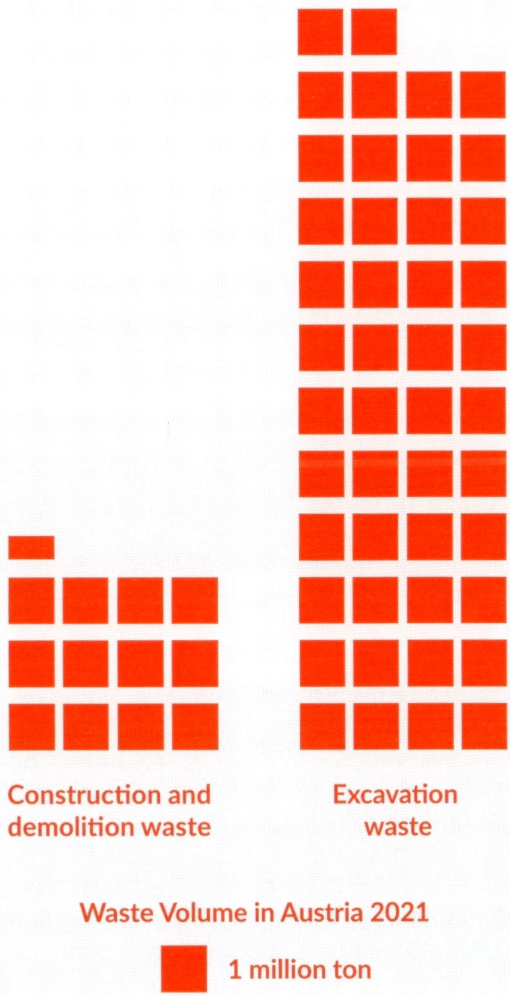

Development of Waste Volume

BMK (2023): Bundes-Abfallwirtschaftsplan Statusreport 2023

“The smaller the cycle, the better”

Interview with Dominik Wiedenhofer, Carolin Bellstedt & Felix Heisel

Dominik Wiedenhofer is a Senior Scientist at the Institute for Social Ecology at the University of Natural Resources and Life Sciences Vienna (BOKU) and is currently working on a research project on the possibilities and limits of transforming Vienna into a circular economy.

Carolin Bellstedt is a researcher and consultant on urban metabolism and Executive Director of Metabolism of Cities, a non-profit network that aims to systematically reduce the net environmental impact of cities and territories in a socially just and context-specific way.

Felix Heisel is an architect and academic working towards the systematic redesign of the built environment as a material depot of endless use and reconfiguration. He is Assistant Professor and Director of the Circular Construction Lab at Cornell University in New York State.

MetroLab: According to the European Union, we will need three Earths to meet our needs by 2050 if we don’t change the way we use resources: The EU identifies efficient waste management as the first step towards a carbon-neutral, environmentally sustainable and non-polluting economy. But what is waste? How is it defined, and is it the same for different sectors and actors?

Dominik Wiedenhofer: It is ultimately a legal issue. There is waste legislation in the EU. The basic idea is that waste is something that most actors want to get rid of because it might be toxic, for example. This definition is the first problem for circular thinking, because once something is classified as waste, all waste legislation applies in terms of health and safety regulations: How to handle it, how to treat it. You cannot just take something out of the waste stream and reuse it. This is where a material or product becomes waste by conscious choice, even though from a circular economy perspective other industries could still use these materials or by-products for their purposes. This is often referred to as “industrial symbiosis”.

Therefore, decisions need to be made, for example, not to classify materials as waste if they are still useful for other purposes, i.e. the line where something becomes waste should not be so easily crossed. For circular economy considerations, we need changes in waste legislation. Basically, once something is collected, it is waste and we are not allowed to reuse it or put it back into the cycle. A lot of organisational practices may also need to change to move towards a circular economy.

MetroLab: In our current economy, we extract materials to produce goods or enable services, and since processes are still largely linear, most of these materials end up as waste. A net zero approach would require a shift to a more circular economy. What do we really mean by circularity and a circular economy, as it is not a well-defined term?

Felix Heisel: The one definition I usually refer to is the one published by the Ellen MacArthur Foundation, which talks about a restorative and regenerative system by design that keeps components, products and materials at their highest utility and value at all times, and distinguishes between the technical and the biological cycle.

For me as an architect, the most important part of this definition is "by design": the kind of call to action that we, as curators of the built environment, can go to the beginning of the cycle and design something that takes waste out of the equation. And a system by design means understanding that we're not making something slightly better by changing the filter in the coal-fired power station, but by designing something that doesn't have emissions, that doesn't have waste as a kind of conceptual component.

D.W.: In our work, we find that the circular economy is an interesting concept because it connects silos that have not been connected before. The circular economy itself is not new, these ideas have been around for decades, but it is a nice new narrative that connects existing concepts and kind of gives new momentum to this idea that our resource use is connected to the way we live and the way we produce waste and treat nature.

It creates momentum and a lot of people can relate to it. Because a lot of people can relate to it and create their own interpretation, there are multiple definitions out there, which is good for the larger discussion, but also bad if you want to evaluate circularity strategies and should be talking about the same thing. So there is a tension between having a broad umbrella that brings everyone in, but then actually agreeing on something. Because that is usually the point where certain groups or certain stakeholders might not like the concept so much, when you actually start to confront those in power to change material flows or change design or change legislation, because all of that is going to be necessary. Circularity is a systems approach, not a quick fix.

MetroLab: What are the biggest barriers to reusing and recycling materials in general?

D.W.: Firstly, we could look at products and materials where recycling and circularity work as a good example, such as plastic and glass bottles in Europe. The main advantage of this is that it is a fairly standardised product, with legislation dictating what it has to look like. Basically, it is a standardised product and the producers get their own product back, which leads to high recycling rates.

When it comes to complex products like electronics, it becomes virtually impossible. If we had infinite amounts of renewable energy, we might be able to separate all the parts again, but that is not the case. Usually you only recover gold, for example, and the rest ends up as waste. It becomes extremely difficult to actually recycle these products in the end.

This brings us back to the question of design: Can we design these products so that they can be repaired, refurbished and recycled as a last resort? That would require clear legislation and standards. But I am always worried that the circular economy discussion boils down to recycling, because that is the last resort of all the strategies we have. First you have to reject and reduce what you need, then make it more efficient, reuse it, repair it, and only then recycle what is left. You cannot recycle everything, instead we have to start at the beginning and ask ourselves how many resources do we actually use and how many do we need? ▸

How do we manage what happens to those resources? Circularity in itself does not mean sustainability—a closed loop can require huge amounts of energy and greenhouse gas emissions to circulate.

It is important to understand that within the circular economy, the smaller the cycle, the better. I think that is a good way to measure it. If you look at recycling, it is currently a global system because we need economies of scale to make recycling viable. We collect the waste and ship it somewhere where the recycling plant can operate at an efficient level. This global system of moving materials around the world is how the linear economy works, recycling is an extension of that. But in many ways it is not circular, because if we started to recycle locally we would have a different system with different problems and challenges.

MetroLab: Felix Heisel, your focus is particularly on the architecture and construction sector, which generates massive amounts of waste through demolition and construction processes.
You have worked with urban mining and the development of structures from waste materials, and have also developed a computer programme to calculate circularity in early design stages. Where do you see the potential for such measures?

F.H.: We work through many different phases of a building, from conceptual design through to the use phase, upgrading and, ideally, deconstruction or adaptive reuse of that building to prolong its performance.

The tools and measures you just mentioned are usually introduced too late in the design process. When we implement circularity indicators, the understanding is that you usually need a lot of data and certainty in the design process, which leads to a very late implementation in the design process. The design is usually done in such a way that this feedback comes much too late. At that point in the process, changes are very expensive. So we are trying to move that much earlier into the design process where you can get quick feedback. The tool we are working on, Rhino Circular, brings visual feedback to the drawing canvas at the mass model stage.

Data can be very important at the end of a building's life to build a materials marketplace where you can suggest quantities of a particular material with detailed specifications. To be able to start designing with these materials even before deconstruction, to close the time gap between deconstruction and new design, which is key to really closing the loop. We need data and we need new tools to close the loop.

MetroLab: Carolin Bellstedt, you are working with different cities to generate data and knowledge to bring the issue of urban metabolism into a broader discourse. Could you tell us about the challenges in your process of data collection and analysis and its importance?

Carolin Bellstedt: The first challenge is that waste data is usually simply not available because it is not registered or collected at city level. Often cities only have waste data for households, not for industrial or commercial waste, such as supermarkets. Often data is available but not standardised or registered.

But collecting data is important because we need to know where a city is, what the status quo is, in order to start making changes. And then it is important to make the data available to other researchers. A lot of resources within a research process go into collecting data. Making data available is important for knowledge transfer, for cities to learn from each other.

MetroLab: It is not easy to look at a city in a kind of closed bubble. How do you limit the data that you can get, and is it even possible to look at a city within its administrative boundaries, or do you have to look at it together with its surroundings?

C.B.: For our analysis we look at the administrative borders, but of course they are not functional in this sense for the circular economy. We live in a globalised world, we cannot look at a city in isolation, there are many dependencies on other countries and self-sufficiency can hardly be achieved by just one city. You have to look at a much larger context and the systems that are connected to it, which are just so large today.

D.W.: In the case of Vienna, the city focuses a lot on the built environment because that is something that the city can intervene in. If you think about other waste streams like electronics, for example, the city of Vienna cannot do anything about that because that is legislation at the European level. We need to look at this as a multi-scalar issue and think about at what spatial scale, at what administrative scale you can improve circularity and improve the performance of the whole system. ▪

MetroLab Podcast
Episode WASTING in Climate Neutral City Regions

Listen to our podcast on all platforms!

International Perspective

Zero Carbon City Regions Forum

The MetroLab Zero Carbon City Region Forum took place in May 2024 in Vienna. The Forum aimed to foster dialogue and cooperation on the role of metropolitan regions in tackling the climate crisis and achieving climate neutrality. It focused on the Vienna metropolitan region as a case study, with insights and presentations from international experts from Italy, France, Germany and Spain.

The forum included an excursion and guided tour of the Biofabrique project as part of the Vienna Climate Biennale. The tour focused on the bioregional approach to transform unused local resources into materials for architecture and design, and to promote a shift towards more circularity in the building sector.

Another part of the forum was a lecture series with international experts and a forum discussion. MetroLab shared key findings from their research on the project Mapping the Zero Carbon City Region, offering a creative mapping tool for climate neutral metropolitan planning. This was followed by insightful presentations from international

Excursion to Climate Biennale Vienna © MetroLab

Excursion to the Biofabrique project, focusing on the bioregional approach to transforming unused local resources into materials for architecture and design, and promoting a shift towards more circularity in the building sector.

experts such as **Carolin Bellstedt** *(Metabolism of Cities)*, **Ombretta Caldarice** *(Politecnico di Torino)*, **Laia Guillén Soley** *(Àrea Metropolitana de Barcelona)*, **Marion Perret-Blois** *(French Movement for Frugality in Architecture and Landcare)* focusing on different strategies and insights for the transformation towards zero carbon metropolitan regions in Europe.

The event concluded with a panel discussion involving both international experts and stakeholders from the Viennese context, such as **Bernhard Steger** *(City of Vienna)*, **Andreas Hacker** *(City Region Management Vienna-Lower Austria)* **and Thomas Romm** *(Architect with a focus on circularity)*.

The panel explored goals, challenges and tools to accelerate the transformation towards a zero carbon city region, combining global perspectives with local realities. An interactive discussion allowed for a dynamic exchange of ideas, with feedback from experts on climate neutrality in metropolitan areas.

On the following pages you will find features on some of the exciting talks, as well as other interesting articles that delve into international expertise and different perspectives.

Panel Discussion at the Zero Carbon City Region Forum © MetroLab

A panel discussion combining global perspectives and local realities with international experts and stakeholders from the Viennese context to explore goals, challenges and tools to accelerate the transformation towards zero carbon city regions.

Climate Biennale Vienna: The Bioregional Design Approach

MetroLab

The bioregional approach to design, particularly in architecture and materials development, offers a way to transition from globalized, resource-intensive building practices to more sustainable, localized systems. This approach focuses on harnessing unused or under-utilized local resources and transforming them into materials for architecture and design. This shift not only promotes circularity - minimizing waste and reusing materials - but also promotes regional specificity, deeply connecting building practices to their environmental and cultural contexts. Two prominent projects that embody this vision are Atelier LUMA in Arles, France, and Biofabrique Vienna, a pilot project and collaboration with Atelier LUMA that took place during the Climate Biennale 2023 in Vienna (Climate Biennale Vienna 2024).

Atelier LUMA, an interdisciplinary research and design laboratory in Arles, France, is a pioneer in the development of bioregional practices. By focusing on the specific environmental and cultural contexts of the Arles bioregion, they have developed innovative materials from underutilized resources such as salt, algae and rice straw. Their work illustrates how local ecosystems can provide abundant materials that can replace traditional, resource-intensive construction processes (LUMA Arles, n.d.). Going beyond a conventional circular economy, Atelier LUMAs focus is on creating interconnected networks of stakeholders—scientists, designers and local communities—who ensure that sustainable solutions are deeply rooted in their respective regions (LINA, the European Architecture Platform 2024).

Similarly, the Biofabrique Vienna project extends these principles by applying them to the urban and regional context of the Vienna metropolitan area. During the Climate Biennale, Biofabrique Vienna demonstrated how leftover materials from local industries, such as excavated soil and industrial by-products, can be reused in new architectural materials (Vienna Design Week 2024). An interdisciplinary team of students, scientists, architects and designers experimented with building and designing with these local materials. The project was a collaboration between Atelier LUMA, the Vienna Business Agency and the Vienna University of Technology. The aim was not only to develop innovative materials, but also to promote a new model of local production in line with the bioregional approach (Klima Biennale Vienna 2024).

The bioregional approach also emphasizes the importance of going beyond the conventional circular economy. While circularity focuses on minimizing waste and closing resource loops, Atelier LUMA aims to build resilient, interconnected production networks that are deeply rooted in the specific conditions of a bioregion and that connect and create collaboration between different types of stakeholders. These networks will contribute to resilience in the face of the climate crisis and societal pressures by enabling new ways of doing things. This method makes use of a region's unique environmental assets to create sustainable solutions that respond to both local and global challenges (LINA, the European Architecture Platform 2024).

Both projects demonstrate the versatility and potential of bioregional design in different contexts. Biofabrique Vienna addresses the challenges of the urban-rural relationship between Vienna and its surroundings, demonstrating that bioregional solutions can be adapted to different scales and contexts. In their work, collaboration between creative industries, academia and local businesses is key to fostering innovation and ensuring that material production is both sustainable and regionally specific.

Bioregional design practices offer a promising path towards more sustainable, place-based and circular approaches to architecture and design. Projects such as Atelier LUMA and Biofabrique Vienna demonstrate how we can rethink the use of local resources to create architecture that is not only environmentally responsible, but also deeply connected to the local resources, culture and needs of its specific location. (Events & Workshops - Business Agency (LUMA Arles n.d.).

Experimenting with materials at Biofabrique Vienna as part of the Climate Biennale Vienna at Nordwestbahnhof © MetroLab

Bridging the Urban-Rural Divide: Sustainable Development Strategies for City Regions

Roland Krebs & Nadia Carboni

Roland Krebs is an urban planner and develops strategic action plans to help cities manage their growth. He studied Urban and Regional Planning at the Vienna University of Technology and holds an MBA in Strategic Management from the Universidad de Belgrano, Argentina. Krebs has international experience in urban planning and design and is co-founder of superwien urbanism.

Nadia Carboni, PhD in Comparative and European Politics, is Head of the Department of Economic Development and Smart Cities at the Union of Romagna Faentina. A former researcher at the Italian National Research Council (CNR), she has taught public administration and business organisation at the University of Bologna since 2003.

The development of rural areas within the European Union presents a unique set of challenges and opportunities. The European Commission's Rural Vision underscores the significance of rural territories, which constitute 83% of the EU's land area, encompassing agricultural land, forests, and natural spaces. However, despite their vast natural resources and strong sense of community, rural regions face persistent obstacles, including aging populations, a lack of services, and economic and educational disparities. Another factor is that population in rural regions is expected to fall by 7,9 million inhabltatants in contrast to the urban regions are projected to increase by 24,1 million inhabitants .

This situation calls for innovative strategies for sustainable urban development in rural areas like the promotion of sustainable mobility, digital coverage to enable economic growth, and social cohesion while connecting urban and rural areas in more meaningful ways.
In this context, the URBACT Action Planning Network econnecting seeks to explore how rural and urban regions can work together to ensure the holistic development of these territories. econnecting is a city network led by Unione della Romagna Faentina in Italy with seven regional agencies and small- to mid-sized towns in Europe that is implemeted between 2023 and 2025.

** The partners of econnecting are Unione della Romagna Faentina, Italy, Razvojno raziskovalni center Ormož, Slovenia, Nagykálló, Hungary, West Mani, Greece, Comunidade Intermunicipal Viseu Dão Lafões, Portugal, Tori Vallavalitsus, Estonia, Ennis Municipal District, Ireland, Berane, Montenegro*

THE 30-MINUTE TERRITORY: ECONNECTING AND URBAN-RURAL LINKAGES

The concept of the 30-minute territory represents a new paradigm for urban and rural development. In a 30-minute territory, essential social services, workplaces, and recreational spaces are conveniently reachable within a 15- to 30-minute radius of walking, cycling, or public transportation. This model promotes accessibility through a public transport network that links rural areas to hub cities while minimizing the environmental impact of car use.

The 30-minute territory prioritizes a humanized and sustainable approach to mobility, creating pedestrian-friendly zones, efficient public transportation options, and eco-friendly commuting alternatives. It also fosters urban and rural connectivity by incorporating Public-Private Partnership (PPP) models, where private businesses contribute to subsidized public transport and mobility-on-demand services.

In addition to improving mobility, the 30-minute territory serves as a social cohesion solution. By ensuring accessibility to essential services for both older residents and younger generations, this model supports intergenerational connections and promotes social inclusion. The implementation of carpooling and sharing models further reduces the carbon footprint of rural areas, contributing to the creation of environmentally conscious and interconnected communities.

CHALLENGE 1: SUSTAINABLE MOBILITY AND ACCESSIBILITY IN THE 30-MINUTE TERRITORY

A critical element in rural development is enhancing mobility and accessibility. Rural areas often suffer from a lack of reliable public transportation and over-reliance on private cars. This creates barriers to employment, education, and essential services, particularly for disadvantaged groups such as the elderly, women or low-income families who face limited job opportunities due to caregiving responsibilities and a lack of childcare facilities. To overcome these obstacles, the project econnecting proposes a shift toward sustainable mobility models that prioritize connectivity through public transport between rural and urban regions. econnnecting partner city-region agency Viseu Dão Lafões already implemented an on demand public transportation service called "IR e VIR" (Portuguese for come and go) due to the high costs of a bus serives in a scattered, low density landscape in the Portuguese region of Viseu (Image 1 and 2). Since the beginning of the service, it has been used by around 30 thousand passengers. The initiative has been increasing its scope and currently involves almost 100 taxis in the region. The service allows inhabitants of the Viseu Dão Lafões region to travel by taxi, in a comfortable and quick way for the price of a simple bus ticket, in locations that are not efficiently served by the public buses network. The service benefits, in particular, the population of remote areas and is also very relevant in the summer, when there is a reduction in the usual public transport service.

"IR e VIR" service prodived by econnecting partner regional agency of Viseu Comunidade (CIM) Intermunicipal Viseu Dão Lafões, Portugal. © CIM Viseu Dão Lafões

"IR e VIR" on demand transportation service has the pick-up at designated areas © MetroLab

Our hypothesis at the econnecting network is to develop integrated transportation networks that connect rural areas with nearby urban centers. This can be achieved through the creation of hub cities, which act as transit points and centers of economic and social activity for the surrounding rural areas. By promoting car-sharing, bike rentals, and enhanced public transportation options such as electric buses and transit on demand products, rural residents can access essential services and employment opportunities without relying on private vehicles. In doing so, these strategies also contribute towards the zero-carbon region and minimize the environmental impact of car use and promoting more sustainable forms of mobility.

Moreover, fostering active modes of transportation, such as walking and cycling, can further improve accessibility in rural areas. The development of pedestrian-friendly zones and bike infrastructure in villages and towns can help residents meet their daily needs within close proximity, reducing the need for long commutes and enhancing the overall quality of life. econnecting partner city Ennis in Ireland is currently creating shared streets in the historic and commercial centre of the town with new trees and improving the walkability of the town. They prioritize pedestrians over car-use with a clear strategy for mobility and public space regeneration in the town (Image 3). The town center is currently experiencing vacancy and a decline in commercial activity. However, the Ennis 2040 Economic & Spatial Strategy presents a comprehensive investment plan aimed at revitalizing public spaces and fostering the vision of Ennis as a welcoming city.

CHALLENGE 2: CREATION OF HUB CITIES IN A WIDER REGIONAL NETWORK

Hub cities, typically mid- to small-sized urban centers, play a crucial role in connecting rural and urban areas. These cities provide a unique and complex landscape in terms of mobility and transport management, serving as focal points for economic activity, services, and transportation. Given that 83% of Europe's territory is rural and only 21 % of the population of the EU lives in rural areas, however 72 % of those rural towns and villages are located close to bigger cities. Those towns could serve as urban hubs, because they are essential for fostering connectivity and sustainable development across regions.

econnecting advocates for a collaborative approach to regional planning, where hub cities work together with rural communities to create integrated mobility solutions that meet the needs of both areas. This collaboration can enhance the economic competitiveness of the region while addressing environmental and social challenges, such as reducing car dependency and promoting green infrastructure.

By positioning hub cities as centers of innovation and sustainable mobility, econnecting aims to create vibrant, accessible, and environmentally conscious communities in a zero carbon region. This approach not only benefits local residents but also contributes to broader regional development objectives, fostering a more balanced and sustainable approach to urban-rural linkages.

Public spaces tranformation of the Irish town of Ennis, before the implementation of the project © MetroLab

CHALLENGE 3: GREEN COMMUNITIES AND REDUCED CAR DEPENDENCY

Reducing car dependency is a key strategy for creating more sustainable, resilient rural communities. econnecting promotes the concept of green communities, where residents can meet their daily needs within walking or cycling distance or at least with a bus or on-demand transportation, thereby reducing the reliance on cars and minimizing the environmental impact of transportation. One of the most effective ways to achieve this is through the reimagining of public spaces and the development of community hubs. These hubs can serve as centers for social, economic, and environmental activities, providing residents with access to essential services, green spaces, and sustainable mobility options. By activating public spaces, such as community gardens and tree-lined streets, green communities can enhance the sense of place and improve the local environment. econnecting partner Ormoz in Slovenia has implemented a vibrant town center with an outstanding cultural centre and music school that was completed in 2011 (image 4). Now, they the city is developing ideas for a new town square that will prioritize pedestrians over cars in the public space design and that will help to revitalize the all empty ground floor zones.

A notable example of econnecting is the Bike-to-Work initiative launched by the City of Faenza. Historically, residents had not embraced cycling as a commuting option, but this project has dramatically increased the number of bike users traveling from home to work. Participants are reimbursed for every kilometer traveled by bicycle, with their progress tracked through a dedicated app. The app also features competitive rankings and a reward system for top performers, which have been crucial to the initiative's success. Co-financed by the Municipality of Faenza and the Emilia-Romagna Region, the project has inspired three spin-offs: one supported by a local company for its employees, another

Ormoz cultural center designed by arrea d.o.o. arhitektura
© MetroLab

targeting middle and high school students called "Bike to School", and a third recently adopted and fully funded by Castel Bolognese, a municipality within the Union of Romagna Faentina, just like Faenza.

Another topic is the integration of green economy principles into rural development can help foster a holistic approach to community buildings. This includes promoting sustainable conservation of vacant buildings and enable the conversion into public buidlings like libraries with co-working spaces. By creating green communities that prioritize environmental sustainability and social cohesion, econnecting seeks to build resilient and harmonious communities that safeguard the natural environment while enhancing the well-being of residents.

CHALLENGE 4: DIALOGUE-ORIENTED PROCESSES TO RESOLVE CHALLENGES

A key component of econnecting's approach to urban-rural linkages is fostering dialogue-oriented processes that involve all stakeholders in decision-making. This participatory approach ensures that the needs and aspirations of local communities are considered in the development of proximity-based territories and sustainable mobility solutions.

Good governance is essential for the successful implementation of these strategies. econnecting emphasizes the importance of promoting transparent decision-making processes, fostering citizen engagement, and integrating sustainable development goals into local policies. By encouraging collaboration between municipalities, regional authorities, and private sector partners, the network aims to create a framework for long-term social, economic, and environmental sustainability. econnecting partner Tori from Estonia initiated a small-scale action in October 2024 to engage residents of Jõesuu in a dialogue about the town's development. This effort focused on identifying the changes the community desired and exploring ways for residents to participate in co-creating ideas for their village.
The inclusion of cultural considerations in urban governance models is crucial for driving holistic transformations. By recognizing culture as a key enabler of urban development, the econnecting seeks to create vibrant, inclusive, and accessible communities that reflect the unique identities of their residents.

MAKING THE 30-MINUTE TERRITORY IN THE ZERO-CARBON-REGION WORK

The 30-minute territory concept offers a promising vision for bridging the urban-rural divide and fostering sustainable development across the European Union. By focusing on accessibility, sustainable mobility, green communities, and dialogue-oriented processes, econnecting aims to create vibrant, resilient, and interconnected regions that meet the needs of both urban and rural residents.

Through initiatives like econnecting, which promotes the development of green communities and sustainable mobility networks,

Tori implemented small-scale-actions to activate the community to participate in the development of their village
© Helle-Triin Hansumäe

the 30-minute territory has the potential to transform rural areas into thriving, inclusive, and accessible spaces. By embracing these strategies and fostering collaboration between municipalities, regional authorities, and private sector partners, we can ensure that rural regions remain vital contributors to the social, economic, and environmental well-being of the European Union.

In the end, the success of the 30-minute territory depends on the active involvement of all stakeholders in creating flexible, adaptive, and sustainable urban-rural linkages. By promoting good governance, fostering cultural identity, and prioritizing accessibility and sustainability, econnecting tries top help realize the full potential of urban-rural linkages, creating a more connected and resilient future and zero-carbon regions.

Circular Strategies for a Zero Carbon City

Thomas Romm & Sebastian Hafner

Thomas Romm works as a civil engineer and freelance architect with a focus on the environmental effectiveness of planning and construction. He is an expert in circular economy and one of the founders of BauKarussell, a cooperative network of socio-economic companies for the dismantling of building components for reuse, as an employment and qualification project with an environmental policy background.

Sebastian Hafner is part of forschen planen bauen—Thomas Romm ZT and works on circular mass strategies in urban planning and landscape design. In the context of the research project Trustmaking he was involved in the co-creative development of green infrastructures.

To establish a climate-neutral circular economy, the carbon footprint of the metropolitan region must be reassessed. The sectoral allocation of emitters follows the internationally established "source-oriented" approach. Allocating the pollutant inventory of emission shares to cross-sector processes such as construction can help to realise the circular economy potential of the metropolitan region's metabolism. The construction industry as a permanent part of production in the city is significant in all emission sectors. At € 9 billion, around one third of the Austrian construction volume is realised in the Vienna metropolitan region (VIBÖ n.d.).

CONSTRUCTION AND THE URBAN METABOLISM OF THE METROPOLITAN REGION

Precisely because the construction industry is strongly reflected in the metabolism of the urban environment, it is an important lever for a Zero Carbon city and it is worth looking at the sectors in detail: Around two thirds of heavy goods traffic in Vienna is construction site-related. 75% of all waste is generated by the construction industry in Austria. Excavated soil alone accounts for 60 % of the waste stream. Of the 33 million tons of excavated soil recorded each year for waste management purposes, 80% goes to landfill (BMK 2023). Dealing with waste streams from construction has become a central problem for metropolitan regions. Landfill space in the east of Austria is becoming increasingly scarce and waste from Vienna is largely transported to the surrounding areas of the capital. At the same time, the majority of resources for the construction industry are extracted in the urban hinterland: The extraction sites for sand and gravel are in competition with other land uses and are moving further and further away as transport distances increase. However,

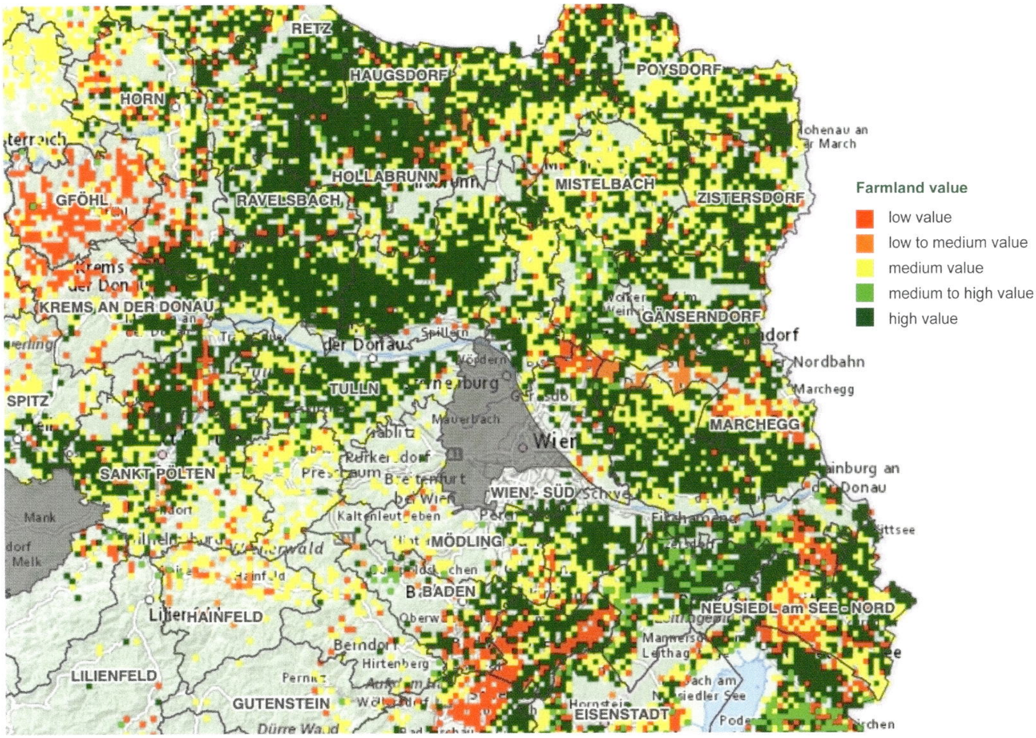

Soil quality in the Vienna Metropolitan Area (bodenkarte.at)

bricks and cement are also still predominantly produced in the metropolitan region and account for a considerable proportion of emissions.

Emissions from industry also include construction machinery, which emits around 0.5 million tons of CO_2e/a. In addition, there are 3 million tons of CO_2e/a from construction-related heavy goods traffic in Austria (Chamber of Labour 2014). When analysing the life cycle of a building, it is assumed that transport accounts for 10% of greenhouse gas emissions during construction. Roughly extrapolated to the construction volume in Austria, this would mean a share of 15 million tons of CO_2e in building construction (55% of the construction volume) and 10 million tons of CO_2 in underground construction (45%) for the construction sector. This would be a third of Austria's total CO_2 emissions and includes raw material extraction, building material production, construction site emissions and supply chains for supply and disposal. Not included are the reductions in CO_2 sequestration as a result of soil loss.*

**A plausibility check of the emissions from cement production (3 million tons of CO_2e/a) and from structural steel (another 3 million of the 12 million tons of CO_2e/a for steel production), as well as from lime, gypsum, magnesite and brick production, makes 12.5 million tons of CO_2e/a of emissions credible for the shell. The shell construction accounts for 50% of the GWP of the construction. The construction industry therefore accounts for 25 million tons of CO_2e/a across all sectors.*

Soil loss is to be taken literally: 50% of soils classified as A1—i.e. suitable for recultivation in agriculture—are landfilled. Unfortunately, this applies to all uncontaminated excavated soil: of 40 million tons of potential secondary raw materials, 22 million tons are landfilled every year.

MATERIAL FLOW MANAGEMENT IN URBAN DEVELOPMENT

This calls for circular economy strategies, especially because urban planning has so far paid little attention to the conditions of its materialisation. Criteria for urban growth have always been decoupled from soil quality. The cause cannot be changed, but the effect can: in the metropolitan region, a circular soil strategy can contribute to a nutrient turnaround. It is precisely in the northern and southern areas surrounding Vienna ("Agricultural Core" and "Bio Valley") that degraded soils are in agricultural use. With the addition of biochar from emission-free electricity and heat generation, these soils can be improved and scaled up in terms of their function as a CO_2 sink and longterm nutrient store. At the same time, we find the highest quality soils in Austria in the urban development areas. A systematic strategy preserves humus-rich topsoil by ensuring that it is properly recultivated. Recovery and transfer of soil to third parties for the improvement of low-value agricultural land are at the forefront of this. Cooperative and local utilisation paths in the sense of a leveled mass balance for soil in the metropolitan region make a significant contribution to ensuring that its ecosystem functions are not only maintained, but also improved with regard to aspects such as rainwater management, food production or CO_2 sequestration.

In addition to these climate-relevant strategies for 3 million tons of A1 classified topsoil per year, the circularity of the aforementioned 20 million tons of potential secondary raw materials for construction recycling is another important contribution to the Zero Carbon City. These are, for example, cohesive soils from deeper layers of soil that are suitable for calcination and should be structurally integrated into brick and cement production. Vienna's underground railway construction, for example, is a suitable starting point for a regionalisation of the construction (materials) industry due to its mass movement in earthworks.

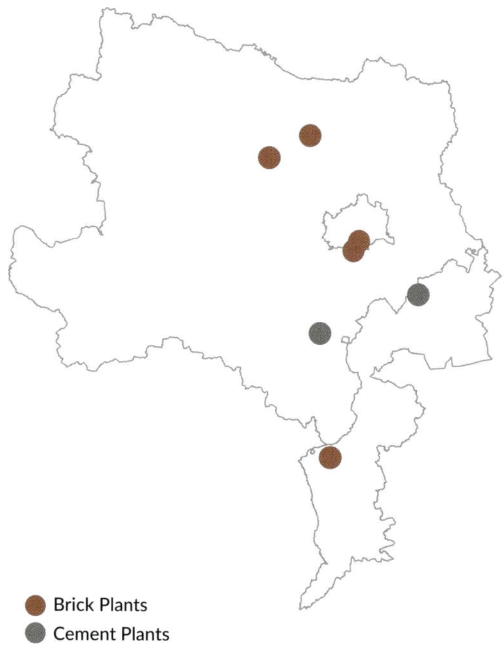

Brick and cement plants © Thomas Romm & Sebastian Hafner

Non-cohesive soils can usually even be processed on site as concrete aggregate. The highest possible quality recycling of secondary resources on site—i.e. where they are produced—is ideal in terms of climate protection and cost factors. The development area in Seestadt Aspern in Vienna is a best practice example. One million tons of gravel produced during the excavation of construction pits and the lake were crushed and used as aggregate for the production of in-situ concrete in addition to the construction of road embankments. The circular use of local resources enabled an environmentally friendly construction process that saved over 100,000 heavy goods vehicle journeys and the associated emissions.

The mapping of a zero-carbon city must capture the components of the urban metabolism. Soil is just as much a part of this as traffic flows, nutrient and food cycles. In addition to avoiding sealing, closing local soil cycles in the case of excavation is an imperative. Excavated soil is an example of what is fundamentally true for material flows in construction: there is a continuous flow of materials and energy between the city and the surrounding area. In Austria in particular, construction is a relatively localized affair due to a good supply of raw materials. Using secondary raw materials for this exchange in the future is the major paradigm shift facing the construction industry.

VISION CIRCULAR CARBON ECONOMY

The high proportion of combustion in our material flows is an obstacle to circularity. Burning material flows generally prevents their re-circulation. Moreover, the circular economy can only make a contribution to climate protection if combustion is also ruled out at the end of technical or biotic life cycles. Circular change therefore cannot avoid comprehensive decarbonisation. A Zero Carbon City also means creating the conditions for a circular carbon economy that aims to close carbon cycles by closing resource cycles. Pyrolysis of biogenic waste streams for the production of technical carbon is a contribution to this. Its application in conjunction with the circular management of material flows in the metropolitan region shows that the built environment, like soil, can be understood as carbon sinks and thus become climate-positive. In contrast, fields of activity such as transport or consumption are at best climate-neutral in their environmental impact through decarbonisation. Metropolitan regions must become aware of their materiality and its metabolism. By conceptually combining the circular economy with aspects such as transport and emissions reduction as well as CO_2 sequestration, it contributes to climate improvement and the vision of the urban environment as a CO_2 sink.

The Role of Urban Planning in Decarbonizing the Metropolis

Laia Guillén i Soley

Laia Guillén i Soley is an architect from the Universitat Politècnica de Catalunya (UPC). She is part of the Urban Planning Department (APUEN) at the Metropolitan Area Administration (AMB) and works on the Urban Master Plan (PDUM) as part of the Green Infrastructure and Urban Metabolism Office.

In a world that continues to grow in population, emissions as well as other impacts are steadily increasing. At the same time, the biocapacity of the land to absorb these impacts is continuously decreasing. This creates an imbalance and is responsible for climate change and other impacts such as the loss of biodiversity, the depletion of finite resources or water scarcity. Reducing carbon emissions and increasing the capacity of the territory to absorb them contributes to rebalancing this equation and it is key to mitigating climate change. However, some of the impacts are unavoidable, and adapting to the new conditions is a pressing challenge today. This critical task has to be addressed at different levels and across disciplines, such as urban planning.

Metropolitan areas are hubs of concentrated activity, where large amounts of energy and materials are consumed, resulting in high levels of carbon emissions. However, this very concentration also increases the effectiveness of mitigation efforts and the potential for significant emissions reductions. The metropolitan area of Barcelona exemplifies this phenomenon, and its pioneering approach to addressing these challenges through urban planning is the focus of this article.

The metropolitan area of Barcelona is formed by 36 municipalities, including Barcelona and its surroundings. It covers an area of 636km^2 and has a population of 3.347.881 inhabitants and a GDP of 120.799M€. It is a very lively city, with a great diversity of highly consolidated urban fabrics and others that are more dispersed. It is a metropolitan area with 48% of the urbanized land and 52% of the land occupied by open spaces.

The Àrea Metropolitana de Barcelona, AMB, is the public administration of the metropolitan area of Barcelona. It is responsible for the urban planning of its territory and is in charge with drafting the metropolitan area Urban Master Plan (PDUM). This Master Plan, which is currently being drafted, is the instrument that aims to regulate and guide the development of the metropolis for the next decades, with a horizon of 2050.

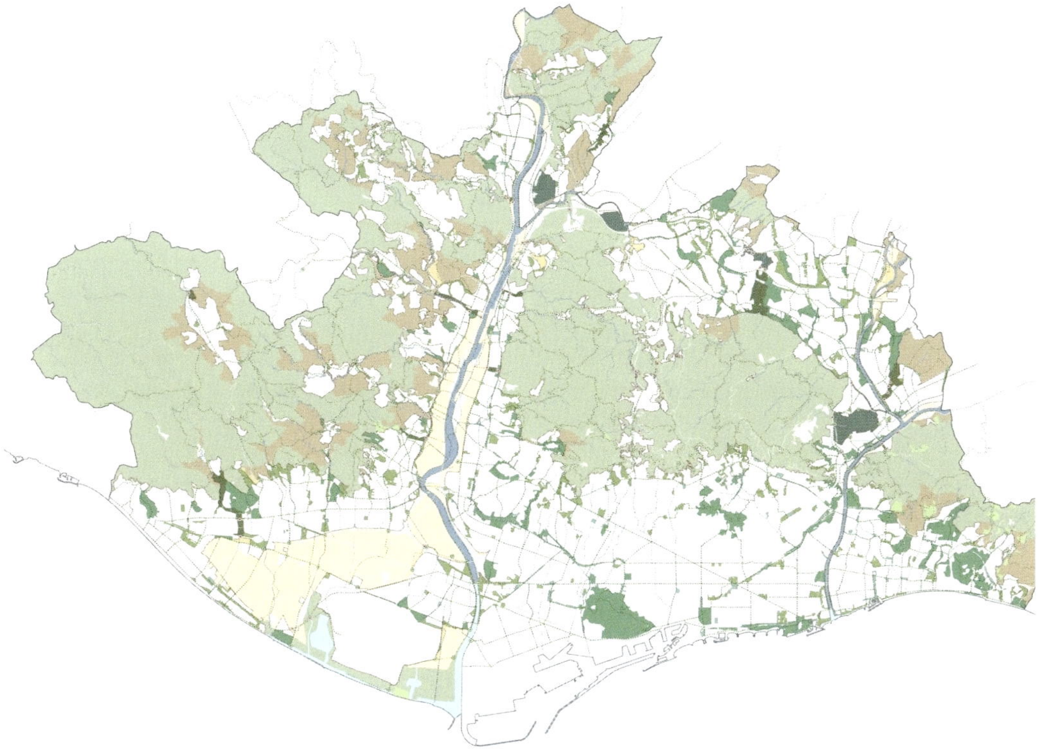

The enhancement of the green infrastructure © AMB

Open spaces

Core Area

Agroforestry mosaic

Agricultural plan

Open space connection

Border parc

Private green of transitional traditional interest

Door to open spaces

Critical point for ecological connectivity

Blue infrastructure

Coastal system

River connection

Urban blue axis

Structuring water channel

Green infrastructure

Connecting park

Structuring park

Equipped structuring park

Square and structuring garden

Structuring green axis

Structuring path

The objective of this Master Plan is to achieve an urban development that integrates the current diversity into a common project, promoting environmental sustainability, economic efficiency and social cohesion. This development must respond to the needs of the population based on the capacity of the territory.

To achieve this urban development, the PDUM defines a model of a mixed, dense and compact city. To achieve this, PDUM defines structural and metropolitan scale aspects of the territory in relation to three main actions: the imrovement of the green infrastructure, the development of a new urban model and the planning of environmental infrastructures.

Each action is a key piece to address some of the issues mentioned above: reducing carbon emissions, increasing the territory's capacity to absorb them and adapting to climate change and in this article we will underline the aspects that contribute to the decarbonize the metropolis.

1–THE ENHANCEMENT OF THE GREEN INFRASTRUCTURE

The PDUM identifies and defines three key components of green infrastructure and proposes strategies for each of them. First, the open spaces, which are composed mainly of agrarian areas, forest areas, agro-forestry mosaic, and biodiversity connectivity areas. In this case, the PDUM protects the biophysical matrix, promotes agriculture activities and improves their ecological connectivity. Second, the green structure, which is composed of all the natural spaces that are found within the urbanized areas, such as parks and green streets. In this case, the PDUM calculates the natural spaces that the city and its inhabitants need and identifies suitable areas to develop new ones when needed. Moreover, it connects the green areas through the green axis, which makes it easier for people to access them. Thirdly, the blue structure, which is constituted by rivers, and other structural waterways, by coastal systems and by zones of interest to protect, manage and improve the entire water cycle.

The capacity of the green infrastructure to absorb all the carbon emissions generated by the metropolitan area of Barcelona is logically, limited. However, this infrastructure plays a very significant role when we consider other environmental aspects such as ecosystem services and the adaptation to climate change.

2–THE DEVELOPMENT OF A NEW URBAN MODEL

As for the urban settlements, the plan addresses two different realities: the development of new centralities and the improvement of the existing areas.

Regarding the first, the PDUM proposes to concentrate new developments in 15 new centralities. These centralities are distributed throughout the territory and will accommodate part of the growth rate. At the same time, the PDUM identifies other existing urban areas that are suitable for the intensification of land use and that can accommodate additional population. The energy efficiency of new construction in these areas will result in a 1% reduction in GHG emissions. (46,632 tons of CO_2e).

For the existing areas, PDUM proposes nine different urban strategies to enhance the built environment. These strategies aim to improve the areas physically and functionally, increase social cohesion, and promot high urban environmental quality. The strategy with the greatest impact on decarbonization is the rehabilitation and renovation strategy, which focuses on improving both the quality and the energy efficiency of buildings. The energy renovation of the buildings is expected to reduce greenhouse gas emissions by 2% (154,826 tons of CO_2e).

The new urban model, proposed through urban strategies, intensification areas and

The development of a new urban model © AMB

Structuring roads

Metropolitan avenue
Structuring street
Structuring connector
Structuring path

Green structure in settlements

Structuring green axis
Structuring park
Equipped structuring park
Parc connection

Metropolitan avenue and structuring green axis

Structuring equipment

Structuring equipment

Actions of urban transformation within the metropolitan area

Area of metropolitan centrality

Existing centralities

Metropolitan centrality
Local centrality

new centralities, creates a city that is more mixed, dense and compact. This transformation promotes active mobility and increases the efficiency and competitiveness of public transport, leading to the development of a healthier and more sustainable new mobility model.

To accompany this new mobility model, the PDUM proposes an urban and social structure that connects the territory across different municipalities, emphasizing public transport and active mobility. This network is composed of different civic roads: Metropolitan Avenues, Structural Streets, Connecting Roads, and Green Streets.

In this new mobility model, segregated mobility also plays a important role. With regard to the highway system, the PDUM promotes the incorporation of pedestrian infrastructure and active mobility in segregated mobility roads, to transform these roads into metropolitan avenues. Regarding the rail network, the PDUM proposes new lines and stations to ensure that new developments are be well served by public transportation. This new mobility model enables the reduction of 50% of private vehicle trips. This reduction is expected to reduce the associated emissions by 20%. (1,569,916 tons of CO_2e)

3–THE PLANNING OF ENVIRONMENTAL INFRASTRUCTURES

Due to the population growth rate and the effects of climate change, it is estimated that there will be an increase in metabolic demands and a more limited availability of resources.

To meet these demands and minimize the associated environmental impacts, the PDUM intervenes in three distinged resource flows: water, energy and waste. The proposal maintains the existing infrastructure and compares with the future needs. In the cases where this infrastructure is insufficient, it identifies and protects areas where new facilities can be installed.

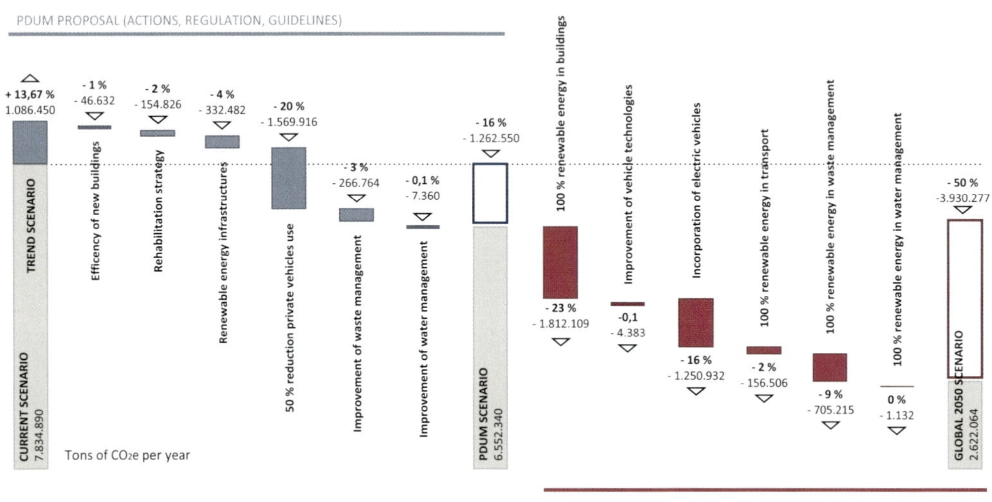

Emission reduction in the 2050 scenario: the Barcelona metropolitan area © AMB

For example, the energy transition will lead to an increased electrification of energy demand, requiring the installation of more renewable energy generation facilities and electrical substations. The PDUM identifies and protects suitable locations for their installation. As another example, one of the main impacts of climate change in the region is the increased periods of water scarcity. To address this, the PDUM is proposing designated areas for the installation of new water regeneration stations.

The implementation of these new infrastructures will have a positive impact on reducing emissions. Specifically, the installation of renewable energy systems in the metropolis is expected to decrease emissions by 4% (332,482 tons of CO_2e). Additionally, improvements in waste and water management are expected to reduce emissions by 3% (266,764 tons of CO_2e) and 0.1% (7,360 tons of CO_2e), respectively.

CONCLUSIONS

As we have seen in the previous sections, the PDUM, as an urban planning tool, has the capacity and power to protect the biophysical matrix of the territory, that provides resources and ecosystem services to the population. It can also organize anthropic systems, such as urban settlements that consume resources, to make them more efficient. To connect these two systems, the PDUM works to develop an efficient network and integrated it into the territory.

Thanks to this ability of urban planning to make the urban metabolism more efficient, the PDUM achieves a total reduction of 16% in CO_2e emissions compared to the current situation and, even more importantly, a reduction of 29.67% in CO_2e compared to the trend scenario.

On the other hand, technological trends and sectoral goals, such as the achievement of 100% renewable energy in buildings, transport, and waste and water management, as well as the enhancement and integration of the electric vehicles, also play a relevant role in the decarbonization of the territory. In addition, technological progress in gas substitution introduces a number of uncertainties that make the transition to zero emissions less clear in certain sectors, such as industry.

Although it is not the only tool, urban planning is essential to create more efficient and resilient territories and to achieve the goal of carbon neutrality by 2050.

All information regarding the PDUM can be found on the website www.urbanisme.amb.cat

The French Movement for Frugality in Architecture and Land-Caring

Marion Perret-Blois

Marion Perret-Blois is an urban planner and environmental scientist focused on creating more coherent ways to inhabit our territories. She is part of the movement for frugality, works as a consultant, teaches at architecture schools on integrating biodiversity in urban projects, researches the ecological and housing crises.

FRUGA… WHAT ? THE FRENCH MOVEMENT FOR FRUGALITY IN ARCHITECTURE AND LAND-CARING

The "Mouvement pour une Frugalité heureuse & créative dans l'architecture et le ménagement des territoires" (www.frugalite.org) is a movement of professionals and citizens that promotes "the metamorphosis of the act of building" through "frugal architecture" and "land care" in planning practices. It operates through a decentralized network of local or thematic groups and aims to develop best practise projects, while organizing webinars, conferences, site visits, trainings, petitions, exhibitions, festivals, international prizes and publications such as the collection "Frugal Architecture in…" with a selection of 25 references of frugal architecture and renovations in each region, as well as collective writings.

The Movement was born out of a short manifesto published in January 2018 by two architects and an engineer—a manifesto that publicly acknowledges the "strong role of builders" in the current ecological and social disasters and advocates a new way for architecture and spatial planning: The way of frugality. This group of founders has actually been involved in ecological architecture and engineering for a very long time, having founded other organizations such as the Institute for Eco-Responsible Buildings (ICEB), while also designing many projects and writing numerous books. It looks like this time it was the right time and the right way to publish their call in this manifesto, not as a closed association to join, but as an open invitation to come together and act. In each region, some signatories began to meet and create local groups for frugal architecture and planning; organizing conferences and visits, followed by the organization of national meetings. The Movement for Frugality was born and has become a very active, dynamic and decentralized movement with more than 16,000 signatories, consisting of two-thirds of professionals such as architects, urban planners, engineers, landscape designers, environmental scientists, as well as developers and another one third of citizens concerned by the way their territories are developed. They are organized in about 40 groups: Either local groups in France and

Illustration by Laura Folmer for Topophile, 2022: topophile.net/savoir/la-frugalite-nest-pas-la-sobriete/

abroad (e.g. Belgium, Vietnam), or thematic groups such as the "Frugal Renovations" group or the "Frugal Territories" group, which deals with issues of frugality on a metropolitan scale. The movement is also proud to be part of a wide network of sectoral associations (e.g. for biobased materials, etc.) and to be part of a new "international coalition" with 10 similar associations around the world, such as the British "ACAN Architects for Climate" or the German "Architects for Future", through a joint statement for the last climate change conference COP28.

FRUGAL ARCHITECTURE AND LAND-CARING PLANNING

But what are the concrete ideas of our movement and what are we promising? First, we take a quick look at the word "frugality", which is a bit different from the more commonly used word "sobriety". If "sobriety" is often reduced to accounting, especially carbon accounting, and reduction or even deprivation, the word "frugality" has a broader and probably more hopeful approach; it comes from the Latin word for "fruit", and we like to define it, after the Roman philosopher Apuleius, as "the fair harvest of the fruits of the earth". It is about the wisdom of the harvest, the pursuit of sufficiency rather than reduction, and the emphasis on local resources, long-term environmental stewardship, and social justice. The harvest can be abundant, but it is tied to a territory, it has to be careful about the next harvest, and it has to be fair to the people. Our first collective book—a hundred contributors—came out with 4 commitments, 4 key switches, which are not dogmas, but quite radical questions:

- "No longer manage or administrate: get involved!" focuses on the personal level, and in fact the movement pays a lot of attention to the human aspects as an important driving force for change, as we are very careful to build convivial relationships between people.
- "No longer consume: create meaningful content!" is understood as a call for creative and happy ways of satisfying our needs and recognizing sufficiency

- "No more building: rehabilitate!" This is one of the most polemical commitments, with the big question: Should we still, should we always build? Or, in other words, is the answer to all our needs always a new building? The idea is to consider rehabilitation in depth, in all its meanings, as bringing back into esteem places, people, materials, techniques, while learning to appreciate and take care of all that is already there.

- "No longer see land as a mere support for development, but as a caretaker of land!" focuses on the shift from land development to land care planning. It's about going back to caring for places, people, buildings, other living things and everything that's already here, and seeing land as our living ecosystem to be shared with all people and all other living things.

But above all, beyond theory, we want to be a network of doers, who are committed to acting, experimenting and implementing right now, no longer waiting for laws or fashions, implementing for real frugal building projects, frugal and fruitful gardens, frugal and fruitful territorial strategies, as proof that we already know and can design and inhabit our territories in a responsible way. Therefore, we present numerous realized projects that have achieved frugality in resources, frugality in energy, frugality in technologies and frugality in territories, for a zero-land take planning, while fulfilling happiness and creativity.

TOWARDS "ZERO CARBON CITY REGIONS" AND A "FUTURE PROOF PLANNING"?

First, we believe that planning must be based on solid scientific and ecological knowledge (even though planning is and will remain a political practice, not a scientific one). There are many innovations in these new approaches: for example, the integration of ecosystem services assessments into planning, so that each neighbourhood can plan not only how to provide enough housing, jobs, transportation, etc., but also how to provide safe water, food, climate comfort, a healthy environment, clean air, mitigation and adaptation to natural risks, and so on. Some cities are beginning to experiment with ecological planning tools: For example, in Geneva, a green infrastructure planning tool; in Lyon, a planning approach based on planetary boundaries. As a researcher, I'm also part of a research program ("EcoModAm") exploring new ecological balances for developments, not only counting abstract square meters but also considering environmental issues. At the other hand it is important to not rush into a hopeless race for data, evaluations, monitoring etc. It takes a lot of energy, and it is very fragile, for example in terms of biodiversity, we think it should never just be about counting and managing everything. It seems to us that the attitude of frugality, and to care for the land as well as the attitude of care for what is already here, is already within our reach, and much more powerful, without delay.

TACKLING TOGETHER THE CLIMATE AND BIODIVERSITY CRISIS, AS WELL AS THE NEED FOR HOUSING

A second point would be to move beyond the false opposition between human needs and ecological wisdom, and to address together the climate and biodiversity crises, as well as the need for housing.

The questions is again: Is the answer to all our needs always new buildings? And is the housing crisis only a question of quantity? That would leave us with only 2 options: Either densification or urban sprawl, which would mean more new buildings. It's time to rethink. We have urbanized so much—in France, the rate of urban sprawl is more than 3 times the rate of population growth—and yet the housing crisis is worse than ever. There are, of course, economic, social and cultural factors. First of all, the housing crisis is linked to the distribution and metropolitanization of jobs, because you need housing where the

"It's still time, it's always time, to sign the Manifesto for Frugality in Architecture and Land Care; to support our actions; and to join or create a group!"

Clay bricks workshop © Pierre-Yves Brunaud

jobs are, but obviously just building more new houses won't solve the problem. Instead, what if we focused our urban projects on relocalizing and building a stronger circular economy, for example by favouring local and organic materials, which also greatly enhance skilled employment. The Viennese philosopher Ivan Ilich wrote that scarcity is an invention, a creation of the markets. Second, the housing crisis is related to prices, i.e. it is a crisis of housing affordability. In this regard, several academic studies have shown that housing prices in today's real estate markets are very poorly related to the quantity of housing.* So again, the answer has to be economic, it's not about building on the whole surface of the earth, it's about sharing, it's about developing non speculative housing: Vienna is still a very inspiring avant-garde on these issues, and it has to move forward.

As both an urban planner and an environmentalist, I often find it funny that from an ecological perspective, land is undoubtedly a common good, but from a social and economic perspective, it remains a very controversial struggle. Is it a challenge to combine ecology and social justice?

** J. Friggit (CGEDD), March 2021: Based on estimates in the literature, the elasticity of housing prices in relation to the number of dwellings is -1 to -2. Therefore, if there were 370,000 additional dwellings in France (or 1% of the total housing stock, which comprises 37 million dwellings), the price of housing would be only 1% to 2% lower, all other things being equal.*

Turin's Transition towards a Post-Fordist, Post-Pandemic, and Post-Carbon Metropolis

Ombretta Caldarice

Ombretta Caldarice is an Assistant Professor in Urban and Regional Planning at Politecnico di Torino. Her research focuses on urban and territorial resilience, planning rules, and integrating climate change adaptation into planning and design. With over ten years of international experience, she has contributed to the UN-Habitat 2022 Report on Urban Climate Action and co-edits the "Resilient Cities" book series.

Over recent decades, the question of metropolitan cities in planning and governance has been at the centre of the political and academic debate. Given that the term "metropolitan" is commonly used to indicate an urbanized territory extending beyond the core city (Da Cruz et al. 2020), the critical question to address lies in searching for a correspondence between the functional dimension and the institutional structure of the metropolitan level (Lefévre 1998). This issue has been the subject of intense debate, and currently, metropolitan areas are freighting with multiple challenges and tensions regarding their role in competing globally in terms of agglomeration, economies of scale, and industrial specialisation (Tosics 2007). In Italy, metropolitan cities were recognised after various attempts during the 1990s and 2000s. This process is the result of a troubled history that culminated in the approval of the so-called Delrio Reform, which introduced in 2014 metropolitan cities in the Italian Constitution with the purpose of managing the strategic development of the metropolitan territory (Casavola et al. 2023). At the same time, several key challenges still need to be addressed (Vinci 2019). Among all, the absence of a straightforward metropolitan political programme able to put into force the effectiveness of metropolitan cities in dealing with crucial issues of the European agenda and the Cohesion Policy, such as climate protection goals (Brunetta & Caldarice 2024).

Among the 14 Italian metropolitan cities, the Turin metropolitan city is the largest as it brings together 312 municipalities and about 2.3 million inhabitants, covering a very large and heterogeneous territory composed of the urban pole of Turin City, periurban area, hills and the mountain areas in the Alps. This regional diversity gives rise to a strong potential for proposing a new alliance between the City of Turin and its regions to ensure the same opportunities for all the inhabitants of the metropolitan city. In this paradigm shift, the Turin metropolitan city is moving from a post-Fordist to a post-pandemic and, most recently, to a post-carbon metropolis. These are three not consequential steps but different titles of the same transition process.

The **post-Fordist metropolis** transition dates back to the Nineties when the strong industrialisation specialisation in the manufacturing sector started to crack, leading to deindustrialisation, as FIAT is moving away from Turin and, at the same time, reducing its connections with the more dynamic productive system of the rest of Piedmont and Northern Italy (Bagnasco et al. 2020). This dynamic asks for a new model of urban development that overcomes the Fordist image of the Turin metropolitan area. Governa and Salone (2023) outlined that Turin attempts to overcome the Fordist legacy through three Strategic Plans for the Turin metropolitan area, anticipating the institutionalisation of the Turin metropolitan city. The first Plan (1997), which managed the underway transition of Turin as the Italian one-company town, was updated in 2006 to apply the knowledge economy paradigm as a "key recipe" for 21st-century Turin. The Third Strategic Plan (2016) focused on a "new manufacturing economy" connected to a neo-industrial paradigm that aims to translate the traditional industrial legacy into innovative forms leading to technological urban smartness. In other terms, the Turin metropolitan city worked towards a productive metropolis from secondary to the advanced tertiary sector through technology transfer, cooperation in business networks, process and product innovation and the promotion of the region and its products. To run this strategy, the Turin metropolitan city launched the TRENTAMETRO project to boost new productive activities and promote the reuse of 30 abandoned areas recognised as strategic for the Turin metropolitan area.

Later, the Turin Metropolitan Strategic Plan (2021–2023) seizes upon the scenario "Turin Augmented Metropolis", envisaging the construction of a new alliance between the city of Turin and the surrounding region following the objectives defined by the Italian Recovery Resilience Plan. Augmentation is the transition towards a **post-pandemic metropolis**, which harmoniously combines the natural and the artificial environment, developing the potential of both to build equity, well-being and sustainability (Robiglio et al. 2021). The Augmented Metropolis coincides with a "90-minute metropolis", making the gateways of metropolitan interest more accessible from all points in the region and promoting a differentiated use of collective transport over medium and long distances and of alternatives to the private car over medium and short distances. This vision is arranged into six areas: (i) a more productive and innovative Turin metropolis (digitalisation, innovation and competitiveness); (ii) a greener and more ecological Turin metropolis (green revolution and ecological transition); (iii) a more mobile, accessible and connected Turin metropolis (infrastructures for sustainable mobility); (iv) a Turin metropolis that learns more (education and research); (v) a more attractive, fair and equal Turin metropolis (inclusion and cohesion); and (vi) a healthier Turin metropolis (healthcare).

Today, the Turin metropolitan city is working to lead the transition towards a **post-carbon metropolis** that deals with climate change mitigation and adaptation. The most significant climate-change-related issues cover mitigation and the adaptation to extreme temperatures, droughts, flooding and water scarcity to preserve the capacity of soils for food and wood production, regulate the microclimate in urban environment, and improve the ecological functionality contrasting the decline of species and ecosystems using Nature-based Solutions (Goličnik Marušić et al. 2023).

The Turin metropolitan city is setting four relevant strategies to be integrated into the future metropolitan spatial plan: (i) contrasting consumption and soil waterproofing by identifying densely built areas, transition areas, and free areas (in which any type of new building is prohibited as urban green or public spaces can contribute to mitigation and adaptation to climate change); (ii) improving ecological functionality and increase forest to foreseen an ecological network project by allocating 45 m^2/inhabitant of green areas; (iii) rationalising

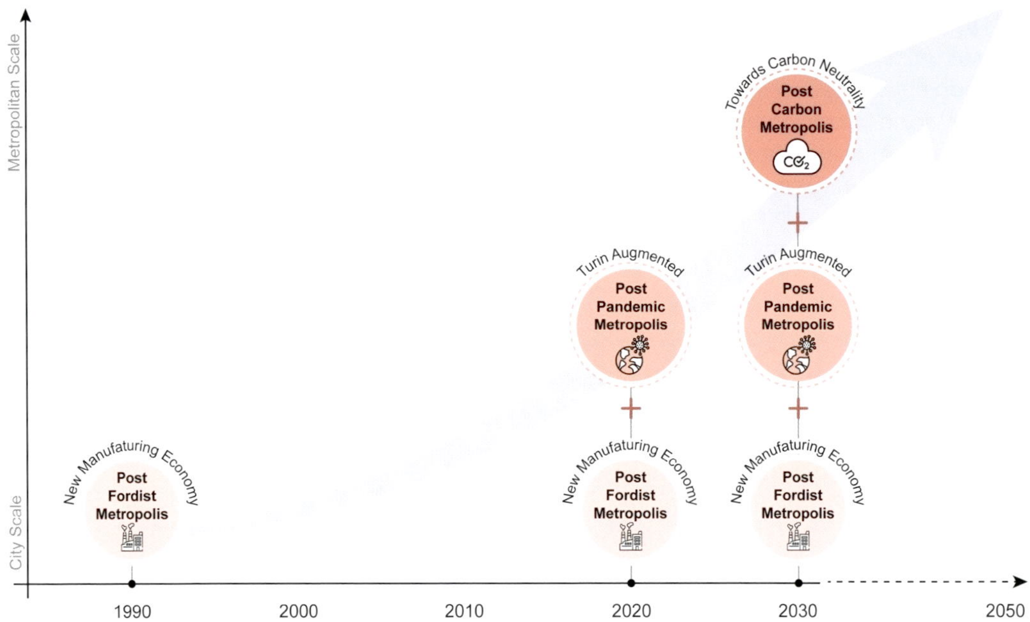

The Turin never-ending transition to a post-Fordist, to a post-pandemic and to a post-carbon metropolis © Bruna Pincegher, Politecnico di Torino

the exploitation of water resources, to ensure a balanced availability of water for hydroelectricity, agriculture and the protection of biodiversity; and (iv) enhancing energy efficiency and district heating. Despite this great effort, the Turin metropolitan city reflects the dominant trend, according to which adaptation as a policy and planning problem is essentially under the responsibility of municipalities (Gori Nocentini 2024). At the same time, we can consider this as the first attempt of the Turin metropolitan city could support Turin's path towards climate neutrality by 2030.

Italian metropolitan cities are generally on a long journey because the institution reorganisation process is still underway. This is why a genuine criticism of decision-making and planning processes on the metropolitan scale is emerging. In this scenario, the metropolitan city of Turin is passing through a never-ending transition to a post-Fordist, post-pandemic, and recently to a post-carbon metropolis *(see figure above)*. In this process of turns and twists overcoming the Fordist image, the Turin metropolitan city could assume a key role in developing a shared understanding of the spatial pathways towards climate neutrality. This path is one of the most pressing challenges of our time that needs to be addressed at the metropolitan scale; this may help strengthen the role of metropolitan actors and provide an opportunity to rethink regional-scale planning practices.

Mapping Future Scenarios

Developing an Integrated Perspective

The Emerging Phenomena Atlas highlights the main trends in greenhouse gas emissions in different sectors in the Vienna Metropolitan Region. By mapping these trends, the Atlas visualizes the complex spatial patterns, relationships and functional linkages that are emerging in the metropolitan region and the relationships between its urban, suburban and rural areas. This information is critical for developing integrated strategies to transform the region into a zero-carbon city. However, addressing the interconnected challenges of the climate crisis requires holistic, integrated strategies that focus on more than just one sector at a time.

The MetroLab team has used the findings of the Emerging Phenomena Atlas as a basis for developing comprehensive strategies (chapter "Strategies for a zero-carbon city region").

To facilitate change, MetroLab takes these strategies and translates them into specific actionable tools to reduce greenhouse gas emissions through spatial change in the Vienna metropolitan region. These tools are described not only in terms of their potential to reduce carbon emissions, but also in relation to the physical spaces they affect. This approach creates a comprehensive "toolbox" to guide climate neutral development on a metropolitan scale, as detailed in the chapter "Toolbox for a Zero Carbon City Region". Because creating a zero carbon city region requires a coordinated approach that crosses both physical and administrative boundaries, these tools are most powerful when they work together as part of interconnected systems.

These tools and systems are then applied to the spatial context of the Vienna metropolitan region, resulting in five different scenarios that show the potential for change (chapter "From Tools to Systems to Future Scenarios"). These scenarios present new pathways towards climate neutrality at the metropolitan scale:

1. Establishing 30-Minute Proximity Territories
2. Favoring Density and Restricting Land Consumption
3. Empowering a Network of Multifunctional Centralities
4. Fostering Local Food Cycles and Self-Sufficiency
5. Protecting Natural Resources and Landscapes

This creative, cross-sectoral and interdisciplinary approach, working with metropolitan strategies, tools and systems, can be applied to other city regions and make the necessary measures tangible.

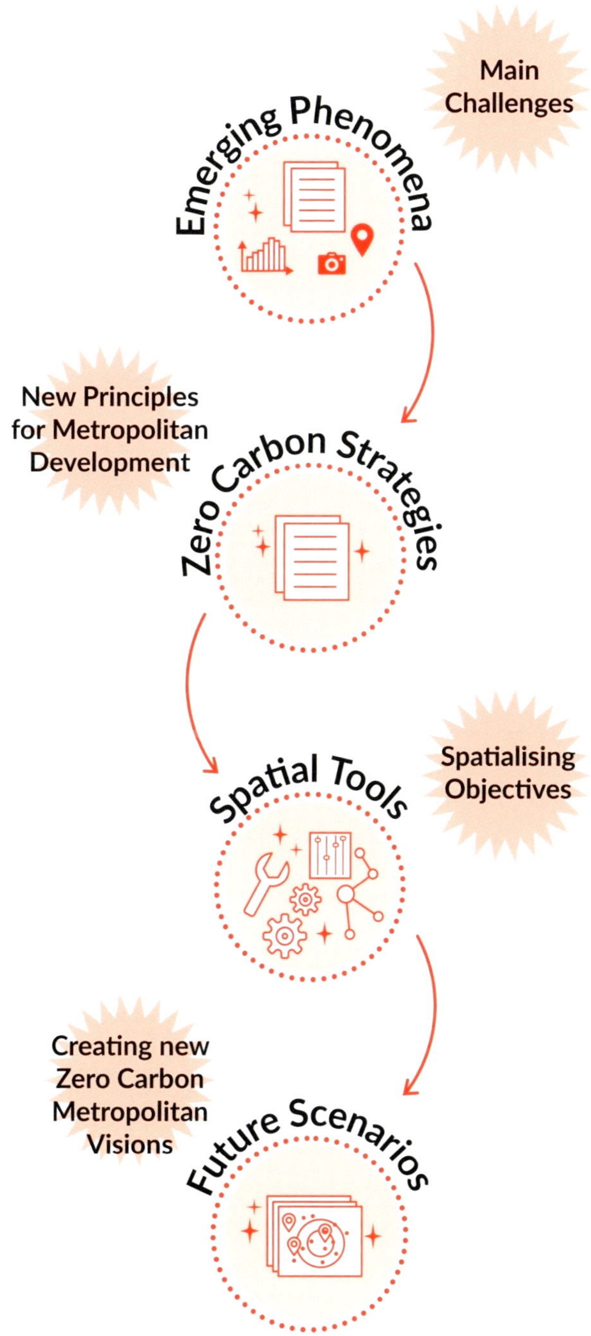
Main Challenges
Emerging Phenomena
New Principles for Metropolitan Development
Zero Carbon Strategies
Spatial Tools
Spatialising Objectives
Creating new Zero Carbon Metropolitan Visions
Future Scenarios

Phenomena

Moving

M1 Greenhouse gas emissions are increasing further, we are still failing to change the modal split towards climate-friendly mobility.

M2 Most ways between Vienna and the region are done by car, and the number of commuters as well as travel-distances in the region are increasing.

M3 Networks are still not ready for a mobility transition and policies are still funding carbon-intensive mobility.

M4 The international train network still cannot rival with the connections by plane from Vienna International Airport.

M5 In Austria, 78% of goods are transported by road.

Living

L1 Areas with a high population density have lower greenhouse gas emissions per person.

L2 The region is not able to keep track of its vacancy rate, and as a result, it is unaware of its current statistics.

L3 Ongoing construction is increasingly taking up space on undeveloped land. The trend towards larger homes and more living space leads to land use, energy use and emissions.

L4 The typology and size of dwellings significantly influence our energy consumption, we are still highly depending on fossil energy to heat our living spaces.

L5 Current constructions are still primarily using carbon intensive materials.

Producing

P1 Nearly 20% of emissions are due to two production sites and energy plants.

P2 Food production requires a very high land footprint, but the majority of the required land is not available within the region.

P3 The Metropolitan Region does not produce the diversity of food that it consumes, resulting in inefficient import-export flows.

P4 A quarter of agricultural land in the Metropolitan Region is cultivated organically.

P5 Free allocations within the EU Emissions Trading System to industry have hindered substantial reductions of emissions in the region.

Consuming

C1 Our current diet causes an average of 1.5 t of CO_2 equivalents per person per year and needs 0.18 ha per person, especially due to our meat- and dairy heavy diet.

C2 Only part of the emissions due to food consumption are in reality emitted in Austria, and 90% of these emissions are caused by animal-based products.

C3 Consumption based emissions are highly influenced by our lifestyle-choices.

C4 Our current lifestyle does not match our available land.

C5 The consumption of ressources in the Metropolitan Region is responsible for resource consumption in other parts of the world.

Wasting

W1 Austria's municipal waste generation is above EU average.

W2 Austria has only achieved its 2025 recycling goals for certain materials, others are still well below EU average.

W3 98% of the resources that Vienna needs for food, energy and the economy comes from other countries.

W4 Most of Austrias waste volume goes to landfill.

W5 Construction waste accounts for 16.1% of Austrias waste volume, when taking into account excavation waste even 75.1%.

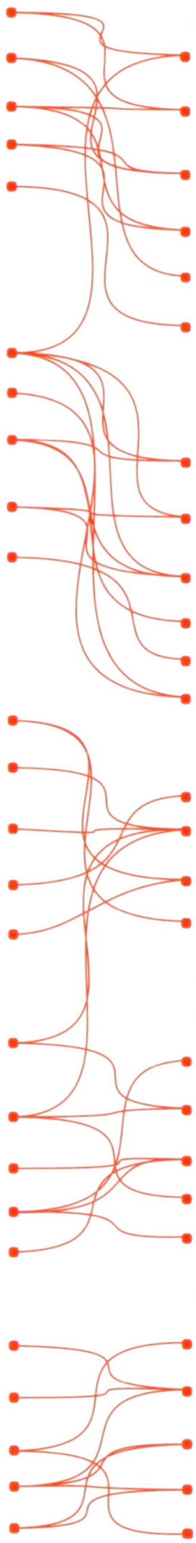

Strategies

Creating strategies for proximity and sustainable mobility

- Build a 15-Minutes City and a 30-Minutes Territory for shorter ways, better connections and a higher quality of life.
- Create a Street Grid that strengthens the Active Mobility Network and makes walking and biking more attractive.
- Develop a well-functioning public transportation system that provides sustainable and fast connections over long distances and serves as the backbone of metropolitan development.
- Reallocate public funds to invest in innovative Zero-Carbon mobility systems.
- Develop decentralized multi-functional mobility systems and last mile concepts that include public transport on demand.
- Create efficient rail-based logistics systems with transition to local systems.

Designing dense and flexible neighborhoods

- Create resilient, multi-functional and accessible public spaces for all.
- Promote a new qualitative density with a high quality of life and flexibility through new ways of living together that focus on more common space.
- Avoid any construction of new single family housing and focus on denser housing with a high quality of life.
- Favor qualitative and flexible stock development instead of designating new construction land.
- Develop strategies to build with low-carbon materials only.
- Program multi-functional spaces to strengthen and diversify local centralities.

Promoting regional production cycles

- Create Metropolitan landscapes that produce and regenerate.
- Foster local and responsible responsible agricultural systems for metropolitan self-sufficiency.
- Decarbonize and decentralize metropolitan energy production.
- Integrate industry in the urban fabric and foster production symbioses.

Fostering responsible consumption patterns

- Create Metropolitan Landscapes for Leisure & Recreation within the Region.
- Foster a societal shift towards a primarily plant-based planetary health diet.
- Support a transition of consuming habits towards the limits of our ecological footprint.
- Create conditions for regional food circularity.
- Encourage a shift to a sharing society that takes care of commons.

Closing metropolitan ressource cycles

- Establish a metropolitan system that reuses and recycles materials.
- Prioritize local ressources and minimize external dependencies.
- Develop local industrial production cycles that promote the reuse of ressources.
- Put systems in place that enable circularity of building materials.
- Shift from a linear to a circular water system.

Tools

Future Scenarios

Strategies towards a Zero Carbon City Region

In order to effectively address the challenges highlighted in the Emerging Phenomena Atlas, the MetroLab team has used its findings to develop comprehensive strategies that are no longer categorized in the five areas of life, but rather in an integrated way. These strategies are designed to address multiple issues simultaneously, ensuring a more holistic approach to achieving a zero-carbon metropolitan region.

By considering the broader context and interconnected nature of these challenges, the MetroLab team aims to create solutions that are sustainable and resilient in the face of the climate crisis, and that can be applied to other metropolitan regions.

» Creating Strategies for Proximity and Sustainable Mobility

Build a 15-minute city and a 30-minute territory for shorter journeys, better connections and a higher quality of life.

Based on the model of Carlos Moreno, a 15-minute city allows its citizens to satisfy all basic needs and have access to services within a walkable or bikeable distance: People should be able to eat, learn, work, run errands, care and enjoy nature within a small radius of their home (Moreno et al. 2021). This essentially avoids long commuting distances and strengthens active mobility, saving carbon emissions and having a social as well as health benefit. It ensures that all citizens have an equal access to services. Expanding this idea to the metropolitan area and its different densities may oblige to widen the radius: Within less dense and more suburban areas, 30-minute territories would already mean a significant shift in accessibility. Establishing 15-minute cities and 30-minute territories throughout the metropolitan area means promoting a city model based on proximity, accessibility and mixed-use.

Create a street grid that strengthens the active mobility network and makes walking and biking more attractive.

In support of the objective of 15-minute cities and 30-minute territories, our way of organizing streets should change towards more space for walking, biking and nature. Today, the street network of the city region is still designed for car use, this has to change to lead the towards climate neutrality. This means more space for bikes, more pedestrianized streets, limited access regulations for cars as well as planting trees and introducing greenery to streets in dense areas. It facilitates commuting by bike or foot for metropolitan residents and thus saves CO_2.

Develop a well-functioning public transportation system that provides sustainable and fast connections over long distances and serves as the backbone of metropolitan development.

The functional interconnectedness of the metropolitan area requires new solutions for public transportation: Housing and jobs should be developed only in close proximity to existing public transportation. Every resident of the metropolitan area should have easy access to public transportation.

Relocate public funds to invest in innovative zero-carbon mobility systems.

The funding system today still fosters the use of carbon-intensive mobility and lacks incentives to live and work close by. Public money is still funding the construction of new roads while in the past years, train lines with little frequency have been shut down. Public funds should shift to support sustainable modes of transport such as biking, walking and public transport infrastructure, especially since these infrastructures need a rapid development and require large amounts of funding.

Develop decentralized multi-functional mobility systems and last mile concepts that include public transport on demand.

Everyone in the metropolitan area should have access to public transportation: In lower density areas, flexible solutions are needed to ensure an efficient network. Active mobility infrastructure such as bike lanes and bike sharing, as well as other innovative solutions, must be improved to support last-mile solutions.

Create efficient rail-based logistics systems with transition to local systems.

With the vast majority of freight moving by truck, there is a need to move to new rail-based logistics systems that also offer flexible local transitions and allow for carbon-neutral transportation of goods.

» Designing Dense and Flexible Neighbourhoods

Create resilient, multi-functional and accessible public spaces for all

Public Spaces are not only spaces of encounter in an urban context, but also a common good on the metropolitan scale.

Promote a new qualitative density with a high quality of life and flexibility through new ways of living together that focus on more common space.

Our current housing practices require a high amount of land consumption, also due to increase of individual living space. This is also a threat to energy efficiency. Creating a new qualitative density that emphasizes the importance of common space would mean to gain in quality of life while being able to live in smaller private spaces, saving energy and carbon emissions.

Avoid any construction of new single family housing and focus on denser housing with a high quality of life.

For a zero-carbon housing future, we need to reconsider our housing typologies: Single family homes are still the dominant housing typology in the metropolitan region. But they are neither efficient in regards of space, nor in regards of energy consumption, therefore with the aim of becoming climate neutral, we cannot continue to build single family homes anymore. This should be reflected in zoning codes and policy. Existing areas of single family homes should be punctually densified or adapted. Leaving this housing model behind also means keeping city centers alive and reducing possible commuting distances.

Develop strategies to build with low-carbon materials only.

Currently, carbon-intensive materials are widely used in construction processes. While the construction sector should solely focus on adapting the existing building stock in the future, used materials should be changed to low-carbon materials.

Program multi-functional spaces to strengthen and diversify local centralities.

The region is diverse in its territories and does not only rely on a single large urban center. However, the development of strong local cores has been overlooked in the past years, leading to empty city and town centers and thriving commercial centers in the peripheries.

Favor qualitative and flexible stock development instead of designating new construction land.

In the past years, large surfaces have been artificialized for new constructions. This is a threat to existing carbon sinks and precious agricultural land that is needed to sustain the region. New constructions also have a significant impact on carbon emissions: It is therefore by far more sustainable the work with the existing built environment. Densifying and adapting the building stock in our cities in a qualitative manner reduces additional land consumption and is necessary to accommodate our growing population.

» Promoting Regional Production Cycles

Create metropolitan landscapes that produce and regenerate.

It is essential to secure metropolitan landscapes that are serving as carbon sinks and play an important role in renewable energy and food production. This requires strategies and rules on the metropolitan level to pursue a common strategy and is a necessary step towards more self-sufficiency in the food system as well as in decarbonizing energy production.

Foster local and responsible responsible agricultural systems for metropolitan self-sufficiency.

Currently, the metropolitan region is not nearly self-sufficient regarding its food consumption. Therefore, strategies to encourage regional food circularity are needed. The Vienna city region has a very fertile and productive agricultural hinterland and can thus strive to achieve a high degree of self-sufficiency concerning food.

Integrate industry in the urban fabric and foster production symbioses.

Spatial planning can work towards creating spaces that allow production symbioses between different actors and integrate workplaces in existing urban environments, so that they are easily accessible for employees.

Decarbonize and decentralize metropolitan energy production.

Fossil energy plants are amongst the regions biggest emitters of greenhouse gases. Progress has been made in the field of renewable energy for the past decades, with Burgenland being more than self-sufficient concerning renewable energy. However, to achieve climate neutrality, energy production needs to be entirely renewable. In dense urban regions, this means also finding new creative solutions to combine different land uses, such as agriculture and energy production.

» Fostering Responsible Consumption Patterns

Create metropolitan landscapes for leisure & recreation within the region.

Our leisure activities are strong emitters of greenhouse gas emissions: Creating attractive natural landscapes for leisure and recreation can create a local offer for recreational activities with low carbon intensity. They should be well connected to sustainable mobility systems. This is an important part in creating a zero-carbon metropolitan region that nevertheless offers more quality of life than ever.

Foster a societal shift towards a primarily plant-based planetary health diet.

Influencing consumption patterns is a difficult task, but to move forward to a more sustainable food system, a shift in our diet is necessary. A diet based on primarily plant-based produce can save a considerable amount of greenhouse gas emissions: Through a food strategy, the Metropolitan region should steer consumption on a big scale and change the supply system of public canteens and cafeterias as well as work with private partners. This strategy should take into account both the consumption as well as production aspect of food: It should work with farmers to transition to mostly plant-based agriculture in the region, that can thus develop a high degree of self-sufficiency for a more sustainable diet.

Support a transition of consuming habits towards the limits of our ecological footprint.

Individual consumption behaviour is not an easy topic to address and depends on multiple social factors. But metropolitan planning can address it by developing a spatial model that favours the provision with universal basic services for all rather than mass consumption, as it is now the case. The rapid development of vast consumption spaces has left its mark on numerous urban and suburban areas in the Vienna region. The ambition of a Zero Carbon City Region forces one to rethink these spaces and their role in a carbon neutral future.

Encourage a shift to a sharing society that takes care of commons.

An essential shift in our consumption patterns is to move to a society that shares as many goods as possible rather than consuming them individually: Sharing means reducing and becoming more efficient in our consumption of resources. For example vehicles, tools and equipment can be shared, but also spaces like community kitchens and guest rooms. Exchange spaces with the aim of encouraging sharing can also become important social spaces within neighbourhoods.

» Closing Metropolitan Resource Cycles

Prioritize local resources and minimize external dependencies.

The use of local resources reduces emissions from transport and favours a more responsible use of resources, that minimizes the externalized emission footprint of the region. This encourages a bioregional approach, that can develop a creative use of local resources for new purposes.

Establish a metropolitan system that reuses and recycles materials.

Currently, our use of resources and materials consists of a rather linear system: Our management of resources and waste should make it easily possible to reuse resources and as a last resort, recycle them. It is essential to think systems on a metropolitan scale in order to efficiently be able to steer material use.

Put systems in place that enable circularity of building materials.

The construction sector is one of the biggest emitters of greenhouse gases and the largest generator of waste. The linear practices of construction and demolition are not future-proof due to their excessive use of resources. Introducing regional circularity in our practices has the potential to drastically reduce waste and emissions in the construction sector.

Shift from a linear to a circular water system.

Water is a precious resource that will gain in importance in the future due to climate change. Today, our cities lack a common management of water, rainwater and wastewater. The metropolitan scale allows to maximise potential uses of water.

Toolbox for a Zero Carbon City Region

In order to bring about meaningful changes in the way we live, the integrated strategies are translated into concrete, practical tools aiming to reduce greenhouse gas emissions by creating new, sustainable spatial cross-border patterns and relationships that foster climate neutrality in the Vienna metropolitan Region. The Integrated Metropolitan Toolbox is a set of 24 tools that address the sources of greenhouse gas emissions in a multi-faceted way, covering all areas of life but tackling the challenges in an integrated way. They are described not only in terms of their potential to reduce carbon emissions, but also in relation to the physical spaces they affect when applied in the spatial context. Because achieving a zero-carbon city requires coordinated efforts that cross boundaries and integrate multiple sectors, these tools are most effective when used together as part of interconnected systems, as will be described in the following afterwards.

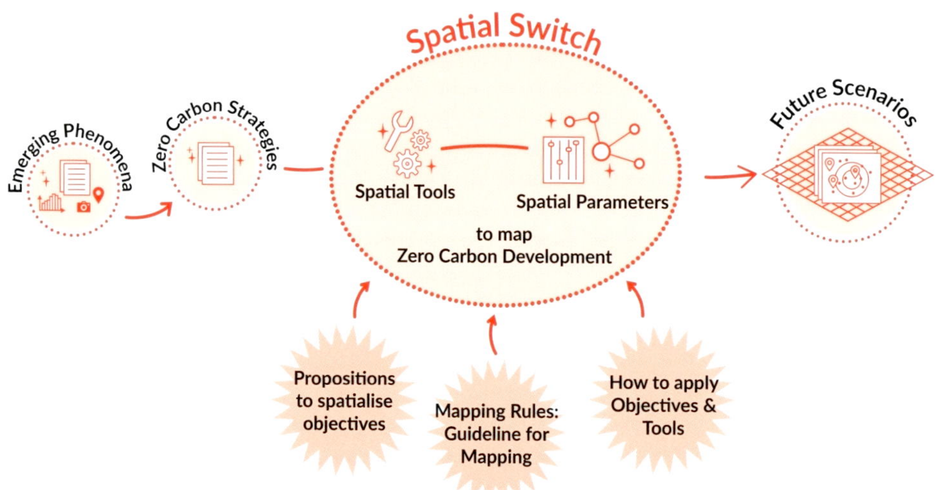

Tools

Metropolitan Bike Highway Network

30-Minute Territories

Multimodal Mobility Hubs

Metropolitan Public Transport System

Zero-Carbon Street Grid

Qualitative Redensification

Zoning Codes limiting Urban Sprawl

Metropolitan Vacancy Agency

Multifunctional Energy Production

Buildings as Energy Producers

Cooling Districts

Industrial Symbiosis

Circlular Material Platform

District Farms

Market Hubs

Distribution Hubs

Rail-based Regional Good Distribution System

Bio Valley

Resilient Public Spaces

Organic Protection Barriers

Land that Recreates, Regenerates and Produces

Circular Water Systems

Multifunctional Centralities

Programmers of Space

Small-scale Local Transportation Modes

Limited Traffic Zones

Market Hubs

Provide local and regional food distribution circuits and short transportation routes

Market hubs aim to provide products as locally as possible, strengthening regional ties and reducing external dependencies. They are located in urban areas as well as in rural communities and provide regional and local food. Accessibility by public transport and active mobility needs to be given. Through their creation throughout the metropolitan territory, they make it possible for all inhabitants of the region to have at least a weekly market in proximity that offers them fresh, local produce.

Spatial Dimension

» Every city with more than 2,500 inhabitants should have a farmer shop
» Every city with more than 5,000 in habitants should have a farmers market hall

Carbon Impacts

» Regionalize food supply and reduce distribution distances between producer and consumer
» Create consciousness for sustainable nutrition & consumption practices, encourage a sustainable diet

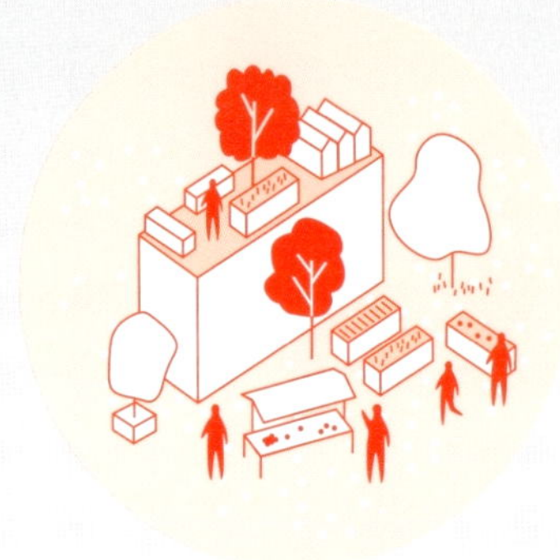

District Farms

Rebalance metropolitan food demand and supply in its quantity and diversity

District farms focus on regional food production to create new producer-consumer relations, they are located between urban and agricultural areas and have an educational dimension concerning food and sustainable diets. They value the idea of regional food production and local sourcing while being active producers. Farms can receive extra public funding for their special concepts and can also serve as testing grounds for new forms of agriculture and become "Agricultural Living Labs", creating new social links by creating proximity between consumers and producers.

Spatial Dimension

» Every settlement with more than 5,000 inhabitants
» On the verge between agricultural and urban areas

Carbon Impacts

» Regionalizing food supply saves greenhouse gas emissions from transport
» A more direct producer-consumer relation creates efficient supply that saves food waste and thus green house gas emissions

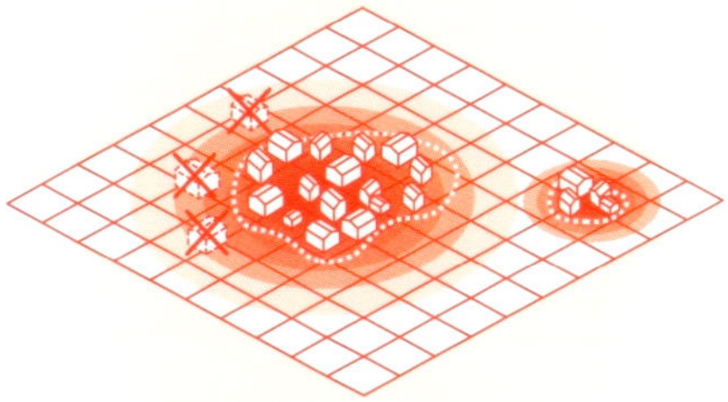

Zoning Codes Limiting Urban Sprawl

Create dense urban areas for proximity and limit land consumption to enhance carbon capture capacities

Land consumption is a major issue: Precious green and agricultural land is artificialized and loses its carbon capture capacities. Therefore, new constructions should only be allowed under strict conditions and spatial limits for urban growth should be set, in form of strict zoning borders. Zoning codes should ban the constructions of single family housing: This typology still is widely popular today while being very inefficient in terms of needed land, low density and creating longer journeys and high (ecological) costs.

Spatial Dimension

- Limit new constructions to areas that are in proximity of public transport
- No new constructions outside existing settlement borders and no constructions of single-family homes

Carbon Impacts

- Preserve carbon capture capacities of the soil, reducing carbon emissions from inefficient construction typologies

30-Minute Territories

Promote accessibility and short journeys in a metropolitan context and create a polycentric structure that fosters proximity

The goal is to promote the accessibility of basic services, goods and needs as well as workplaces within a radius of 30 minutes by sustainable modes of mobility, taking the idea of the 15-minute city to a suburban and rural spatial context. On metropolitan level, this means strengthening sustainable mobility and regional sub-centres across municipal borders that are well connected to public transport and their surrounding cities and villages.

Spatial Dimension

- Develop the 30-minute territories alongside public transport infrastructure
- Strengthen regional sub-centres above 5,000 inhabitants and connections to surrounding towns within a 30-minute bike radius

Carbon Impacts

- Shorter journeys can reduce CO_2 emissions from everyday mobility

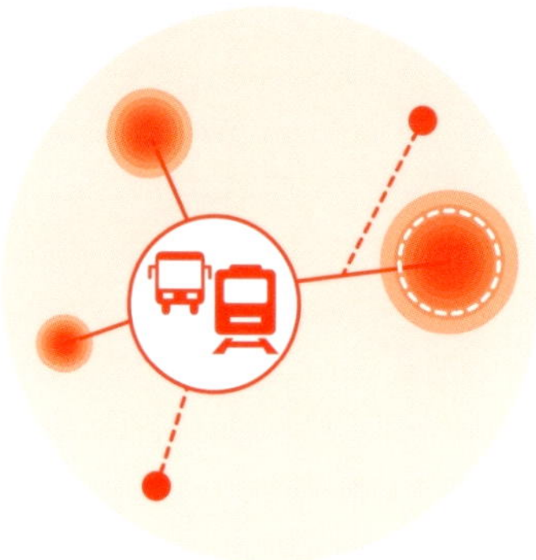

Metropolitan Public Transport System

Develop public transport infrastructure on metropolitan level as the backbone of development

On metropolitan level, a uniform public transport network should be widely accessible and multimodal. Instead of favouring new long-term and large-scale infrastructure projects, metropolitan planning should concentrate on improving existing infrastructure, by introducing more frequency and accessibility. An efficient network throughout the metropolitan territory is the base for integrated metropolitan planning.

Spatial Dimension

» Improve existing infrastructure and increase frequency on existing lines
» Plan connections on metropolitan level as well as develop local offers

Carbon Impacts

» Switching commutes from private cars to public transport is a main lever in the mobility sector to reduce carbon emissions

Multimodal Mobility Hubs

Provide intermodal hubs to facilitate transition between different mobility offers

Mobility hubs are strategically located at key points in transit networks and local centers, linking sustainable transport options. Built around high-capacity nodes, they offer safe, convenient spaces for seamless transfers. A consistent, region-wide system is essential, with small hubs in neighborhoods and larger, more versatile hubs near major nodes. Obsolete fossil-fuel structures like gas stations could be repurposed, and hubs can integrate social functions as well.

Spatial Dimension

» Hubs in centralities and on the nodes of sustainable mobility networks
» Different sizes of hubs according to the importance of the hub

Carbon Impacts

» Facilitating a sustainable modal split and offering new transportation choices is essential to reducing emissions

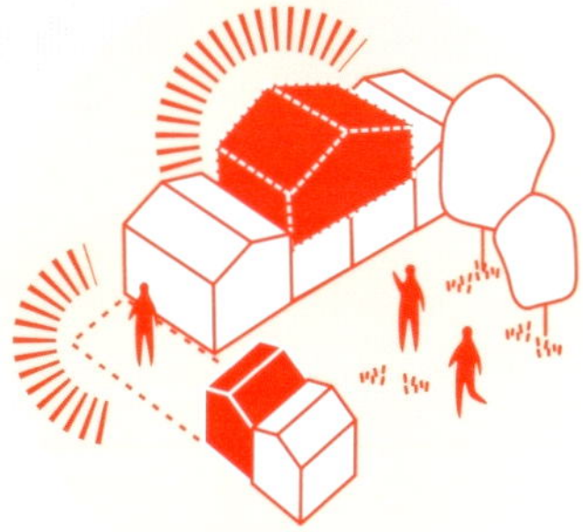

Metropolitan Bike Highway Network

Connect major centralities and make biking an easy and fast mode of transport

Bike highways change the modal split towards active mobility on routes for everyday commutes as well as for leisure purposes within an easily recognizable, uniform system throughout the city region. They need to be separated from motorized traffic, have adequate lighting and shade and be at least 4 meters wide. The track should be straightforward, bikers should have priority at crossings.

Spatial Dimension

» Every city with more than 2,000 inhabitants and major mobility nodes need to be connected to the bike highway network
» Existing bike connections need to be used and improved. New connections should use existing infrastructure to a maximum

Carbon Impacts

» Carbon emissions from commuting and everyday mobility related to cars can be reduced drastically.
» Carbon emission from leisure commutes can be reduced and intermodal mobility is encouraged

Qualitative Redensification

Create dense local neighbourhoods and centres with a high quality of life

While the metropolitan region is expected to grow in population, the goal is to not consume more land but rather create a more dense, efficient urban fabric that favours climate neutral compatible forms of housing in a qualitative manner, paying attention to green spaces, free spaces and common infrastructures. Neighbourhoods should gain in quality of life. Through redensification, local cores can be redeveloped into local centres, which is essential for the polycentric structure on a metropolitan level.

Spatial Dimension

» Create higher density in more populated areas (Cities with over 5,000 inhabitants)
» Create higher density in areas that are close to public transport infrastructure

Carbon Impacts

» Fostering dense neighborhoods with short distances and great proximity is essential to reducing carbon emissions

Bio Valley

Create territories that promote organic food production

The aim of the bio valley is to create a territory within the region that becomes the main organic food producer and, in the end, offers exclusively organic agriculture as a unique selling point. This brings benefits for biodiversity and public health due to a reduction of fertilizers, along with less emissions of greenhouse gases and enhanced carbon capture capacities.

Spatial Dimension

» Establish a pilot bio-valley in an area that is densely populated while also having large agricultural areas and natural areas nearby

» Possibility to extend concept after pilot phase

Carbon Impacts

» The reduction of the use of chemical and artificial fertilizers has a positive impact on greenhouse gas emissions

» Other positive effects include benefits for biodiversity

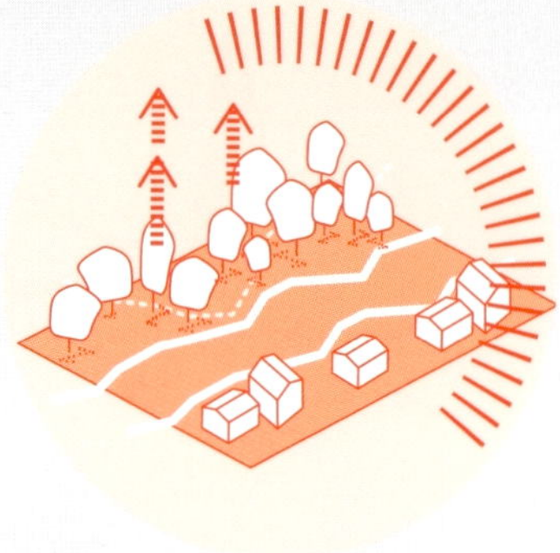

Organic Protection Barriers

Protect natural and ecological resources and ecosystems

Important natural areas and resources should be protected from the impacts of artificial fertilizers, intensive agricultural production and industrial emissions. Therefore, organic protection barriers aim to convert areas next to important ecosystems to exclusively organic agriculture, analogous to the bio valley. This again means reducing the emission impact from our food system and positive effects for biodiversity.

Spatial Dimension

» Areas in the immediate surroundings of natural parks, protected areas, important ecosystems

Carbon Impacts

» The reduction of the use of chemical and artificial fertilizers has a positive impact on greenhouse gas emissions

» Positive effects for biodiversity

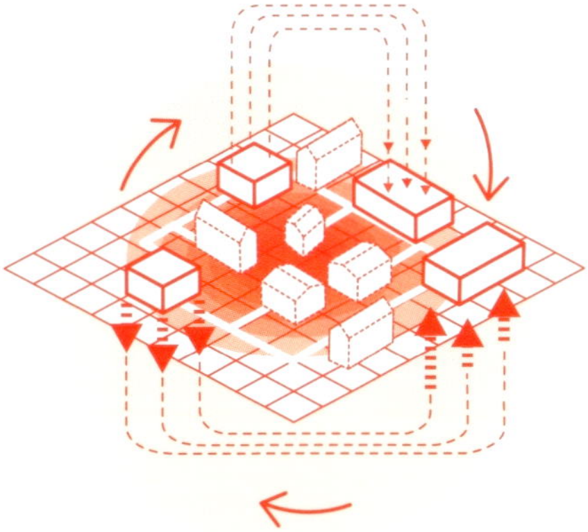

Industrial Symbiosis

Promote the exchange, reuse and recycling of resources in industrial agglomerations

Industrial symbiosis implies the strategic integration of business agglomerations that complement each other through synergies in resource use and exchange into urban landscapes. This relies on careful urban planning with robust regulations, mixed-use developments, seamless infrastructure integration and innovation in industrial processes. Urban planning needs to recognize the potential and design industrial zones with a possible circularity of resources in mind.

Spatial Dimension

» Mixed-use development based on symbiosis potential in industrial zones

Carbon Impacts

» Saving greenhouse gas emissions through reuse of resources (heat, waste, etc. from industrial processes)

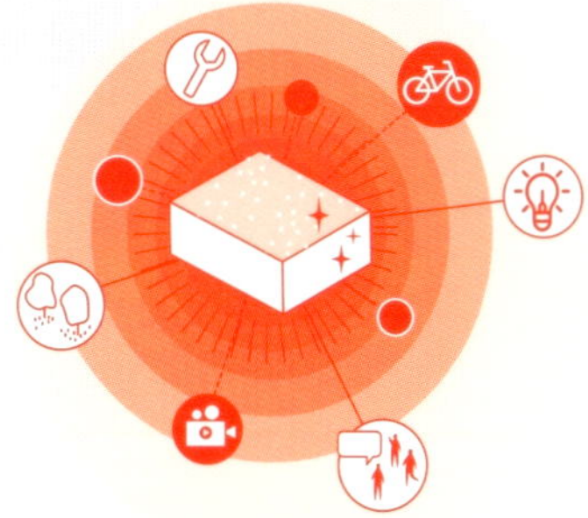

Programmers of Space

Support the creation of activity centres for local communities and neighbourhoods

The purpose is to foster community building and neighbourhood activities in accessible locations. Existing buildings can be reactivated with community uses that foster a more sustainable use of resources. Non-profit sharing activities, repair spaces, workspaces, libraries, cultural facilities or many other uses are possible. They are new centres of neighbourhoods that currently lack of central meeting points.

Spatial Dimension

» In all neighbourhoods and towns with over 2,500 inhabitants
» Different types possible according to centrality of the location

Carbon Impacts

» Environmental benefit through community actions (sharing, reusing, working in sustainable areas)

Circular Material Platform

Create a platform for implementing circular economy practices in the construction industry

The goal is to reduce waste and emissions from the construction sector and coordinate the use of building resources on the metropolitan scale. The platform facilitates resource allocation, collaboration, and sustainability by connecting those who have surplus resources with those who need them, fostering efficient resource utilization. Materials are made easily accessible in different quantities to respond to different demands. This type of platform can be built up in various sectors, from sharing economy apps to business-to-business resource exchange. This type of approach can also be applied at neighbourhood level and combined with an educational and community approach.

Spatial Dimension

» A local hub needs to be in cities with more than 5,000 inhabitants

Carbon Impacts

» Through the circularity of building materials, emissions in construction processes can be reduced, as well as emissions from waste treatment

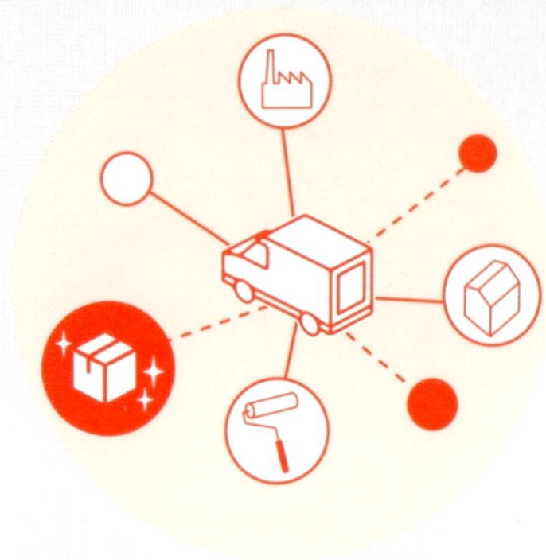

Small-Scale Local Transportation Modes

Provide sustainable last mile transportation solutions

In order to efficiently work together with larger-scale rail based distribution systems for goods, it is key to reduce emissions on the last mile and put flexible systems in place that largely rely on cargo bikes and other emission-free vehicles and forms of transportation. This system should work across municipal borders, supported by distribution hubs located throughout the territory. This is also important for the local provisioning with food produce.

Spatial Dimension

» Especially in dense urban areas and local centres

Carbon Impacts

» Saving energy and reducing emissions from transport

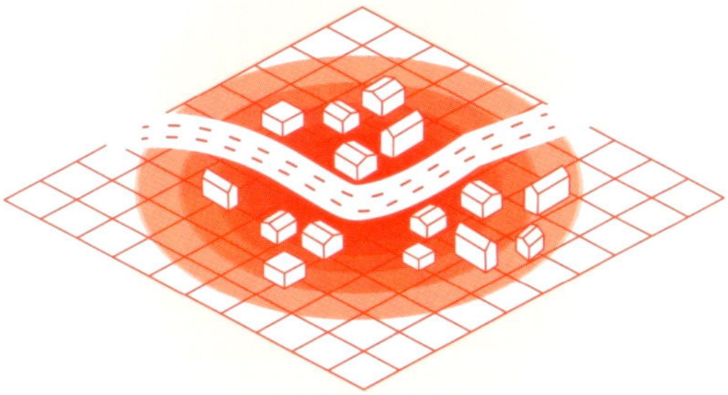

Circular Water System

Enhance a circular use of water

Water does not know administrative borders and will be an even more precious resource in the future that must actively be dealt with to limit our wasteful use, characterized by a rather linear than circular paradigm. Decentralized systems adapted to the different spatial contexts of the metropolitan region work together, reducing the need for large-scale facilities to treat water and subsequently also reducing energy consumption, as well as reducing the risks of floods.

Spatial Dimension

- Adaptation of urban areas for circular water systems
- Renaturalization of rivers and green spaces

Carbon Impacts

- Reduction of energy need to treat wastewater
- Efficient water use minimizes footprint of water use
- Enhanced carbon storage capacities

Landscapes for Recreation, Regeneration and Production

Secure multifunctional natural landscapes with ecological and social benefits

On metropolitan level, large natural landscapes that cross administrative boundaries need to be preserved to be able to fulfill a multitude of functions that bring both environmental as well as social benefits. Natural landscapes can serve as carbon sinks, areas for food production, energy production and individual recreation. These functions can often be combined.

Spatial Dimension

- Large-scale, interconnected natural landscapes need to be preserved and their functions strengthened
- Their accessibility for recreational purposes needs to be enhanced

Carbon Impacts

- Enabling local food and energy production and securing carbon capture capacities
- Creating land for recreational leisure activities with a low footprint

Distribution Hubs

Establish an efficient rail-based food logistics system

Currently, the transport of food is usually organized with motorized vehicles since rail infrastructure is not efficient enough. Distribution hubs tackle these problems by being located on strategic locations in agricultural areas to gather the fresh produce to load them on rail infrastructure, and being located as well as in urban centres to redistribute food to consumption and vending locations. They are inscribed in a larger strategy to promote a maximum of food self-sufficiency within the region and decarbonizing the food supply.

Spatial Dimension

» Strategic locations in rural areas next to agricultural areas
» Locations in every city with more than 5,000 inhabitants

Carbon Impacts

» Facilitate the transport of local food and encourage local food circles
» Decarbonize food transport by switching to rail-based transportation

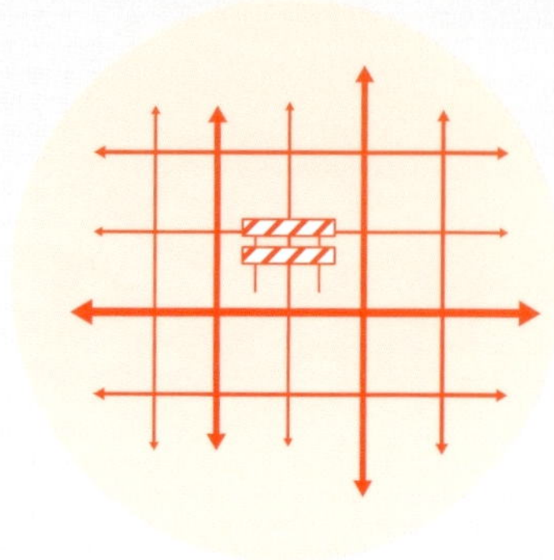

Zero-Carbon Street Grid

Adapt streets and roads for active mobility

Current mobility infrastructure consists mainly of roads for motorized vehicles. In order to change our ways of moving, this has to change: Our network has to provide space for pedestrians and bike users alike, existing spaces need to be rethought and redistributed. The environment has to be made attractive to bike, through providing shadows, planting trees and unsealing concrete land. On a smaller level, this approach is based on the concept of the "Superblock" but transferred to smaller cores of towns and villages. Only few roads stay accessible for motorized traffic, while smaller streets are reserved for residents and active mobility. This creates more liveable streets with important potential for greenery.

Spatial Dimension

» Reorganize motorized traffic and reserve smaller neighbourhood streets for active mobility

Carbon Impacts

» Reduce emissions from motorized traffic
» Encourage active mobility as a main mode of transport

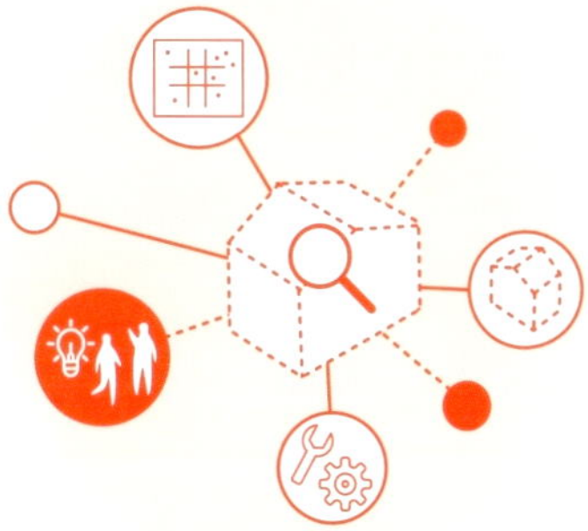

Metropolitan Vacancy Agency

Tackle the issue of vacant buildings

The agency working on metropolitan level should manage and activate the empty building stock and encourage new uses as well as activate empty apartments for housing needs. This is also essential in finding solutions to accommodate population growth on a large territory while working with the existing built urban fabric and revitalizing monofunctional areas with potential for new uses.

Spatial Dimension

- Create higher density in more populated areas (Cities with over 5,000 inhabitants)
- Create higher density in areas that are close to public transport infrastructure

Carbon Impacts

- Saves CO_2 by reducing new constructions and preserving soil that captures CO_2
- Creates denser territories along mobility infrastructure and facilitates sustainable modes of transport

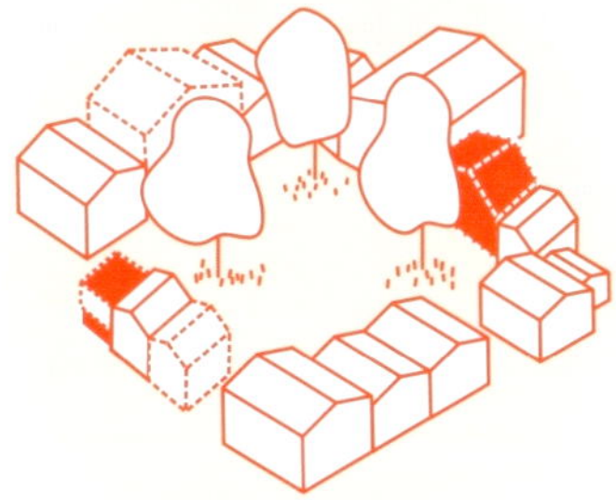

Multifunctional Centralities

Creating local centres with a diverse offer

Today, the metropolitan region relies on a few large centres of attraction that are characterised by a diverse offer of jobs, public, health, cultural and educational institutions to name a few. This creates long journeys for residents and large amounts of traffic. Creating local multifunctional centralities is thus necessary to develop an attractive offer near the home of residents and enable them to fulfill their needs within a small radius. Centres should be supported in their development since they play a role in a larger development of a polycentric metropolitan region.

Spatial Dimension

- According to the city size, every centre should fulfill a number of basic functions

Carbon Impacts

- Saving greenhouse gas emissions from transport through shortening everyday commutes

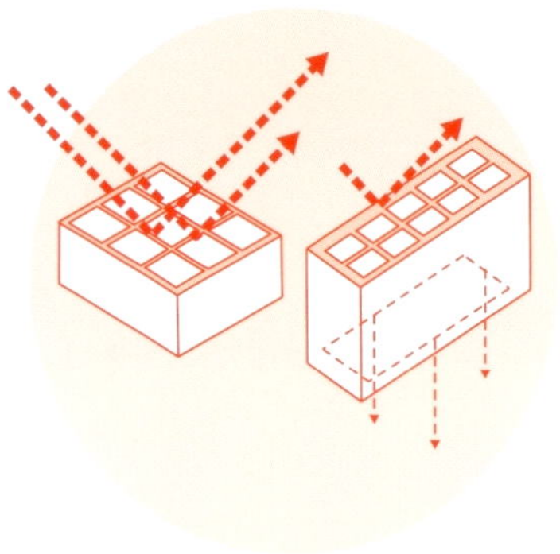

Buildings as Energy Producers

Transform the building stock to a collective power plant

On a metropolitan scale, buildings can be an important source of renewable energy production. To overcome individual actions and achieve a collective transformation, a larger strategy is needed, that takes the adaptation of power networks into account and maximizes incentives for transformation. New constructions need to produce more energy than they consume.

Spatial Dimension

» Adapt the existing building stock
» Strongly regulate new constructions
» Decentralize power networks

Carbon Impacts

» Reduce consumption of fossil resources

Multifunctional Energy Production

Find individual solutions for areas to produce renewable energy

Given that the energy supply should be entirely renewable in the future, large areas are required for energy production. In a densely populated region with limited space available, this calls to find solutions to combine energy production with other uses, such as agriculture. This multifunctional use of space permits to secure the integrity of important natural landscapes while advocating for an efficient use of space.

Spatial Dimension

» In agricultural areas with fitting land uses
» Combine infrastructure and industry with energy production

Carbon Impacts

» Expand renewable energy production and reduce need for fossil energy

Limited Traffic Zones

Reduce motorized traffic in dense areas to favour active mobility and public transport

Within the zone, which can be implemented quickly, motorized traffic is prohibited and a fee is charged for entering the zone. Exact regulations can vary and be temporarily reinforced. Stronger regulation of motorized traffic could have positive effects on public space and its redistribution to sustainable forms of mobility, as well as reducing pollution in dense urbanized areas. Liberated public space should be redistributed and opened up.

Spatial Dimension

» In urban centres of more than 10,000 inhabitants

Carbon Impacts

» Reduce greenhouse gases from motorized traffic, especially for commuting purposes

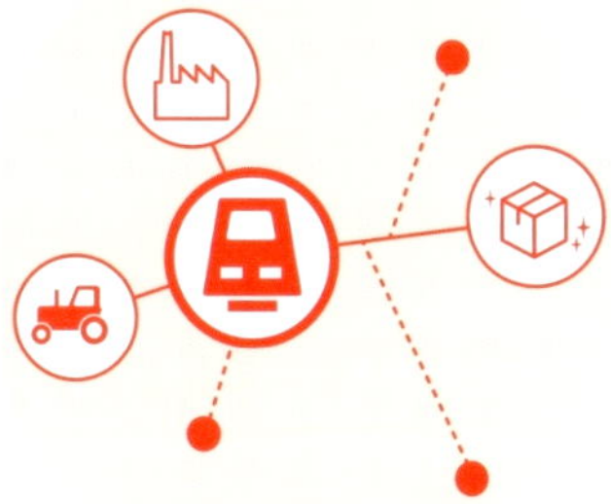

Rail-based Regional Good Distribution System

Establish sustainable regional distribution systems

To reduce carbon emissions from freight transport, goods need to be transported by rail rather than by road for longer (regional) distances. This is a significant step in reducing motorized traffic and mobility related emissions. This system works in connection with local distribution hubs and small scale concepts for the last mile. The rail system should be adapted to the centres of local food production.

Spatial Dimension

» Transport goods and produce along the existing railway lines in connection with local distribution hubs

Carbon Impacts

» Save carbon emissions caused by motorized freight transport

From Tools to Systems to Future Scenarios

To demonstrate the impact of the integrated tools for a zero carbon city region and to create visions in the specific spatial context, the developed tools are applied to the spatial context of the Vienna city region. In this way, future visions and new pathways towards a zero carbon city region will be demonstrated.

Achieving a zero-carbon metropolitan region requires coordinated efforts across sectors and boundaries. The tools presented are most effective when they work together as part of interconnected systems. It is within these systems that the tools can have a more powerful and coherent impact on the region's transition to climate neutrality. The application of the tools and systems to the spatial context results in innovative mappings that vividly illustrate the potential for transformative change in future scenarios, and by doing so, show new ways to achieve climate neutrality at the metropolitan scale. These scenarios are not just visual representations; they serve as powerful tools for understanding how spatial changes can lead to significant reductions in greenhouse gas emissions across the region and, more importantly, present visions of what a zero-carbon future could look like in the Vienna Metropolitan Region.

This approach is particularly effective because it is cross-sectoral and interdisciplinary, drawing on the comprehensive data collection of the Emerging Phenomena Atlas as well as expertise and policies from different sectors to create a coherent vision for climate action at the metropolitan level. By using tools developed through extensive research, dialogue, knowledge sharing and best practice collection, the approach ensures that the strategies and tools are not only effective and integrated, but also adaptable to the unique challenges and opportunities of other city regions. This makes the actions outlined in the toolbox and the scenarios more tangible and applicable beyond the Vienna context, providing a model that other metropolitan areas can follow to achieve similar goals.

Scenarios

1 Establishing 30-Minute Proximity Territories
2 Favoring Density and Restricting Land Consumption
3 Empowering a Network of Multifunctional Centralities
4 Fostering Local Food Cycles and Self-Sufficiency
5 Protecting Natural Resources and Landscapes

Scenario 1

Establishing 30-Minute Proximity Territories

The “Establishing 30-Minute Proximity Territories” scenario for the Vienna metropolitan area envisions a connected, sustainable mobility network that reduces car dependency and improves accessibility. By improving the frequency of existing public transport, creating safe cycle routes, and establishing multimodal mobility hubs, residents can access essential services, jobs, and leisure activities within a 30-minute commute. This polycentric approach strengthens regional sub-centers, encourages active mobility, revitalizes local economies, and promotes social equity, creating a balanced, accessible metropolitan region centered on sustainable, multimodal transportation options.

Findings Atlas

» 43.2% of the working population in the region does not work and live in the same municipality, but 68.1% commute only up to 20 km.

» The mobility sector accounts for 33.9 percent of greenhouse gas emissions in the metropolitan region.

» Density saves precious land: Even though 35% of Vienna’s permanent settlement area is sealed, the average sealed surface per inhabitant in Lower Austria and Burgenland is over 7 times as high.

Strategies

» **Build a 15-minute city and a 30-minute territory for shorter journeys, better connections and a higher quality of life.**

» **Create a street grid that strengthens the active mobility network and makes walking and biking more attractive.**

» **Develop a well-functioning public transportation system that provides sustainable and fast connections over long distances and serves as the backbone of metropolitan development.**

» **Develop decentralized multi-functional mobility systems and last mile concepts that include public transport on demand.**

» **Create efficient rail-based logistics systems with transition to local systems.**

» **Program multi-functional spaces to strengthen and diversify local centralities.**

Spatial Dimension

Connected mobility across city boundaries is essential to shift metropolitan mobility from the individual car to a multimodal network that combines active mobility infrastructure with the main public transport artery that serves as the backbone of metropolitan development.

Metropolitan Public Transport System

» The public transport system is the backbone for metropolitan mobility. Together with the metropolitan bike highway network it serves as the foundation for the 30-minute territories. Existing Infrastructure needs to be analysed, improved and extended in order to connect main centralities and transport as many citizens as posssible on a metropolitan and local level.

30-Minute Territories

» Based on the public transport infrastructure, 30-minute territories should be developed across municipal borders through the strengthening of regional sub-centres above 5,000 inhabitants and connections to surrounding towns within a 30-minute bike radius. The aim is to facilitate shorter journeys and save greenhouse gas emissions from everyday mobility.

Multimodal Mobility Hubs

» Multimodal mobility hubs are located in centralities and on the nodes of mobility networks (e.g. major crossings of bike highways and public transport network). They vary in size according to its strategic importance within the mobility system and are responsible for the transition towards local central as well as decentral mobility modes.

Metropolitan Bike Highway Network

» The network of metropolitan bike highways serves as a central mobility infrastructure that supports and complements the public transportation system wihtin the metropolitan region. The network should connect every town with more than 2,000 inhabitans with each other and main mobility nodes. Existing bike connections need to be used and improved.

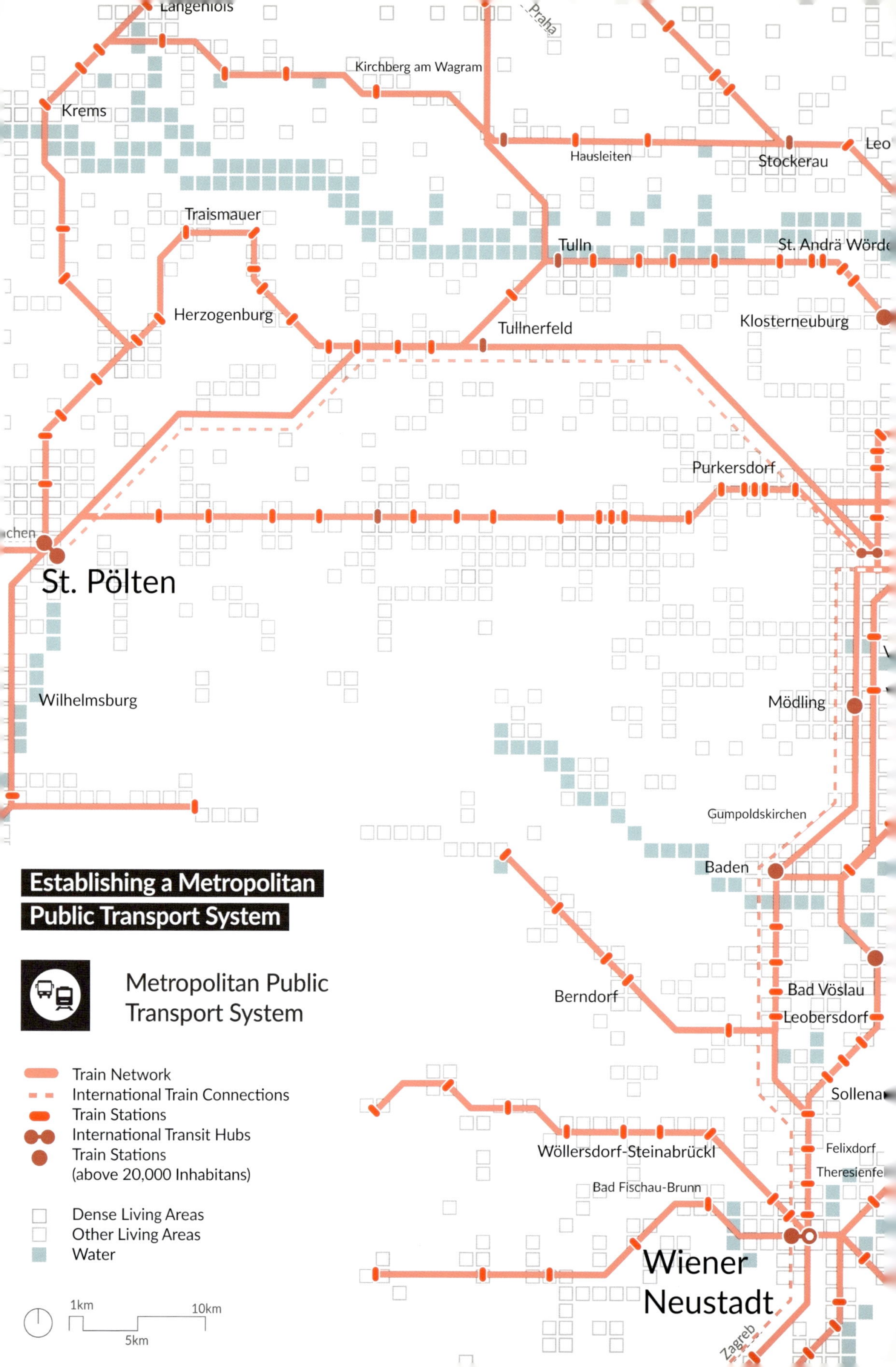
Establishing a Metropolitan
Public Transport System
Metropolitan Public
Transport System
Train Network
International Train Connections
Train Stations
International Transit Hubs
Train Stations
(above 20,000 Inhabitans)
Dense Living Areas
Other Living Areas
Water
1km
5km
10km
Langenlois
Praha
Kirchberg am Wagram
Krems
Hausleiten
Stockerau
Traismauer
Tulln
Herzogenburg
Tullnerfeld
Klosterneuburg
Purkersdorf
St. Pölten
Wilhelmsburg
Mödling
Gumpoldskirchen
Baden
Berndorf
Bad Vöslau
Leobersdorf
Wöllersdorf-Steinabrückl
Felixdorf
Bad Fischau-Brunn
Wiener
Neustadt
Zagreb

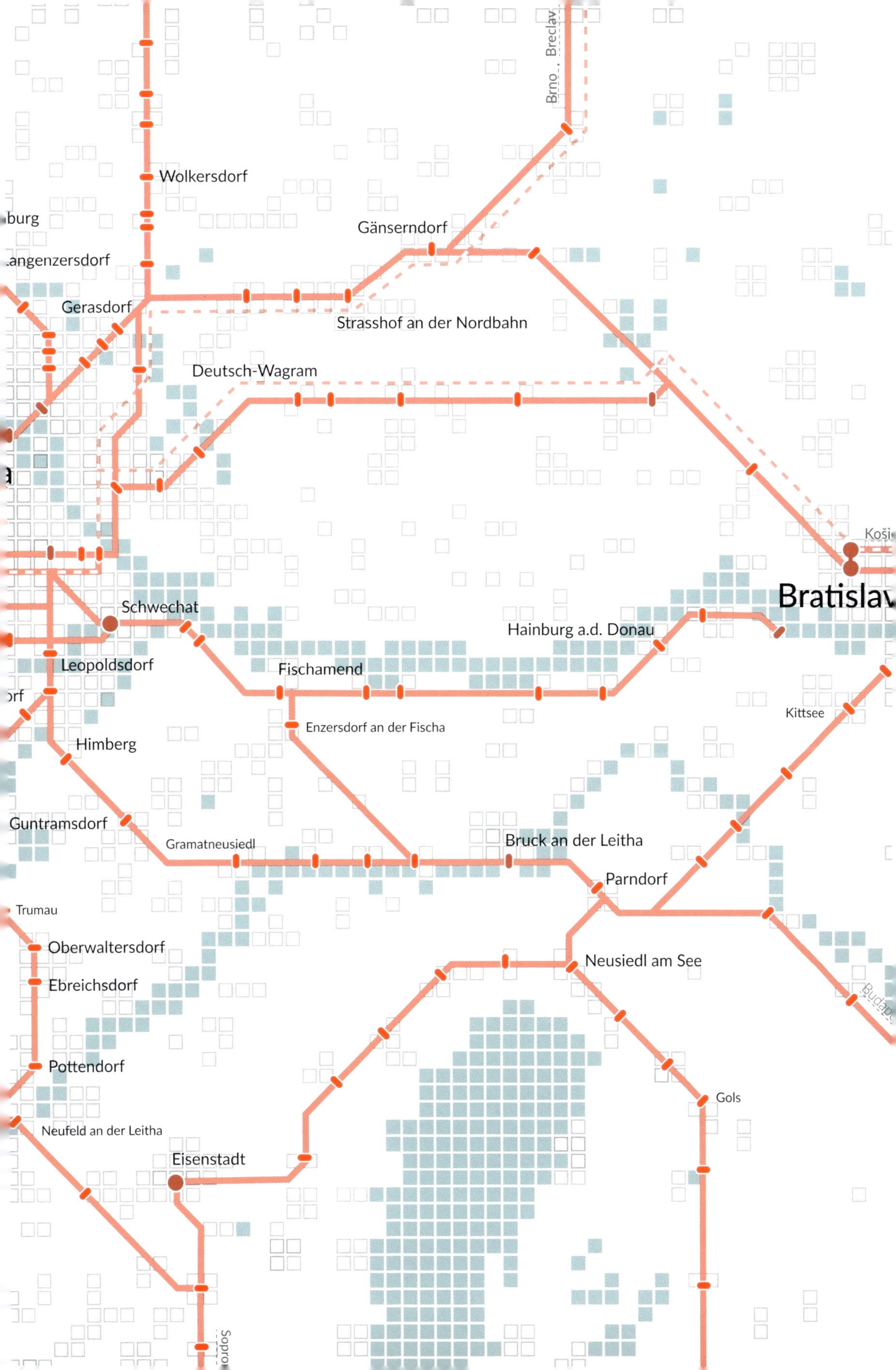

Brno
Breclav
Wolkersdorf
burg
Langenzersdorf
Gänserndorf
Gerasdorf
Strasshof an der Nordbahn
Deutsch-Wagram
Koši
Bratislav
Schwechat
Hainburg a.d. Donau
Leopoldsdorf
Fischamend
orf
Enzersdorf an der Fischa
Kittsee
Himberg
Guntramsdorf
Gramatneusiedl
Bruck an der Leitha
Parndorf
Trumau
Oberwaltersdorf
Neusiedl am See
Ebreichsdorf
Budap
Pottendorf
Gols
Neufeld an der Leitha
Eisenstadt
Sopro

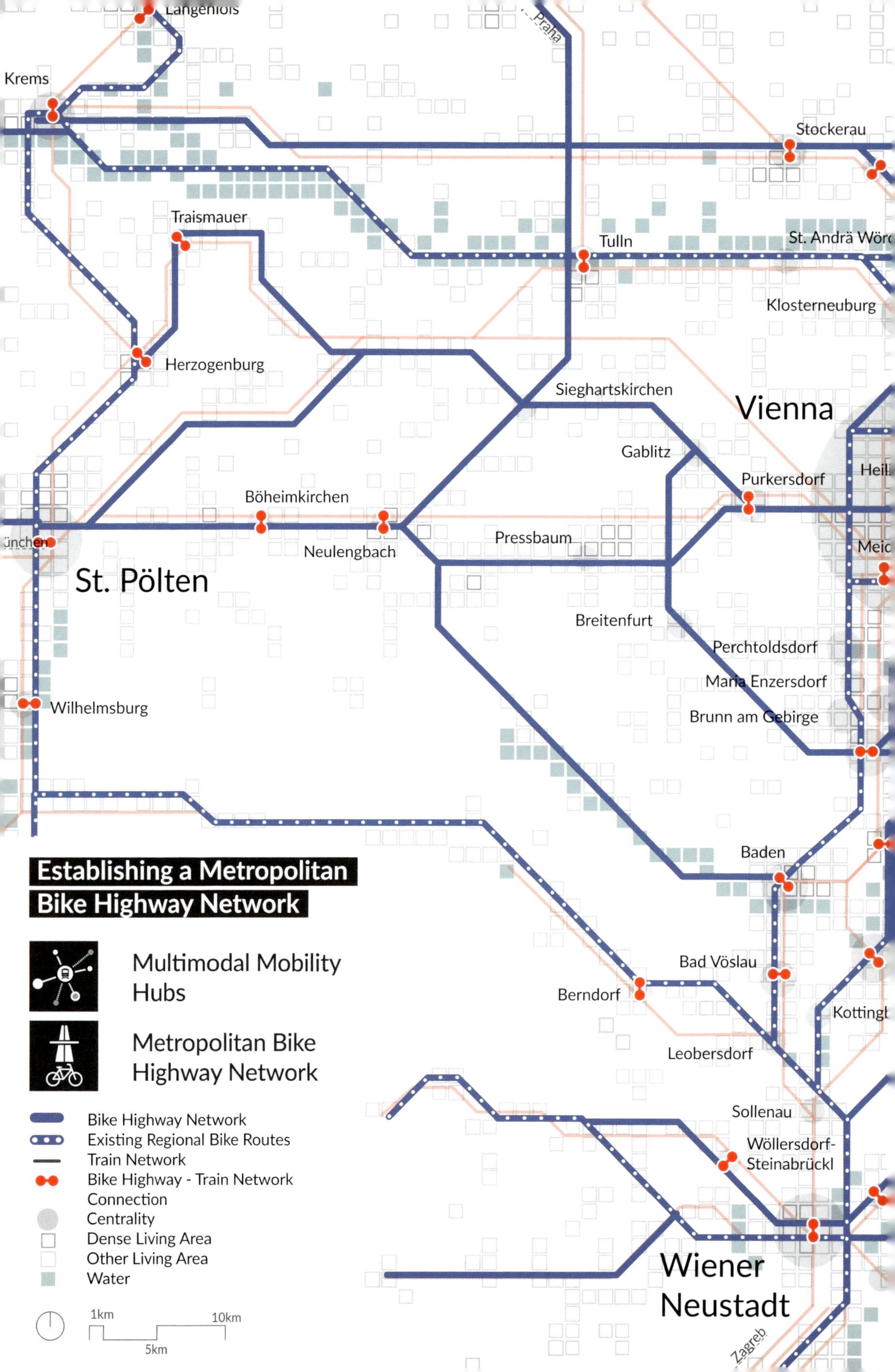

Establishing a Metropolitan Bike Highway Network
Multimodal Mobility Hubs
Metropolitan Bike Highway Network
Bike Highway Network
Existing Regional Bike Routes
Train Network
Bike Highway - Train Network Connection
Centrality
Dense Living Area
Other Living Area
Water
1km
5km
10km
Langenlois
Krems
Praha
Stockerau
Traismauer
Tulln
St. Andrä Wörd
Klosterneuburg
Herzogenburg
Sieghartskirchen
Vienna
Gablitz
Purkersdorf
Heili
Böheimkirchen
Pressbaum
Meid
ünchen
Neulengbach
St. Pölten
Breitenfurt
Perchtoldsdorf
Maria Enzersdorf
Brunn am Gebirge
Wilhelmsburg
Baden
Bad Vöslau
Berndorf
Kottingb
Leobersdorf
Sollenau
Wöllersdorf-Steinabrückl
Wiener Neustadt
Zagreb

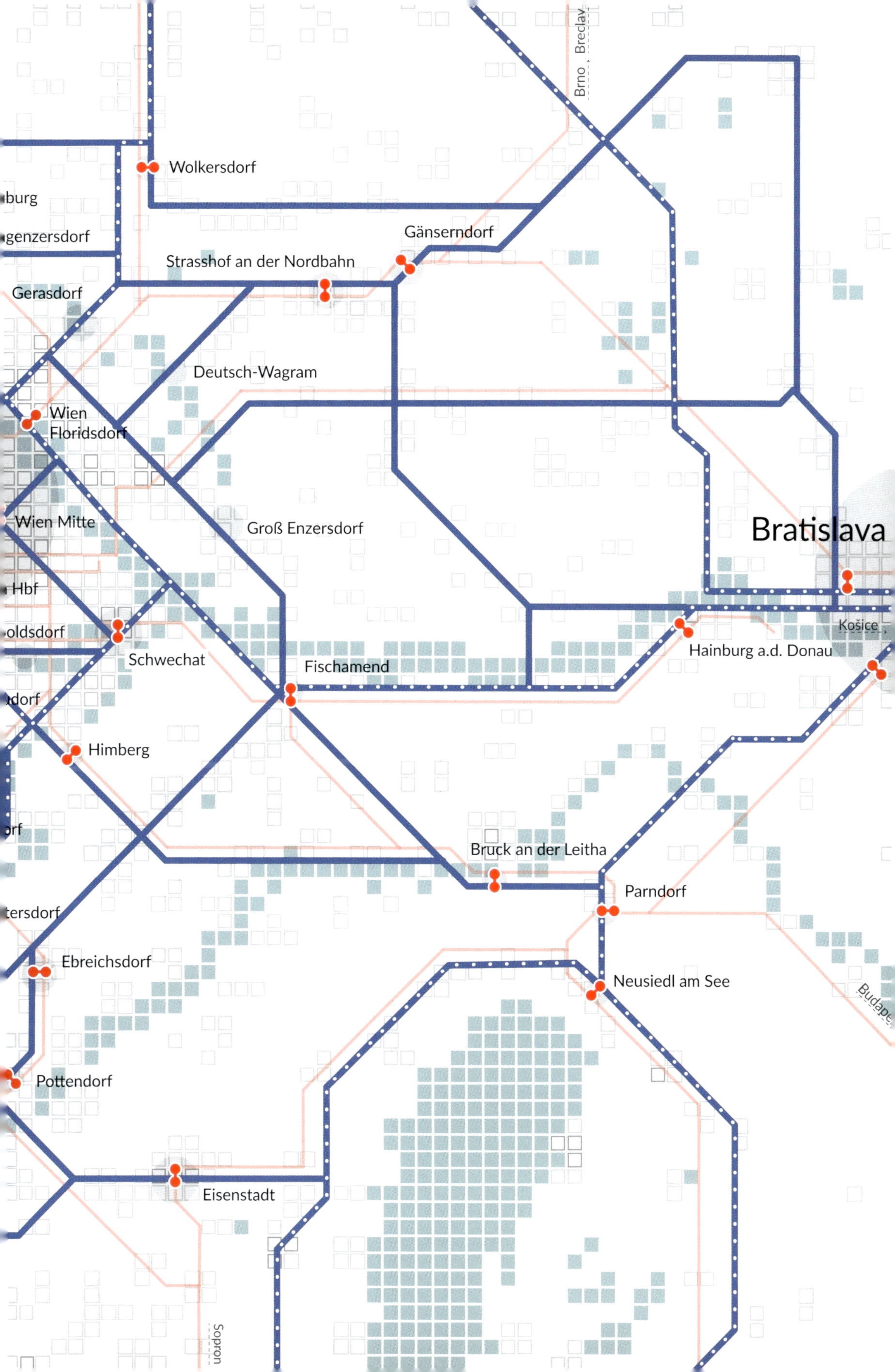
Brno , Breclav
Wolkersdorf
burg
genzersdorf
Gänserndorf
Strasshof an der Nordbahn
Gerasdorf
Deutsch-Wagram
Wien Floridsdorf
Wien Mitte
Groß Enzersdorf
Bratislava
Hbf
oldsdorf
Schwechat
Fischamend
Košice
Hainburg a.d. Donau
dorf
Himberg
orf
Bruck an der Leitha
Parndorf
tersdorf
Ebreichsdorf
Neusiedl am See
Pottendorf
Eisenstadt
Sopron

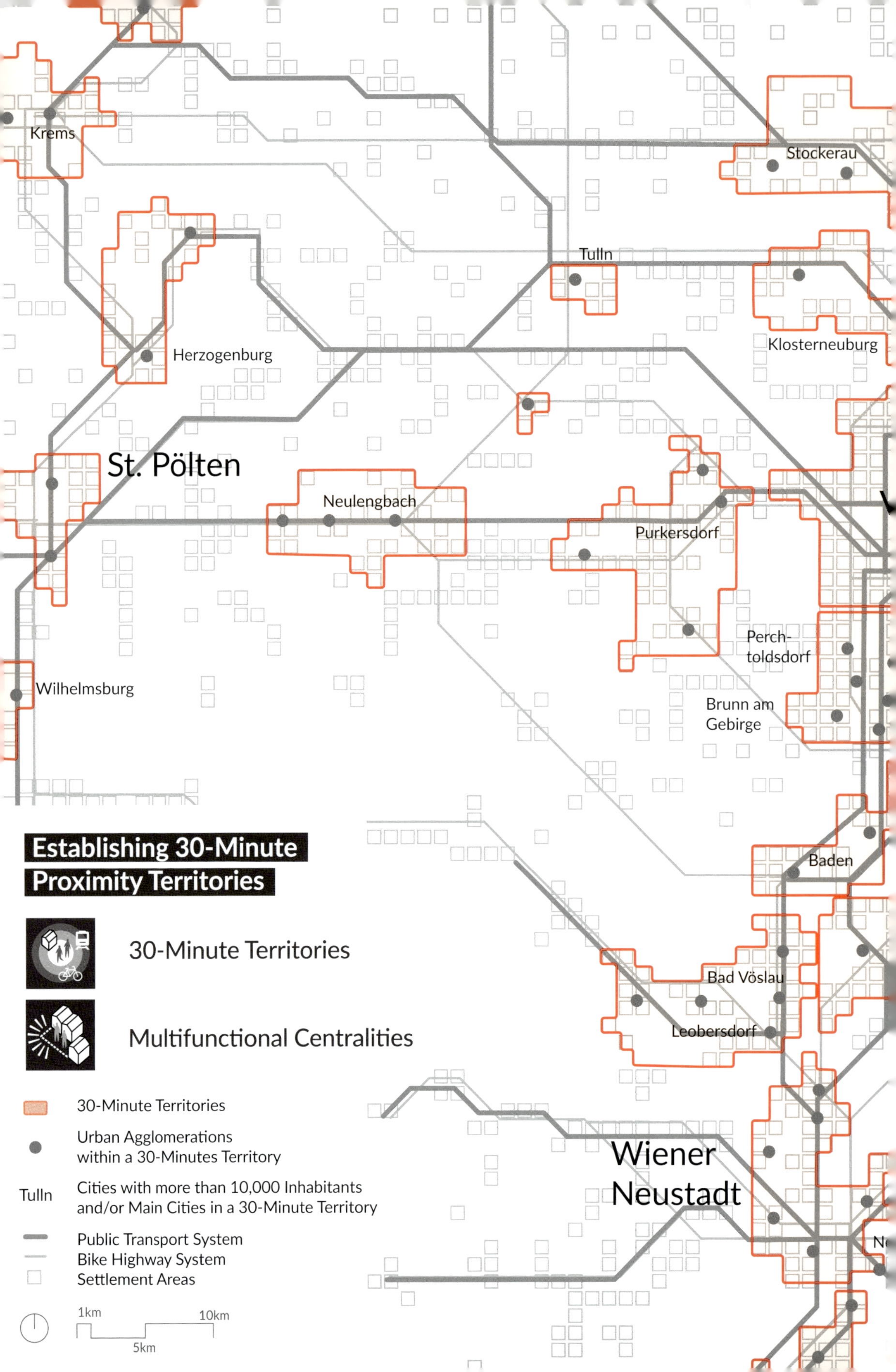
Krems
Stockerau
Tulln
Herzogenburg
Klosterneuburg
St. Pölten
Neulengbach
Purkersdorf
Perch-
toldsdorf
Wilhelmsburg
Brunn am
Gebirge
Baden
Bad Vöslau
Leobersdorf
Wiener
Neustadt
Establishing 30-Minute
Proximity Territories
30-Minute Territories
Multifunctional Centralities
30-Minute Territories
Urban Agglomerations
within a 30-Minutes Territory
Tulln
Cities with more than 10,000 Inhabitants
and/or Main Cities in a 30-Minute Territory
Public Transport System
Bike Highway System
Settlement Areas
1km
5km
10km

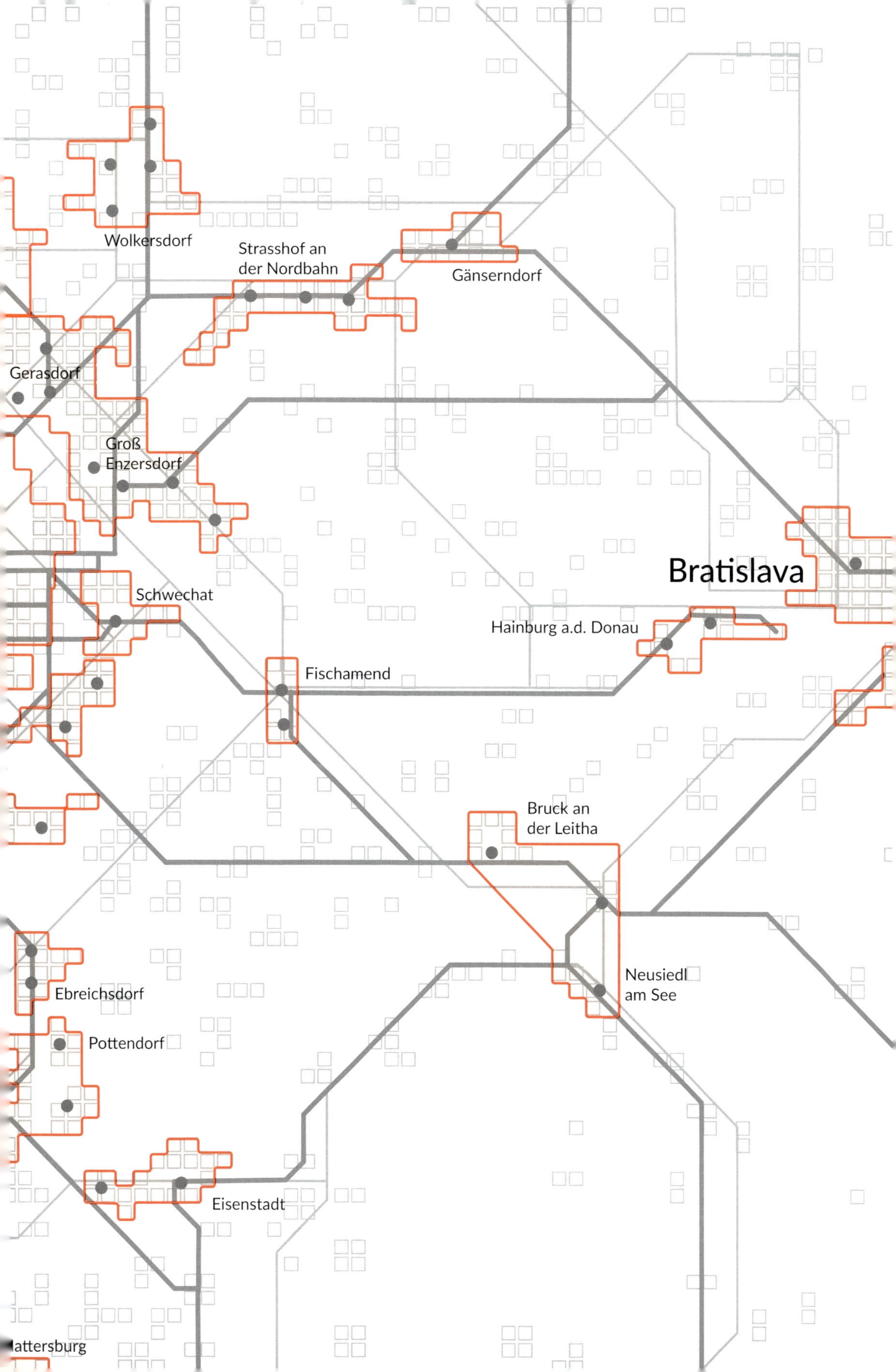

Wolkersdorf
Strasshof an der Nordbahn
Gänserndorf
Gerasdorf
Groß Enzersdorf
Bratislava
Schwechat
Hainburg a.d. Donau
Fischamend
Bruck an der Leitha
Neusiedl am See
Ebreichsdorf
Pottendorf
Eisenstadt
attersburg

Scenario 2

Favoring Density and Restricting Land Consumption

The scenario "Favoring Density and Restricting Land Consumption" promotes sustainable growth by densifying urban spaces and limiting land consumption. To support this, vacant buildings and underused spaces are reused to minimize the need for new construction, reducing environmental impacts while creating vibrant, mixed-use local centers. Strict zoning codes will limit urban sprawl and protect green and agricultural lands essential for carbon sequestration and biodiversity. New development will focus on high-density housing and ban inefficient, land-intensive single-family homes to reduce environmental costs and support public transit. A Metropolitan Vacancy Agency will manage vacant properties, activating vacant land for housing and revitalizing single-use areas. This coordinated effort will promote a compact, climate-resilient metropolitan fabric that improves quality of life and preserves valuable land and resources for future generations.

Findings Atlas

» More than 425,000 new inhabitants are expected in the region until 2050.

» 24,644 new single family homes were constructed in the metropolitan region between 2020 and 2023 on more than 385 ha of land.

» The region is not able to keep track of its vacancy rate, and as a result, it is unaware of its current statistics

Strategies

» **Build a 15-minute city and a 30-minute territory for shorter journeys, better connections and a higher quality of life.**

» **Develop a well-functioning public transportation system that provides sustainable and fast connections over long distances and serves as the backbone of metropolitan development.**

» **Create resilient, multi-functional and accessible public spaces for all.**

» **Avoid any construction of new single family housing and focus on denser housing with a high quality of life.**

» **Favor qualitative and flexible stock development instead of designating new construction land.**

Zoning Codes limiting Urban Sprawl

» New constructions are limited to areas in proximity to existing public transport offers. Strong, binding settlement borders limit constructions. No constructions of new single-family homes are allowed.

Densification and strict zoning are essential to keep distances short and to save land for agriculture, renewable energy production, and carbon sequestration. Redensification of the existing building stock and activation of vacant land reduces the construction of new buildings.

Qualitative Redensification

» To limit urban sprawl and encourage short distances, a focus lies on the qualitative redensification of the existing building stock. Towns with more than 5,000 inhabitans should be densified in their inner cores and areas close to public transportation must open for densification as well.

Metropolitan Vacancy Agency

» The metropolitan vacancy agency serves as a platform to collect data of vacant spaces and homes locally and in the following steps initiate temporary and permanent uses for them, to activate the building stock to a maximum.

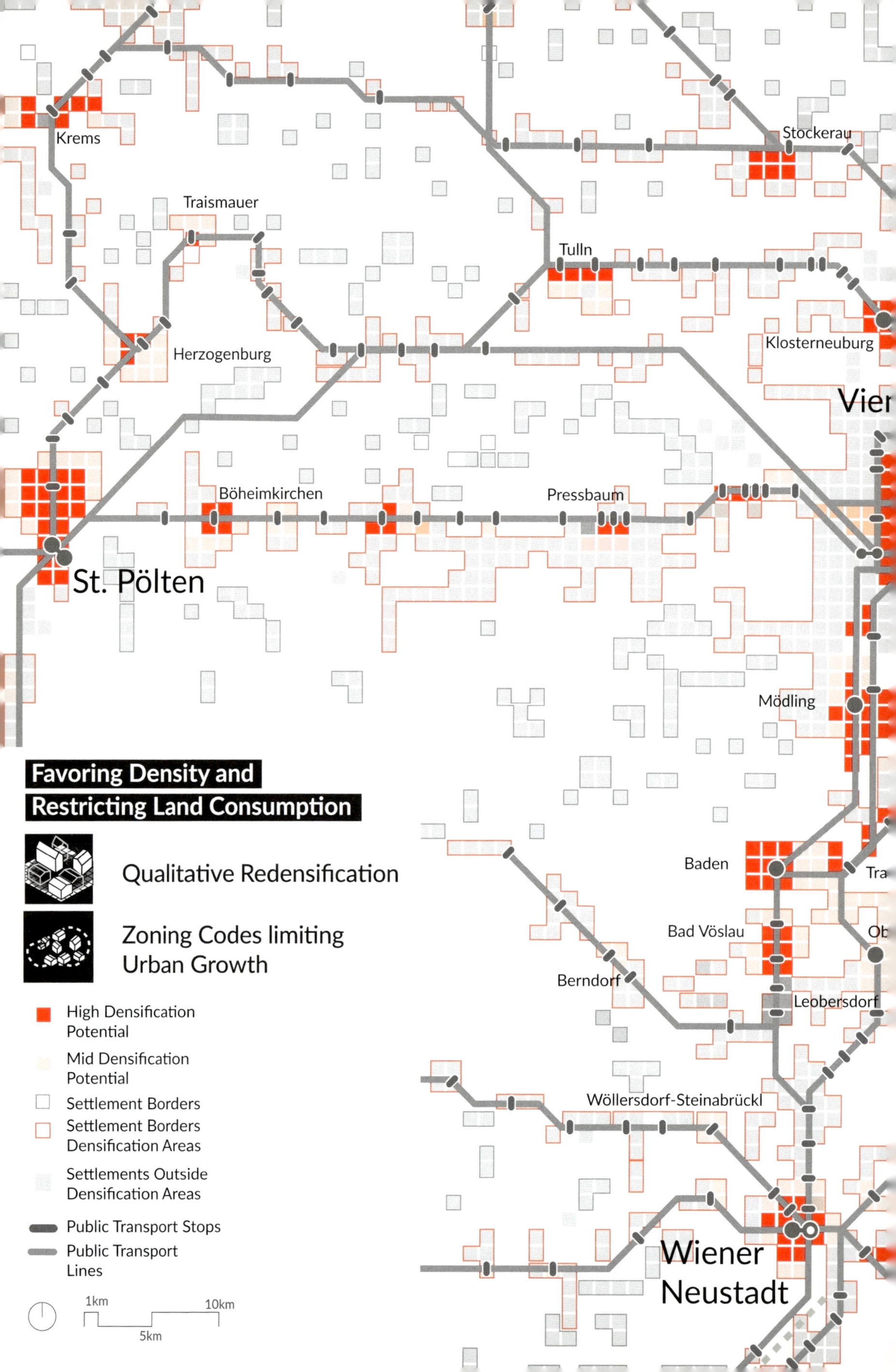

Krems
Stockerau
Traismauer
Tulln
Herzogenburg
Klosterneuburg
Vien
Böheimkirchen
Pressbaum
St. Pölten
Mödling
Favoring Density and
Restricting Land Consumption
Qualitative Redensification
Zoning Codes limiting
Urban Growth
Baden
Tra
Bad Vöslau
Ob
Berndorf
Leobersdorf
High Densification
Potential
Mid Densification
Potential
Settlement Borders
Settlement Borders
Densification Areas
Settlements Outside
Densification Areas
Wöllersdorf-Steinabrückl
Public Transport Stops
Public Transport
Lines
Wiener
Neustadt
1km
10km
5km

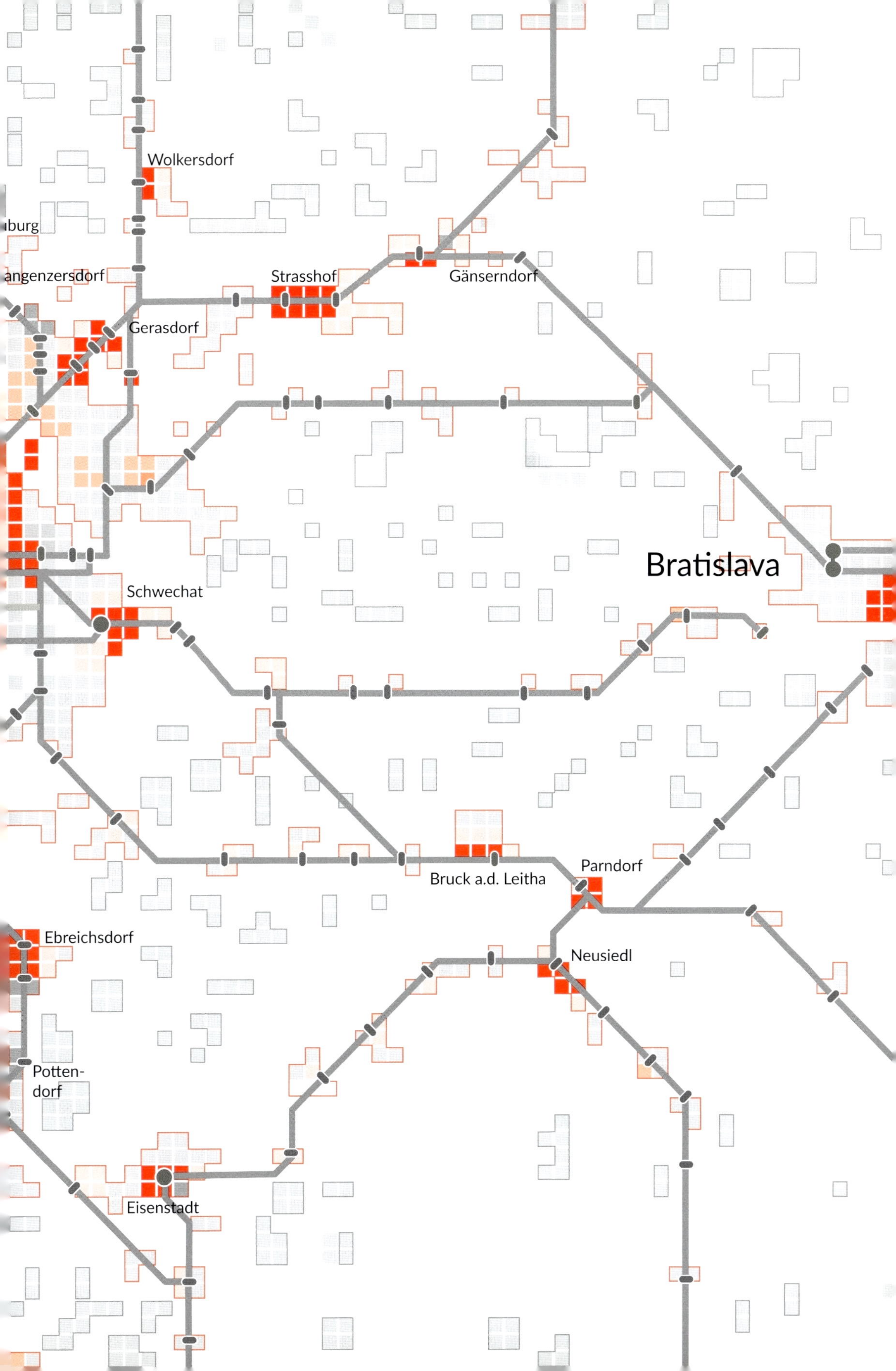
Wolkersdorf
ıburg
angenzersdorf
Strasshof
Gänserndorf
Gerasdorf
Bratislava
Schwechat
Bruck a.d. Leitha
Parndorf
Ebreichsdorf
Neusiedl
Potten-
dorf
Eisenstadt

Scenario 3

Empowering a Network of Multifunctional Centralities

This scenario envisions a polycentric metropolitan region where residents in suburban and rural areas can access essential services, health care, education, employment, culture, recreation, and amenities within 30 minutes by bicycle or public transit. By developing local hubs and centers with diverse amenities in suburban and rural areas, this approach reduces the need for long commutes to urban centers, reduces emissions, and improves the quality of daily life. Strengthening regional subcentres fosters an interconnected network of communities, ensures equitable and convenient access to resources, and promotes a sustainable, resilient, and accessible metropolitan landscape.

Findings Atlas

» Most journeys between Vienna and the region are done by car, and the number of commuters as well as travel-distances in the region are increasing.

» Areas with a high population density have lower greenhouse gas emissions per person.

Strategies

» **Build a 15-minute city and a 30-minute territory for shorter journeys, better connections and a higher quality of life.**

» **Develop a well-functioning public transportation system that provides sustainable and fast connections and serves as the backbone of metropolitan development.**

» **Relocate public funds to invest in innovative zero-carbon mobility systems.**

» **Program multi-functional spaces to strengthen and diversify local centralities.**

» **Promote a new qualitative density with a high quality of life and flexibility through new ways of living together that focus on more common space.**

» **Favor qualitative and flexible stock development instead of designating new construction land.**

Spatial Dimension

30-Minute Territories

» Based on the public transport infrastructure, 30-minute territories should be developed across municipal borders through the strengthening of regional sub-centres above 5,000 inhabitants and connections to surrounding towns within a 30-minute bike radius. The aim is to facilitate shorter journeys and save greenhouse gas emissions from everyday mobility.

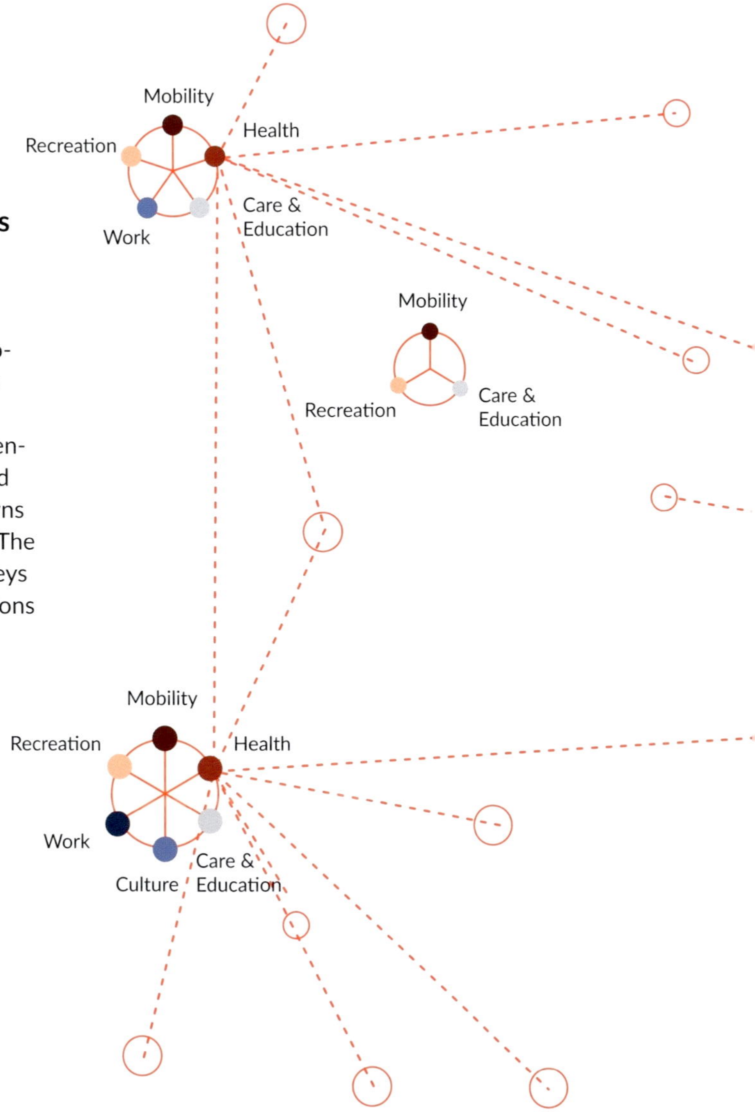

Multifunctional Centralities

» Centres in the metropolitan area should provide a number of essential functions according to their size. A polycentric network of multifunctional centralities saves long commuting distances throughout the region and promotes proximity.

The requalification and creation of multifunctional centralities is essential for the balanced development of the entire region, ensuring the accessibility of basic services and needs, thus saving greenhouse gas emissions by reducing long commutes, and ultimately improving the quality of life of citizens.

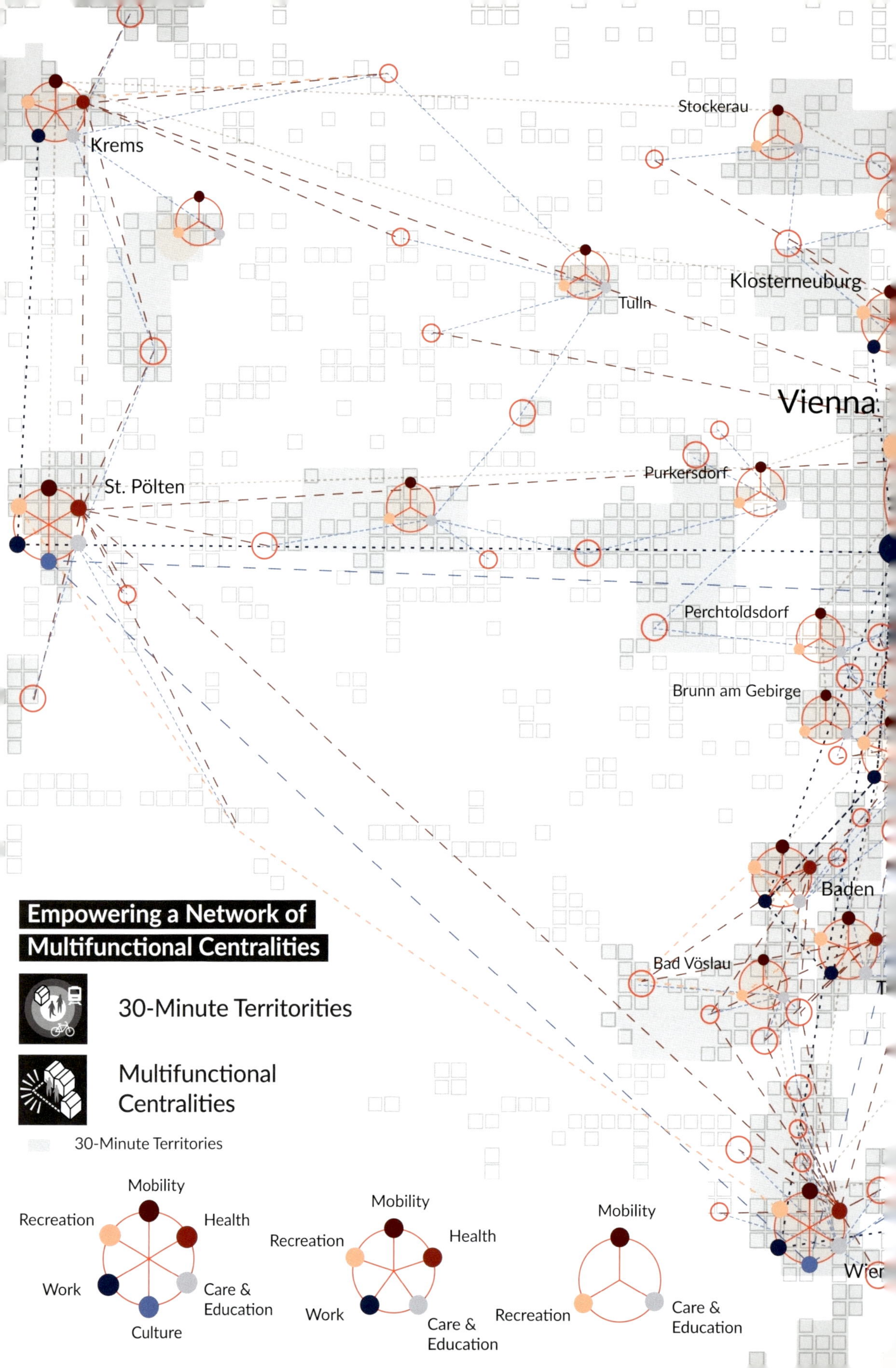
Krems
Stockerau
Tulln
Klosterneuburg
Vienna
Purkersdorf
St. Pölten
Perchtoldsdorf
Brunn am Gebirge
Baden
Bad Vöslau
Empowering a Network of Multifunctional Centralities
30-Minute Territories
Multifunctional Centralities
30-Minute Territories
Mobility
Recreation
Health
Work
Care & Education
Culture
Mobility
Recreation
Health
Work
Care & Education
Mobility
Recreation
Care & Education

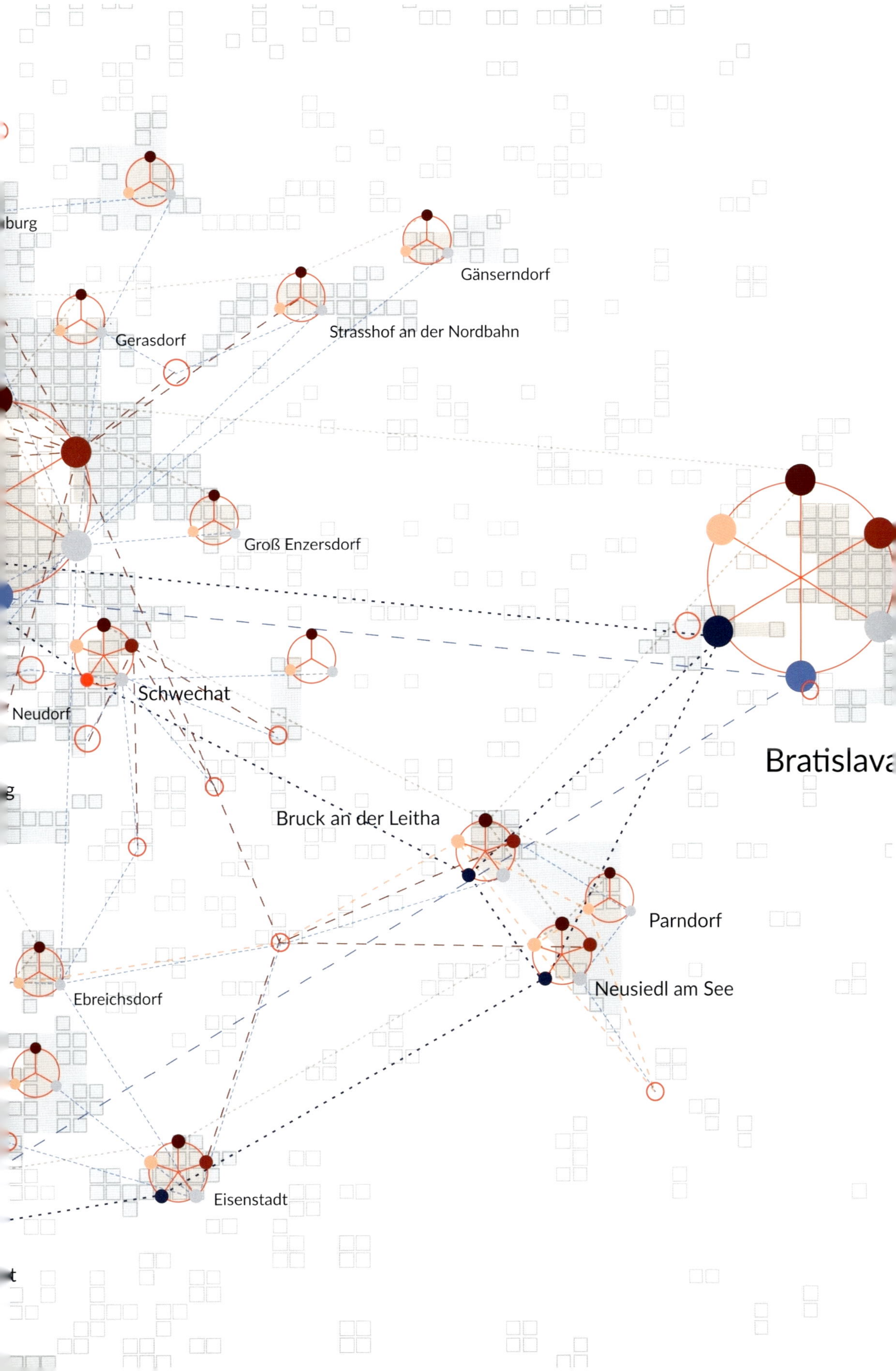

burg
Gänserndorf
Gerasdorf
Strasshof an der Nordbahn
Groß Enzersdorf
Schwechat
Neudorf
Bratislava
Bruck an der Leitha
Parndorf
Neusiedl am See
Ebreichsdorf
Eisenstadt

Scenario 4

Fostering Local Food Cycles and Self-Sufficiency

In the “Fostering Local Food Cycles and Self-Sufficiency” scenario, the Vienna metropolitan area transitions to a resilient, low-emission food system based on regional self-sufficiency and stronger producer-consumer linkages. District farms, located between urban and rural areas, serve as agricultural hubs, increasing local food production and promoting sustainable agriculture through education and public engagement. These farms serve as “agricultural living laboratories”, testing sustainable farming techniques and reconnecting consumers and producers. A rail-based distribution network efficiently transports locally grown produce from these farms to locally distributed District Market Hubs, reducing carbon emissions and food imports. Accessible District Markets provide locally grown, plant-based food, encouraging healthier eating habits and strengthening local economies. Together, these interconnected systems create a sustainable, self-sufficient, and health-promoting food cycle that connects urban and rural areas within a cohesive, resilient regional food system.

Findings Atlas

» Vienna’s current food consumption requires 639,000 ha, but only 8% of Vienna’s food consumption footprint is located within its region.

» Austrians eat 12.5 times as much red meat as reccomended in the Planetary Health Diet, that combines health aspects with planetary boundaries.

» In Austria, 78% of goods are transported by road.

Strategies

» **Create metropolitan landscapes that produce and regenerate.**

» **Foster local and responsible responsible agricultural systems for metropolitan self-sufficiency.**

» **Foster a societal shift towards a primarily plant-based planetary health diet.**

» **Support a transition of consuming habits towards the limits of our ecological footprint.**

» **Create conditions for regional food circularity.**

» **Establish a metropolitan system that reuses and recycles materials.**

» **Prioritize local resources and minimize external dependencies.**

Spatial Dimension

Distribution Hubs

Rail-based Regional Good Distribution System

» Distribution hubs, located next to agricultural areas, in connection with a rail based system enable a decarbonization of food transport to the urban areas of the region.

By strengthening the links between urban and agricultural areas and creating proximity in food supply, a decarbonization of the food system becomes possible. The supply of food in markets encourages a shift to a predominantly plant-based, locally sourced diet.

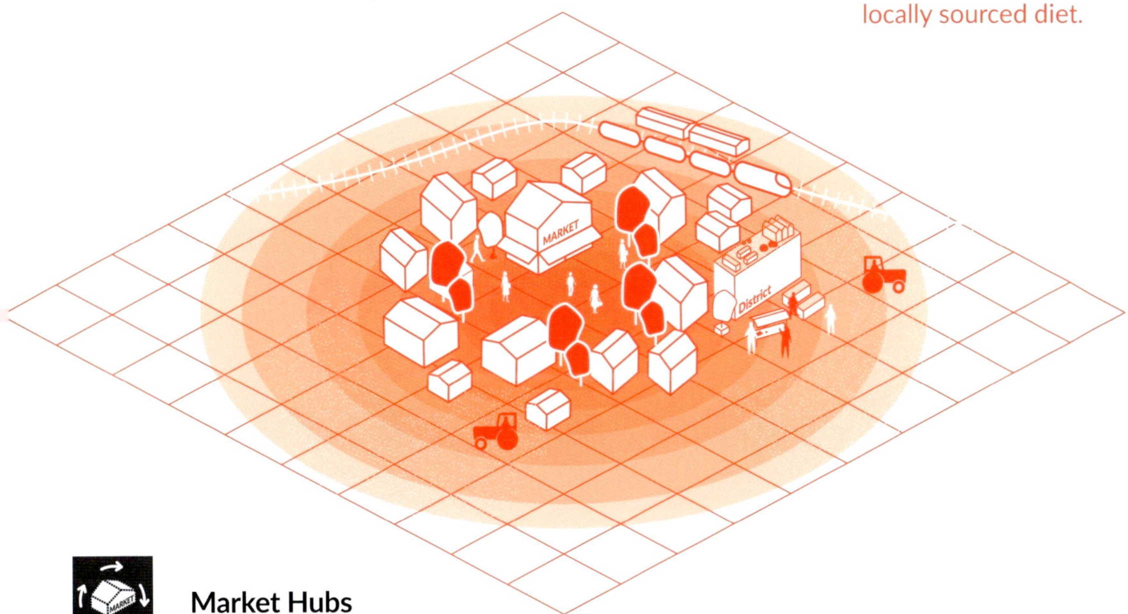

Market Hubs

» Every town with more than 3,500 inhabitants should have a farmer shop and every city with more than 5,000 inhabitants should have a farmers market hall, to reduce the distance between production and consumption of food. This saves transport emissions and is a lever to promote a healthier diet on metropolitan level.

District Farms

» Every town with more than 5,000 inhabitants should have a district farm, it should be located on the verge between urban and agricultural areas, creating a social link between producer and consumer. They are pioneers in regionalizing food supply and testing grounds for new forms of agriculture.

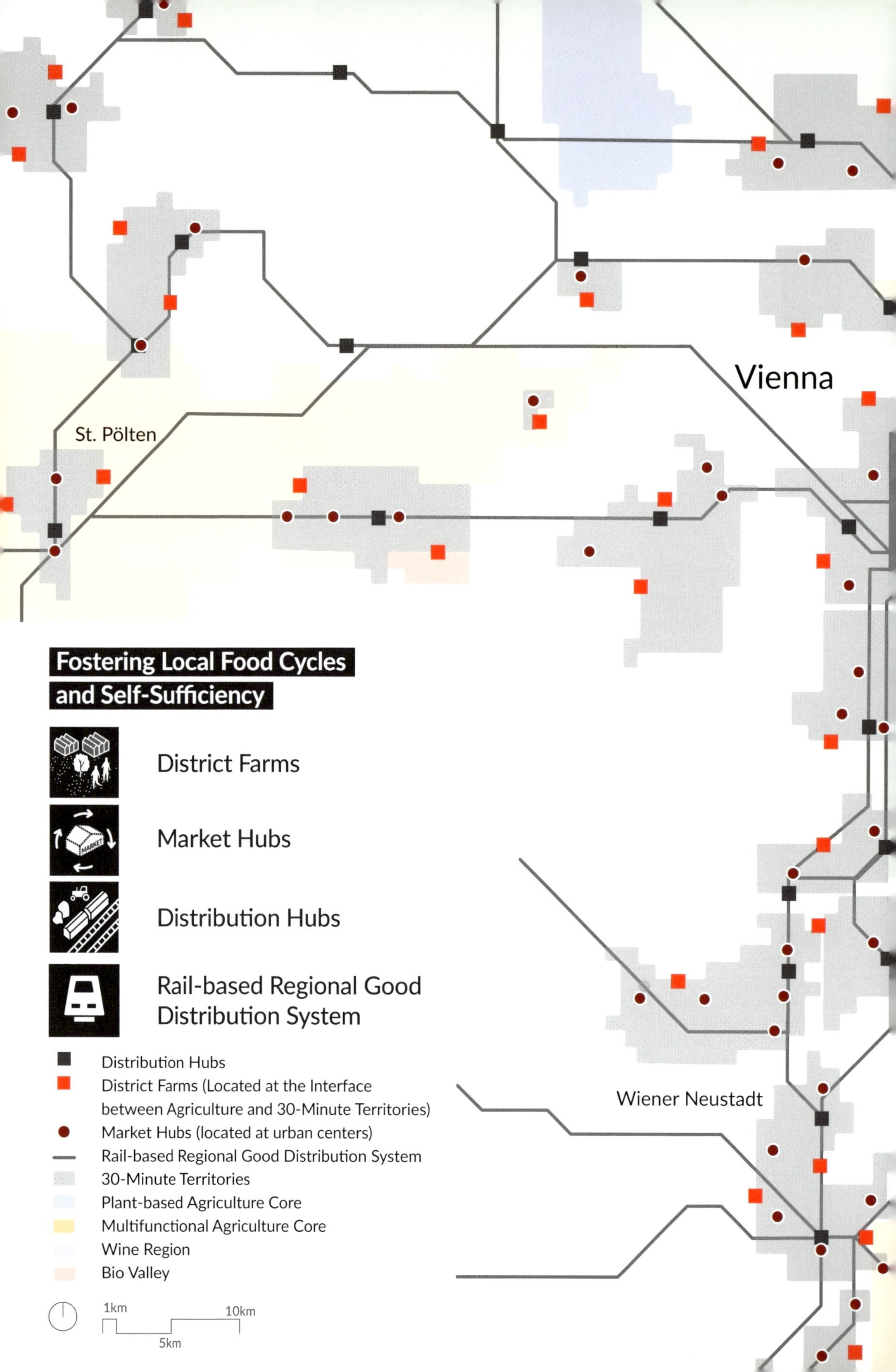
Vienna
St. Pölten
Wiener Neustadt
Fostering Local Food Cycles and Self-Sufficiency
District Farms
Market Hubs
Distribution Hubs
Rail-based Regional Good Distribution System
Distribution Hubs
District Farms (Located at the Interface between Agriculture and 30-Minute Territories)
Market Hubs (located at urban centers)
Rail-based Regional Good Distribution System
30-Minute Territories
Plant-based Agriculture Core
Multifunctional Agriculture Core
Wine Region
Bio Valley
1km
10km
5km

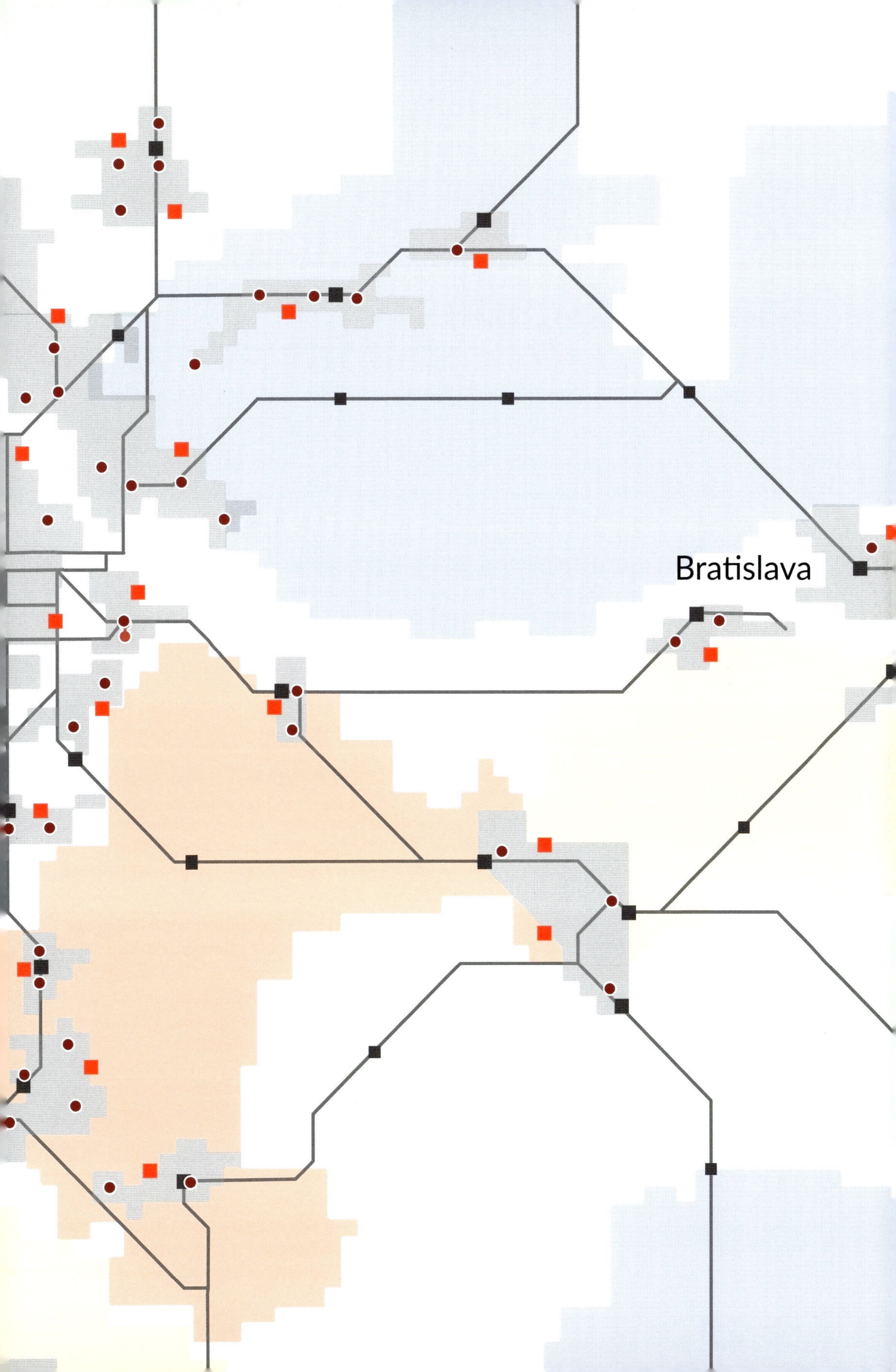
Bratislava

Scenario 5

Protecting Natural Resources and Landscapes

The "Protecting Natural Resources and Landscapes" scenario creates a sustainable, self-sufficient urban-rural ecosystem by integrating organic agriculture, multifunctional energy production, renewable energy buildings and circular water systems. Organic buffer zones around key natural landscapes preserve biodiversity by allowing only organic farming practices, reducing greenhouse gases and promoting ecological balance. Multifunctional energy production combines renewable energy production with agricultural land use, optimising space while maintaining landscape integrity. Buildings contribute to energy self-sufficiency by producing more renewable energy than they consume, transforming urban areas into an interconnected power grid. Finally, circular water systems prioritise the efficient recycling of waste and rainwater, conserving vital water resources and reducing overall energy consumption. Together, these elements create a resilient, sustainable blueprint for metropolitan areas.

Findings Atlas

» In 2021, Austrian forests captured 10.4 million tons of CO_2 equivalents, while artificialisation of land was responsible for 500,000 tons of CO_2 emissions.

» 2% of Austria's surface for wind production would produce more energy than Austria currently consumes.

Strategies

» **Create metropolitan landscapes that produce and regenerate.**

» **Decarbonize and decentralize metropolitan energy production.**

» **Create metropolitan landscapes for leisure & recreation within the region.**

» **Support a transition of consuming habits towards the limits of our ecological footprint.**

» **Prioritize local resources and minimize external dependencies.**

» **Shift from a linear to a circular water system.**

» **Avoid any construction of new single family housing and focus on denser housing with a high quality of life.**

Spatial Dimension

Bio Valley

Organic Protection Barriers

» The bio valley concept fosters biodiversity and saves greenhouse gases through promoting exclusively organic agriculture. First established as a pilot in an area that is both densely populated and important for agricultural production, it can then be extended further to other areas. Protection Barriers around important natural landscapes protect their biodiversity through allowing only organic agriculture.

Circular Water Systems

» Water will even be a more precious resource in the future: Efficient waste and rainwater cycles save energy and drinking water.

Buildings as Energy Producer

» This project transforms buildings into renewable energy producers, turning the building stock into a coherent energy generation network. By reimagining buildings not just as consumers but as contributors to energy networks, this approach promotes a self-sustaining urban environment.

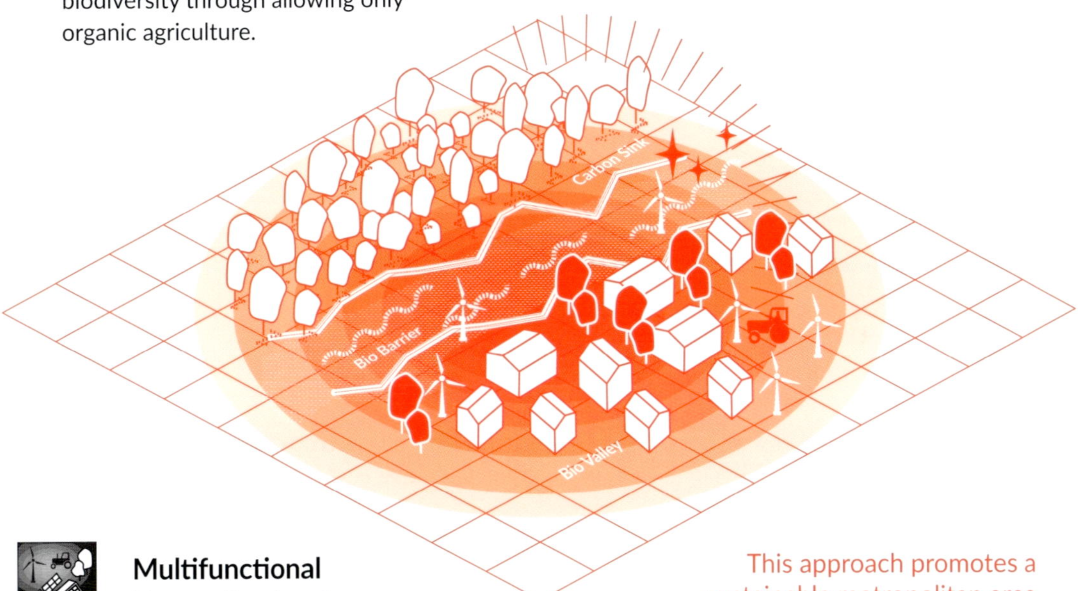

Multifunctional Energy Production

» To be able to meet our energy demand and be self-sufficient through renewable energy sources exclusively, energy production should be combined with other land uses, such as agriculture. This secures the integrity of natural landscapes and promotes an efficient use of space.

This approach promotes a sustainable metropolitan area by integrating organic barriers protect biodiversity, while multifunctional energy production combines agriculture and renewable energy to optimise land use. Buildings generate surplus energy and circular water systems recycle resources, creating a resilient, self-sustaining urban-rural environment.

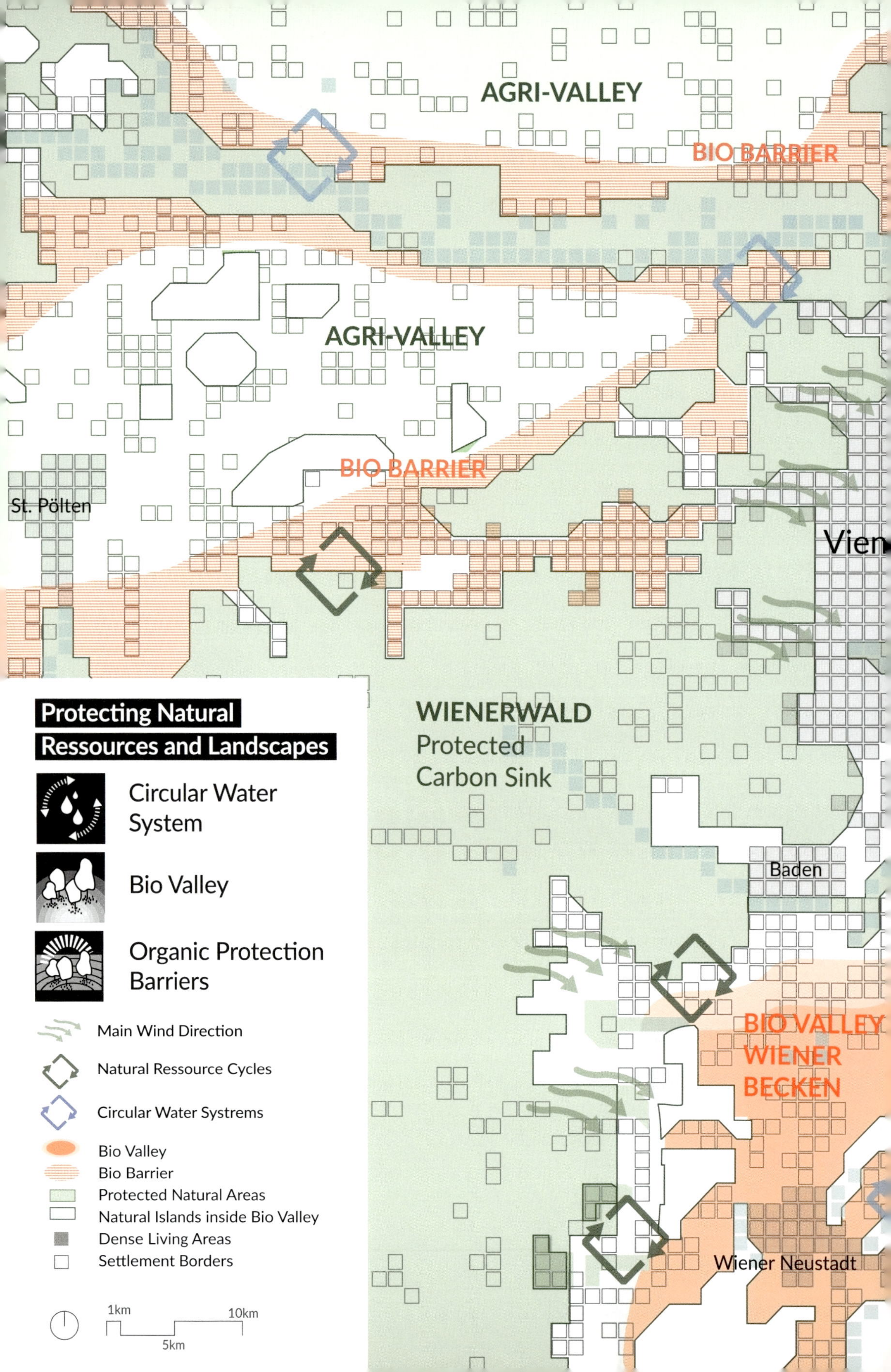

AGRI-VALLEY
BIO BARRIER
AGRI-VALLEY
BIO BARRIER
St. Pölten
Vien
WIENERWALD
Protected
Carbon Sink
Baden
BIO VALLEY
WIENER
BECKEN
Wiener Neustadt
Protecting Natural
Ressources and Landscapes
Circular Water
System
Bio Valley
Organic Protection
Barriers
Main Wind Direction
Natural Ressource Cycles
Circular Water Systrems
Bio Valley
Bio Barrier
Protected Natural Areas
Natural Islands inside Bio Valley
Dense Living Areas
Settlement Borders
1km
5km
10km

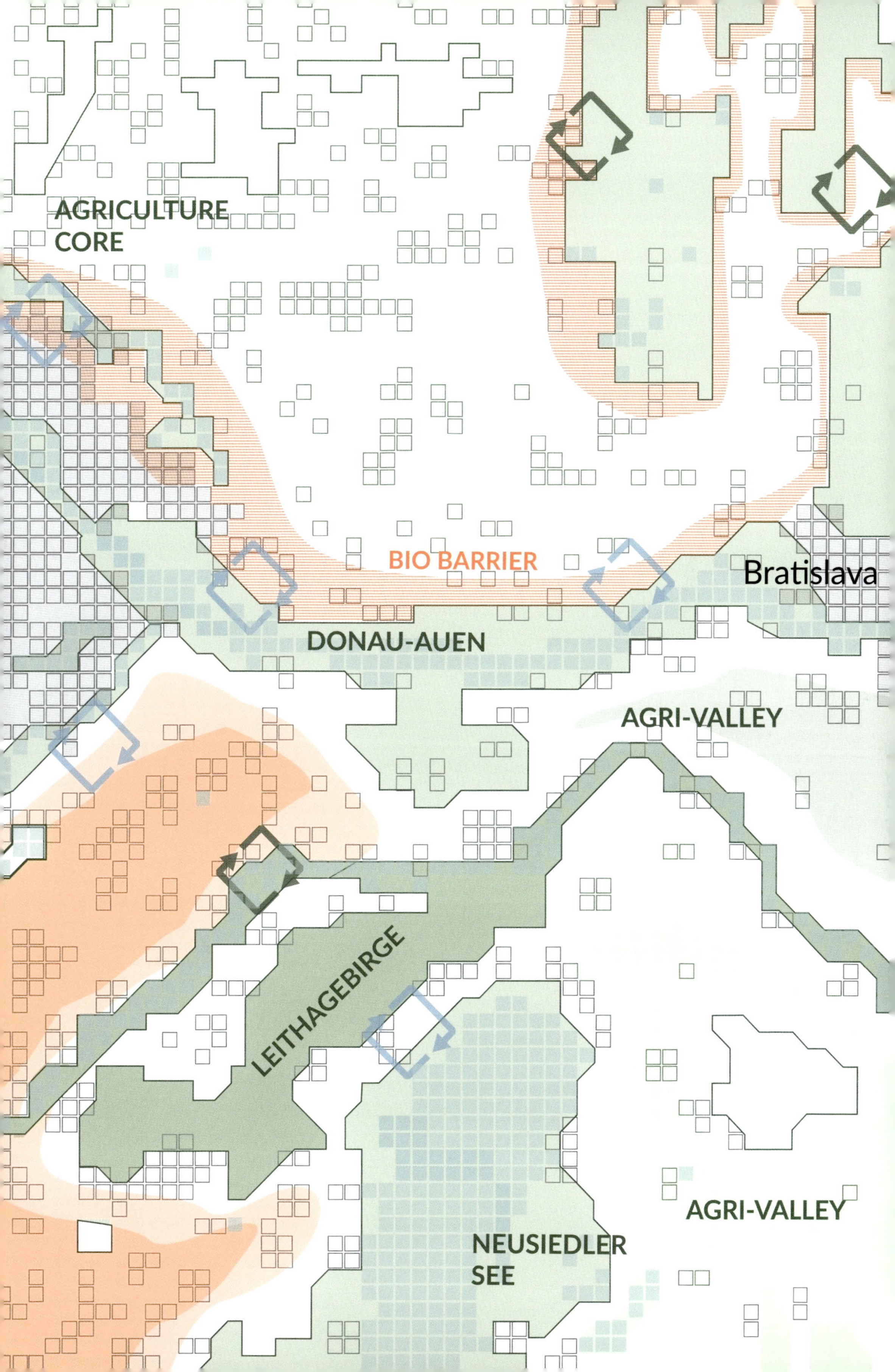
AGRICULTURE
CORE
BIO BARRIER
Bratislava
DONAU-AUEN
AGRI-VALLEY
LEITHAGEBIRGE
NEUSIEDLER
SEE
AGRI-VALLEY

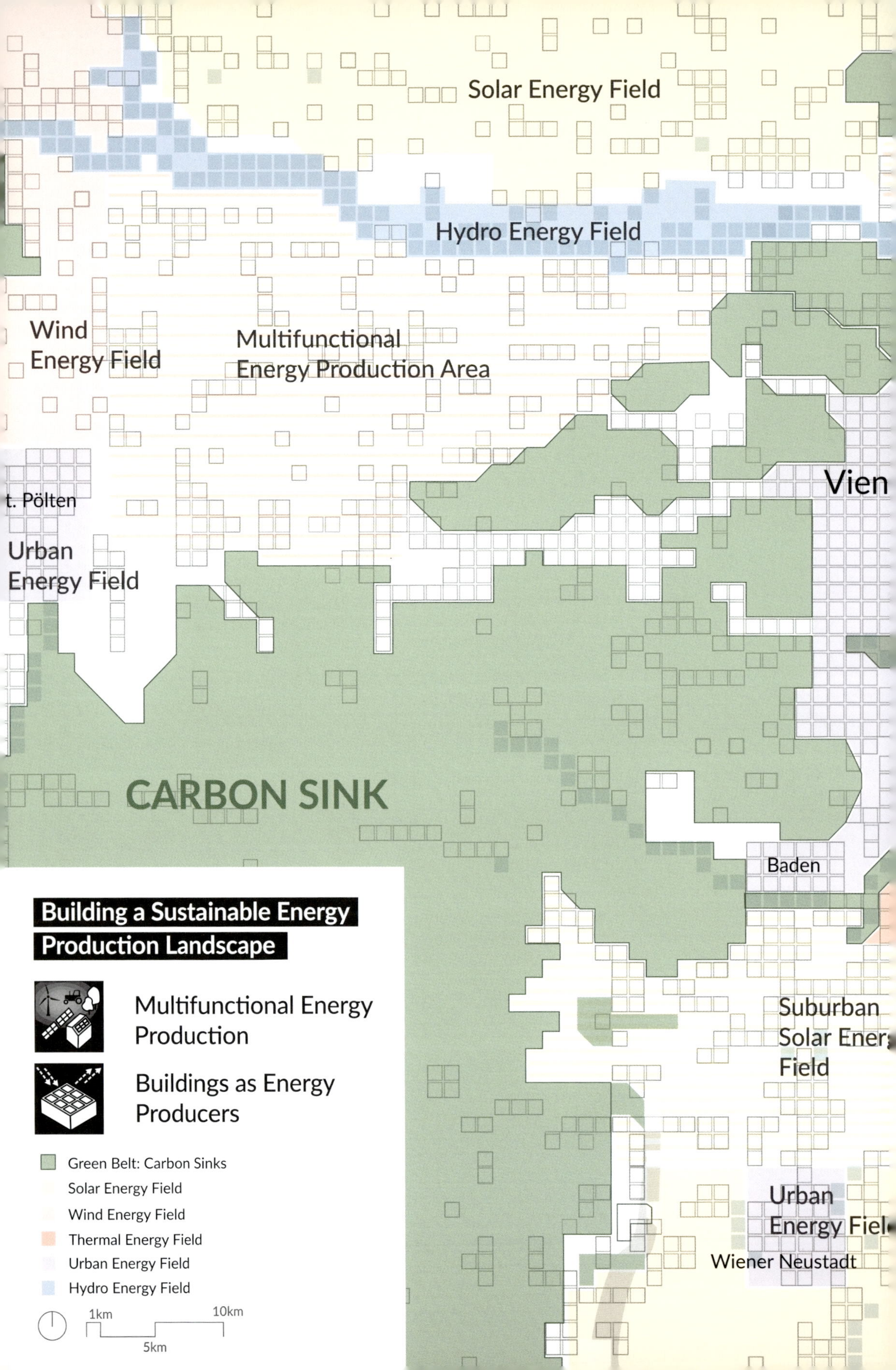
Solar Energy Field
Hydro Energy Field
Wind Energy Field
Multifunctional Energy Production Area
t. Pölten
Urban Energy Field
Vien
CARBON SINK
Baden
Suburban Solar Ener Field
Urban Energy Fiel
Wiener Neustadt
Building a Sustainable Energy Production Landscape
Multifunctional Energy Production
Buildings as Energy Producers
Green Belt: Carbon Sinks
Solar Energy Field
Wind Energy Field
Thermal Energy Field
Urban Energy Field
Hydro Energy Field
1km
10km
5km

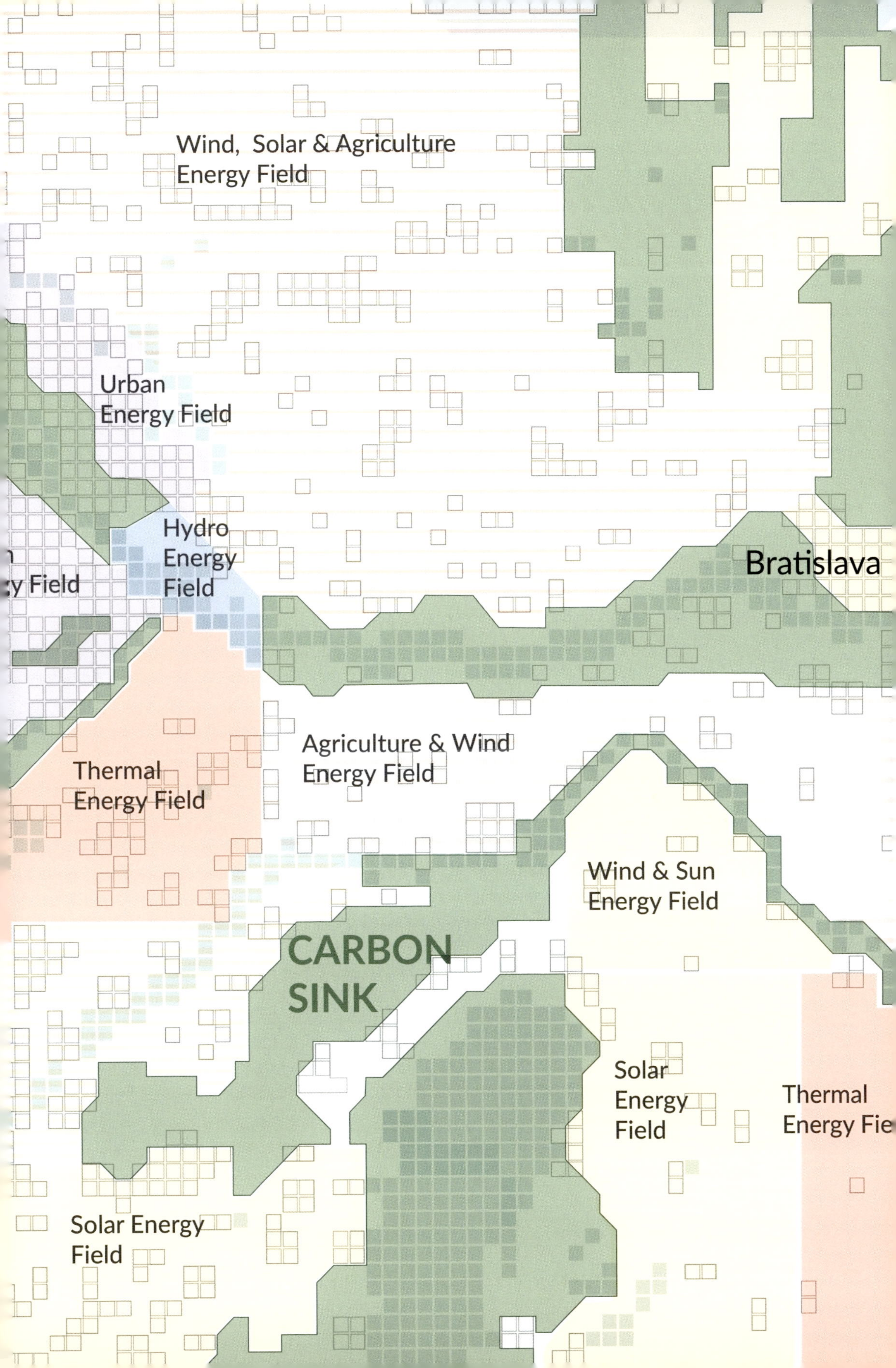
Wind, Solar & Agriculture Energy Field
Urban Energy Field
Hydro Energy Field
y Field
Bratislava
Agriculture & Wind Energy Field
Thermal Energy Field
Wind & Sun Energy Field
CARBON SINK
Solar Energy Field
Thermal Energy Fie
Solar Energy Field

The Power of Mapping

MetroLab's work highlights the critical role of mapping in assessing, analyzing, envisioning, and designing concrete actions for the Zero Carbon City Region. Throughout the planning cycle, mapping facilitates dynamic discussions and continuous dialogue among stakeholders, fostering a deeper understanding of the metropolitan area. This approach, rooted in integrated urban planning, is especially important in the pursuit of climate neutrality.

At the metropolitan level, mapping tools provide actionable insights for pursuing carbon neutrality by simulating possible future scenarios and visualizing strategy outcomes. These maps reveal areas of challenge, opportunity, and growth, enabling informed decision-making and helping policymakers to prioritize interventions based on geographic evidence. The visual aspect fosters a shared vision, rallying diverse groups around common climate goals. By simplifying complex policy implications, mapping tools allow decision-makers to communicate strategic priorities without overwhelming detail. This shared understanding is crucial for coordinated action on complex challenges like climate change.

Mapping serves two main purposes: visualizing data from dialogue-oriented, qualitative co-creative processes and presenting findings from data-driven, quantitative assessment and analysis. By translating these inputs into accessible visual narratives, mapping clarifies pathways toward a zero-carbon city region and broadens participation in climate action, making solutions more tangible and actionable.

Mapping simplifies complex data and abstract policies, rendering them in clear, visual formats that invite engagement and understanding. By transforming extensive data on energy use, transport patterns, land use, and climate risks into accessible visuals, mapping enables stakeholders to comprehend the nuances of urban systems and policies more readily. Maps help communicate potential outcomes of various planning scenarios, fostering richer engagement among policymakers, urban planners, businesses, and the public. This visual language demystifies urban policies, making it easier to communicate both challenges and opportunities. Importantly, mapping as a tool empowers stakeholders to engage in meaningful discussions on climate adaptation and mitigation strategies, enabling an inclusive process in which diverse voices can contribute to reimagining urban transformation. This approach not only helps align stakeholders but also encourages the co-creation of strategies that respond to the unique characteristics and climate needs of the metropolitan area, establishing a shared commitment to sustainable urban futures.

Maps are an essential step toward place-based solutions at the neighborhood level, where multi-level governance is important in translating regional policies into local action. Local investment can be stalled by unpopular decisions, such as limiting urban sprawl. However, regional policies like intra-municipal collaboration enables regional strategies to be implemented effectively at the local scale. Aligned with the principles outlined in the Urban Agenda for the EU and the New Leipzig Charter, mapping supports place-based solutions that address specific needs within functional urban areas. These frameworks emphasize integrated, participatory approaches to urban planning, ensuring that policy interventions are tailored to local contexts rather than one-size-fits-all. Through mapping, stakeholders can visualize how policy measures—such as sustainable mobility, climate adaptation, and social inclusion—apply to distinct functional areas within a metropolitan region. This localized focus enables tailored solutions that address each area's unique social, economic, and environmental conditions, fostering resilience and sustainability. By aligning with the EU's policy goals for balanced territorial development, mapping also enhances cross-border cooperation between urban and rural areas, strengthening cohesion within metropolitan areas and empowering regions to make strategic, climate-positive transformations.

After all, the creation of maps and narratives requires an innovative co-creative process, where the imagination and ideas of stakeholders shape a shared regional vision and goals through open dialogue. This creative, cross-sectoral, and interdisciplinary approach was tested in Vienna through the MetroLab and can be applied to other city regions, making necessary climate actions clear and achievable.

Glossary & Network

Glossary

The glossary consists of a wide range of different terms related to the Zero Carbon City Region topic. The following is an attempt to classify the different terms from above and to relate them to each other.

The basic terms of sustainability describe the basics and how they work, which are important for a better understanding of climate change and its consequences. Building on this, the basic terms of climate change describe more detailed terminology in the debate on climate change mitigation and adaptation, climate neutrality and climate justice. This raises the question of how to measure climate neutrality, which is more accurately described by the term carbon footprint, which, once defined, raises further questions about how to measure it for an entire metropolitan area. On this basis, different strategies for climate-resilient urban development are presented and defined, such as climate-sensitive urban design, the concept of the circular city, water-sensitive urban development and more. In addition, more detailed basic concepts of urban resilience are described as concrete measures for the strategies described above. These are different strategies and measures that can contribute to the Zero Carbon City Region as single approaches or in combination.

BIO-CLIMATIC
(Architecture and Urban Design)

Bioclimatology is the science that studies the influence of climatic factors on humans, animals and plants. Bioclimatic architecture and urban design aim to create buildings and spaces which respect the environment and live in accordance with it. It considers the local climatic conditions—sun, wind, rain, etc.—to reduce the environmental impact of a building or space. The goal is to achieve optimal thermal comfort inside architectural elements that avoid complete dependence on mechanical systems.

IBERDROLA (2022): Bioclimatic architecture, buildings that respect the environment
BioclimaticX (n.d.): Bioclimatic Architecture.

BIODIVERSITY

Biodiversity is one of the most important foundations of our life. A balanced and functioning environment is based on biodiversity, which comprises three aspects: the diversity of ecosystems, genetic diversity and the richness of species in animals, plants, fungi and microorganisms.
Material cycles, clear water and clean air, food production, adaptability to changing environmental conditions, human recreation in nature, all these are based on biodiversity. So for our survival, we need to use biodiversity and protect it at the same time. On the other hand, we exert a strong influence—partly promoting, partly destroying—on biodiversity.
The main direct drivers of biodiversity loss today are: land use change, climate change, areal nutrient and sheep pollution, overexploitation of natural resources, emergence of invasive species

Environment Agency Germany (2014): Biodiversity

CARBON FOOTPRINT

Greenhouse gas emissions are used as an indicator of human impact and are a term for all those anthropogenic emissions that contribute to global warming: in addition to carbon dioxide (CO_2), for example, also methane, nitrous oxide, chlorofluorocarbons or SF6. They are abbreviated to CO_2 equivalents, since carbon dioxide is the reference value.

The CO_2 footprint is the result of an emissions calculation or CO_2 balance. It indicates the amount of greenhouse gases released by an activity, process or action. A CO_2 footprint can be specified for business or production processes of companies, for example.

The Product Carbon Footprint (PCF) is also such an abbreviation. This is because by no means only a carbon balance (carbon = carbon) is drawn up here, but more precisely a greenhouse gas balance, whereby in addition to CO_2, the other greenhouse gases mentioned above are also included.

A carbon footprint can also be calculated for many other activities and processes, for example, for an overnight stay at a hotel, a business trip, an event, or the provision of a specific service.

Hottenroth et al. (2013): Carbon footprints for products
The Nature Conservancy (2022): Calculate Your Carbon Foodprint
First Climate (2022): What is a Carbon Footprint?

CIRCULAR CITY

Transition from a linear to a circular economy through an integrated approach in all its functions, as they are directly related to each other (waste, energy, mobility, land, wastewater, food)

The idea is that through integrated management, in cooperation with citizens, local governments, businesses and the research community, interactions between the individual sectoral cycles are optimally taken into account to achieve high efficiency and effectiveness of resource utilization.

This means in practice to promote economic behaviors that decouple resource use from economic activity by maintaining the value and utility of products, components, materials, and nutrients for as long as possible.

Through this transition, cities aim to improve human well-being, reduce emissions, protect and enhance biodiversity, and promote social equity, in line with the Sustainable Development Goals.

Circular Cities Declaration (2022): Cities and the Circular Economy
Verbücheln et al. (2013): Szenarien für eine integrierte Nachhaltigkeitspolitik – am Beispiel nachhaltige Stadt 2030

CIRCULAR ECONOMY

A production and consumption model in which existing materials and products are shared, leased, reused, repaired, refurbished and recycled for as long as possible, extending the life cycle of products. When a product reaches the end of its service life, its materials are left in the economy wherever possible. The idea is to use them productively again and again, creating further value. This is a transformation from the traditional, linear economic model based on the "take-make-consume-discard" pattern, which relies on large quantities of cheap, readily available materials and energy.

Measures such as waste prevention, ecodesign and re-use could save money while also reducing the total amount of annual greenhouse gas emissions.

European Parliament (2022): Circular ecnomy: definition, importance and benefits.

CLIMATE ADAPTATION

Climate protection aims to reduce emissions of climate-relevant greenhouse gases such as carbon dioxide and methane in order to minimize the advance of climate change in accordance with the precautionary principle. Climate adaptation, on the other hand is about taking precautionary action to deal with the unavoidable consequences of climate change and extreme weather events:

» Minimizing risks
» Avoiding damage
» Adapting to the expected changes

Climate impact adaptation includes heavy rain and storm preparedness to prevent or mitigate flooding and other risks in settlement areas. Another focus is heat and health preparedness to minimize risks to vulnerable populations. Other important precautionary aspects include early active adaptation to expected climatic changes and the "creeping" changes already observed, for example in urban, green and building planning. This also includes a continuous improvement of risk awareness and change capacity of all social groups.

On the way to a climate-friendly, sustainable city, there is no "either or" of climate protection and climate adaptation. Both fields of action are important for livable communities in the future. The goal must be to create synergies between the two and to defuse possible conflicts at an early stage through integrated measures.

DIFU (2021): Was ist eigentlich... Klimaanpassung/ Klimaschutz?

CLIMATE CHANGE

Scientific accepted term for the cooling or warming of the Earth's climate over a long period of time. Climate change is not a new phenomenon. It describes the long-term changes in factors such as temperature, precipitation, and ocean currents. These changes have been demonstrated by numerous studies and observations around the world in recent decades.

It is the long-term trends that are critical, which means that even in a long-term warming trend, there will always be outliers up or down. Importantly, if a year turns out to be colder than expected, this does not call into question the existence of climate change.

Global warming is one example of climate change. And here, the human influence is clear, because the climate has never warmed up as fast as in the time since the industrial revolution.

Causes: The climate changes mainly due to the greenhouse effect: The sun's rays that hit the earth are absorbed by natural gases and clouds, and some of them are reflected back to the planet. In this way, they keep it warm.

But climate change, which poses a threat to life on earth, is predominantly man-made: industrialization and the associated burning of fossil fuels such as lignite, hard coal and petroleum are causing twice the amount of CO_2 to enter the atmosphere than would be the case without human intervention.

CARE Deutschland (n.d.): Klimawandel: Definiton, Ursachen, Folgen
Greenpeace (n.d.): Klimakrise – wenn das Klima kollabiert

CLIMATE CRISIS

For some years now, various NGOs and activist groups (Greenpeace, Fridays for future, etc.) have been calling for climate change to be called the climate crisis: Although climate change is one of the greatest threats of our time, it still plays too small a role in public and political debates.

The climate crisis demands immediate action and endangers the existence of the entire human race.

Spark Neuro (2020): Rebranding Climate Change
Utopia (2022): Klimakrise und Klimakatastrophe: Warum wir nicht mehr über den Klimawandel reden sollten
Kirchner, L. (2022): Defnitionsansätze für den Begriff Nachhaltigkeit

CLIMATE-FRIENDLY LIFESTYLE

Climate-friendly lifestyle permanently secures a climate that enables a good life within planetary boundaries. Climate-friendly living strives for a high quality of life while respecting planetary boundaries for all people. It's about an equal, good and secure life.

APCC (2023): Zusammenfassung für Entscheidungstragende

CLIMATE JUSTICE

The dramatic changes in climate change threaten the livelihoods of millions of people, especially in the Global South. They are leading to more poverty, greater marginalization of people, more flight and consequently to more conflicts over vital resources and the rise of nationalist tendencies in our societies.

From the perspective of climate justice, behind the 1.5-degree limit is a conflict of freedom for different people—also in different parts of the world and as members of different generations.

For climate change is likely to affect people in the future and in the countries of the global south that have contributed very little to the problem hit particularly hard.

The term environmental justice refers to a socio-spatially balanced distribution of environmental burdens. It is to be distinguished from the term "ecological justice", which refers to the consideration of future generations in the use of natural resources.

An environmental justice-oriented policy combines elements of social policy, health care, and ecology. It seeks to ensure that all citizens, regardless of their income, background, and place of residence, enjoy equal rights of protection from harmful environmental impacts and health hazards, and equal opportunities to participate in political decision-making processes regarding the distribution of environmental burdens.

Rosa Luxemburg Stfitung (n.d.): Dossier Climate Justice
BpB (2019): Klimaschutz und gesellschaftlicher Wandel
DIFU (2021): Was ist eigentlich... Umweltgerechtigkeit?

CARBON NEUTRALITY

Climate neutrality means achieving a balance between carbon emissions and the absorption of carbon from the atmosphere into carbon sinks. To achieve net zero emissions, all greenhouse gas emissions worldwide must be offset by carbon sequestration. A carbon sink is a system that absorbs more carbon than it emits. The most important natural carbon sinks are soils, forests, and oceans. According to estimates, natural sinks remove between 9.5 and 11 gigatons of CO_2 per year. In 2019, annual global CO_2 emissions were 38 gigatons.
To date, there are no man-made carbon sinks that can remove carbon from the atmosphere at the rate needed to combat global warming.

Carbon stored in natural sinks such as forests is released back into the atmosphere through fires, land use changes or deforestation. For this reason, CO_2 emissions must be reduced in order to implement the climate neutrality target.

European Parliament (2019): What is carbon neutrality and how can it be achieved by 2050?

CLIMATE-SENSITIVE PLANNING

Climate-sensitive planning means tackling climate issues through planning. It aims to make cities and metropolitan areas climate resilient and adaptable to the changing climate, while at the same time promoting climate protection. Climate change will affect different local geographic and settlement-specific conditions. Therefore, its effects are also varied. The right answers for early adaptation must therefore be found locally on site.

Tasks of climate-sensitive planning can be:

Flood protection in river basins
Link water-sensitive urban planning with precipitation and water management.
Incorporate habitat management for species and biotope protection.
Secure fresh air corridors (parks, green spaces and tree-lined streets) in the urban area (through planning) and link them with regional green corridors.
Take measures to protect areas, buildings and settlement-related infrastructures from erosion, landslides or undercutting, depending on the terrain.

Environment Agency Germany (2015): Planen im Klimawandel

ECOSYSTEM

An ecosystem is a geographic area where plants, animals, and other organisms, as well as weather and landscape, work together to form a bubble of life. Ecosystems contain biotic or living, parts, as well as abiotic factors, or nonliving parts. Biotic factors include plants, animals, and other organisms. Abiotic factors include rocks, temperature, and humidity.

Ecosystems can be very large or very small. The whole surface of Earth is a series of connected ecosystems. Ecosystems are often connected in a larger biome. Biomes are large sections of land, sea, or atmosphere.

Ecosystems are not delimited, but have fluid boundaries. Ecosystems can be seen globally (Earth), continentally (Arctic) and locally (Swabian Alb). Additionally, they can be broken down much smaller into the garden pond, the compost, the greening strip along a road.

Humans depend on functioning ecosystems, on biodiversity in general. What we benefit from and what nature provides us with is referred to as "ecosystem services".

National Geographic Resource Library (n.d.): Ecosystem
OroVerde (2021): Ökosysteme

ENERGY TRANSITION

The prosperity of our society depends on a functioning energy supply. The goal of the energy transition is therefore to realize a secure, economical and environmentally compatible energy supply. Research into technologies and social concepts for sustainable energy generation, conversion and distribution are therefore key for the energy transition

For a sustainable energy supply, the consumption of fossil energy sources, such as crude oil, natural gas and coal, must be reduced. Burning these fossil fuels produces energy in the form of heat as well as the greenhouse gas carbon dioxide, which is highly polluting and an important contributor to global warming. The key to greater climate protection is an energy turnaround that saves fossil fuels through the expansion of renewable energies and greater energy efficiency.

In the course of the energy transition, renewable energies such as hydroelectric and solar power, wind energy, geothermal energy and renewable raw materials are continuously replacing fossil fuels.

The aim is to switch the energy supply to renewable energies—in the electricity sector, but also in heating and transport.

BMBF (n.d.): Energiewende.
Press and Information Office of the Federal Government Germany (n.d.): Intergenerational contract for the climate.

GREENHOUSE GASES

Greenhouse gases trap heat and make the planet warmer. Human activities are responsible for almost all of the increase in greenhouse gases in the atmosphere over the last 150 years.

Greenhouse gases are: Carbon dioxide (CO_2), Methane (CH_4), Nitrous oxide F-gases, Carbon = Carbon (C)

Greenhouse gases are released mainly through the use of fossil fuels such as coal and petroleum. Industrial processes and livestock farming are also relevant emission sources. Rising levels of greenhouse gases warm the earth's atmosphere, leading to climate change.

At the 2015 Climate Summit in Paris the international community agreed to limit the temperature increase to 1.5 °C when possible and to keep it below 2 °C. This can only be achieved if global greenhouse gas emissions are rapidly reduced.

Environment Agency Germany (n.d.): Indicator: Greenhouse gas emissions

RENEWABLE RESOURCES NON-RENEWABLE RESOURCES

RENEWABLE RESOURCES

Renewable Resources obtain their nutrients from organic waste that is cycled through natural processes in such a way that as much is recycled as is harvested in the same period of time. This means, then, that renewable resources, such as forest and fish stocks, can regenerate in the time period relevant to human planning.

There are also resources that are fundamentally renewable and can also be regrown. In practice, these are not renewed and consequently cannot grow back in the same form, since harvesting or clearing takes place, but there is no compensatory release of substances.

NON-RENEWABLE RESOURCES

Non-renewable resources such as energy sources (e.g., oil, coal, or natural gas) and mineral resources (e.g., iron or nickel) are characterized by the fact that they cannot regenerate in the time and at the rate in which we extract them from the earth. Thus, each quantity of an exhaustible resource that is extracted in the present reduces the future available stock by exactly that quantity. This therefore creates a rivalry between the present and the future.

Aachener Stiftung Kathy Beys (2023): Lexikon der Nachhaltigkeit

RESILIENCE

Resilience is derived from the Latin word "resilire" and means "to bounce back", "to rebound". The term describes the ability of a system to behave in the face of internal or external influences in such a way that it is able to return to its original state. It is therefore about the resilience, fault tolerance or self-regulation of a system.

The term, which originated in psychology and became known within ecological theories, has recently also been used in other research disciplines, for example in urban research.

Within social psychological research, it refers to the circumstance of responding to and appropriately coping with sociocultural challenges by using available resources.

In general, however, "resilience" nowadays refers to the capacity of individuals or institutions to maintain a desirable state by developing effective self-protection mechanisms.

European Parliament (2019): What is carbon neutrality and how can it be achieved by 2050?

URBAN RESILIENCE

The technical term resilience inside sustainability studies describes the ability of a system to maintain or restore its ability to function in the event of a disruption or disturbance. Urban resilience thus describes the ability of different actors (institutions, business, individuals) to adapt to changing conditions, to survive and even to continue to grow.

Urban resilience describes the ability of an urban system and its population to respond resiliently in the face of crises or disasters, while adapting and transforming itself in terms of sustainable urban development.
As part of integrated urban development policy, cities and municipalities are encouraged to coherently reduce known risks, prevent new risks, manage crises more effectively in the future, and shape urban development—robust, adaptive and sustainable.

BMI (2021): Memorandum Urbane Resilienz.
DIFU (2021): Was ist eigentlich...Resilienz?
Göhlich, V. (2022). Urbanismus: Was ist urbane Resilienz?

SUFFICIENCY/SELF-SUFFICIENCY

SUFFICIENCY

In climate protection and sustainability studies, sufficiency stands for the "enough". Aware of limited natural resources (climate change and the threat of species loss), it aims to minimize the consumption of raw materials and energy.

The idea is to produce and consume within planetary boundaries by crictically reflecting consumption patterns (e.g. in the energy and material sector).

SELF-SUFFICIENCY

Production of goods or cultivation of agricultural products not for export, but for domestic use. People primarily produce for themselves what they need to live – they are able to maintain one's owns needs without external assistance. It can mean: to produce the food withing the same region in which it is consumed or that most waste should be treated or disposed within the region of origin.

It is primarily characterized by regional and local relationships and social networks and less by national or even international markets.

European Environment Agency (n.d.): Principle of self-sufficiency
Barghorn, L. (2020): Subsistenz: Das bedeutet der Begriff in der Nachhaltigkeitsforschung
BUNDjugend (n.d.): Suffizienz
BpB (n.d.): Subsistenzwirtschaft

SUSTAINABILITY

"Sustainability" is a very fuzzy, ambiguous and complex term for which there are several definitions or approaches to definition. The principle of sustainability states that no more should be consumed (degraded) than can be regrown. Often, it is mainly about longevity, durability, shelf life or stability, while the term is also closely linked to resource scarcity or climate and environmental protection.

For us, Sustainability or sustainable development means meeting the needs of the present in such a way that the opportunities of future generations are not restricted. In this context, it is important to consider the three dimensions of sustainability—economically efficient, socially just, ecologically viable—on an equal footing. In order to preserve global resources in the long term, sustainability should be the basis of all political decisions.

Perez-Diehl, N. (2024): Was bedeutet Nachhaltigkeit?

TRANSFORMATION

Transformation refers to a fundamental and profound change. From a social perspective, it encompasses sudden shifts in political, economic, or technological development. These shifts may be driven by new technical and economic possibilities or significantly altered societal needs. Transformation is a long-term learning and search process, often spanning several decades and marked by uncertainty. It concludes only when new system structures become permanently established and stabilized.

Urban transformations are complex and cannot simply be controlled. They can only be guided in a socially accepted direction through negotiation processes. In this, politics and municipal administration are expected to take on a coordinating role.

European Parliament (2019): What is carbon neutrality and how can it be achieved by 2050?

ZERO CARBON CITY REGION

A zero-carbon city refers to an urban area where no carbon emissions are produced from its activities, including energy generation, transportation, and industrial processes. It relies entirely on renewable energy sources like wind, solar, and nuclear power, which do not create carbon emissions when used to produce electricity. This concept generally extends to include the elimination of all greenhouse gases.

Zero-carbon cities aim to reduce carbon emissions to a minimum, ideally achieving zero or even negative emissions. Any remaining emissions are balanced through carbon storage or offset mechanisms. Globally, more than 500 cities have committed to low-carbon and net-zero carbon targets, aiming to significantly reduce greenhouse gas emissions over the coming decades.

However, because a city's supply chains extend far beyond its physical borders, Princeton University's High Meadows Environmental Institute advocates for a broader definition. A net-zero carbon city should also include net-zero carbon infrastructure and food provisioning systems, addressing all sources of emissions that support urban living.

NESO (n.d.): What is net zero and zero carbon?
High Meadows Environmental Institute (2021): What is a net-zero city? Depends on how you count urban carbon emissions

MetroLab Team

Stefan Mayr
Architect ZT, Co-Managing Director *superwien urbanism*, Co-Founder of *MetroLab*

Roland Krebs
Urban and Regional Planner ZT, Co-Managing Director *superwien urbanism*, Co-Founder of *MetroLab*

Claudia Staubmann
Architect DETSV, Co-Managing Director *CoCo architecture*, Co-Founder of *MetroLab*

Cédric Ramière
Architect DPLG, Co-Managing Director *CoCo architecture*, Co-Founder of *MetroLab*

Lena Diete
Urban Designer at *MetroLab* and *superwien urbanism*

Marie-Theres Schwaighofer
Architect at *MetroLab* and *CoCo architecture*

Paul Klema
Junior Urban and Regional Planner at *MetroLab* and *superwien urbanism*

Daniel Wally
Junior Urban and Regional Planner at *MetroLab* and *CoCo architecture*

Larissa Hollub
Junior Urban and Regional Planner at *MetroLab* and *superwien urbanism*

International Network

Carolin Bellstedt
Metabolism Researcher & Consultant at Metabolism of Cities

Joan Caba
Senior Urban Planner Àrea Metropolitana de Barcelona

Ombretta Caldarice
Assistant Professor in Urban & Regional Planning at Politecnico di Torino

Nadia Carboni
Head of the Department of Economic Development and Smart Cities at the Union of Romagna Faentina

Nicolas Fontaine
General Manager of the Greater Grenoble Area Mobility Authority

Laia Guillén i Soley
Architect at Àrea Metropolitana de Barcelona

Andreas Hacker
SUM Vienna Metropolitan Agency Vienna/Lower Austria

Sebastian Hafner
Architect at forschen planen bauen

Lautaro Iriarte
Representative of the Austrian Klimavolksbegehren

Andrea Jany
Architect and Researcher

Helga Kromp-Kolb
Professor at the Institute of Meteorology and the Centre for Global Change and Sustainability at the University of Natural Resources and Life Sciences, Vienna

Jaqueline Matijevic
Head of the Mobility and Transport Technologies Department at BMK Austria

Helene Pattermann
Head of the Community and Circular Economy Department at the Climate Lab

Marion Perret-Blois
Urbanist and Ecologist, Co-president of the Happy & Creative Frugality Movement

Alexander Prinsen
Circular Innovation and Transition Expert and Founder of Scope Matters

Thomas Romm
Architect at forschen planen bauen, Expert of Circularity in Construction Processes

Carolyn Steel
Architect, Author and leading Thinker on Food and Cities

Bernhard Steger
City of Vienna, MA21

Martin Strele
Managing Director at Kairos Impact Research & Development

Paraskevi Tarani
Site Project Manager Ri-Connect

Ivan Tosics
Institute of Metropolitan Research, Budapest

Carmo Tovar
Senior Executive at Área Metropolitana do Porto

Yvonne Lötscher
Head of Sustainable Nutrition in Zurich

BIBLIOGRAPHY

Aachener Stiftung Kathy Beys (2023): Lexikon der Nachhaltigkeit. https://www.nachhaltigkeit.info/

Abart-Heriszt, L. und Reichel, S. (2022): Energiemosaik Austria. Austria-wide modelling and web-based visualization of energy consumption and CO2 emissions at municipal level. Vienna, Salzburg. Licence: CC BY-NC-SA 3.0 AT. www.energiemosaik.at

Agenda Austria (2018): Commuters. https://www.agenda-austria.at/tags/pendler/

APCC (2023): Zusammenfassung für Entscheidungstragende. [Aigner, E., C. Görg, V. Madner, A. Muhar, A. Novy, et al.]. In: APCC Special Report: Strukturen für ein klimafreundliches Leben (APCC SR Klimafreundliches Leben) [Görg, C., V. Madner, A. Muhar, A. Novy, A.

Austrian Emissions Trading Registry (n.d.): Copliance status. https://www.emissionshandelsregister.at/oeffentlicheberichte/standdereinhaltung

Austrian Parliament (2022): Parliamentary Correspondence No. 1267. https://www.parlament.gv.at/aktuelles/pk/jahr_2022/pk1267

Bagnasco A., Berta G., Pichierri A. (2020): Chi ha fermato Torino? Una metafora per l'Italia, Torino, Einaudi.

Barghorn, L. (2020): Subsistenz: Das bedeutet der Begriff in der Nachhaltigkeitsforschung. https://utopia.de/ratgeber/subsistenz-das-bedeutet-der-begriff-in-der-nachhaltigkeitsforschung_188099/

BioclimaticX (n.d.): Bioclimatic Architecture. http://bioclimaticx.com/bioclimatic-architecture1/

BMAW (2022): Housing policy and the housing industry in Austria. https://www.bmaw.gv.at/dam/jcr:a227f25b-9e99-4353-b8ff-4ade6ac8f6d4/Handbuch-Wohnungspolitik-Wirtschaft-0205.pdf

BMBF (n.d.): Energiewende. https://www.bmbf.de/bmbf/de/forschung/energiewende-und-nachhaltiges-wirtschaften/energiewende/energiewende_node.html

BMI (2021): Memorandum Urbane Resilienz. https://www.nationale-stadtentwicklungspolitik.de/NSPWeb/SharedDocs/Publikationen/DE/Publikationen/memorandum_urbane_resilienz.pdf?__blob=publicationFile&v=4

BMK (2020): Resource Use in Austria 2020. Volume 3. https://www.bmk.gv.at/themen/klima_umwelt/nachhaltigkeit/ressourceneffizienz/publikationen/bericht2020.html

BMK (2022): Renewable energies 2020. https://www.bmk.gv.at/themen/energie/publikationen/erneuerbare_energie20.html

BMK (2022): The Austrian climate protection strategy/policy. https://www.oesterreich.gv.at/themen/bauen_wohnen_und_umwelt/klimaschutz/1/Seite.1000310.html

BMK (2023): Bundes-Abfallwirtschaftsplan Statusreport 2023. https://www.bmk.gv.at/themen/klima_umwelt/abfall/aws/bundes_awp/bawp2023.html

BMF (2023): Commuting Calculator. https://pendlerrechner.bmf.gv.at/pendlerrechner/query.exe/dn?ld=std1.a&seqnr=1&ident=0f.01535250.1676563262&

BpB (2019): Klimaschutz und gesellschaftlicher Wandel. Themenblätter im Unterricht Nr. 122

BpB (n.d.): Subsistenzwirtschaft. https://www.bpb.de/kurz-knapp/lexika/lexikon-der-wirtschaft/20793/subsistenzwirtschaft/

Brunetta G., Caldarice O. (2024, in press): Protezione climatica e dimensione metropolitana nella politica di coesione. A che punto siamo?. Territorio.

BUNDjugend (n.d.): Suffizienz. https://www.bundjugend.de/glossar/suffizienz/

CARE Deutschland (n.d.): Klimawandel: Definiton, Ursachen, Folgen. https://www.care.de/schwerpunkte/klimakrise/klimawandel/

Casavola D., Cotella G., Staricco L., Vitale Brovarone E. (2023): "Territorializzare la politica di coesione alla scala metropolitana. Il caso di Torino". In: Pasqui G., Tedesco C. (eds, 2023), Governance territoriale tra cooperazione e varietà, Atti della XXIV Conferenza Nazionale SIU Dare valore ai valori in urbanistica, Brescia, 23-24 giugno 2022, vol. 04, Planum Publisher e Società Italiana degli Urbanisti, Roma-Milano 2023, pp. 16–23.

Chamber of Labour (2014): Modal Split in heavy goods traffic. https://www.arbeiterkammer.at/infopool/wien/Verkehr_und_Infrastruktur_52_neu.pdf

Chamber of Labour Vienna (2022): Housing boom in Vienna 2018–2021. https://wien.arbeiterkammer.at/interessenvertretung/meinestadt/wohnen/Studie_Wohnbauboom_Wien_2018-2021.pdf

Circular Cities Declaration (2022): Cities and the Circular Economy. https://circularcitiesdeclaration.eu/cities-and-the-circular-economy/what-is-a-circular-city

City of Vienna (2024): Geodata viewer of the Vienna City Survey. https://www.wien.gv.at/ma41datenviewer/public/

Climate Biennale Vienna (2024): Biofabrique Vienna. https://www.biennale.wien/projekte/biofabrique

Climate and Energy Fund (2023): Fact check sustainable construction. https://faktencheck-energiewende.at/wp-content/uploads/sites/4/FCNB16Broschrefinal.pdf

Climate Dash Board (2023): Facts and figures on the climate crisis in Austria. https://klima-dashboard.at/

Da Cruz N.F., Oh D.Y., Choumar N.B. (2020): The metropolitan scale. Cities, 100(102644). https://doi.org/10.1016/j.cities.2020.102644.

DIFU (2013): Was ist eigentlich...Resilienz? https://difu.de/nachrichten/was-ist-eigentlich-resilienz

DIFU (2013): Was ist eigentlich... Umweltgerechtigkeit? https://difu.de/nachrichten/was-ist-eigentlich-umweltgerechtigkeit

DIFU (2021): Was ist eigentlich... Klimaanpassung/Klimaschutz? https://difu.de/nachrichten/was-ist-eigentlich-klimaanpassung-klimaschutz

EcoTransit (2021): Methodology Report EcoTransIT World. https://www.ecotransit.org/wordpress/wp-content/uploads/20210531_Methodology_Report_EcoTransIT_World.pdf

Environmental Agency Austria (2017): SUM-Food. Regional food paths using the example of the city of Vienna for the vegetable product group. https://www.umweltbundesamt.at/fileadmin/site/publikationen/REP0621.pdf

Environment Agency Austria (2018): Factsheet greenhouse gas balance: a comparison of vacation types https://www.umweltbundesamt.at/fileadmin/site/aktuelles/2018/treibhausgasbilanz_urlaubsreisevergleich_factsheet2018.pdf

Environment Agency Austria (2020): Renovation rate in Austria: proposal for new calculation. https://www.umweltbundesamt.at/news200428-1

Environment Agency Austria (2021): Land take in Austria 2020. https://www.umweltbundesamt.at/fileadmin/site/themen/boden/flaecheninanspruchnahme_2020.pdf

Environment Agency Austria (2022a) : Emissions figures data basis 2022. https://www.umweltbundesamt.at/fileadmin/site/themen/mobilitaet/daten/ekz_pkm_tkm_verkehrsmittel.pdf

Environment Agency Austria (2022b): Federal states air pollutant inventory 1990–2020. https://www.umweltbundesamt.at/fileadmin/site/publikationen/rep0817.pdf

Environment Agency Germany (n.d.): Indicator: Greenhouse gas emissions. https://www.umweltbundesamt.de/en/data/environmental-indicators/indicator-greenhouse-gas-emissions#at-a-glance

Environment Agency Germany (2014): Biodiversity. https://www.umweltbundesamt.de/das-uba/was-wir-tun/forschen/umwelt-beobachten/biodiversitaet#umweltschutz-und-biodiversitat

Environment Agency Germany (2015): Planen im Klimawandel. Stadt- und Freiraum schützen und aufwerten. Anpassungsmaßnahmen rechtzeitig planen und umsetzen. https://www.umweltbundesamt.de/sites/default/files/medien/376/publikationen/planen_im_klimawandel.pdf

Environment Agency Germany (2021): European Emissions Trading. https://www.umweltbundesamt.de/daten/klima/der-europaeische-emissionshandel#vergleich-von-emissionen-und-emissionsobergrenzen-cap-im-eu-ets

ERCST, Wegener Center, BloombergNEF und Ecoact (2021): 2021 State of the EU ETS Report. https://ercst.org/wp-content/uploads/2021/05/20210506-DE_2021-State-of-the-EU-ETS-Report_JH61.pdf

European Commission (n.d.-a): Member states emission targets. https://climate.ec.europa.eu/eu-action/effort-sharing-member-states-emission-targets_en

European Commission (n.d.-b): The European Climate Law. https://climate.ec.europa.eu/eu-action/european-climate-law_en

European Commission (2021): Ten-T Core Network Corridors. https://ec.europa.eu/transport/infrastructure/tentec/tentec-portal/site/maps_upload/SchematicA0_EUcorridor_map.pdf

European Council (2022): European Green Deal. https://www.consilium.europa.eu/en/policies/green-deal/

European Environment Agency (n.d.): Principle of self-sufficiency. https://www.eea.europa.eu/help/glossary/eea-glossary/principle-of-self-sufficiency

European Environment Agency (2023): Copernicus Land Monitoring, CORINE Landcover https://land.copernicus.eu/pan-european/corine-land-cover

European Environment Agency (2024): Greenhouse gases viewer. https://www.eea.europa.eu/data-and-maps/data/data-viewers/greenhouse-gases-viewer

European Parliament (2019): What is carbon neutrality and how can it be achieved by 2050? https://www.europarl.europa.eu/topics/en/article/20190926STO62270/what-is-carbon-neutrality-and-how-can-it-be-achieved-by-2050

European Parliament (2022): Circular ecnomy: definition, importance and benefits. https://www.europarl.europa.eu/news/en/headlines/economy/20151201STO05603/circular-economy-definition-importance-and-benefits

Eurostat (2021): Freight Statistics – Modal Split. https://ec.europa.eu/eurostat/statistics-explained/index.php?title=Freight_transport_statistics_-_modal_split#Modal_split_of_freight_transport_by_country_in_2021

Eurostat (2022): What are the main destinations of EU export of waste? https://ec.europa.eu/eurostat/web/products-eurostat-news/-/ddn-20220525-1

Eurostat (2023): Built-up areas. https://ec.europa.eu/eurostat/cache/digpub/housing/bloc-3b.html?lang=en

FAO (2023): Per capita consumption of meat. https://ourworldindata.org/grapher/meat-supply-per-person

Federal Ministry for Transport, Innovation and Technology (2016): Austria on the move 2013–2014. https://www.bmk.gv.at/dam/jcr:fbe20298-a4cf-46d9-bbee-01ad771a7fda/oeu_2013-2014_Ergebnisbericht.pdf

Federal State of Lower Austria (2020): Mobility in Lower Austria. Results of the 2018 mobility survey. https://www.noel.gv.at/noe/NOELRU7_Mobilitaetserhebung_2018_Barrierefrei.pdf

First Climate (2022): What is a Carbon Footprint? https://www.firstclimate.com/was-ist-ein-co2-fussabdruck?lang=en

Flightconnections B.V. (2023): Flights from Vienna (VIE). https://www.flightconnections.com/de/fl%C3%BCge-ab-wien-vie

Frey, V. & Bruckner, M. (2021). The global carbon footprint of Austria's consumption of agricultural (food and non-food) products. Ecological Economic Papers No. 41/2021. https://doi.org/10.57938/7cd7ee70-111e-4784-80e9-84965bf2a371

Google Maps (2023): Routing Function. https://www.google.com/maps/dir/

Göhlich, V. (2022). Urbanismus: Was ist urbane Resilienz? https://urbanauth.de/Artikel/2021/urbanismus-was-ist-urbane-resilienz/

Goličnik Marušić B. et al. (2023): DISTENDER D 9.1 Case Studies. Retrieved: https://distender.eu/resources/

Gori Nocentini M. (2024): The governance of climate adaptation in metropolitan regions: A systematic review of emerging themes and issues. Urban Climate, 55(101944). https://doi.org/10.1016/j.uclim.2024.101944

Governa F., Salone C. (2023): Lost in Transition: Turns and Twists of Turin's Post-Fordist Governance. IGLUS QUARTERLY, 8(4), pp. 6–15.

Greenpeace (n.d.): Klimakrise – wenn das Klima kollabiert. https://www.greenpeace.de/klimaschutz/klimakrise

Greenpeace (2020): Climate injustice in Austria. https://mobilitaet.greenpeace.at/assets/uploads/assets/uploads/GP_ReportKlimaungerechtigkeitAT.pdf

High Meadows Environmental Institute (2021): What is a net-zero city? Depends on how you count urban carbon emissions. https://environment.princeton.edu/news/what-is-a-net-zero-city-depends-on-how-you-count-urban-carbon-emissions/

Hottenroth et al. (2013): Carbon footprints for products. Handbuch für die betriebliche Praxis kleiner und mittlerer Unternehmen. https://www.hs-pforzheim.de/fileadmin/user_upload/uploads_redakteur/Forschung/INEC/Dokumente/Hottenroth_et_al_Carbon_Footprints_fuer_Produkte_web.pdf

IBERDROLA (2022): Bioclimatic architecture, buildings that respect the environment. https://www.iberdrola.com/innovation/bioclimatic-architecture-passivhaus

IG Windkraft (2022): Wind power in Austria. https://www.igwindkraft.at/fakten/?mdoc_id=1027482

Interrail (2023): Timetable. https://www.interrail.eu/en/plan-your-trip/interrail-timetable#/

Kirchner, L. (2022): Defnitionsansätze für den Begriff Nachhaltigkeit. https://www.nu3.de/blogs/special/definition-klimakrise

Lauk et al. (2022): Demand side options to reduce greenhouse gas emissions and the land foot-print of urban food systems: A scenario analysis for the City of Vienna. in: Journal of Cleaner Production, Volume 359.

Lefèvre C. (1998): Metropolitan government and governance in western countries: a critical review. International Journal of Urban and Regional Research, 22, pp. 9–26.

LINA, the European Architecture Platform (2024): Bioregional Design Practice. https://lina.community/programme/event/111/bioregional-design-practice/

LUMA Arles (n.d.): About Atelier LUMA. https://www.luma.org/en/arles/atelierluma/atelier-luma.html

Moran, D., Kanemoto K; Jiborn, M., Wood, R., Többen, J., and Seto, K.C. (2018): Environmental Research Letters. Carbon footprints of 13,000 cities. DOI: 10.1088/1748-9326/aac72a.

Moreno, C.; Allam, Z.; Chabaud, D.; Gall, C.; Pratlong, F. (2021): Introducing the "15-Minute

City": Sustainability, Resilience and Place Identity in Future Post-Pandemic Cities. Smart Cities 2021, 4, 93–111. https://doi.org/10.3390/smartcities4010006

National Geographic Resource Library (n.d.): Ecosystem. https://education.nationalgeographic.org/resource/ecosystem

NESO (n.d.): What is net zero and zero carbon? https://www.nationalgrideso.com/future-energy/our-progress-towards-net-zero/net-zero-explained/what-net-zero-and-zero-carbon

OpenStreetMap 2022. https://download.geofabrik.de/europe/austria-latest.osm.pbf

OroVerde (2021): Ökosysteme. https://www.regenwald-schuetzen.org/fileadmin/user_upload/pdf/Projekt/Vielfalt/LI/Lehrerinfo_2d_oekosysteme.pdf

ÖWAV (2020): Recycling targets 2025/2030. Measures to achieve the planned recycling targets. https://www.oewav.at/Kontext/WebService/SecureFileAccess.aspx?fileguid={7a7c03af-2693-45e3-a314-ecb5019f49fb}

Perez-Diehl, N. (2024): Was bedeutet Nachhaltigkeit? Definition, Modelle & Co. ZEIT---GEIST.DE. https://zeit---geist.de/magazin/was-bedeutet-nachhaltigkeit-definition/#n-1https://www.bmz.de/de/service/lexikon/nachhaltigkeit-nachhaltige-entwicklung-14700

Press and Information Office of the Federal Government Germany (n.d.): Intergenerational contract for the climate. https://www.bundesregierung.de/breg-de/schwerpunkte/klimaschutz/klimaschutzgesetz-2021-1913672

Ritchie, H. & Roser, M. (2022): Environmental Impacts of Food Production. Published online at OurWorldInData.org. https://ourworldindata.org/environmental-impacts-of-food

Robiglio M., Russi N.P., Governa F., Scellato G. (2021): "Turin Augmented Metropolis". In: Coricelli F., Marini L., Robiglio M. (eds., 2021): The Future Urban Legacy Lab. A Report. 2017-21, Politecnico di Torino, Torino, pp. 174–181.

Rosa Luxemburg Stfitung (n.d.): Dossier Climate Justice. https://www.rosalux.de/dossiers/klimagerechtigkeit

Schlatzer M. und Lindenthal, T. (2020): Einfluss von unterschiedlichen Ernährungsweisen auf Klimawandel und Flächeninanspruchnahme in Österreich und Übersee (DIETCCLU). Endbericht von StartClim2019.B in StartClim2019: Weitere Beiträge zur Umsetzung der österreichischen Anpassungsstrategie, Auftraggeber: BMLFUW, BMWF, ÖBf, Land Oberösterreich

Seidl, R., Plank, L., & Kadi, J. (2017): Airbnb in Vienna: An analysis. Interactive research report 2017. http://hdl.handle.net/20.500.12708/39217

Smetschka, B., Wiedenhofer, D., Egger, C, Haselsteiner E., Moran, D., Gaube V. (2019): Time Matters: The Carbon Footprint of Everyday Activities in Austria, in Ecological Economics, Volume 164, https://doi.org/10.1016/j.ecolecon.2019.106357.

SNCF Connect (2022): Calculation of CO2 emissions on your train journey. https://www.sncf-connect.com/en-en/help/calculation-co2-emissions-your-train-journey

Spark Neuro (2020): Rebranding Climate Change. https://media.sparkneuro.com/rebranding-climate-change/

Statistics Austria (2020): Farm Structure Survey 2020: Agricultural and forestry holdings increased in size. https://www.statistik.at/fileadmin/announcement/2022/07/20220712AS2020EN.pdf

Statistics Austria (2022): Harvest survey. https://www.statistik.at/fileadmin/pages/161/Gemuese-prodInsgBL2019bis2022.ods

Statistics Austria (2022): Housing census. https://www.statistik.at/en/about-us/surveys/register-based-census/housing-census

Statistics Austria (2022): Housing conditions. https://www.statistik.at/statistiken/bevoelkerung-und-soziales/wohnen/wohnsituation

Statistics Austria (2022): Stock of motor vehicles. https://www.statistik.at/statistiken/tourismus-und-verkehr/fahrzeuge/kfz-bestand

Statistics Austria (2022): Supply balance sheet for vegetables 2020/21

Statistics Austria (2022): Transport statistics. https://www.statistik.at/fileadmin/publications/Verkehrsstatistik-2021.pdf

Statistics Austria (2023): Aviation. https://portal.statistik.at/statistik.at/ext/statcube/jsf/tableView/tableView.xhtml

Statistics Austria (2023): Building permits, dwellings as of 2010. https://www.statistik.at/en/statistics/population-and-society/housing/building-permits

Statistics Austria (2023): Commuters (place of work) https://www.statistik.at/statistiken/arbeitsmarkt/erwerbstaetigkeit/arbeitsort-und-pendeln

Statistics Austria (2023): Economic Accounts for Agriculture. https://statcube.at/statistik.at/ext/statcube/jsf/tableView/tableView.xhtml

StatisticsAustria (2023): Microcensus; main residence dwellings as of 2004

Statistics Austria (2023): Population. https://portal.statistik.at/statistik.at/ext/statcube/jsf/tableView/tableView.xhtm

Statistics Austria (2023): Private households. https://portal.statistik.at/statistik.at/ext/statcube/jsf/tableView/tableView.xhtml

Statistics Austria (2023): Regional divisions. https://www.statistik.at/services/tools/services/regionales/regionale-gliederungen

Steininger, K. W., Munoz, P., Karstensen, J., Peters, G. P., Strohmaier, R., & Velázquez, E. (2018): Austria's consumption-based greenhouse gas emissions: Identifying sectoral sources and destinations. Global Environmental Change, 48, 226–242. https://doi.org/10.1016/j.gloenvcha.2017.11.011

Technical University Graz, ISV (2023): Kordonerhebung Vienna 2022. https://www.vor.at/fileadmin/CONTENT/Downloads/KordonerhebungWien_2022_barr..pdf

The Nature Conservancy (2022): Calculate Your Carbon Foodprint. https://www.nature.org/en-us/get-involved/how-to-help/carbon-footprint-calculator/

Tosics I. (2007), City-regions in Europe: the potentials and the realities. Town Planning Review, 78(6), pp. 775–796.

Utopia (2022): Klimakrise und Klimakatastrophe: Warum wir nicht mehr über den Klimawandel reden sollten. https://utopia.de/ratgeber/klimawandel-klimakrise-klimakatastrophe-experiment/

Verbücheln et al. (2013): Szenarien für eine integrierte Nachhaltigkeitspolitik – am Beispiel nachhaltige Stadt 2030. Band 2: Teilbereicht "Kreislaufstadt" https://www.umweltbundesamt.de/sites/default/files/medien/461/publikationen/4456.pdf

VIBÖ (n.d.): Bauproduktion Jahresrückblick 2020 bis 2023. https://www.viboe.at/Downloads/Statistik/Baustatistik/Produktionsstatistik/Bauproduktion_OEsterreich_10-Jahres-UEbersicht/Jahresrueckblick_2020_bis_2022.pdf

Vienna Airport (2023): Traffic figures. https://www.viennaairport.com/unternehmen/investor_relations/news/verkehrsergebnisse

Vienna Design Week 2024: Biofabrique Vienna. https://www.viennadesignweek.at/en/archive/2024/biofabrique-vienna/

Vinci I. (2019): Governing the Metropolitan Dimension: A Critical Perspective on Institutional Reshaping and Planning Innovation in Italy. European Journal of Spatial Development, 17(1), 1–21.

WIFO (2020): A (De-)Carbonisation Map for Austrian Manufacturing. https://www.wifo.ac.at/wp-content/uploads/upload-2401/s_2020_dekarbonisierung_66573.pdf

WIFO (2022): Analysis of climate-counterproductive subsidies in Austria. https://www.wifo.ac.at/wp-content/uploads/upload-2332/s_2022_klimakontraproduktive_subventionen_69687_.pdf

WKO (2022): Rail freight transport. https://www.wko.at/branchen/transport-verkehr/schienenbahnen/Schienengueterverkehr.html

WKO (2023): Housing subsidies. https://www.wko.at/branchen/k/information-consulting/immobilien-vermoegenstreuhaender/2022-FV-Steine-Wohnbaufoerderung-2021[64].pdf

Wohnungsbörse (2023): Rental prices Vienna 2024. https://www.wohnungsboerse.net/mietspiegel-Wien/16688

Wohnungsbörse (2023): Rental prices Weidhofen an der Thaya (Lower Austria) 2024. https://www.wohnungsboerse.net/mietspiegel-Waidhofen-an-der-Thaya/17389

Wolbart, N. (2019): Greenhouse gas emissions of Austrian diets in comparison. https://boku.ac.at/fileadmin/data/H03000/H73000/H73700/Publikationen/Working_Papers/WP176_Web.pdf

Wüstenrot Stiftung (Ed.): Jocher, T.; Loch, S.: Raumpilot Basics (2012) https://wuestenrot-stiftung.de/publikationen/raumpilot-grundlagen-pdf/

WWF (2023): EU emissions trading. https://www.wwf.de/themen-projekte/klimaschutz/klimaschutz-europa/eu-emissionshandel

METROLAB
RESEARCH | DEVELOPMENT | SERVICE

The *MetroLab* is a metropolitan Think Tank and consulting service for the integrated urban development of metropolitan areas and city regions. It introduces participative, integrative and creative-artistic elements and develops innovative metropolitan strategies as well as place-based solutions. Based on a co-creative and dialogue-oriented planning and design approach, it fosters not only placemaking interventions, but also the transfer of cutting-edge knowledge in creative urban planning and bureaucracy. Facing the immensity of contemporary urban challenges, the *MetroLab* works with an elaborated toolbox of metropolitan planning.

The *MetroLab* team consists of the partnering offices Superwien urbanism, based in Austria, and CoCo architecture, based in France and Austria. The joint MetroLab office in Vienna was founded in 2020.

SUPERWIEN
architecture urbanism

superwien is a studio for architecture and urbanism based in Vienna, Austria. The office supports public and private institutions in order to achieve sustainable urban change. Besides developing strategic plans, masterplans and public space projects, Superwien specialises in participatory and dialogue-oriented planning techniques from the national to the global scale.

COCO
architecture, urbanisme, *etc.*

CoCo architecture was founded in the Dordogne by French-Austrian architects in 2005. The architecture and urban design office employs new methods of practicing architecture through ambitious and varied projects all around the globe. CoCo architecture aims to be a catalyst for social change, putting environmental and lifestyle values at the heart of human endeavour. Its architecture reflects local thinking and traditional attitudes as well as modern approaches.

Imprint

An imprint of Walter de Gruyter GmbH, Berlin/Boston
Texts by kind permission of the authors.
Pictures by kind permission of the photographers/holders of the picture rights.

Cover: WHY. Studio for Concept and Design

Authors: Roland Krebs, Stefan Mayr, Cédric Ramière, Claudia Staubmann
Editorial Team: Lena Diete, Larissa Hollub, Paul Klema, Marie-Theres Schweighöfer, Daniel Wally
Guest Authors: Ombretta Caldarice, Nadia Carboni, Laia Guillén i Soley, Sebastian Hafner, Marion Perret-Blois, Thomas Romm
Copy-Editing and Proofreading: Celene Kay-Russell
Research: MetroLab
Design and Setting: MetroLab
Photographs: MetroLab
Illustrations: MetroLab

Printed in the European Union.

For questions regarding the General Safety Product Regulation, please contact productsafety@degruyterbrill.com.

Bibliographic information published by the Deutsche Nationalbibliothek
The Deutsche Nationalbibliothek lists this publication in the Deutsche Nationalbibliografie; detailed bibliographic data are available on the Internet at http://dnb.d-nb.de

jovis Verlag
Genthiner Straße 13
10785 Berlin

www.jovis.de

jovis books are available worldwide in select bookstores. Please contact your nearest bookseller or visit www.jovis.de for information concerning your local distribution.

vienna business agency

MetroLab is supported by the Vienna Business Agency

www.metrolab.design
www.superwien.com
www.cocoarchitecture.fr

ISBN 978-3-98612-195-2